EF169485
£14.95

Statistics for the
Social Sciences

STATISTICS FOR THE SOCIAL SCIENCES
With Computer Applications

Anthony Walsh

Boise State University

HARPER & ROW, PUBLISHERS, New York
Grand Rapids, Philadelphia, St. Louis, San Francisco,
London, Singapore, Sydney, Tokyo

1817

Sponsoring Editor: Alan McClare
Project Editor: Donna Conte
Art Direction and Cover Coordination: Heather A. Ziegler
Cover Design: Jung Sok Yo
Production: Beth Maglione

STATISTICS FOR THE SOCIAL SCIENCES: With Computer Applications

Library of Congress Cataloging-in-Publication Data

Walsh, A. (Anthony)
    Statistics for the social sciences : with computer-based
applications / Anthony Walsh.
       p.   cm.
    Includes bibliographical references.
    ISBN 0-06-046894-7
    1. Social sciences—Statistical methods. 2. SPSS X (Computer
program) 3. SAS (Computer program) I. Title.
HA29.W33574   1990
300′.01′5195—dc20   89-26814
                                                                                          CIP

90 91 92 93 9 8 7 6 5 4 3 2 1

Contents

CHAPTER 3   CENTRAL TENDENCY AND DISPERSION   33

CHAPTER 4   PROBABILITY AND THE NORMAL CURVE   54

CHAPTER 8   TWO-WAY ANALYSIS OF VARIANCE   144

CHAPTER 9   HYPOTHESIS TESTING WITH CATEGORICAL DATA: CHI-SQUARE   165

**CHAPTER 15   A BRIEF INTRODUCTION TO SOME ADVANCED
STATISTICS 317**

**CHAPTER 16   INTRODUCTION TO THE COMPUTER AND SPSSx
AND SAS LANGUAGES 340**

**APPENDIX A   AREAS UNDER THE NORMAL CURVE: VALUES OF $A(z)$
BETWEEN ORDINATE AT MEAN (Y_0) AND ORDINATE
AT z 349**

Preface

Statistics is a fascinating field of study, especially when it is used in exploring "real-world" problems. I treat statistics as a laboratory science. Students learn the logic and computation of the statistics in lectures and then apply what they have been taught in the computer lab.

The teaching and learning of statistics have changed tremendously over the last few decades. As high-speed computers, hooked to individual terminals, replaced card sorters and key punchers, we became able to do increasingly sophisticated things with our data. Unfortunately, statistics texts, on the whole, have not kept pace with the increasing capabilities.

The major advantage of this book is the opportunity for students to gain "hands on" experience with real data. Instructors who use this book may obtain four computer-ready data sets of floppy disks to facilitate this practical experience. These data sets contain a total of 153 variables, ranging from the self-esteem of multiple-sclerosis patients to the sex acts of convicted criminals, and from IQ scores of juvenile delinquents to measures of support of the Supreme Court by the elderly. The range of variables provided are of interest to a variety of social science disciplines.

I introduce the theory and logic underlying each statistical technique through narrative and simple computational examples. It is my firm belief that it is still absolutely necessary for students to solve small problems with their calculators in order to gain a grasp of the techniques. In most cases, both definitional and computational formulas are given. I then use either an SAS* or SPSS-X Data Analysis System** computer printout

---

* SAS is a registered trademark of SAS Institute Inc., Cary, NC, USA. Output from SAS procedures is printed with the permission of SAS Institute Inc., Cary, NC, USA. Copyright © 1983.

** SPSS-X is a registered trademark of SPSS Inc. of Chicago, Illinois, for its proprietary computer software. Output from SPSSx procedures is printed with the permission of SPSS Inc. of Chicago, IL.

to further explore the technique. The printouts are based on one of the data sets provided with the text. The proper interpretation of these computer printouts can be confusing, even to advanced students, but we go through each printout in a step-by-step fashion. This is the first introductory text that integrates theoretical and computational material with "guided tours" through the intricacies of a computer printout.

This method of teaching statistics gives students the opportunity to gain closure with the statistical concepts developed in the classroom by using the computer to run their own jobs. In my own classes, I have students choose a topic from one of the data sets and follow it all the way through from the simple descriptive level to multiple regression. This continuity of topics gives students a strong intuitive grasp of the utility of statistical analysis at the various levels of sophistication (for instance, they may find that a conclusion arrived at via bivariate analysis does not hold up under multivariate analysis). This methodology goes a long way in helping students to grasp the interrelatedness of the statistics that he or she will be using. This text's emphasis on continuity and interrelatedness of the various statistical techniques leads many students to appreciate the symmetry and beauty of statistics.

Another strong point of this text is the presentation of both SAS and SPSSx computer package programs throughout. Although I do not claim to have condensed into one book all the information contained in a dozen expensive SPSSx and SAS manuals, much essential introductory information is provided. Students are given the precise instructions necessary to run their statistical jobs in both languages and the information necessary to interpret the output. A special chapter on the use of the computer in social science research has been included for those who are using the computer in conjunction with the text (see Chapter 16).

I have included only the most popular and frequently used statistics in this text, excluding, for example, the largely meaningless average deviation. An in-depth understanding of the major statistical tools is superior to a nodding acquaintance with a smorgasbord of techniques, few of which are ever seen in professional journals. Class time is limited; the students' understanding of the major tools of their trade should not be. On the other hand, some statistical techniques not usually found in introductory texts are presented where they further the interpretation of traditional techniques. For instance, the odds ratio is presented in conjunction with chi-square, and eta is presented in conjunction with the t test and ANOVA.

A strong emphasis is placed on correlation and regression techniques. A perusal of any quantitative social science journal will convince the reader that these techniques, by a wide margin, are the most frequently used of all statistics. I have also included a chapter on advanced statistics (path analysis, logit regression, and factor analysis), since these techniques are frequently encountered in the literature today (see Chapter 15). Emphasis in Chapter 15 is placed on the logic of the techniques, providing students with the instructions to obtain these statistics from the computer and providing them with an interpretation of the computer printout.

A Note on Using This Text

Statistics for the Social Sciences (With Computer Applications) is a comprehensive and flexible text that is suitable for a wide variety of teaching styles and orientations toward the subject matter. Although I use the computer in my introductory classes, many instructors may not desire to integrate computer applications into their course. Having students run computer jobs and requiring them to interpret what they have found is time consuming and necessarily detracts from other things that some instructors may feel are more important for beginning students. This book can stand on its own as a traditional instructional text without the computer material, which is presented in addition to, not instead of, the usual statistical material. Even if the computer is not actually used by students, instructors may find the discussions that are related to the printouts to be a useful teaching tool.

In recognition of the wide variety of statistics classes that an instructor may teach, I have developed four suggested teaching outlines for those using this book based on: (1) the teaching preference (with and without the computer) for a one-semester course, (2) a two-semester sequence, and (3) a one-semester graduate course. These suggested outlines follow. The topics suggested for omission under certain course outline suggestions are usually the more advanced topics associated with a particular technique.

Suggested Outlines for Various Types of Courses

The following is a suggested outline for a one-semester introductory course in which a computer is not used and for which a broad survey of basic techniques is desired.

Chapter 1

Chapter 2

Chapter 3

Chapter 4

Chapter 5

Chapter 6

Chapter 7   (probably omitting multiple comparison tests)

Chapter 9

Chapter 10   (probably omitting certain techniques)

Chapter 11

Chapter 12   (probably omitting certain topics)

Chapter 13

The following is a suggested outline for a one-semester introductory course that emphasizes practical research, in which a computer is used in most chapters. (With this emphasis, Chapters 1 through 5 may have to receive less consideration than is optimally desirable.)

Chapter 1

Chapter 2

Chapter 3   (computer exercise: central tendency and dispersion)

Chapter 4

Chapter 5

Chapter 6   (computer exercise: t test)

Chapter 7 (optional chapter)

Chapter 9 (computer exercise: chi-square)

Chapter 10 (computer exercise: crosstabulation)

Chapter 11

Chapter 12 (probably omitting certain topics) (computer exercise: bivariate correlation and regression)

The following is a suggested outline for a two-semester introductory sequence.

Chapter 1

Chapter 2 (computer exercise: histogram and bar chart)

Chapter 3 (computer exercise: central tendency and dispersion)

Chapter 4

Chapter 5

Chapter 6 (computer exercise: t test)

Chapter 7 (computer exercise: ANOVA)

Chapter 8 (computer exercise: two-way ANOVA)

Chapter 9 (computer exercise: chi-square)

Chapter 10 (computer exercise: crosstabulation)

Chapter 11 (computer exercise: elaboration techniques and partial gamma)

Chapter 12 (computer exercise: bivariate correlation and regression)

Chapter 13 (computer exercise: multiple regression)

Chapter 14 (optional)

Chapter 15 (optional)

The following is a suggested outline for a one-semester graduate course. (Chapters 1 through 5 may be addressed briefly for "brush-up" purposes.)

Chapter 1

Chapter 2

Chapter 3 (computer exercise: central tendency and dispersion)

Chapter 4

Chapter 5

Chapter 6 (computer exercise: t test)

Chapter 7 (computer exercise: ANOVA)

Chapter 8 (computer exercise: two-way ANOVA)

Chapter 9 (computer exercise: chi-square)

Chapter 10 (computer exercise: crosstabulation)

Chapter 11 (computer exercise: elaboration techniques and partial gamma)

Chapter 12 (computer exercise: bivariate correlation and regression)

Chapter 13 (computer exercise: multiple regression)

I would like to acknowledge a debt of gratitude to professor Paul Hatab of the Department of Mathematics at Boise State University for his thoughtful reading and criticism of the manuscript. We spent many hours together discussing a number of statistical topics. I would also like to acknowledge my former statistical mentors: Dr. Ira Wasserman of Eastern Michigan University, Dr. Neil Palmer of the University of Toledo, and Drs. Kenneth Rothrock and Richard Zeller of Bowling Green State University.

I would also like to thank the following professors who reviewed part or all of the manuscript in various stages of its development. Their suggestions were important and I appreciate their efforts.

Kenneth J. Mietus, Western Illinois University

Michael Hughes, Virginia Polytechnic and State University

Kenneth Wilson, East Carolina University

Gregory L. Weiss, Roanoke College

Ernest Kurnow, New York University

Debra Friedman, University of Arizona

Satish Sharma, University of Nevada, Las Vegas

Ronald S. Edari, University of Wisconsin

Thanks are also extended to my sponsoring editor, Alan McClare, for having faith in this project and to my project editor, Donna Conte, for her scrupulous attention to detail. Thanks also to the students in my statistics classes who suffered through various drafts of this book (especially Grace Balazs, who did a lot of proofreading).

Special thanks to all members of my immediate family—my wife, Patricia Ann, my sons, Robert and Michael, and their wives, Dee and Sharron—for their support throughout this project.

Anthony Walsh

Statistics for the Social Sciences

Chapter 1

Introduction to Statistical Analysis

1.1 WHY STUDY STATISTICS?

As civilizations become more complex and technical, it becomes increasingly necessary for the thinking of the average person to become more complex and technical. The Industrial Revolution was the beginning of the end of a long period in history in which people could feel comfortably at home in their culture with only strong backs and the authority of received opinion to sustain them. It soon became imperative for citizens to understand, interpret, and analyze the written words of their culture. People who did not have the opportunity or the ability to adjust to this new requirement for full cultural participation were, by and large, condemned to lives of poverty and ignorance. They were considered to be "illiterate" and assigned society's least meaningful roles. H. G. Wells, writing in the nineteenth century, stated that "statistical thinking will one day be as necessary for efficient citizenship as the ability to read or write." I believe that day has arrived.

We hear much talk today about computer literacy, and much dire talk about the consequences of being left behind in the race to acquire it. The computer is a tool, however, a repository of the techniques that enable us more quickly and thoroughly to understand, interpret, and analyze data about phenomena. Its function is analogous to that of the library, a tool and a repository of the written word. To use the library, one must first learn the symbols of the written word that convey knowledge to us. If one cannot read, the library is not a tool; it is just another building. If one does not understand the symbols generated by the computer, it too is not a tool—it is just another fancy electronic gadget. It is our belief that an understanding of statistics will be as important to the educated person of the future as reading was to our great grandfathers, and for much the same reason.

1

Most people have an aversion to statistics—known as "the killer course" in my student days—and they have a tendency to mask their fears by denigrating and poking fun at it. It is a lot easier to think of some sharp and witty reasons for avoiding our fears than to confront and master them. For instance, there is British Prime Minister Benjamin Disraeli's famous dictum that "there are three kinds of lies: lies, damned lies, and statistics." W. H. Auden admonished his fellow poets: "Thou shalt not with statisticians sit, or commit a social science." These are attempts to dignify ignorance. We do not deny that people lie with statistics. But this is precisely why one should understand its possibilities and limitations.

1.2 THINKING STATISTICALLY

The following are some statistical "findings" of the type we run into almost every day as consumers of information, both inside and outside the university. After reading these findings, see if you can think of ways in which the conclusions based on them could be in error.

1. It appears that gender is a substantial cause of TV watching. We found that women watch significantly more TV than men (up to 50 percent more).

2. Researchers from the First Fundamentalist Church University have found a highly significant relationship between a preference for rock music and unwed motherhood. The researchers suggest that rock music be banned from the home as detrimental to the morals of young people.

3. Rampant racism still pervades our criminal justice system. Our findings indicate that, on the average, black defendants receive significantly more severe sentences than white defendants.

4. Fifty percent more teachers in the 1986 sample said that U.S. educational standards were declining than said so in the 1985 sample. It is a sad fact that U.S. education standards continue to fall behind those of other industrial nations.

The first three statements are examples of what social scientists call "misspecified models." *Misspecification* is the omission of crucial explanatory variables from the model. No doubt women do watch more TV than men, but not because they are women per se. Since women are less likely to be employed than men, they simply have more opportunity to watch TV. Similarly, I would not argue with a finding that reports a strong link between a preference for rock music and unwed motherhood. However, both a preference for rock music and unwed motherhood are also strongly associated with age. So age can be said to "cause" both musical preference and unwed motherhood. Nor would I particularly disagree with a finding that blacks are punished more severely than whites by the criminal justice system. But I would certainly like to know if the possibility that the blacks in the sample may have committed more serious crimes and possessed more serious prior records than the whites in the sample was taken into account.

Notice that I had no argument with any of the simple statements of statistical findings—they are what they are. Where problems arise, they arise with faulty interpretations based on incomplete information. We avoid this type of problem by including other theoretically relevant variables in the model: employment status in the first case, age in the second, and crime seriousness and prior records in the third.

The problem with finding 4 is the way it is presented. It doesn't tell me a thing. What were the answer categories? Perhaps 10 percent said they were declining, 50 percent said they were not declining, and 40 percent actually said they were improving. What were the sample sizes? Perhaps the 1986 sample was considerably increased over the 1985 sample, and this alone accounted for the additional 50 percent. If I don't know the answers to these questions, the statement is meaningless.

The avoidance of these and many other kinds of poor statistical reasoning is taught at various places in this book. A number of interesting examples of statistical bumbling, and sometimes downright statistical chicanery, are contained in Darrell Huff's (1954) entertaining little classic, *How to Lie with Statistics*.

If you are going to graduate school or aspire to be an administrator, it is even more important to come to grips with statistical reasoning. Statistics is the language of science. It is a mathematical language that enables us to draw logical conclusions within known boundaries of error from a set of data. **Data** (singular, **datum**) are simply a set of numerical scores relating to the phenomenon under investigation. Statistics enables us to reduce thousands of separate pieces of numerical information to a few easily understood summary statements. For instance, the primary data base that we will be working with throughout this book consists of 637 males convicted of felony crimes. Fifty-one separate pieces of information associated with the criminal and his case were collected on each of the 637 cases, for a total of 32,487 pieces of data. Once we have organized them by the techniques of statistics, these data enable us to make a multitude of statements about crime and punishment.

1.3 DESCRIPTIVE AND INFERENTIAL STATISTICS

1.3.1 Descriptive Statistics

A major function of all statistics is to describe the phenomenon under investigation. By convention, statisticians have reserved the label **descriptive statistics** for information that can be organized and presented in rather simple and direct ways. We are all familiar with such basic descriptive statistics as baseball batting averages, the annual rainfall in an area, the number of Japanese cars on American roads, divorce rates, and so forth. Percentages, ratios, proportions, frequencies, charts, tables, and graphs are some of the ways we organize, summarize, and describe these data. Descriptive statistics are limited to the data at hand and do not involve any inferences or generalizations beyond them.

1.3.2 Inferential Statistics

Inferential statistics are statistical techniques that enable us (given that certain assumptions can be made) to make inferences or generalizations about a large group on the basis of data taken from a subset of that group, called a sample. When we have sample data we are not really interested in the sample per se; we are interested in the population from which the sample came. If we have data on an entire population (i.e., a complete tabulation of some characteristics of interest from all elements in a population) we have a **census**.

Census refers to not only the enumeration of the populace that the government undertakes every decade but also any comprehensive tabulation of many different kinds of populations. The term **population** does not necessarily mean a body of people, although in social science it almost always does. *Population* refers to all cases about which a researcher wishes to make inferences. If we want to make general statements about U.S. citizens, the entire population of the United States is the population. If we are interested in the religious practices of Mormons, all Mormons are the population. If we are interested in the recreational activities of members of the New York City Police Department, the NYPD is the population.

For virtually all statistical research in the behavioral sciences, the intention is to use information derived from a representative **sample** in order to make statements about the population from which the sample was drawn. Technically, we say that we use sample **statistics** to estimate population **parameters**. Both a statistic and a parameter are numbers, the former being a proxy for the latter. Actually, we all make decisions based on samples even if we are not aware that we are doing so. Many students go to two or three different sections of an introductory course to "sample" the teaching style and class requirements of different professors. On the basis of the sample, the student decides which section he or she will enroll in. The student infers from the sampling of classes what the remainder of the classes will probably be like in terms of subject matter, requirements, and level of difficulty. Likewise, it is hardly necessary to eat the whole cow before deciding that the meat is tough. This is the point of scientific research and inference; we do not need to take the time or endure the cost necessary to obtain information relevant to our research from all elements of the population before we can draw conclusions. Statistical techniques allow us to estimate population parameters within precisely known margins of error.

The relationship between samples, parameters, populations, and statistics is presented graphically in Figure 1.1. In the example shown in the figure, we are attempting to estimate the average self-esteem score of all multiple sclerosis patients in the state of Idaho (the parameter) from the average self-esteem score (the statistic) of a random sample of those patients. Keep in mind that a statistic is to a sample as a parameter is to a population.

Assuming that our sample of multiple sclerosis patients is representative of all such patients in Idaho, we can say that our best guess of the average level of self-esteem among the population is 35, and we can then place some margin of error around this guess.

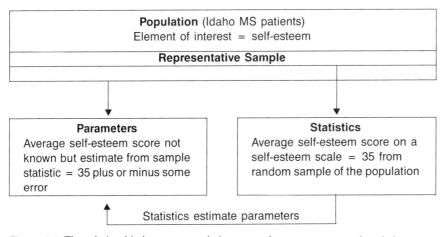

Figure 1.1 The relationship between populations, samples, parameters, and statistics

1.3.3 Statistics and Error

Anytime we measure something, particularly in the social and behavioral sciences, some degree of error is almost inevitable. Error in measurement is basically a function of two things: the accuracy of our instruments and the size of our samples. Obviously, the instrument used to measure self-esteem is not as reliable as is a well-calibrated scale used to measure weight, or a yardstick used to measure height. A person's feeling about his or her self-worth varies from time to time, and people can "fake high" or "fake low" for whatever reasons. Fortunately, these fluctuations tend to cancel one another out. That is, we might reasonably assume that for every person we catch on a bad day, we catch another on a good day, and that for every person faking high, there is another faking low.

Sample size is the other factor influencing the degree of error. The larger the sample the smaller the error. If we wanted to determine the height of all men in the U.S. Marine Corps, a sample size of 1000 would be better than one of 150, which is better than one of 50. This should be obvious to you, for the larger the sample you take, the more likely you are to include some rare or atypical cases (such as male marines shorter than 5'2" or taller than 6'2"). Populations always have more variability than do samples. Populations, by definition, contain all common and all rare cases. The larger the sample, the more likely it is to represent the situation as it exists in the population. But whatever the sample size, there will always be error associated with the sample statistics we use to estimate population parameters. Recognizing this, we place some margin of error around the estimates. We might conclude from our study of self-esteem among multiple sclerosis patients that the average self-esteem score is 35, plus or minus 3 points, or between 32 and 38. Statistical procedures for assessing the degree of error are included in this book, especially in Chapter 5.

1.3.4 Parametric and Nonparametric Statistics

Statistical methods that enable us to estimate population parameters are known as *parametric statistics*, which make certain assumptions about the population parameters. A second family of statistics requires no assumptions about the population parameters: *nonparametric statistics*. It would not be appropriate at this stage to go into the advantages and disadvantages of these two types of statistics. These issues will be addressed later.

1.3.5 Operationalization

The measurement of such physical constructs as height and weight is unproblematic. But what about such social science concepts as self-esteem, social frustration, religiosity, or alienation? No one has yet invented an alienation meter to measure the ingredients of that concept. If we are serious about the social science enterprise, first we have to be clear about what we want to measure. Then we have to design a series of operations that yield suitable measurements. Clarifying what it is we wish to measure—the process of refining and sharpening our conceptualizations of a phenomenon—does not concern us here. Designing a series of operations to measure those conceptualizations does. In doing so we say that we are "operationalizing the ingredients of the concept."

The process of operationalization is often a difficult one for students to grasp. Let us first distinguish between a conceptual definition and an operational definition. A conceptual definition is a verbal statement relating our understanding of a phenomenon: "Blood pressure is the pressure exerted on the arterial walls by the pumping action of the heart." This is an accurate verbal definition, but what if I want to compare the blood pressure of a number of individuals in an attempt to determine whose pressure is higher (more) or lower (less)? The ideas of "higher" and "lower" and "more" and "less" are at the heart of measurement. As we all know, there is a well-established series of operations to measure the ingredients of the concepts of the "more and less" of blood pressure, which is measured by a sphygmomanometer. The operational definition of blood pressure is "The height of a column of mercury in standard units recorded at the first Korotkoff phase (the first audible sounds) and the fifth Korotkoff phase (termination of audible sounds)." The Korotkoff phases give us systolic and diastolic readings, respectively. We now have measured numbers that we can compare and contrast with other numbers obtained by the same operations. Thus, an **operational definition** is the definition of a concept in terms of the operations used to measure it.

Suppose a social science researcher makes the proposition that people with high self-esteem tend to be successful. Contained in the proposition are two concepts—self-esteem and successful—that have to be operationally defined if the researcher is to test the proposition. *Self-esteem* can be defined operationally as the score an individual obtains on a questionnaire that asks various questions relating to how that person feels about himself or herself. Such scales usually contain multiple indicators of the concept it is attempting to measure. *Success* may be operationally defined in terms of occupational prestige, amount of money in the bank, the kind of house lived in, or many other indicators.

No matter how many indicators we use to measure a concept, we never exhaust its meaning. For instance, an IQ test is an operationalization of the concept of intelligence, but it doesn't get at the "essence" of the concept of intelligence. Nevertheless, for the purpose of research, the operational definition of the concept *is* the concept for all practical purposes. You may be an excellent student in all respects, but you won't get an A in most courses unless you achieve a cumulative score of 90 percent or more (the operational definition of the concept of academic excellence) on your examinations.

Researchers wish to be sure that the instruments used to measure their concepts are reliable and valid. *Validity* refers to how well the measures derived from the operation reflect the concept. *Reliability* refers to the consistency with which repeated measures produce the same results across time and across observers. The validity of a blood pressure gauge is determined pragmatically. That is, individuals whose blood pressure is consistently high, say 180/95, have very different cardiovascular histories than individuals whose blood pressure is normal or low, say 120/75. (Note that the concepts "high" and "low" in this context have definite numbers.) This is pragmatic or predictive validity because, based on the numbers obtained, the physician makes treatment decisions and well-founded predictions about the consequences of not adhering to the treatment he or she prescribes. A blood pressure gauge is reliable if two or more health workers obtain the same reading with the same patient or if the same researcher obtains identical readings from a different gauge.

The assessment of reliability and validity of a social science instrument, such as a scale to measure self-esteem, is usually done mathematically. Other social science variables, such as race, sex, number of children, or whether or not an immigrant is a U.S. citizen, are straightforward and measured by simple observation or by a single question. Whatever the concept we are operationalizing, we assign numbers to our observations. In other words, we measure them.

1.4 MEASUREMENT

Measurement is the process of assigning numbers to observations according to a set of rules. The observations being measured are **variables**, or anything that can change in value from case to case. Sex is a variable because cases vary from male to female. Self-esteem is a variable because scores obtained on a self-esteem scale can be arranged on a continuum from those scoring lowest to those scoring highest. Being male is an attribute of the variable sex. Being male is therefore a constant; it does not change. In the sex offender data to be used throughout this book, all offenders are male. Thus, "sex of offender" is a constant in this data set.

Variables can be discrete or continuous. **Discrete variables** classify observations according to the kind or quality of their characteristics. Yes/no, black/white, male/female are examples of dichotomous (division of two) variables. Discrete variables can take on more divisions than two; religious affiliation, ethnic origin, and income category are examples of multicategory discrete variables. **Continuous variables** can theoretically take on any value between two points on a scale and be classified according to the magnitude and quantity of their characteristics, for example, age. It is possible to divide age into any number of values on the continuum, including weeks, days, and hours. Discrete variables, however, have sharply demarcated distinct values; you cannot have 1.5 yes answers or 2.45 males, nor can you sell 25.35 cars per month.

The rules we use to assign numbers to observations result in various levels of measurement. Information comes to us from the real world in many forms, ranging from crude to very refined. The statistics we use in our research depend greatly on the relative crudity or refinement of our measures. There are four levels of measurement with different properties that are important for us to understand: nominal, ordinal, interval, and ratio. These levels are hierarchical and cumulative in that each higher level, in addition to having its own special characteristic, incorporates the characteristics of those levels beneath it. Nominal and ordinal variables are qualitative variables, meaning that they differ in kind but cannot be expressed numerically except in an arbitrary fashion. Interval and ratio measures are quantitative, meaning that they can be expressed numerically. Let us look at these four levels of measurement one at a time.

1.4.1 Nominal Level

The **nominal level** of measurement is the crudest form of measurement and is used only to classify, that is, to name observations that are different in some qualitative way. The categories of the classification scheme should be mutually exclusive (being in one category automatically excludes inclusion in another) and exhaustive (all possible categories of a variable should be included). For example, if we are interested in the variable of sex, both males and females should be included, and being placed in one category automatically excludes being placed in the other.

The numbers assigned to nominal-level data are arbitrary. The researcher may assign the number 0 to males and 1 to females. If the researcher is interested in religion, he or she might code Catholics 1, Protestants 2, and Jews 3, or any other sensible coding system. It should be apparent that we cannot perform mathematical operations such as adding, subtracting, dividing, and multiplying with this kind of nonquantitative data (you cannot multiply Catholics by Protestants and arrive at some meaningful third value). Numbers assigned to categories in this way are nothing more than labels masquerading as numbers. Statistical formulas for variables measured at this level make use of category frequencies (how many males, females, Catholics, etc., in the data), not the numeric code value used to identify a particular category of the variable.

1.4.2 Ordinal Level

Ordinal-level data are somewhat of an improvement on nominal data in that we can order them in addition to naming them. That is, we can put the data in an order that ranges somewhere from the bottom to the top. We may also be able to see a middle to the data or gradation of the middle. For example, we can ask all the people in the classroom to stand. We can then arrange them in a line based on descending order of height. Notice that when we do this we have a rank order, but we do not have the precise measures of the differences among the heights of the individuals. We know that the tallest person is at the top and the shortest person is at the bottom and that every other person is located in his or her proper ascending or descending location. We do not have the precise heights of the tallest person or the shortest person, or any person; we just have the right order.

Examples of ordinal-level data are class standing (freshman, sophomore, junior, senior) and social class (low, medium, high). These categories can be perceived only as "more" or "less" since we cannot validly assign an arithmetic interval separating them. Attitudinal and opinion scales (disagree, undecided, agree) are technically also ordinal scales. However, we can, and many researchers do, treat such scales as interval data without seriously biasing results.

1.4.3 Interval Level

The **interval level** is the next highest level of measurement. At this level, in addition to classification and order, we have equal units of measurement. That is, there are precisely defined intervals between and among the observations; the interval between 6 and 7 is exactly the same as the interval between 24 and 25, and both are identical in magnitude to the interval between 1155 and 1156. An example of an interval-level variable is IQ. Consider four individuals with IQ scores of 70, 140, 75, and 145. We can say that the differences between 70 and 140 and between 75 and 145 are exactly the same, but we cannot say that the second person is twice as intelligent as the first. All we can say is that those with the higher scores are more intelligent (insofar as IQ tests measure intelligence) than those with the lower scores. What we lack with an interval scale is a stable starting point (an absolute zero), and consequently, the scale values cannot be interpreted in any absolute sense. However, we can perform a large number of mathematical operations with interval data not possible with nominal and ordinal data.

1.4.4 Ratio Level

The **ratio level** has all the properties of the lower measurement scales in addition to an absolute zero point. In other words, we can classify it, we can place it in proper order, the numbers we use to measure it are of equal magnitudes, and it starts at an absolute zero point. Examples include feet and inches, ounces and pounds, years of education, and income (although some may assert that strictly speaking years of education and income are discrete variables). It should be obvious that we can use all sorts of mathematical procedures with ratio-level variables. Someone with an income of $50,000 makes precisely twice as much as someone with an income of $25,000. This is a meaningful ratio of 2:1.

It is important to be aware of the level at which you have measured your variables because the choice of statistical analysis depends on it. However, I must point out that there are arguments between statistical purists and more liberal statisticians regarding level of measurement issues. The main bone of contention is whether or not it is permissible to treat certain ordinal variables as interval-level variables in order to take advantage of superior statistical techniques. An alienation scale ranging from a possible low of 0 to a possible high of 40 would be treated by most researchers as an interval-level scale, although such a scale only approximates the equidistant functions of "true" interval scales. That is, although scores on an alienation scale are continuous, they have properties that lie somewhere between ordinal and interval levels of measurement. Whether or not you would use an interval-level technique with such data depends more on your statistical philosophy than on some absolute principle. Stanford Labovitz (1970), among others, has shown that the assignment of a linear scoring system to "partial interval" data results in negligible error and that the advantages of doing so far outweigh the disadvantages.

This does not mean that any ordinal variable is properly treated as an interval-level variable. Generally, the greater the number of ranks or categories of the measured ordinal variable the greater confidence we may have in treating the variable as an interval. Scores on an alienation scale ranging from 0 to 40, for example, can be much more validly treated as an interval variable than if they were divided into low, medium, and high levels of alienation. A further consideration is the approximation to the equidistant function. A scoring system that looks like 0, 1, 2, 3, 4, 5,... is much better than one such as 0, 8, 9, 16, 28, 102,... The latter scoring system is far from equidistant and begins to look very much like discrete ordered categories.

Table 1.1 illustrates the cumulative and hierarchical character of the four levels of measurement.

TABLE 1.1   CHARACTERISTICS OF LEVELS OF MEASUREMENT

Levels of Measurement	Classify	Order	Equal Units	Absolute Zero
Nominal	yes	no	no	no
Ordinal	yes	yes	no	no
Interval	yes	yes	yes	no
Ratio	yes	yes	yes	yes

1.5 ORGANIZATION OF THIS BOOK

This book is organized to facilitate a number of important goals: (1) an understanding of the basic assumptions behind each statistic, (2) an understanding of the logic and computations underlying each solution, (3) an understanding of the utilities and limitations of each statistic, (4) the ability to use the computer to run statistical analyses and to check computations with the UDOIT program in either SAS or SPSSx language, and (5) the ability to understand the important elements provided by the computer printout. Points 4 and 5 are special attributes of this book and are designed to make it possible for students actually to do research with real data on topics of interest to them.

Each chapter contains three kinds of instructional material. To facilitate understanding of the logic and computations of the statistics, we first present examples based on fictitious data and small numbers of cases. These kinds of examples allow ease of computation and are designed to be neat and clean in terms of interpretation. The assumption is that these real research examples will be more readily interpretable after you have mastered the logic presented in the idealized "error-free" fictitious examples. The real research examples are in computer printout format and are followed by explanations of the meaning of each of the statistics presented. We then present information needed to run the programs that are the basis for the examples in both SAS and SPSSx computer language, after which we give a detailed description of the printout. Thus, theory and practice are integrated throughout.

Of course, some instructors choose not to integrate the use of the computer into the course. The computer instructions are in addition to, not instead of, a thorough explication of the statistical techniques. For this reason I have placed computer instructions for each chapter into chapter appendices rather than in the body of the chapter. For those using the computer with this book, Chapter 16 provides an introduction to the use of the two most popular statistical languages in social science today, SPSSx and SAS. The emphasis in this book is on SPSSx since this statistical package appears to be somewhat more popular than SAS at the present time.

1.6 SUMMARY

Statistics is becoming an increasingly important field of study. As a consumer of statistics you should be aware of the many ways that the producers of statistics, either purposely or inadvertently, can mislead you. This book will make you a more sophisticated consumer, as well as a producer, of statistics.

Descriptive statistics describe data in simple and direct ways by using graphs, charts, percentages, proportions, ratios, and rates. Inferential statistics make inferences about a population from information derived from a sample. A population is the totality of all observations that are of interest, and a sample is a subset of the population. We estimate population characteristics, called parameters, from sample characteristics, called statistics. In our estimation of parameters there will always be a certain amount of error, although we can quantify this error and take it into account.

However, before we can estimate any parameter, such as the average self-esteem of a population, we have to be able to measure it. Before we can measure it we have to define it operationally, that is, in terms of the operations used to measure it.

Measurement is the assignment of numbers to observations according to rules. We measure variables (defined as some characteristic or trait that takes on different values across observations) at four different levels of measurement.

Nominal-level variables, the crudest level, have mutually exclusive and exhaustive categories that differ from one another only qualitatively. There is no implied order or equality of distance between the categories. The ordinal level of measurement allows for the rank ordering of categories, but not with respect to equal distance. The interval level of measurement has categories of equal distance between continuous variables, but they lack a true zero point. The ratio level of measurement is the highest form of measurement in that it contains all the attributes of the lower levels in addition to having a true zero point. Only interval- and ratio-level variables are amenable to mathematical operations. Each level of measurement has the attributes of lower levels as well as its own.

Most researchers today assign an interval scoring system to what are, strictly speaking, ordinal variables. This is considered valid to the extent that the scoring system approximates the equidistant function and there are a relatively large number of ranks or categories such as one finds in attitude scales. Researchers do this because they are able to use more high-powered statistics and because it has been shown that the benefits of doing so far outweigh any error, which tends to be negligible.

PRACTICE APPLICATION: VARIABLES AND LEVELS OF MEASUREMENT

A teacher decides to generate a statistical description of a class of eight students on four variables: sex, class standing, IQ, and weight. These measurements are made and placed in the following table.

VARIABLE AND LEVEL OF MEASUREMENT

Student	Sex (Nominal)	Class Standing (Ordinal)	IQ (Interval)	Weight (Ratio)
Bill	0	2	90	200.0
Mary	1	3	110	110.5
Tony	0	3	130	152.6
Ingrid	1	2	98	100.0
Susan	1	2	120	110.4
Sam	0	4	100	165.0
Kurt	0	3	104	171.1
Alice	1	4	180	123.7

Coding: Sex: 0 = male, 1 = female. Class standing: 1 = freshman, 2 = sophomore, 3 = junior, 4 = senior. IQ = continuous. Weight = continuous.

The first variable, sex, is a discrete, dichotomous, qualitative variable measured at the nominal level. It has no quantitative value, and all we can do arithmetically is count the numbers of males and females in the sample.

The second variable, class standing, is a discrete, ordered, qualitative variable measured at the ordinal level. Alice and Sam are of higher class standing than Mary, Kurt, or Tony, who are themselves of higher standing than Bill or

Ingrid. Here we can talk about higher and lower, but nothing else. We cannot, for instance, add Bill and Ingrid together to get an Alice or a Sam. If there were a direct one-to-one relationship between the number of years spent in college and class standing we could conceptualize this variable as ratio level and make statements such as "Alice has been in school twice as long as Bill." However, as the variable is presently conceptualized, we cannot even assume that Alice has been going to school as long as Bill. Her superior IQ, especially in relation to Bill's, makes it possible that she could have passed more classes than Bill in less time.

The third variable, IQ, is a continuous, quantitative variable measured at the interval level. Since we have equal units, we can say that the difference between Mary's and Tony's IQ scores (20 points) is exactly the same as the difference between Susan's and Sam's. However, even though Alice's IQ score is numerically twice that of Bill's, we cannot say that she is twice as intelligent because IQ scales lack a precise absolute zero. I should point out that some people believe that IQ is more an ordinal- than an interval-level variable. Their argument is that the substantive difference between IQ scores of 80 and 100 is much greater than the difference between 120 and 140, although mathematically the difference is still 20.

The final variable, weight, is a continuous, quantitative variable measured at the ratio level. Since weight has an absolute zero, we can validly say that Bill weighs exactly twice as much as Ingrid. Note again that the ratio level of measurement contains all the attributes of the lower levels (name, order, equal units) in addition to having an absolute zero point.

REFERENCES

Huff, D. (1954). *How to lie with statistics*. New York: W. W. Norton.

Labovitz, S. (1970). The assignment of numbers to rank-order categories. *American Sociological Review*, 35:515–524.

Chapter 2

Describing Data

2.1 PRESENTATION AND SUMMARIZATION OF DATA

This chapter examines methods of **univariate analysis**, that is, the analysis of one (*uni* means "one") variable as opposed to the simultaneous analysis of two variables (bivariate) or more than two variables (multivariate). Although researchers are often anxious to get right down to the task of bivariate and multivariate analysis, good researchers first want to get a "feel" for their data through univariate analysis.

The objective of data presentation is to communicate to the readers of the research the informational content of the data. When researchers complete the process of collecting data, they have a mass of raw numbers, which won't tell them much unless the data are arranged and displayed in a meaningful way. Researchers cannot discern trends until some order or structure is imposed on the data. The researchers first have to organize the data into formats that can be meaningfully interpreted, and they must then choose a way of summarizing the data to allow assimilation of the information conveyed.

By convention, statisticians have reserved the label *descriptive statistics* for information that can be organized and presented in rather simple and direct ways, such as frequencies, histograms, bar graphs, and pie charts. These are pictorial representations of data, utilizing the old adage that "a picture is worth a thousand words." The particular graphic technique chosen by the researcher depends on a number of considerations, including the purpose of the research and what the researcher wants to convey and emphasize, the assumed level of sophistication of the readers, and the type of data being described.

In addition to presenting data graphically, it is also important to be able to summarize them numerically. Numeric summarization provides more precise descriptions of the data and complements the visual impact of the pictorial presentation. It also emphasizes the features of the data most relevant to the research. Common numeric descriptions include percentages, ratios, proportions, and rates. We will begin with frequency distributions.

2.1.1 Types of Frequency Distributions

A **frequency distribution** is simply the frequency or number or times that a particular value or class of a variable appears in a distribution of scores. Suppose we asked 20 persons to provide information about their gender and the number of children they have. We would obtain the information given in Table 2.1.

To describe this small data set initially a researcher would say that the number of observations equals 20, sample size equals 20, or $N = 20$. The total number of children in the families of these respondents equals 44, and there are 12 females and 8 males in the sample. We are only interested for the moment in the number of children in this data set. To obtain a clearer picture of the group we will arrange the observations in ascending order and tally them. Each value is symbolized by x, and a tally is placed next to each occurrence of that value. There are two respondents with no children, two with one child, eight with two children, six with three children, and two with four children. The result of this exercise is a frequency distribution (see Table 2.2). The notation (f equals frequency) and $cum.f$ symbolize the cumulative frequency, which is obtained by adding the number of the observations in each category to the score values preceding it. The cumulative frequency of respondents is 20, and the number of children these 20 people report is 44.

We will now look at a more complicated frequency distribution using the offender data supplied with this text. These data were collected from the files of a probation department in a large metropolitan county in the Midwest (Walsh, 1986). (Detailed information regarding the data set is provided in the workbook accompanying this text.) For this example we will use the frequency distribution

TABLE 2.1 FREQUENCY DISTRIBUTION OF NUMBER OF CHILDREN AND SEX OF RESPONDENT

Obs.	Number of Children	Sex	Obs.	Number of Children	Sex
1	1	F	11	0	M
2	0	M	12	4	F
3	2	F	13	1	F
4	2	F	14	2	M
5	2	M	15	3	M
6	3	F	16	2	F
7	3	M	17	2	F
8	4	F	18	3	M
9	3	M	19	3	F
10	2	F	20	2	F

TABLE 2.2   TABULATION OF FREQUENCIES AND CUMULATIVE FREQUENCIES OF
RESPONDENTS AND NUMBER OF CHILDREN REPORTED

x	tally	f	cum.f	Number of Children
0	//	2	2	0
1	//	2	4	2
2	//// ////	8	12	16
3	//// //	6	18	18
4	//	2	20	8
				44

of the ages of victims of violent crime (sexual and nonsexual). This frequency
distribution is presented in Table 2.3 and is taken directly from the SPSSx computer printout.

2.1.2 Interpreting the Printout

The SPSSx printout shown in Table 2.3 is an array of the data on victims' ages
ordered from the youngest victim (1 year) to the oldest (71 years). The first term
we encounter identifies the variable on which the frequency distribution is based
(VAGE   AGE OF VICTIM). We next see the terms VALUE LABEL and FREQUENCIES.   The first value label is age 1 and there is one victim in that
category, so the frequency equals 1. Running down the distribution to value label
12, we see that there were 43 victims in this age group. This number constitutes
10.2 PERCENT of the entire distribution. The term VALID PERCENT is printed
out in case we have missing values in the data. In this case the valid percent is
identical to the percent because we have eliminated from consideration those
cases in which we did not have information on the victim's age. The final term,
CUM PERCENT, is simply an alternative to reporting cumulative frequencies as
raw numbers and will always culminate at 100 percent.

2.1.3 Frequency Distribution of Grouped Data

It is sometimes desirable to group continuous data such as the victims' age into
discrete groups, or intervals. The data in Table 2.3 contain 42 different values,
and we may feel that they could be better comprehended if we had fewer values
for graphical presentation. In a grouped frequency distribution, a group of scores
is associated with a particular frequency, whereas in a regular frequency distribution each single score is associated with a frequency. Thus, a grouped frequency
is the sum of all the frequencies in the group. For example, if we decided to place
ages 1 through 6 into a single group, the frequency for this group would be 1 +
1 + 2 + 2 + 10 + 10 = 26. Groups of scores such as these are referred to as
class intervals.

TABLE 2.3 FREQUENCY DISTRIBUTION OF THE AGES OF CRIME VICTIMS

VAGE   AGE OF VICTIM (SPSSx Printout)

VALUE LABEL	VALUE	FREQUENCY	PERCENT	VALID PERCENT	CUM PERCENT
	1	1	.2	.2	.2
	2	1	.2	.2	.5
	3	2	.5	.5	.9
	4	2	.5	.5	1.4
	5	10	2.4	2.4	3.8
	6	10	2.4	2.4	6.2
	7	10	2.4	2.4	8.5
	8	8	1.9	1.9	10.4
	9	22	5.2	5.2	15.6
	10	24	5.7	5.7	21.3
	11	23	5.5	5.5	26.8
	12	43	10.2	10.2	37.0
	13	26	6.2	6.2	43.1
	14	37	8.8	8.8	51.9
	15	32	7.6	7.6	59.5
	16	11	2.6	2.6	62.1
	17	15	3.6	3.6	65.6
	18	25	5.9	5.9	71.6
	19	25	5.9	5.9	77.5
	20	12	2.8	2.8	80.3
	21	9	2.1	2.1	82.5
	22	11	2.6	2.6	85.1
	23	4	.9	.9	86.0
	24	11	2.6	2.6	88.6
	25	5	1.2	1.2	89.8
	26	6	1.4	1.4	91.2
	27	3	.7	.7	91.9
	28	2	.5	.5	92.4
	29	2	.5	.5	92.9
	30	5	1.2	1.2	94.1
	31	5	1.2	1.2	95.3
	32	3	.7	.7	96.0
	34	3	.7	.7	96.7
	40	4	.9	.9	97.6
	49	3	.7	.7	98.3
	50	2	.5	.5	98.8
	55	1	.2	.2	99.1
	56	1	.2	.2	99.3
	62	1	.2	.2	99.5
	69	1	.2	.2	99.8
	71	1	.2	.2	100.0
	TOTAL	422	100.0	100.0	

2.1.4 Limits, Sizes, and Midpoints of Class Intervals

For the purposes of illustration we have decided to divide the data into seven class intervals, each containing six values. A class interval is a segment of the frequency distribution containing certain score values. Each interval has three values we have to calculate—the real lower limit, the real upper limit, and the midpoint. The apparent limits of a group of scores are the lowest and highest scores. In a class interval containing the scores 8, 9, 10, 11, and 12, the apparent lower and upper limits are 8 and 12, respectively. The **real lower limit** of a class interval is one-half of the distance between the apparent lower limit of that class interval and the apparent upper limit of the preceding class interval. Likewise, the **real upper limit** is one-half of the distance between the apparent upper limit of that class interval and the apparent lower limit of the next class interval. To explain the reasoning behind the need to determine real limits of class intervals, suppose we had entered the values of victims' ages in years and months rather than rounding off to the nearest whole year. Further suppose that an individual was scored as being 12.8 years of age. Would you place that individual into the class interval 8, 9, 10, 11, 12 or into the class interval 13, 14, 15, 16, 17? You would probably round 12.8 to the nearest number, and in doing so you would be implicitly recognizing that the real lower limit of the number 13 is 12.5. The practice of determining real class limits resolves the dilemma of deciding in which of two adjacent class intervals a given score belongs. Figure 2.1 illustrates this concept.

To obtain the **size** of the class interval we simply subtract the real lower limit of the interval from its real upper limit. The size of interval 1 is $12.5 - 7.5 = 5$, and the size of interval 2 is $12.5 - 17.5 = 5$. Thus, the size of each interval is 5. The **midpoint** of a class interval is located precisely at its center and is obtained by adding one-half of the size of the class interval to the lower real limit. The midpoint for interval 1 is one-half its size $2.5 + 7.5 = 10$, and for interval 2 it is $2.5 + 12.5 = 15$.

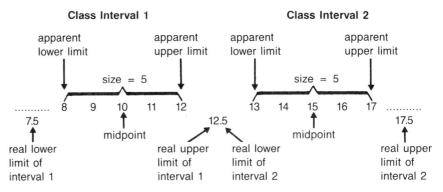

Figure 2.1 Apparent and real limits of two adjacent class intervals

2.1.5 Bar Charts and Histograms

Bar charts and histograms are graphic methods of displaying data. You will often see this method employed in newspapers and magazines when the writers wish to convey such information as the percentage of house owners versus renters, the percentage of those who agree with the outcome of the Baby M case versus those who disagree and who had no opinion, and so forth. **Bar charts** are vertical bars proportional in height to the number of cases or observations in a particular frequency. Bar charts are suitable only for the graphical presentation of nominal and ordinal data or grouped continuous data.

A **histogram** is similar to a bar chart but is suitable for the presentation of interval and ratio data as well as nominal and ordinal data. Another important difference between the bar chart and the histogram is that there are no spaces between the categories in a histogram. This difference reflects the continuous nature of the data presented as opposed to the discrete nature of the data in a bar chart. In histograms the categories are usually listed on the horizontal axis and the frequencies on the vertical axis. However, both SAS and SPSSx printouts reverse the placement of the axes. Of course, this makes no substantive difference to the interpretation of the data. Figure 2.2 shows a typical bar chart.

It is easy to assess the visual impact imparted by Montgomery's bar chart. The relative height of the bars certainly indicates that American prison officials rely on force to end prison riots to a far greater extent than Canadian officials.

A bar chart of our grouped data is presented in Figure 2.3, and a histogram of the same data is given in Figure 2.4. To obtain these graphs from a computer using SPSSx, use command 2.1 as explained in the chapter appendix.

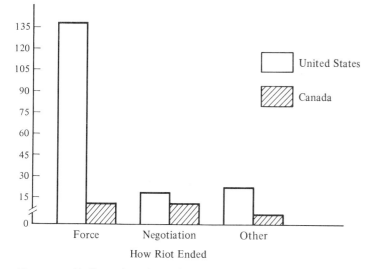

Figure 2.2 Ending prison riots, 1971–1983, United States and Canada (*Source*: From Reid H. Montgomery, Jr., "Costly Prison Riots: United States and Canada," *Journal of Justice Issues,* 1987, vol. 2, p. 63)

VAGE	AGE OF VICTIM				
VALUE LABEL		VALUE	FREQUENCY	PERCENT	VALID PERCENT	CUM PERCENT
		1	26	6.2	6.2	6.2
		2	130	30.8	30.8	37.0
		3	146	34.6	34.6	71.6
		4	72	17.1	17.1	88.6
		5	23	5.5	5.5	94.1
		6	11	2.6	2.6	96.7
		7	14	3.3	3.3	100.0
		TOTAL	422	100.0	100.0	

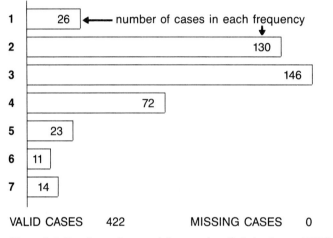

VALID CASES   422   MISSING CASES   0

Figure 2.3 Bar chart of grouped frequencies of victims' ages (SPSSx)

VAGE	AGE OF VICTIM	
COUNT OCCURRENCES	VALUE	ONE SYMBOL EQUALS APPROXIMATELY 4.00
26	1.00	*******
130	2.00	*********************************
146	3.00	*************************************
72	4.00	******************
23	5.00	******
11	6.00	***
14	7.00	****

Figure 2.4 Histogram of grouped frequencies of victims' ages (SPSSx)

2.1.6 Frequency Polygon

A **polygon** is similar to a histogram. Instead of bars it uses dots placed above the midpoint of each class interval, the adjacent points being connected by a straight line. We will show in Figure 2.5 a polygon with our grouped data of victims' ages (see Table 2.4). Recall that the midpoint is the precise center of the class interval and can be determined by adding one-half of the size of the interval to its lower real limit. Our first task is to determine the real limits, interval sizes, and midpoints, for the data from Table 2.3. Note that the small number of cases in which the victims were 38 or older necessitates a class interval size for these observations that greatly exceeds the size of the other intervals.

Note that the line connecting the data points is taken all the way down to intersect the bottom of the graph on the horizontal line, known as the **abscissa**, and that the height of the dots on the vertical line, the **ordinate**, correspond to the frequency of observations in a class interval.

TABLE 2.4   GROUPED FREQUENCY DISTRIBUTION OF THE DATA IN TABLE 2.3 WITH REAL LIMITS, INTERVAL SIZES, AND MIDPOINTS

Class Interval	Real Limits	Interval Size	Midpoint	Frequency
1–6	0.5–6.5	6	3.5	26
7–12	6.5–12.5	6	9.5	130
13–18	12.5–18.5	6	15.5	146
19–24	18.5–24.5	6	21.5	72
25–30	24.5–30.5	6	27.5	23
31–37	30.5–37.5	7	34.0	11
38–71	37.5–71.5	34	54.5	14

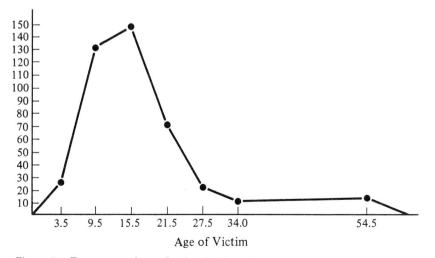

Figure 2.5 Frequency polygon for data in Figure 2.3

2.1.7 Pie Charts

A **pie chart** is another way of graphically presenting your data. Pie charts are especially useful if you want to compare each category (slice of the pie) with the total rather than comparing one category with another, as with bar heights. For this example, rather than dividing our data into approximately equal frequencies as we did before, we will divide it in terms of some theoretical interest. Suppose that we wished to show the relative numbers of people who are sexually victimized based on age categories. We might divide the distribution into four categories: young children of 13 years of age and younger, older children between 14 and 17, young adults between the ages of 19 and 29, and adults over 30. To obtain a pie chart showing this distribution command 2.3 is required.

The pie chart in Figure 2.6 is divided into pieces that are proportional in size to the corresponding categories. Since any circle has 360 degrees, each 3.6 degrees corresponds to 1 percent of the total. The share of the pie for the older adults, the group least likely to be victimized, is thus $6.99\% \times 3.6 = 25.2$ degrees.

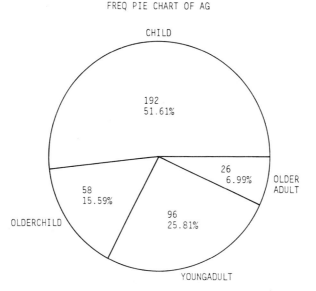

Figure 2.6 Pie chart of sexual assault victims' ages in four groups

2.1.8 Advantage and Disadvantage of Grouping Data

Whenever you group data you must consider the advantage and disadvantage. The advantage is that grouping reduces data to manageable sizes, which allows a more pleasing visual representation and ease of computation when that hurdle is approached. A major disadvantage is that the more we reduce data in order to summarize it, the more information we lose. Returning to our discussion of levels of measurement in Chapter 1, what we have done by grouping data is to render a good ratio variable (victims' ages) in the form of ordinal data. With victim's ages rendered in the original metric, we could validly say that a victim of age 20 is twice as old as one of age 10. However, we cannot say that the victims in grouped category 4 are twice as old as those in grouped category 2; we can only say that they are older. By grouping the data we have lost the ability to make precise statements about the data. The problem is magnified as the size of the class intervals becomes larger. You will learn later that the more powerful statistics can only be applied to interval and ratio data; and if there is a cardinal sin in statistics, it is to group this kind of data, thereby necessitating the use of weaker statistical methods when the more powerful ones could have been fruitfully utilized. However, if the data are collected initially in ungrouped form, we can just as easily group them if necessary to do so.

2.1.9 Histogram with Ungrouped Data

Table 2.5 presents a histogram of victims' ages with ungrouped data. In this example we have again selected only victims of sexual assault. The histogram in Table 2.5 enables you to see the shape of the distribution of scores in their raw form. As we will see in the next chapter, this is an important consideration. Often the first step in any social scientist's research is to run a frequencies program such as this.

An important first step in any data analysis is to run a set of frequencies. Not only does this give a feel for the data, it also is an important step in cleaning up the data (searching for miscoded variables and so forth). To illustrate, suppose that you ran a frequencies program on race and the distribution looked like this:

	RACE VALUE	FREQUENCY
WHITE	1	250
BLACK	2	175
MEXICAN	3	55
OTHER	4	6
	5	1
	8	2

Values 5 and 8 were miscoded when the data were entered. You know this since *white, black, Mexican,* and *other* exhaust the racial types you have in the data. To locate these miscoded cases you would have to give the computer the following command: SELECT IF (RACE EQ 5 RACE EQ 8). You would then type in the command FREQUENCIES VARIABLES = SID. SID stands for "subject's identification number." The frequencies printout will identify which cases have been miscoded. You can then go back to the original data and enter the correct code value.

TABLE 2.5 FREQUENCIES AND HISTOGRAM OF SEXUAL ASSAULT VICTIMS' AGES IN THE ORIGINAL METRIC (SPSSx)

VAGE	AGE OF VICTIM	FREQ	CUM. FREQ	PERCENT	CUM. PERCENT
1	*	1	1	0.31	0.31
2	*	1	2	0.31	0.62
3	**	2	4	0.62	1.25
4	**	2	6	0.62	1.87
5	*********	10	16	3.12	4.98
6	******	6	22	1.87	6.85
7	*********	10	32	3.12	9.97
8	********	8	40	2.49	12.46
9	******************	18	58	5.61	18.07
10	*******************	19	77	5.92	23.99
11	******************	19	96	5.92	29.91
12	*********************************	33	129	10.28	40.19
13	*****************	17	146	5.30	45.48
14	**************************	26	172	8.10	53.58
15	**************************	26	198	8.10	61.68
16	********	8	206	2.49	64.17
17	*********	10	216	3.12	67.29
18	*********************	22	238	6.85	74.14
19	******************	18	256	5.61	79.75
20	*********	9	265	2.80	82.55
21	****	4	269	1.25	83.80
22	*********	9	278	2.80	86.60
23	****	4	282	1.25	87.85
24	********	8	290	2.49	90.34
25	*****	5	295	1.56	91.90
26	****	4	299	1.25	93.15
27	**	2	301	0.62	93.77
28	*	1	302	0.31	94.08
29	**	2	304	0.62	94.70
30	****	4	308	1.25	95.95
31	**	2	310	0.62	96.57
34	**	2	312	0.62	97.20
40	*	1	313	0.31	97.51
49	**	2	315	0.62	98.13
50	**	2	317	0.62	98.75
55	*	1	318	0.31	99.06
56	*	1	319	0.31	99.38
69	*	1	320	0.31	99.69
71	*	1	321	0.31	100.00

```
     5    10    15    20    25    30
            FREQUENCY
```

The choice of what kind of graphical display of data to use rests on the nature of the data and the researcher's preference. Pictorial displays of data add nothing to the data that is not already there, so unless there is a compelling reason to present data in this way, one rarely sees graphic displays in the journals today.

2.1.10 Line Graphs

Another basic type of pictorial presentation is the **line graph**, which is particularly useful for describing the movement of some qualitative variable over time, such as birthrates, crime rates, marriage rates, and sales rates. Like a frequency polygon, plotted points in the line graph are joined by a straight line. Unlike the polygon, the line graph does not begin and end on the abscissa. Rather, it begins at the frequency of the phenomenon being investigated for the baseline year.

Figure 2.7 is a line graph of divorce rates in the United States for the years 1925 through 1985 per 1000 married women of 15 years of age and over. The line therefore begins at the divorce rate per 1000 married women in 1925 and ends at 1985.

The divorce rates are presented in two different ways: The continuous line indicates the actual number of divorces per 1000 married women, and the broken line shows the divorce rate per 1000 total population. Obviously, the more people there are, the greater the number of divorces there are likely to be. The continuous line is a better indication of the prevalence of divorce because the number of divorces depends not only on the size of the population but also on the proportion of the population that is married. However, presenting both trend lines together tends to "soften" the dismal picture of soaring divorce rates indicated by the continuous line.

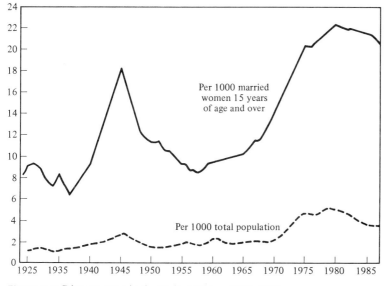

Figure 2.7 Divorce rates in the United States, 1925–1985

2.2 NUMERICAL SUMMATION OF DATA

2.2.1 Proportions, Percentages, and Ratios

In addition to the various types of graphs, researchers often present numerical summaries of their data. The most commonly used techniques are proportions, percentages, and ratios. Percentages standardize the raw data to a base of 100; proportions standardize to a base of 1.00; and a ratio is a comparison between two quantities, such as between two subsamples of a whole sample.

By *standardization* I mean that disparate numbers are changed to conform to a uniform scale for purposes of comparison. For instance, suppose I have a sample of 110 males and 288 females and report that 46 males and 90 females fear a trip to the dentist. I cannot fairly compare males and females in terms of fear and dentistry because the raw numbers are based on different category totals. By standardizing to a base of 100 (percentage), I can say that $46/110 = 41.8$ percent of the males and $90/288 = 31.25$ percent of the females report a fear of dentistry. These percentages are directly comparable to one another in a way that the raw numbers are not. To illustrate these techniques we will again consider the 20 people from whom we requested information regarding family size in Table 2.1.

FREQUENCY DISTRIBUTION OF NUMBER OF CHILDREN AND SEX OF RESPONDENT

Obs.	Children	Sex	Obs.	Children	Sex
1	1	F	11	0	M
2	0	M	12	4	F
3	2	F	13	1	F
4	2	F	14	2	M
5	2	M	15	3	M
6	3	F	16	2	F
7	3	M	17	2	F
8	4	F	18	3	M
9	3	M	19	3	F
10	2	F	20	2	F

A **proportion** compares a part of the distribution with the whole; it is a particular frequency divided by the total number of cases. The formula for calculating proportions is given in Formula 2.1.

$$\text{proportion } (p) = \frac{f}{N} \tag{2.1}$$

where f = frequency

N = number of cases

There are 12 females in our small data set of 20 cases. Thus, the proportion of females in our sample of 20 is $12/20 = .6$. If we computer-code males as 0 and females as 1, we have what is known as a *dummy variable*. Although we said in Chapter 1 that we cannot logically speak of an "average" of a nominal variable such as sex, we can do so statistically through the use of dummy variables that are dichotomous (having just two attributes). A proportion is the average or "mean" value of a dummy variable.

The more familiar **percentage** is simply a proportion multiplied by 100. The formula for computing percentages is given in Formula 2.2

$$\text{percentage}\ (\%) \ = \ \frac{f}{N} \times 100 \tag{2.2}$$

We can now say that females constitute $12/20 \times 100 = 60$ percent of our sample.

A **ratio** is a comparison of two quantities determined by dividing the frequency of one category by the frequency of another. For example, to obtain the ratio of females to males we divide the number of females by the number of males, as shown in Formula 2.3.

$$\text{ratio}\ = \ \frac{f_1}{f_2} \tag{2.3}$$

where $\quad f_1 \ = \ $ frequency of females

$\qquad f_2 \ = \ $ frequency of males

Calculating, we get $12/8 = 1.5$, indicating that there are 1.5 females to every male in the sample and written as 1.5:1.

Other statements that we could make from this small data set are (1) the proportion of all children reported by female respondents is $28/44 = .636$, (2) the percentage of all children reported by males is $16/44 \times 100 = 36.36$, and (3) the ratio of the number of children reported by females compared to the number reported by males is $28/16 = 1.75:1$.

Data reduced to percentages, proportions, and ratios are easier to read and understand, particularly if we wish to compare some variable within samples of different sizes. To illustrate, suppose we have three samples of convicted criminals from three different cities and we want to compare their violent and property offenses. The breakdown of the three separate samples is presented in Table 2.6.

As Table 2.6 shows, it is difficult to compare the raw frequencies from samples with different Ns. Let us compute the summary statistics for these data and place them in Table 2.7.

TABLE 2.6 NUMBER OF VIOLENT AND PROPERTY CRIMES IN THREE CITIES

	City 1 N	City 2 N	City 3 N
Property	147	182	191
Violent	59	75	108
Total	206	257	299

TABLE 2.7 DATA FROM TABLE 2.6 EXPRESSED IN PERCENTAGES, PROPORTIONS, AND RATIOS

Total	City 1			City 2			City 3		
	N	%	*P*	*N*	%	*P*	*N*	%	*P*
Property	147	71.4	.714	182	70.8	.708	191	63.9	.639
Violent	59	28.6	.286	75	29.2	.292	108	36.1	.361
Total	206	100.0	1.000	257.0	100.0	1.000	299.0	100.0	1.000
Ratio of property to violent crime		= 2.49:1			= 2.43:1			= 1.77:1	

We can now make meaningful comparisons clearly and concisely. We can see that the percentages and proportions of violent crimes in cities 1 and 2 are almost identical but that offenders in city 3 appear to be more violence-prone in comparison to their propensity to commit property crimes. We also note that the ratios of violent to property crimes in cities 1 and 2 are also virtually identical. Multiplying these ratios by 100 to eliminate the decimal point, we find that city 1 has 249 property crimes for every 100 violent crimes, city 2 has 243 property crimes for every 100 violent crimes, and city 3 has 177 property crimes for every 100 violent crimes.

2.2.2 Rates

Do these figures indicate that city 3 is the most violent of the three cities? No, they do not. They only indicate that more violent crimes are committed in this city relative to property crimes. To determine which of the three cities is most violence-prone we have to have an additional piece of information. Perhaps city 1 is a small city of 50,000 people, whereas city 3 has 1 million people. If that were the case we might conclude that city 3 is inordinately peaceful. Thus, the information we need to make statements about relative violence is the population size. When we have population size we can compute a rate of violent crime.

Rates are a special form of ratio that compares the frequency with which an event actually occurs to the frequency with which it could potentially occur over a defined period of time (usually one year). All inhabitants of any city are considered potential candidates for committing a crime (not that this is realistically true, for there are the extremely young and infirm who for all intents and purposes lack the potential). However, on the reasonable assumption that the number of people lacking this potential is more or less constant in all cities, the population of those cities can be validly used as a base of potentiality. The formula for computing rates is given in Formula 2.4.

$$\text{rate} = \frac{\text{number of actual occurrences}}{\text{number of potential occurrences}} \times 100,000 \tag{2.4}$$

Since the ratio of actual to potential occurrences is usually quite small, we multiply the quotient of this formula by 100,000 (or some other multiple of 10) to eliminate decimal places. We will now provide the populations of each of our three cities and calculate their violence rates.

population city 1 = 115,000

$$\text{violence rate} = \frac{59}{115,000} \times 100,000 = 51.3$$

population city 2 = 175,000

$$\text{violence rate} = \frac{75}{175,000} \times 100,000 = 42.9$$

population city 3 = 540,000

$$\text{violence rate} = \frac{108}{540,000} \times 100,000 = 20.0$$

After we have computed the violence rates for each of the cities we can see that any initial assumptions about their relative violence would have been hasty. City 3 actually has a violent-crime rate less than half as large as the other two cities.

2.3 SUMMARY

This chapter has discussed data description and display. A frequency distribution is simply a tally of the number of times each value of the variable in the distribution occurs in a group of values. Frequency distributions can be arrayed graphically in a variety of ways. We have emphasized bar charts, histograms, polygons, and pie charts. For researchers who are constructing these graphics by hand, procedures for determining real limits of numbers, midpoints, and sizes of class intervals were discussed.

The numeric description of the distribution of a variable in the form of proportions, percentages, ratios, and rates further enhances the clarity and conciseness of data description. These calculations are very useful in comparing a particular category with the whole array of cases (proportions and percentages) or in comparing one particular category with some other particular category (ratios). Rates are a special kind of ratio that compares the number of actual occurrences of a particular phenomenon with the number of potential or possible occurrences of the phenomenon over a unit of time.

PRACTICE APPLICATION: DISPLAYING AND SUMMARIZING DATA

A researcher collects data on IQ and home status (broken/intact) for 30 juvenile delinquents:

HOME STATUS AND IQ LEVELS OF JUVENILE DELINQUENTS

Obs.	IQ	B.Home	Obs.	IQ	B.Home	Obs.	IQ	B.Home
1	72	yes	11	90	yes	21	100	no
2	78	yes	12	90	no	22	100	no
3	80	yes	13	90	no	23	100	yes
4	81	yes	14	90	yes	24	105	no
5	83	no	15	90	yes	25	111	no
6	84	yes	16	94	no	26	112	yes
7	85	yes	17	94	yes	27	113	no
8	85	yes	18	95	no	28	114	no
9	88	no	19	95	yes	29	120	yes
10	88	yes	20	95	yes	30	120	no

Group the data into intelligence levels (66–79 = borderline, 80–90 = dull normal, 91–110 = average, 111–119 = bright average, 120–127 = superior) and construct a grouped frequency distribution and bar chart.

GROUPED FREQUENCY

Category	f	%	Cum.%
Borderline	2	6.7	6.7
Dull normal	13	43.3	50.0
Average	9	30.0	80.0
Bright average	4	13.3	93.3
Superior	2	6.7	100.0
Total	30	100.0	

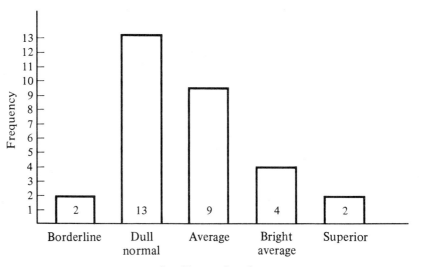

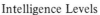

What is the proportion and percentage of juveniles from broken homes?

$$P = f/N = 17/30 = .566 \qquad \% = f/N \times 100 = 17/30 \times 100 = 56.3\%$$

What is the ratio of broken to intact homes?

$$R = f_1/f_2 = 17/13 = 1.3{:}1$$

What percentage of the sample is below the average IQ category?

$2 + 13 = 15$ are below average. Therefore, $15/30 \times 100 = 50.0\%$

What is the ratio of below-average to above-average juveniles?

$$15/6 = 2.5{:}1$$

What proportion of the sample with below-average IQs is from broken homes? We see that 11 of the 13 juveniles with less than average IQs are from broken homes. Therefore,

$$P = 11/13 = .846 \quad (\% = 84.6)$$

APPENDIX: Computer Instructions and Explanations

Command 2.1

```
SELECT IF (VAGE LE 98)
RECODE VAGE (LO THRU 6=1)(7 THRU 12=2)(13 THRU 18=3)
            (19 THRU 24=4)(25 THRU 30=5)(31 THRU 37=6)(ELSE=7)
FREQUENCIES VARIABLES=VAGE/
            BARCHART/
FREQUENCIES VARIABLES=VAGE/
            HISTOGRAM/
```

The SELECT IF command tells the computer to select only those values of victims' ages that are less or equal (LE) to 98. Missing values are coded as 99, we do not want them to be considered. The RECODE command tells the computer the size of the groupings or categories of the VAGE variable. For instance, LO THRU 6 = 1 means that all victims from the youngest to age 6 are combined to form group 1. ELSE = 7 means that all victims older than 37 go into group 7.

Command 2.2

SAS	SPSSX
`IF TCRIM=1;`	`SELECT IF (TCRIM EQ 1)`
`IF VAGE<98;`	`SELECT IF (VAGE LE 98)`
`IF VAGE<=13 THEN AGE=1; ELSE`	`RECODE VAGE (LO THRU 13=1)`
`IF 14<=VAGE<=17 THEN AGE=2; ELSE`	`(14 THRU 17=2)`
`IF 18<=VAGE<=29 THEN AGE = 3; ELSE`	`(18 THRU 29=3)`

```
IF VAGE>30 THEN AGE=4;                (30 THRU HI=4)/
PROC FORMAT; VALUE AGE 1='CHILD'    PIECHART PLOT=VAGE/
2='OLDERCHILD' 3='YOUNGADULT'          TITLE='AGE OF VICTIMS
4='OLDADULT';                           OF SEX OFFENDER: 4 GROUPS'/
PROC CHART;
PIE AGE/DISCRETE;
FORMAT AGE AGE.;
```

Note: The PROC FORMAT; VALUE AGE command enables you to title the pie slices. Without these commands the slices would be identified by the numbers 1, 2, 3, and 4 only.)

Since we want only victims of sexual assault for this illustration, we use the IF or SELECT IF commands to select them out (TCRIM = type of crime: 1 = sex, 2 = non-sex assault, 2 = property crime).

REFERENCES

Montgomery, R. (1987). Costly prison riots: United States and Canada. *Journal of Justice Issues*, 2:53–64.

National Center for Health Statistics. (1986). Advanced report of divorce statistics, 1984. *Monthly Vital Statistics Report*, 35 (No. 6, supplement). Hyattsville, MD: Public Health Service.

Walsh, A. (1986). The sexual stratification hypothesis and sexual assault in light of the changing conceptions of race. *Criminology*, 25:153–173.

Chapter 3

Central Tendency and Dispersion

3.1 MEASURES OF CENTRAL TENDENCY

In studying social phenomena, scientists collect and evaluate data in numerous ways. Organizing the data into frequency distributions, charts, graphs, tables, and figures is often the first important way of visualizing the shape and scope of the data for a single variable, for example, the numbers of births in Idaho, age at marriage for Irish males, suicides in Sweden, and homicides in Canada. However, if we wanted to compare Idaho births with California births, American suicides with Swedish suicides, and so on, we would find visual inspection of frequency distributions somewhat cumbersome and not very precise. When making such comparisons it would be more useful to have mathematically precise summary statements that would tell us the center of each distribution and how the data in each are dispersed or scattered away from their centers. We call such measures measures of central tendency and measures of dispersion.

Measures of central tendency show the centrality of the data, and **measures of dispersion** indicate the spread of the data away from the center. Both measures sacrifice the general view of the data provided by a frequency distribution but more than make up for it by providing very useful summaries.

Measures of central tendency are measures of the average. All of us have an idea about what the average is. But consider the following: A real estate salesperson who is attempting to sell you a house tells you that the average income in the neighborhood is $70,000. The salesperson is hoping to impress you with the "classiness" of the neighborhood and influence you to buy, and you do. The following month you see this person, who lives in the same neighborhood as you do now, stating in a town meeting protesting property taxes that the average income in your neighborhood is $25,000. In neither case was the salesperson lying—only using two different meanings of the word *average*. In the first instance the salesperson was quoting a measure of central tendency called the mean, and in the second, another index of averageness called the median. The salesperson might on some other occasion (when it is profitable, no doubt) tell someone that the average income in the neighborhood is $23,500. In this case the measure of central tendency is called the mode. We will now examine these three measures of central tendency, beginning with the mode.

3.1.1 Mode

The **mode** (symbolized *Mo*) is defined as that score that occurs most frequently in the distribution. Since the mode is the most frequently occurring score, it may appear in a distribution in places other than at the center, although it will always be under the peak of a distribution. It is possible to have more than one mode in a distribution; in such cases the distribution is bimodal or multimodal. The mode is the only valid measure of central tendency for nominal data, but it may be validly used for all other levels as well.

Suppose we asked 30 people to reveal their annual income and we organize their responses in rounded thousands of dollars into ungrouped and grouped distributions as shown in Table 3.1.

TABLE 3.1 ANNUAL INCOME OF 30 RESPONDENTS IN THOUSANDS OF DOLLARS IN UNGROUPED AND GROUPED FORM

Ungrouped				Grouped		
Value	Freq.	Value	Freq.	Class	Freq.	Cum. Freq.
12	1	28	2	10–15	4	4
13	2	29	1	16–20	7	11
14	1	30	2	21–25	4	15
16	4	32	1	26–30	6	21
18	1	35	2	31–35	3	24
19	1	36	1	36–40	4	28
20	1	37	1	— —	—	—
24	1	38	1	— —	—	—
25	3	40	1	95–100	2	30
26	1	97	1			
		99	1			

The mode for these data is 16 because it is the income category that occurs most often (four times). The mode is the least frequently used measure of central tendency in statistics because it does not lend itself to mathematical operations. It is purely a descriptive statistic, which provides useful information regarding the typical case.

3.1.2 Median

The **median** (symbolized *Md*) is defined as that score in the range that divides the scores into two equal parts; it is the middle score of a set of scores that have been arranged in increasing sequence. Consider the following range of scores:

$$1 \quad 3 \quad 4 \quad 5 \quad 8 \quad 9 \quad 11$$

median

The median score is 5 since half of the values are above that number and half are below it. If there are an even number of scores such as 1, 3, 4, 5, 8, 9, 10, and 11, the median is determined by interpolating between the two middle scores by taking their average. For instance,

two middle
scores

$$1 \quad 3 \quad 4 \quad 5 \quad 8 \quad 9 \quad 10 \quad 11 \qquad Md = (5 + 8)/2 = 6.5$$

median = 6.5

To take another example, because there are 30 scores in our annual income data, we must interpolate between the two middle scores, which are 15 and 16. The fifteenth score is 25 and the sixteenth is 26. Thus, (25 + 26)/2 = 25.5; the median income of this group of observations is 25.5.

Computing the Median with Grouped Data The median is not always so easily computed. In the preceding example each value appears only once. If values in a distribution occur more than once, as in the grouped frequency distribution of the same income data to the right of the ungrouped distribution in Table 3.1, we have to use a different formula to compute the median: Formula 3.1. We will make the computations in step-by-step fashion.

$$Md = L + \left[\frac{N/2 - cf}{f} \right] \times w \tag{3.1}$$

where L = the true lower limit of the class interval in which the median is located

$N/2$ = one-half of the total frequency

cf = the cumulated frequency up to but not including the median class interval

f = the frequency of the median class interval

w = the class width

STEP 1. We proceed by first dividing the sample N by 2 (30/2 = 15). So 15 is the number that divides the distribution into two equal parts.

STEP 2.   To determine the value of L, the true lower limit, the class interval containing the fifteenth score must be identified. From the cumulative frequency distribution we see that the class containing the fifteenth score is the 21–25 class. The median is somewhere in this class interval. The lower limit of the number 21 is 20.5. Therefore, $L = 20.5$.

STEP 3.   The value of cf is determined by adding all frequencies down to but not including those in the class containing the median. We note that 11 scores precede this interval, so $cf = 11$.

STEP 4.   The value of f is defined as the value frequency of the class containing the median, so $f = 4$.

STEP 5.   The value of w refers to the width of the class containing the median. The width of the interval is obtained by subtracting the true lower limit from the upper limit of the class ($25.5 - 20.5 = 5$). The class width is 5. Substituting these values into the formula, we get

$$Md = 20.5 + \left(\frac{\frac{30}{2} - 11}{4} \right) \times 5$$

$$= 20.5 + \left[\frac{15 - 11}{4} \right] \times 5 = 20.5 + \left[\frac{4}{4} \right] \times 5$$

$$= 20.5 + (1)(5) = 20.5 + 5 = 25.5$$

This is the same value previously computed from the ungrouped data. Half of our respondents have incomes equal to or below $25,500 and half have incomes equal to or above $25,500.

3.1.3 Mean

The **mean** is symbolized in two different ways, depending on whether we are describing the population mean (μ read *mu*) or the sample mean ($\bar{X}$ read *X bar*). The mean is the measure of central tendency that most of us think about when we hear the term *average*. It is simply the arithmetic average of a distribution of scores. Among the measures of central tendency the mean is used most. Unlike the mode and the median, it is suited to interval and ratio data. The mean is the focal point and entrance to the higher statistics. Before we can calculate any of the interval- and ratio-level statistics we must first know the means of the variables with which we are working. Another nice characteristic of the mean is that it is quite stable across repeated random samples from the same population. The modes and medians of repeated random samples are less stable in that they tend to fluctuate more than the means.

The common formula for the mean is given in Formula 3.2, which simply informs you to add all the individual scores or values together and divide by the sample size. When you see Σ, or sigma, you are instructed to add a series of numbers, usually but not always all the values associated with a variable in the data set. If not all the values are to be summed, a subscript will accompany sigma telling you which values to include.

$$\bar{X} = \frac{\Sigma X}{N}$$ (3.2)

where $\bar{X}$ = the mean

Σ = "the sum of"

X = the values to be summed

N = sample size

The mean annual income is obtained from Table 3.1 by first summing all numbers in the distribution

$$\Sigma X = 12 + 13 + 13 + 14 + \cdots + 99 = 892$$

and then dividing this sum by the number of observations:

$$\bar{X} = \frac{892}{30} = 29.733$$

Computing the Mean from Grouped Data   Just as we computed the median from grouped data, so we can compute the mean. The formula for computing the mean from grouped data is

$$\bar{X} = \frac{\Sigma fm}{N}$$ (3.3)

where fm = the frequency of each class multiplied by its midpoint

Recall that the midpoint of a class interval is halfway between its true lower and upper limits. Therefore, the midpoint for class 1 is between 9.5 and 15.5 and is equal to 12.5. The logic of using the midpoint is that it represents our best estimate of the mean value of the scores in each class interval. There are four observations in this class. The symbol fm instructs us to multiply the frequency of the class by its midpoint, so for the first class we have $12.5 \times 4 = 50$. We continue in this way until we have computed fm for each class.

$$
\begin{array}{llll}
\text{class 1:} & 12.5 \times 4 & = & 50 \\
\text{class 2:} & 18.0 \times 7 & = & 126 \\
\text{class 3:} & 23.0 \times 4 & = & 92 \\
\text{class 4:} & 28.0 \times 6 & = & 168 \\
\text{class 5:} & 33.0 \times 3 & = & 99 \\
\text{class 6:} & 38.0 \times 4 & = & 152 \\
\text{class 7:} & 97.5 \times 2 & = & 195 \\
& \Sigma fm & = & 882 \\
\end{array}
$$

$$\bar{X} = \frac{\Sigma fm}{N} = \frac{882}{30} = 29.4$$

Our mean computed on the basis of grouped data underestimates the "true" mean, which we know to be 29.733. It must be realized that a mean computed from group data is only an estimate of the sample mean. The formula for the mean of grouped data assumes that the class scores are uniformly distributed around the class midpoint. Our data tend to be on the high side of the midpoint. Take the first and last class intervals, for instance. The actual mean of the first interval is 13, not 12.5, and the actual mean of the last class is 98, not 97.5. Although the amount of misestimation is usually quite small, it is always preferable to collect data in the form of raw scores rather than in grouped form if at all possible.

We can further emphasize the desirability of raw over grouped data by pointing out that the mode of grouped data is simply the midpoint of the class interval with the largest frequency. It should be intuitively obvious that this is the best estimate of the mode that we could make from grouped data. The class interval with the largest frequency is class 2, and the midpoint of class 2 is 18. Thus we overestimate the value of the mode, which we know to be 16.

3.1.4 A Computer Example

We will now use the computer to run a frequency program in which these measures of central tendency, as well as measures of dispersion, have been calculated for us. The distribution is from our multiple sclerosis (MS) data collected in Idaho in 1986 (Walsh & Walsh, 1987). The variable is number of years since each respondent's MS has been diagnosed. Command 3.1, given in the chapter appendix, is used to request this job. The SPSSx printout is shown in Table 3.2.

From the output we see that the mode is 1, the median is 7, and the mean is 10.474. We will defer discussion of the other printed values until our discussion of dispersion. Do note, however, that if we smoothed out the histogram derived from these data and stood the resulting distribution on end, we would have a distribution curve that resembled a ski slope, with the mode at the top of the hill and the median and mean located more or less halfway down the hill. In Figure 3.1 I

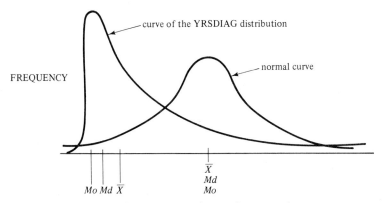

Figure 3.1 MS distribution curve superimposed on normal curve

TABLE 3.2   NUMBER OF YEARS MULTIPLE SCLEROSIS HAS BEEN DIAGNOSED

FREQUENCY BAR CHART

	YRSDIAG		FREQ	CUM. FREQ.	PERCENT	CUM. PERCENT
Mode	1	******************	18	18	13.33	13.33
	2	****	4	22	2.96	16.30
	3	****************	16	38	11.85	28.15
	4	********	9	47	6.67	34.81
	5	******	6	53	4.44	39.26
	6	*************	14	67	10.37	49.63
Median	7	******	6	73	4.44	54.07
	8	********	8	81	5.93	60.00
	9	**	2	83	1.48	61.48
Mean	10	**********	10	93	7.41	68.89
	13	**	2	95	1.48	70.37
	14	**	2	97	1.48	71.85
	15	******	6	103	4.44	76.30
	16	**	2	105	1.48	77.78
	17	****	4	109	2.96	80.74
	18	**	2	111	1.48	82.22
	19	**	2	113	1.48	83.70
	20	********	8	121	5.93	89.63
	21	**	2	123	1.48	91.11
	23	**	2	125	1.48	92.59
	26	***	3	128	2.22	94.81
	29	*	1	129	0.74	95.56
	30	**	2	131	1.48	97.04
	36	*	1	132	0.74	97.78
	40	*	1	133	0.74	98.52
	49	*	1	134	0.74	99.26
	59	*	1	135	0.74	100.00

```
            5    10    15
              FREQUENCY
```

MEAN	10.474	STD ERR	.938	MEDIAN	7.000	
MODE	1.000	STD DEV	10.893	VARIANCE	118.654	
KURTOSIS	6.446	SKEWNESS	2.265	RANGE	58.000	
MINIMUM	1.000	MAXIMUM	59.000	SUM	1414.000	

have superimposed the normal curve (examined in the next chapter) over our MS data curve. The normal curve is perfectly symmetrical, with the mean, mode, and median all being exactly in the center of the distribution. Our MS distribution, however, is highly skewed to the right. A curve skewed to the right is called a *positive skew,* and a curve skewed to the left is called a *negative skew.* The rightward skew of this distribution is a function of a few highly atypical cases at the high end of the distribution. These atypical cases pull the mean toward them at the tail of the distribution. As is usual in such skewed distributions, the median falls between the mode and the mean, and the mean lies closest of the three measures to the tail of the distribution.

3.1.5 Choosing a Measure of Central Tendency

Choosing a measure of central tendency depends on the kind of information you wish to convey to the readers of your research. You should use the mode if you are referring to a variable measured at the nominal level. It would make little sense to talk about the "mean" sex of a sample but quite all right to say that the modal sex was male. As I indicated in Chapter 2, you can use the mean of a dichotomous nominal-level variable (a proportion) that has been dummy-coded. You also use the mode when you wish to point out the "typical." For instance, a politician is much more interested in the typical opinion than in any mean level of opinion, as are most of us when we buttress arguments by saying, "most people would agree with me."

The median is used when the variable to be described is measured at the ordinal level or higher. It is useful when extreme scores distort the mean, as they do in our MS distribution. In such cases the median better reflects central tendency than does the mean. The government uses the median rather than the mean to report the average individual and household income in the United States for just this reason. The income of multimillionaires would pull the mean in the direction of the higher incomes in a very positively skewed distribution. Using the median only makes one-half of the population feel poor, but if the mean were to be used to describe the distribution, a lot more than half of us would fall below "average."

You use the mean only with interval- or ratio-level measures. It is the only measure of central tendency that uses all the information in a distribution, and it is the only one that is mathematically based. This latter quality makes it indispensable to advanced statistics. Variables measured at the interval or ratio levels are not limited to the mean for description, however. It is valid to report all measures of central tendency for such variables. Table 3.3 summarizes the relationship between the measures of central tendency and levels of measurement, ignoring the special case of dummy variables.

Statisticians refer to the mean as the "center of deviations," or the "center of gravity." By this it is meant that deviations from the mean in a distribution of scores, both above and below the mean, will balance each other out. To illustrate,

TABLE 3.3 RELATIONSHIP BETWEEN MEASURES OF CENTRAL TENDENCY AND MEASUREMENT LEVELS

Level of Measurement	Valid to Use		
	Mean	Median	Mode
Nominal	No	No	Yes
Ordinal	No	Yes	Yes
Interval	Yes	Yes	Yes
Ratio	Yes	Yes	Yes

TABLE 3.4   DEVIATIONS FROM THE MEAN, MODE, AND MEDIAN OF A DISTRIBUTION OF SCORES

X	$\bar{X}$	$X - \bar{X}$	X	Md	$X - Md$	X	Mo	$X - Mo$
3	9	−6 ⎫	3	10	−7 ⎫	3	6	−3 ⎫
6	9	−3 ⎬ −15	6	10	−4 ⎬ −19	6	6	0 ⎬ −3
6	9	−3 ⎪	6	10	−4 ⎪	6	6	0 ⎪
6	9	−3 ⎭	6	10	−4 ⎭	6	6	0 ⎭
10	9	+1 ⎫	10	10	0	10	6	+4 ⎫
10	9	+1 ⎪	10	10	0	10	6	+4 ⎪
12	9	+3 ⎬ +15	12	10	+2 ⎫	12	6	+6 ⎬ +30
13	9	+4 ⎪	13	10	+3 ⎬ +10	13	6	+7 ⎪
15	9	+6 ⎭	15	10	+5 ⎭	15	6	+9 ⎭

$$\Sigma(X - \bar{X}) = 0 \qquad \Sigma(X - Mo) = -9 \qquad \Sigma(X - Md) = +27$$

suppose we have the distribution of scores given in Table 3.4. We calculate the mean, median, and mode for these data and find them to be 9, 10, and 6, respectively. We first calculate the deviation scores for the mean. A deviation score is the raw score minus the mean $(X - \bar{X} = x)$, where $x =$ the deviation score. As illustrated, the sum of x will always be equal to zero. However, the deviations from the mode and the median will not be zero unless the distribution is perfectly symmetrical (the mean, median, and mode are identical).

There is one problem regarding the mean that we should note. Although we have said that it is the most stable of measures of central tendency across random samples from the same population, it is affected more than the mode or median by extreme scores in a distribution. In this sense it is less stable than the median. For instance, if we had a thirty-first respondent in our income data set who reported an income of $250,000, it would change the mean considerably (from 29.467 to 36.58), would change the median only from 25.5 to 25.6, and would leave the mode totally unchanged (16 would still be the modal category). Are you now beginning to see how the real estate salesperson could quote two different averages without lying? Quite obviously there are a few families living in the neighborhood with extremely high incomes. These families pull the mean to the high end but have very little effect on the median and none at all on the mode. Thus, whenever a distribution is highly skewed, as in our MS distribution, it might be more appropriate to report the median as the preferred measure of central tendency.

Figure 3.2 presents four distributions (from an infinite number of possible distributions) with the mean, mode, and median in different positions relative to each other. Note that in a positively skewed distribution the mean is greater than the median and the median is greater than the mode. In a negatively skewed distribution the mean is less than the median and the median is less than the mode. Our annual income data would be distributed approximately like curve C, with a mode of 16, a median of 25.5, and a mean of 29.733.

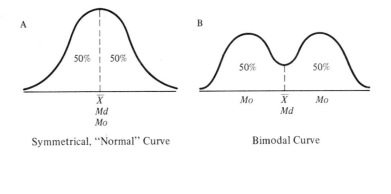

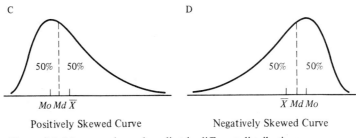

Figure 3.2 Mean, mode, and median in different distributions

3.2 MEASURES OF DISPERSION

The measures of central tendency are very useful in relating indices of typicality, or averageness, of a group of scores. However, it is also most useful to gain some idea of how the individuals or objects in a distribution differ from one another. As we shall see, a measure of dispersion or variability, coupled with the mean, will allow us to compute measures, which will tell us how different two or more individuals or groups are with regard to the variable under exploration. For instance, suppose that the mean income for both a sample of college professors and a sample of criminals is found to be $40,000. Such information standing alone conveys a false impression without a measure of the variability within the respective samples.

3.2.1 Range

The **range** is the simplest measure of dispersion. Unlike the other measures we will be discussing, the range is not a measure of the dispersion from the mean; rather it is simply the difference between the lowest and highest scores in the distribution. In our MS distribution the lowest score is 1, the highest is 59, and the range is 58 (59 − 1 = 58). Even this simple measure of dispersion gives us a better feel for the data than we would have with the mean alone. Returning to our college professors/criminals example, suppose the lowest income is $22,000 and the highest is $55,000 for the professors and $2,000 and $120,000 for the crimi-

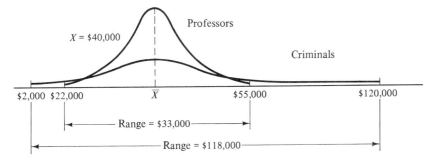

Figure 3.3 Distributions with identical means but different dispersions

nals. Such information gives us a little better feel for the data than the mean alone. Figure 3.3 illustrates the example in which the two distributions have the same mean but different levels of dispersion.

We know there is large variability among the criminals and relatively little among the professors. However, the range is a very crude measure of sample variation that depends entirely on the two extreme values in it. One or both of these values may be so atypical as to render the range most untrustworthy as a measure of dispersion.

3.2.2 Standard Deviation

Although there are a number of other rarely used measures of dispersion, we will concentrate on the three major indices of variability used to assess the spread of interval and ratio data in a distribution about their mean. Although they are "different" measures, they are only made so by mathematical transformations. The most basic of the three is the sum of squares. A measure called the variance is derived from the sum of squares, and the standard deviation is derived from the variance. All three measures are used in their various transformations in statistical analysis of interval- and ratio-level data.

A good and complete measure of dispersion should utilize all the scores in the distribution and describe the typical or average deviation of the scores around their mean. Such a measure would be relatively small in a distribution in which the scores are closely clustered around the center, and relatively large when they are scattered away from it. The **standard deviation** is such a measure. If you study Formula 3.4 for a moment it will become obvious that if all observations had exactly the same value the standard deviation would be zero—there would be no variability in the data. As the observations become more scattered or variable in their individual values, the standard deviation becomes progressively larger. The standard deviation, in effect, reflects the extent to which the mean represents the entire set of observations in a population or sample. If you turn back to Table 3.2 you will see that the standard deviation for years since diagnoses is 10.893. This value is actually larger than the mean (10.474). What this means practically is that the mean is a poor indicator of the central tendency of this distribution.

Like the mean, there are two symbols for the standard deviation. When we are talking about the population standard deviation the lowercase Greek letter sigma (σ) is used, and when we are referring to a sample standard deviation, which is used to estimate the population standard deviation, we use the Roman letter s.

We will demonstrate the computation of the standard deviation by using two small samples of third-world countries, with their military expenditures as the variable of interest. The first set of countries is considered to have democratic forms of government and the second to have dictatorial forms of government. Our task is to determine the mean and dispersion of these data in Table 3.5.

TABLE 3.5 MILITARY EXPENDITURE IN BILLIONS OF DOLLARS

Democratic		Dictatorial	
Obs.	X	Obs.	X
1	2	1	5
2	4	2	5
3	4	3	6
4	4	4	6
5	11	5	8

The formulas for population and sample standard deviations are

Population Standard Deviation

$$\sigma = \sqrt{\frac{\Sigma(X - \mu)^2}{n}}$$

(3.4)

where n = number of cases

   X = each individual case

   μ = population mean

Sample Standard Deviation

$$s = \sqrt{\frac{\Sigma(X - \bar{X})^2}{N - 1}}$$

where N = number of cases

   X = each individual case

   $\bar{X}$ = sample mean

Since we are dealing with samples, we use the sample standard deviation formula. In prose, the formula informs us that the sample standard deviation is equal to the square root of the sum of the squared deviations from the mean divided by the sample size less one. Notice that in the calculation of s the denominator is $N - 1$. In calculating the population σ we use n. The sample standard deviation uses $N - 1$ because s^2 is a biased estimator of σ^2, and reflects the fact that ordinarily a sample has less diversity than is found in its parent population. (A "biased" statistic is one that on the average tends not to yield values that equal the parameter it is estimating.) Using $N - 1$ rather than N adjusts the value of s upward to account for this bias. Therefore, using $N - 1$ makes s^2 an unbiased estimator of σ^2. This adjustment is particularly important for small samples, but the difference between N and $N - 1$ becomes more and more trivial as the sample size gets larger and larger. With a sample size of 10, for instance, the difference between N and $N - 1$ is 10 percent, a rather substantial amount. With a sample size of 100, the difference is only 1 percent. So we see that the difference soon becomes negligible.

For the military expenditure data, the first thing we have to do is calculate the means for each sample. The mean is then subtracted from each individual score. As we have seen, an important property of the mean is that the sum of the deviations from the mean is zero because the negative deviations cancel the positive deviations. An index of dispersion that equals zero is not much use to us. We get out of this dilemma by squaring each deviation, thus eliminating the negative signs. Taking the first value in the democratic distribution, subtracting 5 from 2 gives us a difference of -3. Squaring -3 (multiplying -3 by -3) gives us a value of 9.

Democratic				Dictatorial			
X	$\bar{X}$	$(X - \bar{X})$	$(X - \bar{X})^2$	X	$\bar{X}$	$(X - \bar{X})$	$(X - \bar{X})^2$
2	5	-3	9	5	6	-1	1
4	5	-1	1	5	6	-1	1
4	5	-1	1	6	6	0	0
4	5	-1	1	6	6	0	0
11	5	6	36	8	6	2	4
25		0	48	30		0	6

$$\bar{X} = 25/5 = 5$$
Sum of squares $= 48$

$$\bar{X} = 30/5 = 6$$
Sum of squares $= 6$

At this point we have a value known as the **sum of squares** (the sum of the squared deviations from the mean). The sum of the squared deviations from the mean is smaller than the squared deviations from any other value. The formula for the sum of squares is simply the numerator under the radical in the standard deviation formula:

$$SS = \Sigma(X - \bar{X})^2$$

The sum of squares for the democratic countries is 48 and for the dictatorial countries, 6.

The next step is to calculate the variances of our samples by dividing the sum of squares by $N - 1$. The formula for the **variance** is simply the numerator and denominator within the radical in the formula for s.

$$s^2 = \frac{\Sigma(X - \bar{X})^2}{N - 1} \quad \text{or} \quad \frac{SS}{N - 1} \tag{3.5}$$

The SS for the democratic countries is 48. The formula tells you to divide this number by $N - 1$. N is 5, so $N - 1 = 4$. Therefore, the variance for the democratic countries is $SS/N - 1 = 48/4 = 12$. The variance for the dictatorial countries is $SS/N - 1 = 6/4 = 1.5$. Note that although the mean expenditure of the dictatorial countries is greater than that of the democratic countries, there is a lot more variability among the latter. This illustrates the effects of sample observations that deviate markedly from the mean, as does observation 5 in the democratic sample.

The variance is an important and vital statistic that will be used in many subsequent calculations. However, it is somewhat difficult to conceptualize. For instance, when we say that the variance in military expenditure for democratic countries is 12 squared billions of dollars it could easily be misinterpreted as meaning that the typical deviation from mean expenditure is 12 billion dollars squared. If we performed the calculation on our number of children sample in Chapter 2 and told you that the typical deviation from the mean number of children is 3.5 squared children, you might drop the class. Such statements are not easy ideas to play around with. To get these values back to the same units in which they were originally measured, we take the square root of the variance to arrive at the standard deviation. Since SAS computer packages sometimes use the term *root mean square* ("square root" of the "mean" of the "squared deviations"), we should note that this is another term for the standard deviation as well as a handy mnemonic device for recalling the formula. The standard deviation for the democratic countries is $\sqrt{12} = 3.464$. The standard deviation for the dictatorial countries is $\sqrt{1.5} = 1.225$.

Computational Formula for s Formula 3.4 is the definitional formula for the standard deviation, presented to give you an intuitive appreciation of what is going on. With a large number of cases it is a cumbersome and time-consuming method. Fortunately, there is a computational formula that requires far less time and effort. As you will note from Formula 3.5, you don't have to compute the mean and you will only make one subtraction rather than N subtractions.

$$s = \sqrt{\frac{\Sigma X^2 - \frac{(\Sigma X)^2}{N}}{N - 1}} \tag{3.6}$$

where $\Sigma X^2 =$ the sum of the squared individual scores

$(\Sigma X)^2 =$ the sum of the individual scores squared

Applying this formula to the democratic sample,

STEP 1. Square each observation and sum.

$$\Sigma X^2 = 2^2 + 4^2 + 4^2 + 4^2 + 11^2$$

$$= 4 + 16 + 16 + 16 + 121 = 173$$

STEP 2.   Add each observation and square the resulting sum.

$$(\Sigma X)^2 = (2 + 4 + 4 + 4 + 11)^2 = (25)^2 = 625$$

Substitute these values into the formula.

$$s = \sqrt{\frac{173 - \frac{625}{5}}{4}} = \sqrt{\frac{173 - 125}{4}} = \sqrt{\frac{48}{4}}$$

$$= \sqrt{12} = 3.464$$

And for the dictatorial sample,

$$s = \sqrt{\frac{186 - \frac{900}{5}}{4}} = \sqrt{\frac{186 - 180}{4}} = \sqrt{\frac{6}{4}}$$

$$= \sqrt{1.5} = 1.225$$

The Usefulness of the Standard Deviation   The standard deviation (along with its more unwieldy cousins the sum of squares and the variance) is the bedrock of statistics. It can serve as a summary of the dispersion of a single variable, it can be used to compare dispersion between and among two or more samples of the sample variable, and most important, it is the basis for the calculation of so many statistics we will be examining. Furthermore, since the mean is the reference point for computing the standard deviation, the standard deviation is viewed as the expected amount of error we would make in attempting to guess any score in a distribution from its expected value (the mean). When we discuss the normal curve in the next chapter we will see that more than two-thirds of all observed values will be within 1 standard deviation on either side of their mean. Figure 3.4 shows graphically the dispersion of the scores around their means for our two samples. Note that only the extreme scores (11 and 8) in these samples are outside of the range of plus or minus 1 standard deviation from the mean.

Democratic Countries

$\bar{X} = 5$ $s = 3.464$

$5 - 3.464 = 1.536$
$5 + 3.464 = 8.464$

```
        .
     .  .                      .
 ┌──────────────────────
 1│2  3  4  5  6  7  8│9  10  11

   − 1s       X̄        + 1s
  1.536       5       8.464
```

Dictatorial Countries

$\bar{X} = 6$ $s = 1.225$

$6 - 1.225 = 4.775$
$6 + 1.225 = 7.225$

```
     .  .
     .  .   .
  ┌──────────────
  1  2  3  4│5  6  7│8

       − 1s  X̄  + 1s
      4.775  6  7.225
```

Figure 3.4 Distributions of the two samples around their means

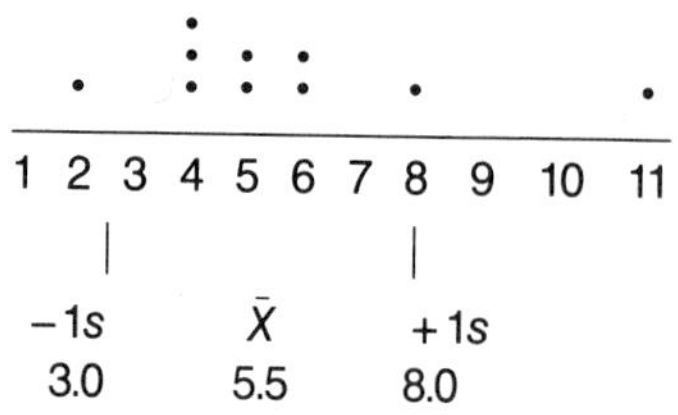

$\bar{X} = 5.5$

1s below the mean = 5.5 − 2.5 = 3

1s above the mean = 5.5 + 2.5 = 8

Figure 3.5 Distribution of combined samples

For a further computational example we will combine the samples and see what happens to the mean and standard deviation. The N of the new combined sample is 10 and the new mean is 5.5. The mean has been pulled in the direction of the extreme scores and the standard deviation is about midway between the two individuals s's. Note that all the scores except the extreme low and extreme high fall within 1 standard deviation on either side of the mean. Also note that some of the gaps in the distribution of scores have been filled in (see Figure 3.5). More such samples of countries would further eliminate the remaining gaps.

$$s = \sqrt{\frac{359 - \dfrac{3025}{10}}{9}} = \sqrt{\frac{359 - 302.5}{9}} = \sqrt{\frac{56.5}{9}}$$

$$= \sqrt{6.278} = 2.5$$

Computing the Standard Deviation from Grouped Data   Suppose the data on military expenditures came in the form of grouped data. In such an instance we would use Formula 3.6 to compute the standard deviation. The first step is to set up a table of five columns showing the class intervals, the frequencies in each class, the midpoint of the classes, the frequencies times the midpoint, and the frequencies times the midpoint times the midpoint. We will assume that the data are grouped into three classes, as shown in Table 3.6. The formula for computing the standard deviation from grouped data is Formula 3.6.

TABLE 3.6 COMPUTATION OF STANDARD DEVIATION FROM GROUPED DATA

Class	f	m	$f(m)$	$fm(m)$
1–4	4	2.5	10	25.00
5–8	5	6.5	32.5	211.25
9–12	1	10.5	10.5	110.25
	10		53.0	346.50

$$\bar{X} = \frac{\Sigma f(m)}{N} = \frac{53.0}{10} = 5.3$$

$$s = \sqrt{\frac{\Sigma fm(m)}{N} - (\bar{X})^2} = \sqrt{\frac{346.5}{10} - 5.3^2} = \sqrt{34.65 - 28.09} \qquad (3.6)$$

$$= \sqrt{6.56} = 2.56$$

Our estimated sample standard deviation is 2.56.

3.2.3 Index of Qualitative Variation

So far we have focused on measures of variation for interval or ratio variables. It is sometimes useful to know how a qualitative nominal or ordinal variable is dispersed. We can gain this knowledge by a measure known as the **index of qualitative variation.** With categorized data, if all the values of a variable are in one category, there is no variation, and the index of qualitative variation (IQV) will be zero. If the values are distributed evenly across the categories, IQV will be 1, its maximum value. The formula for IQV is given in Formula 3.7.

$$\text{IQV} = \frac{k(N^2 - \Sigma f^2)}{N^2(k - 1)} \qquad (3.7)$$

where k = the number of categories

N = the number of cases

Σf^2 = the sum of the squared frequencies

Let us compute and compare the IQV for the marital status variable for both our offender and MS data. First, we must present the category frequencies of the variable. Second, we square each of the frequencies and sum. First, the offender data:

STEP 1. Square the number of cases in each category and sum.

IQV FOR MARITAL STATUS (OFFENDER DATA)

Marital Status	f	f^2
Married	230	52900
Divorced	117	13689
Single	285	81225
Widowed	5	25
	637	147839

STEP 2. Substitute the numbers into the formula ($k = 4$, $N^2 = 637^2 = 405769$, $F^2 = 147839$) and proceed.

$$\text{IQV} = \frac{k(N^2 - \Sigma f^2)}{N^2(k - 1)} = \frac{4(405769 - 147839)}{405769(3)} = \frac{(4)257930}{405769(3)}$$

$$= \frac{1031720}{1217307} = .847$$

Now do the same for the MS data.

IQV FOR MARITAL STATUS (MS DATA)

Marital Status	f	f^2
Married	87	7569
Divorced	28	784
Single	8	64
Widowed	12	144
	135	8561

$$IQV = \frac{k(N^2 - \Sigma f^2)}{N^2(k-1)} = \frac{4(18225 - 8561)}{18225(3)} = \frac{(4)9664}{18225(3)}$$

$$= \frac{38656}{54675} = .707$$

Thus, there is more variation in marital status among the offenders than among the MS patients.

3.3 SUMMARY

Measures of central tendency indicate the centrality of the data, and the measures of dispersion we have examined here indicate the spread of the data away from the mean. The mode, median, and mean each report a summary value of a typical or representative value of the data. The mode is the most frequent value found in the data, the median is the value that splits the distribution exactly in half, and the mean is the arithmetic average of the distribution. The mean is generally the most useful of the three measures. It is the most stable of the three, and it is the entry point for the calculation of higher statistics.

The range is not a measure of the spread of the data away from the mean. Rather it is a measure of the difference between the highest and lowest scores in the distribution. The sum of squares is the most basic of the measures of dispersion away from the mean. It is the sum of the squared deviations of the scores off the mean. The variance is the sum of squares divided by n for the population variance, and $N - 1$ for a sample variance. Using $N - 1$ renders the sample variance an unbiased estimate of the population variance. The standard deviation is the square root of the variance. The standard deviation plays a key role in many of the statistics we will be discussing.

PRACTICE APPLICATION: CENTRAL TENDENCY AND DISPERSION

Compute the mean, mode, and median for the IQ data in the practice application in Chapter 2. The data follow:

HOME STATUS AND IQ LEVELS OF JUVENILE DELINQUENTS

Obs.	X	X^2	Obs.	X	X^2	Obs.	X	X^2
1	72	5184	11	90	8100	21	100	10000
2	78	6084	12	90	8100	22	100	10000
3	80	6400	13	90	8100	23	100	10000
4	81	6561	14	90	8100	24	105	11025
5	83	6889	15	90	8100	25	111	12321
6	84	7056	16	94	8836	26	112	12544
7	85	7225	17	94	8836	27	113	12769
8	85	7225	18	95	9025	28	114	12996
9	88	7744	19	95	9025	29	120	14400
10	88	7744	20	95	9025	30	120	14884

Sum of $X = 2844$, sum of $(X)^2 = 8088336$, and sum of $X^2 = 274298$.
Compute the mean:

$$\bar{X} = \Sigma \frac{X}{N} \qquad \Sigma X = 72 + 78 + \cdots + 120 = 2844$$

$$2844/30 = 94.8$$

The mean $= 94.8$. The modal IQ is 90; more juveniles in the sample have an IQ of 90 than any other IQ value. The mode $= 90$.
Compute the median: Simply take the middle two values (90 and 94), and take their mean.

$$Md = 90 + 94 = 184/2 = 92$$

The median $= 92$. Half the scores are above this value and half are below it.
Compute the standard deviation.

$$s = \sqrt{\frac{\Sigma X^2 - \dfrac{(\Sigma X)^2}{N}}{N-1}} = \sqrt{\frac{274298 - \dfrac{2844^2}{30}}{29}}$$

$$= \sqrt{\frac{274298 - \dfrac{8088336}{30}}{29}} = \sqrt{\frac{274298 - 269611.2}{29}}$$

$$= \sqrt{\frac{4686.8}{29}} = \sqrt{161.614} = 12.713$$

The standard deviation is 12.713.
Graph the distribution.

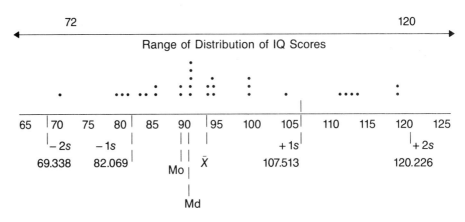

Range of Distribution of IQ Scores

$\bar{X} = 94.8$, $Md = 92$, $Mo = 90$, and $s = 12.713$. One standard deviation below the mean falls at a value of 82.069 and 1 standard deviation above, at 107.513. Twenty observations (66.67 percent) fall within the range of 1 standard deviation on either side of the mean, and all fall within the range of plus or minus 2 standard deviations.

Assume that the data are in the form of the intelligence level groupings in the practice application in Chapter 2 and compute the mode, median, mean, and standard deviation. The grouped frequencies table necessary to make these computations follows:

GROUPED FREQUENCY

Class	f	m	f(m)	fm(m)
66–79	2	72.5	145.0	10512.50
80–90	13	85.0	1105.0	93925.00
89–110	9	100.5	904.5	90902.25
111–119	4	115.0	460.0	52900.00
120–127	2	123.5	247.0	30504.50
	30		2861.5	278744.25

The mode is the midpoint of the category containing the highest frequency. This category is the 80–90 category, and the midpoint is 85. The mode = 85.

Compute the median:

$$Md = L + \left[\frac{N/2 - cf}{f} \right] \times w = 79.9 + \left[\frac{30/2 - 2}{13} \right] \times 10$$

$$= 79.5 + \left[\frac{13}{13} \right] \times 20 = 79.9 + 10 = 89.5$$

The median = 89.5.

Compute the mean:

$$\bar{X} = \frac{\Sigma fm}{N} = \frac{2861.5}{30} = 95.38$$

Compute the standard deviation.

$$s = \sqrt{\frac{\Sigma fm(m)}{N} - (\bar{X})^2} = \sqrt{\frac{278744.25}{30} - 95.38^2}$$

$$= \sqrt{9291.475 - 9097.344} = \sqrt{194.131} = 13.933$$

The standard deviation $= 13.933$.

Using grouped data underestimates the mode and median and overestimates the mean and standard deviation. Data grouped according to some theoretical scheme (such as IQ) rather than into approximately equal groups yield unreliable measures of central tendency.

APPENDIX: Computer Instructions for Measures of Central Tendency and Dispersion

Command 3.1

SAS	SPSSX
PROC UNIVARIATE;	FREQUENCIES GENERAL = YRSDIAG
VAR YRSDIAG;	STATISTICS ALL

REFERENCE

Walsh, P., and Walsh, A. (1987). Self-esteem and disease adaptation among multiple sclerosis patients. *Journal of Social Psychology,* 127:669–671.

Chapter 4

Probability and the Normal Curve

4.1 PROBABILITY

The basis of statistical analysis is the idea of **probability,** which provides a mathematical basis for making predictions. Statistical statements are statements of probability, not of determinism. We do not say that given *A, B* will occur. This is a deterministic statement. Rather, we might make a statement such as "Given *A, B* has a .33 probability of occurring." We are all familiar with probability statements such as "The chances of rolling a 6 in one throw of a fair die are 1 in 6," "There is a 60 percent chance of rain through tomorrow morning," or "The chances of a cancer patient surviving for five years after diagnosis is 55 percent."

The first probability statement, regarding a throw of a die, is an example of classical probability; the second two statements are examples of empirical probability. *Classical probability* is theoretical probability based on a priori knowledge of all possible numerical values. Each throw of a die is a random event, with any one of six die values being equally probable for any toss. The variables (dice, cards, coins, etc.) on which classical probability is based are called random variables because, assuming fairness, each have an equal numerical chance of occurring. That is, each of the six values of a die have a 1/6 probability of coming up, each card in a shuffled deck has a 1/52 chance of being drawn, and a head or a tail is equally likely each time a coin is tossed. This is not to say that it is impossible to get four heads in four tosses of a coin, although it is not very likely. We do expect heads to come up 50 percent of the time in the long run, however. There is something called the law of large numbers, which tells us that the observed proportion will come closer and closer to the expected proportion (in this case, .50) as the number of trials increases.

Empirical probability is based on observation. When meteorologists talk about a 60 percent chance of rain, they mean that based on previous occasions when weather patterns were similar, it rained about 60 times out of 100. Probability in the real world is empirical probability. In other words, outcomes do not rest on pure chance in the same way as the fall of a fair coin does. Although the statistics in the rest of this book result from empirical observations, classical probability is very useful for the demonstration of some basic principles of probability, which we will expand on at various other places in the book.

4.1.1 The Multiplication Rule

Suppose we want to determine the probability of getting two heads on two tosses of a fair coin. For each toss of the coin the probability of getting a head is equal to one-half, or .50. Each successive toss is independent of the outcomes of previous tosses. That is, what happens on the first toss does not in any way influence what happens on the second. The probability of getting a head (or tail) remains .50 regardless of how many times you toss the coin. If you want to determine the probability of two independent events, such as two heads in two tosses of a fair coin, you must multiply the two independent probabilities. This is known as the **multiplication rule**, which has two forms. One is based on mutually exclusive (independent) outcomes, and the other, on nonindependent (conditional) outcomes. For independent outcomes, the rule is this:

MULTIPLICATION RULE.   The probability of two independent events occurring is equal to the product of their respective probabilities.

$$P(AB) = P(A)P(B)$$

where A and B are independent events

The probability of two heads in two tosses is $(.5)(.5) = .25$; the probability of three heads in three tosses is .125; and so on.

If the outcomes A and B are not independent of one another, the rule is this:

MULTIPLICATION RULE.   The probability of two or more dependent events occurring together is the product of the probability of A and the probability of B, given A.

$$P(AB) = P(A) \times P(B/A)$$

where $P(B/A)$ is the probability of B, given A has already occurred.

Behavioral scientists often want to know the probability of joint occurrences far more complex than the simple coin-tossing experiment. For instance, what is the probability that a person is white and an opponent of affirmative action? Suppose we have a random sample of 200 men. Of these, 120 are white and 70 are opposed to affirmative action. The other 80 men are black, 20 of whom are opposed to affirmative action. We select an individual at random from the sample: What is the probability that he is white and opposed to affirmative action? The probability of being white is $120/200 = .6$. The probability of being opposed to affirmative action, given that he is white $= 70/120 = .5833$. Therefore, $P(AB) = P(A) \times P(B/A) = (.6)(.583) = .35$. We can verify our answer with the general probability formula, which is

$$P = \frac{\text{number of ways the event can occur}}{\text{total number of possible outcomes}} = \frac{70}{200} = .35$$

4.1.2 The Addition Rule

Another probability rule you should be familiar with is the **addition rule.** To take a simple example: For the roll of a die, the probability of a 3 or a 5 is simply the sum of their respective probabilities ($1/6 + 1/6 = .333$). We are able to add these probabilities together because there are only six possible mutually exclusive outcomes, and each face of a die has an equal chance of coming up. The addition rule for two independent outcomes occurring is thus $P(A \text{ or } B) = P(A) + P(B)$, or the sum of their respective probabilities.

To go back to our affirmative action example, what if we wanted to determine the probability that a man selected at random from the sample is white *or* an opponent of affirmative action? We know that the probability is .6 that a man in our sample is white. The probability of being opposed to affirmative action is $90/200 = .45$. If we simply sum these two probabilities we get 1.05. This would be the same as summing the number of whites (120) and the number of men opposed to affirmative action (90) and dividing by the total sample N ($210/200 = 1.05$). Such an outcome is a logical impossibility because the probability of anything cannot exceed 1. We have exceeded 1 because there is an overlapping of occurrences of outcomes; they are not mutually exclusive outcomes as die-rolling outcomes are. That is, if we roll a 3 on a die, all other numbers are automatically excluded from coming up for that roll. But being white does not automatically tell us whether a man is in favor of or opposed to affirmative action. In fact, we have counted a number of men twice. Seventy of the 90 men opposed to affirmative action are white, and we have already accounted for all whites when we broke the sample down by race. We cannot count them again when we break the sample down by opposition to affirmative action. To eliminate this overlap of probabilities we have to add the individual probabilities and subtract the probability of their joint occurrence, which we know from the previous example to be .35. This is known as the addition rule for non-mutually exclusive occurrences.

ADDITION RULE.   The probability of either of two mutually exclusive events occurring is equal to the sum of their respective probabilities minus the probability of their joint occurrence.

$$P(A \text{ or } B) = P(A) + P(B) - P(A \text{ and } B)$$

where A and B are not mutually exclusive

Thus, the probability of selecting a man who is white or an opponent of affirmative action is

$$P(A \text{ or } B) = P(A) + P(B) - P(A \text{ and } B) =$$

$$P(A \text{ or } B) = (.6) + (.45) - (.35) = 1.05 - .35 = .70$$

Let us illustrate the two rules of probability for independent outcomes with an interesting sociological example. It has been estimated that fewer than 1 percent of the marriages in the United States are interracial (Reiss & Lee, 1988, p. 297). What if there were no cultural, economic, or psychological barriers to interracial marriage? How many interracial marriages might we expect if marriages were determined simply by chance shots of Cupid's bow? Let us assume that the racial groups in the United States break down according to the following proportions: white = .76, black = .14, and other = .10. Let us also assume that there is an equal number of men and women in each race. Under these conditions the probabilities of inter- and intraracial marriages would be as shown in Table 4.1. The multiplication rule is illustrated by the probabilities of marrying either into one's own race or into another (two independent events under the conditions we have assumed). The addition rule for mutually exclusive events is illustrated in the summation of the proportion of inter- and intraracial marriages expected under the assumed conditions (marrying a person of one race automatically excludes marrying a person of another, at least at the same time). Since they are mutually exclusive events, we can simply sum the individual probabilities.

There is no doubt that the percentage of interracial marriages expected under conditions of pure chance (39.28 percent) is a long way from what we actually

TABLE 4.1   PROBABILITIES OF INTER- AND INTRARACIAL MARRIAGES UNDER ASSUMED CONDITIONS

White/white	(.76)(.76) =	.5776
White/black	(.76)(.14) =	.1064
White/other	(.76)(.10) =	.0760
Black/black	(.14)(.14) =	.0196
Black/white	(.14)(.76) =	.1064
Black/other	(.14)(.10) =	.0140
Other/other	(.10)(.10) =	.0100
Other/white	(.10)(.76) =	.0760
Other/black	(.10)(.14) =	.0140

Sum of probabilities = 1.0000

Proportion of Intraracial Marriages	
White/white =	.5776
Black/black =	.0196
Other/other =	.0100
	.6072

Proportion of Interracial Marriages	
White/black =	.1064
White/other =	.0760
Black/white =	.1064
Black/other =	.0140
Other/white =	.0760
Other/black =	.0140
	.3928

Total marriages = .6072 + .3928 = 1.000

observe. This gap could be considered a good indicator of the sociocultural distance between the races in this country. How can I make this statement? I make it on the basis of the very large difference between the expected and observed percentages. Inferential statistics are built around comparisons of observed and expected phenomena, and the tools enabling us to make such comparisons are theoretical probability distributions.

4.1.3 Theoretical Probability Distributions

Another reason for discussing classical probability is its usefulness in showing how theoretical distributions of common and rare events are constructed. These distributions are actually theoretical probability distributions for random variables. They are not empirical distributions, such as the YRSDIAG and IQ distributions shown in the last chapter. However, theoretical probability distributions are indispensable to the statistical interpretation of empirical distributions, and the most important is the normal distribution for continuous random variables. We will discuss this distribution at length later in this chapter. Another probability distribution is the binomial probability distribution for discrete random variables (*binomial* means two distinct, either/or events, such as coin tossing).

Let us construct a binomial distribution by tossing coins. If I toss three fair coins, there are eight possible outcomes: HHH, HHT, HTH, THH, TTH, THT, HTT, TTT. Suppose I want to determine the probability of getting two heads in three tosses. Checking our eight possibilities, we see that three of them had two heads (HHT, HTH, and THH). As already indicated, for discrete events the probability of any random event occurring is the ratio of the number of ways the event can occur to the total number of possible outcomes. We have determined that two heads can occur three ways, and that the total number of possible outcomes in three tosses is eight. Therefore, the probability of two heads in three tosses = 3/8 = .375.

This example was fairly easy to compute without resorting to a mathematical formula. But what if instead of three tosses I toss the coin 10 times, or even 100 times? Determining the possible number of unique outcomes by listing them as I did with three tosses would be a formidable task. Luckily, there is a simple formula for determining the number of possible outcomes, Formula 4.1.

$$C_r^n = \frac{N!}{r!(N-r)!} \tag{4.1}$$

where C_r^n = number of combinations, outcomes, sequences, or successes

       N = number of trials

       r = number of successes

       ! = factorial (the product of all positive integers from N to 1)

For purposes of illustration, let us apply the formula to the three-toss example. We have three trials, so $N = 3$. We want to determine the number of ways we can get two heads, so $r = 2$. The factorial (!) means that we start at N (3) and determine the product of all positive integers from 3 to 1 ($3 \times 2 \times 1$). The complete calculation is

$$\frac{3 \times 2 \times 1}{2 \times 1(1)!} = \frac{6}{2} = 3$$

The next step is to determine the probability of observing two heads in three tosses by using Formula 4.2.

$$P_r^n = \frac{N!}{r!(N-r)!} p^r q^{n-r} \qquad (4.2)$$

where P_r^n = probability of observing the outcome

   p = probability

   $q = 1 - p$

The p is the probability of success on one toss (.5). The q is $1 - p$, or $1 - .5 = .5$. The formula applied to the problem of the probability of getting two heads in three tosses is

$$P_r^n = \frac{3!}{2!(3-2)!} p^2 q^{3-2}$$

$$= \frac{3 \times 2 \times 1}{(2 \times 1)(1)} .5^2 .5^1 = \frac{6}{2}(.25)(.5)$$

$$= 3(.125) = .375$$

If we were calculating the probability of getting four heads from ten tosses, the calculations would be as follows. Note that p^4 means that the probability of a success (.5) is multiplied by itself four times.

$$P_r^n = \frac{10!}{4!(10-4)!} p^4 q^{10-4}$$

$$= \frac{10 \times 9 \times 8 \times 7 \times 6 \times 5 \times 4 \times 3 \times 2 \times 1}{(4 \times 3 \times 2 \times 1)(6 \times 5 \times 4 \times 3 \times 2 \times 1)}(.5^4)(.5^6)$$

   canceling

$$= \frac{\overset{5}{\cancel{10}} \times \overset{3}{\cancel{9}} \times \overset{2}{\cancel{8}} \times 7}{\underset{1}{\cancel{4}} \times \underset{1}{\cancel{3}} \times \underset{1}{\cancel{2}} \times \underset{1}{1}} = \frac{210}{1}(.0625)(.015625)$$

$$= 210(.00976562) = .2051$$

Pay special attention to the relationship between p and q.

   Let us now construct a binomial distribution by the simple operation of tossing a fair coin ten times. The discrete random variable in this exercise is the number of heads in ten tosses. There are 11 possible outcomes (0 heads, 1 head, 2 heads, ..., 10 heads). Each of these outcomes has a number of ways it can occur, and each probability is computed by Formula 4.2. By the multiplication rule, each outcome has a $p^r q^{n-r} = .000976562$, or 1/1024 chance of occurrence. To arrive at the probability of a given outcome, you multiply the number of ways that outcome can occur by 1/1024. For example, five heads in ten tosses can occur in 252 ways. Therefore, $(252)(1/1024) = .2460937$ is the probability of five heads in ten tosses of a fair coin. Note that zero and ten heads have the same probability of occurrence as does one and nine heads, and so on. The calculations have been done for you and appear in Table 4.2. The first column of Table 4.2 lists the 11 possible outcomes. The second column lists the number of ways each outcome can occur. The third column shows the probabilities for each way. Note that these probabilities are equal, as demanded by the symmetry of $(p)(q)$. The fourth column shows the probability of the outcome.

This probability distribution serves as a standard by which we can judge empirical, or real-life, outcomes. If we wanted to test the fairness of a suspect coin, for instance, we could actually toss it in the air 10 times and compare the observed outcome to the theoretically expected outcome. If the empirical outcome departs significantly (we have ways of quantifying what we mean by "significantly," but this discussion comes in Chapter 6) from the theoretically expected outcome, we reject the notion that the coin is a fair one. As I have previously indicated, inferential statistics are built around comparisons of observed and theoretically expected outcomes.

We will now display all 11 probabilities in a probability histogram (Figure 4.1). Note that the histogram is perfectly symmetrical, indicating that low outcomes (e.g., zero or one head) are just as probable as high outcomes (e.g., ten and nine heads). Its highest point is the most probable outcome, and its lowest

TABLE 4.2 A BINOMIAL PROBABILITY DISTRIBUTION WHERE $n = 10$ and $p = .5$

Number of Heads	C_r^n	$(p^r)(q^{n-r})$	Probability	
0 heads	1	$(1/2)^0(1/2)^{10} = 1/1024*$	1/1024 =	.0009765
1 heads	10	$(1/2)^1(1/2)^9 = 1/1024$	10/1024 =	.0097650
2 heads	45	$(1/2)^2(1/2)^8 = 1/1024$	45/1024 =	.0439453
3 heads	120	$(1/2)^3(1/2)^7 = 1/1024$	120/1024 =	.1171875
4 heads	210	$(1/2)^4(1/2)^6 = 1/1024$	210/1024 =	.2050781
5 heads	252	$(1/2)^5(1/2)^5 = 1/1024$	252/1024 =	.2460937
6 heads	210	$(1/2)^6(1/2)^4 = 1/1024$	210/1024 =	.2050781
7 heads	120	$(1/2)^7(1/2)^3 = 1/1024$	120/1024 =	.1171875
8 heads	45	$(1/2)^8(1/2)^2 = 1/1024$	45/1024 =	.0439453
9 heads	10	$(1/2)^9(1/2)^1 = 1/1024$	10/1024 =	.0097650
10 heads	1	$(1/2)^{10}(1/2)^0 = 1/1024$	1/1024 =	.0009765
Total	1024		1024/1024 =	1.0000000

*Any number raised to the 0 power = 1.

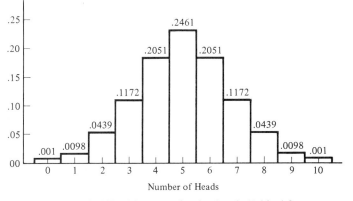

Figure 4.1 A probability histogram for the data in Table 4.2

points are the least probable outcomes. As is always the case, the area underneath the probability histogram is 100 percent, or unity.

If we were to make 1000 tosses of a fair coin rather than 10 we would have 1001 possible values rather than 11. The bars for a histogram for this number of possibilities would be so close together that they would almost describe a smooth, curved line. As the number of possible probability outcomes gets larger and larger, the histogram follows the normal-shaped curve more and more.

4.2 THE NORMAL CURVE

As we noted in the last chapter, the mean and the standard deviation are powerful ways of describing distributions of interval- and ratio-level variables. We also noted that the means of the distributions we have examined so far fall at differing points along the horizontal line (the abscissa) of the frequency distributions, and that about two-thirds of the observations fall between plus and minus 1 standard deviation from their mean. It would be nice if we had some "ideal" distribution against which we could compare our observed distributions. As we have seen, there is such a distribution, called the normal distribution, the bell-shaped curve, or the **normal curve.**

The normal curve is a probability distribution for continuous random variables that is entirely specified by two parameters, its mean (μ) and its standard deviation (σ). By "normal" we don't mean that it is the typical or most-often-observed distribution, although we do find rough approximations with fair regularity in large samples. "Normal" is used in the sense that the curve is a "norm," or idealized version, of a distribution against which we can compare the distributions we obtain in our research. It is a completely hypothetical curve, with a number of special attributes. It is perfectly symmetrical and smooth, and it is unimodal (it has only one mode). The tails of the curve never touch the abscissa. Technically, we say that the normal curve is asymptotic to the X-axis. This property reflects the assumption that any score, value, or outcome is theoretically possible, although extreme values are highly unlikely.

When we say that the normal curve is perfectly symmetrical we mean that each side of a curve split in the middle by its mean occupies exactly one-half of its total area. This means also that precisely 50 percent of the observations are on one side of its center and 50 percent are on the other side. Further, exactly 68.26 percent of the total area of the curve falls between plus and minus 1 standard deviation, exactly 95.44 percent of the area falls betwen plus and minus 2 standard deviations, and exactly 99.74 percent of the area falls between plus and minus 3 standard deviations.

These proportions under the normal curve are not tied to any particular distribution of scores. They are strictly a distribution of probabilities that can be generalized to any empirical distribution more or less regardless of their measurement units and the number of observations involved. Figure 4.2 presents the distribution of the area under the normal curve.

Summing these proportions under the curve, you will note that you get .9974 rather than unity. This result reflects the fact that scores that deviate from the mean further than plus or minus 3 standard deviations are possible. Such highly unlikely scores account for the remainder of the area (.0026, or .0013 on either side). In a sample of 10,000 we would expect only 13 cases more than 3 standard deviations below the mean and 13 cases more than 3 standard deviations above the mean.

It might help you to understand if we conceptualized these proportions or percentages of the area under the normal curve as numbers of observations in a sample. Suppose that we had a random sample of 1000 observations of male heights (a variable that is roughly normally distributed). In such a sample we should find about 683 cases within plus or minus 1 standard deviation of the mean, about 954 between plus or minus 2 standard deviations, and about 997 within 3 standard deviations. If our mean is 5 feet 9 inches and our standard deviation is 3 inches, we would observe the distribution of cases shown in Figure 4.3. With a truly representative sample of all males in the population we would expect to find only about three males that were either shorter than 5 feet 0 inches

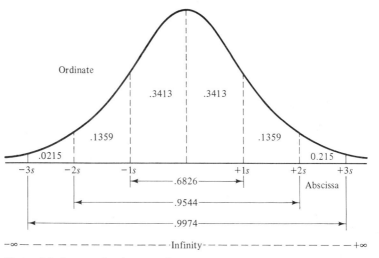

Figure 4.2 Areas under the normal curve

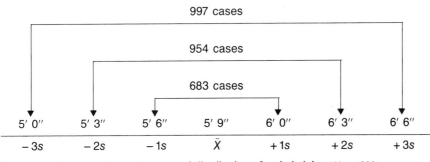

Figure 4.3 Number of cases in a normal distribution of male heights ($N = 1000$)

or taller than 6 feet 6 inches. The unlikelihood of finding extreme cases or scores beyond 2 or 3 standard deviations is something you should thoroughly digest for future reference.

The smoothness of the curve is based on the theoretical assumption of an infinite number of observations. Since the normal curve is a distribution of probabilities rather than empirical frequencies, we observe no peaks, valleys, or gaps in the normal distribution as we did in the empirical distributions in Chapters 2 and 3. This fact has an important implication for research in that it suggests that

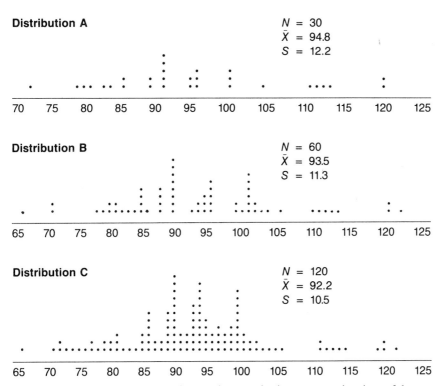

Figure 4.4 Illustrating the effects of increasing sample size on approximations of the normal curve

the larger the sample size the more the distribution of scores will approximate the normal curve if the underlying population distribution is normally distributed. Since this is an important point, we will demonstrate it with the IQ data in the practice application in Chapter 3.

Recall that the practice application asked you to plot the distribution of the 30 IQ scores, and we obtained the distribution given in Figure 4.4. There are lots of peaks, valleys, and gaps in this distribution, although it is a rough approximation of the normal curve. To illustrate the effects of increasing sample size on the increasing approximation of the normal curve, we doubled the sample size to 60 and then doubled it again to 120. Note how many of the gaps are filled in as the sample size becomes larger.

4.2.1 Different Kinds of Curves

A curve may be perfectly symmetrical (i.e., each side of the curve may be the same size and shape) but not be "normal." In fact there are theoretically an infinite number of different symmetrical curves, although they all contain the same proportion of observations within their standard deviation units regardless of their height or width. As mentioned earlier, the shape of the curve is determined entirely by the mean and standard deviation. The formidable-looking equation for the curve might convince you of this if you are a fair mathematician. Note that π and e are constants (they do not vary), so the only values that do vary are μ and σ.

Normal Curve Equation

$$Y = \frac{1}{\sigma\sqrt{2\pi}}e^{-(x-\mu)^2/2\sigma^2}$$

where Y = the height of the curve for a given value of x

   σ = the standard deviation

   π = the ratio of the circumference of a circle to its diameter (3.14159)

   e = the base of Naperian logarithms (2.71828)

Since the function $x - \mu$ is the difference between the height of any ordinate and the height of the ordinate at the mean, $x = 0$ for the ordinate at the mean and we have $0/2\sigma^2 = 0$. Any number raised to the power of zero $= 1$. Thus

$$e^{-0/2\sigma^2} = 1$$

The maximum ordinate height (the ordinate at the mean), then, is obtained by

$$Y\mu = \frac{1}{\sigma\sqrt{2\pi}}1$$

For example, if we assume a standard deviation of 1, the maximum ordinate is

$$Y\mu = \frac{1}{1\sqrt{(2)(3.14159)}}1 = \frac{1}{1\sqrt{6.28318}}1 = \frac{1}{(1)(2.5066)}1$$

$$= \frac{1}{2.5066}1 = (.399)(1) = .399$$

The height of the ordinate at plus or minus 1 standard deviation is

$$Y_1\sigma = \frac{1}{\sigma\sqrt{2\pi}}e^{-(1\sigma)^2/2(1\sigma)^2} = \frac{1}{1/(2)(3.14159)}e^{-(1)/(2)}$$

$$= .399 \times 2.71828^{-1/2}$$

$$= .399 \times \sqrt{\frac{1}{2.71828}}$$

$$= .399 \times .60653 = .242$$

After computing the ordinates at the maximum height and for 1, 2, and 3 standard deviations, we can plot them to form the curve shown in Figure 4.5.

We could go on repeating this calculation to get the height of any x value relative to the mean. This short example should be sufficient at this stage of your statistical education to convince you that curves can differ infinitely according to their means and standard deviations. They may be tall and thin relative to the theoretical normal curve, indicating a small amount of variation around the mean. Such a curve is called **leptokurtic** (from the Greek term *lepto,* meaning "thin"), as is curve B in Figure 4.6. A curve that is wide and flat relative to the theoretical normal curve, indicating a great deal of variation around the mean, is called **platykurtic** (meaning "flat"), as is curve C. A **mesokurtic** ("middle") curve is a curve with a "normal" scatter of observations about its mean, as is the theoretical normal curve shown in Figure 4.2. Notice that the curves in Figure 4.6 have the same mean but different standard deviations. The reason why these curves differ in height is that the area under the curve is unity (100 percent). Therefore, it follows that as the base of the curve expands (indicating a large σ) or shrinks (indicating a small σ), the height must decrease or increase accordingly to keep the area constant.

4.2.2 The Standard Normal Curve

The **standard normal curve** is a special case of the normal distribution curve in that it has a mean of zero and a standard deviation of 1. It was not just for ease of computation that I chose $\sigma = 1$ when I demonstrated the procedure for obtaining

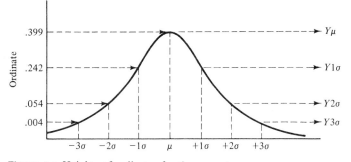

Figure 4.5 Heights of ordinates for the normal curve

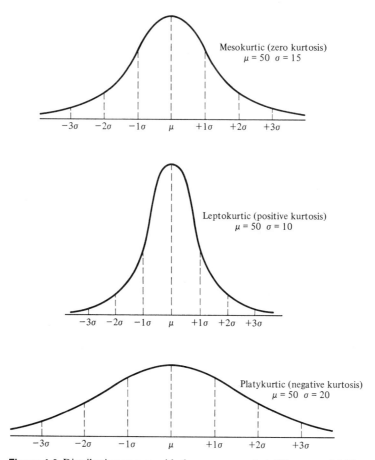

Figure 4.6 Distribution curves with the same mean but different variability

the height of the ordinate for given values of x for the normal curve. The resulting ordinates plotted in Figure 4.2 describe the standard normal curve.

The utility of the standard normal curve is that any normally distributed variable can be transformed into a standardized distribution, allowing a single reference distribution for comparing otherwise noncomparable statistics. For instance, if we wished to compare the IQ of one of our juvenile delinquents from Figure 4.4, distribution C, with the IQ of one of our adult criminals from the sex offender data, it would be difficult because the two different distributions have different means and standard deviations. Standardizing both distributions to a mean of zero and a standard deviation of 1 renders such comparisons meaningful. To do so we will compute what are called z scores. But first we will look at the distribution of IQ scores in our offender data. Since we have 376 cases for which we have IQ data, we can expect a better approximation of the normal curve than those we observed in Figure 4.4. The distribution of IQ scores for the offender data (SAS output) is presented in Table 4.3.

TABLE 4.3   DISTRIBUTION OF OFFENDER IQ (SAS)

```
                    FREQUENCY BAR CHART    SAS
```

Midpoint IQ	Sub IQ Score	Freq	Cum. Freq	Percent	Cum. Percent
60	**	2	2	0.53	0.53
62		0	2	0.00	0.53
64		0	2	0.00	0.53
66	**	2	4	0.53	1.06
68	*****	5	9	1.33	2.39
70	********	8	17	2.13	4.52
72	***	3	20	0.80	5.32
74	*******	7	27	1.86	7.18
76	*************	13	40	3.46	10.64
78	**********	10	50	2.66	13.30
80	***********	11	61	2.93	16.22
82	******	6	67	1.60	17.82
84	*************************	25	92	6.65	24.47
86	***************	15	107	3.99	28.46
88	****************	16	123	4.26	32.71
90	*******************************	31	154	8.24	40.96
92	*******************************	31	185	8.24	49.20
94	**********************************	34	219	9.04	58.24
96	************	12	231	3.19	61.44
98	**********************	22	253	5.85	67.29
100	********************************	32	285	8.51	75.80
102	*********************	21	306	5.59	81.38
104	*********************	21	327	5.59	86.97
106	******	6	333	1.60	88.56
108	************	12	345	3.19	91.76
110	************	12	357	3.19	94.95
112		0	357	0.00	94.95
114	*******	7	364	1.86	96.81
116	*	1	365	0.27	97.07
118	*	1	366	0.27	97.34
120	*****	5	371	1.33	98.67
122	*	1	372	0.27	98.94
124	*	1	373	0.27	99.20
126	*	1	374	0.27	99.47
128		0	374	0.00	99.47
130		0	374	0.00	99.47
132		0	374	0.00	99.47
134		0	374	0.00	99.47
136		0	374	0.00	99.47
138		0	374	0.00	99.47
140	**	2	376	0.53	100.00

```
         5    10    15    20    25    30
```

TABLE 4.3   (continued)

		SAS UNIVARIATE		
VARIABLE = IQ		SUB IQ SCORE		
	N	376	SUM	35179
	MEAN	93.5612	VARIANCE	148.359
	STD DEV	12.1803	KURTOSIS	0.743591
	SKEWNESS	0.182294	RANGE	80
	CV	13.0185	MODE	94
	MEDIAN	94		

This distribution is very close indeed to normal. If we rounded the mean to the nearest whole number the mean, median, and mode would all be 94, as verified by a visual examination of the graph as well as the skewness and kurtosis statistics.

Skewness refers to the symmetry or asymmetry of a distribution. The more asymmetrical the distribution the more it deviates from the normal curve. A positive value of skewness indicates a positive (rightward) skew, and a negative value of skewness indicates a negative (leftward) skew. The skewness for our IQ data (.18) is very small and positive, indicating a slight tendency for the tail of the distribution to be skewed to the right. Compare this value to the positive skew of 2.265 obtained from the MS diagnosis data in Chapter 3. A normal distribution, being perfectly symmetrical, has a skewness equal to zero.

Kurtosis refers to the height or peakedness of the distribution curve. A normal curve is mesokurtic and has a kurtosis of zero. When kurtosis is negative the curve is platykurtic, and when it is positive the curve is leptokurtic. Our kurtosis value (.74) is quite low and indicates a slight tendency toward leptokurtosis. Compare this with the very leptokurtic distribution (kurtosis = 6.446) of our MS data in Chapter 3. The formulas for calculating kurtosis and skewness used by SAS and SPSSx are quite complicated and not necessary for our purposes.

The only statistic given in a SAS univariate printout not yet addressed is the coefficient of variation (*CV*), which is used for assessing relative variation rather than absolute variation. It is useful for comparing variation in two distributions of the same variable having different means, or for comparing two distributions when the same dependent variable is measured in different units (e.g., months versus years). The coefficient of variation is calculated by multiplying the standard deviation by 100 and dividing by the mean. In the present example, [(12.1803)(100)]/93.5612 = 13.01. SPSSx does not give this statistic in its frequency program.

4.2.3 The Practical Value of the Normal Curve: The *z* Score

The usefulness of the normal distribution comes into play when we identify the parameters of the normal curve with the parameters of an empirical distribution.

The *z* **scores** are a basic illustration of this process of tying the theoretical distribution to empirical raw scores. When we convert raw scores into *z* scores the distribution of scores is standardized to the theoretical normal curve. There is nothing esoteric about standardizing scores. We did it in Chapter 2 when we standardized violent crime rates by population. Banks do it when they standardize or convert foreign currency to the U.S. dollar so that they can have a common basis for comparing the value of British pounds, German marks, French francs, Mexican pesos, and so on. The point is that standardizing doesn't in any way alter the value of the underlying variable: The distance from point *A* to point *B* is the same whether rendered in miles or kilometers. The formula for converting raw scores to *z* scores is

$$z = \frac{X - \mu}{\sigma} \quad \text{for populations, and} \quad z = \frac{X - \bar{X}}{s} \quad \text{for samples}$$

A *z* score tells us the number of standard deviations a score lies above or below its mean. A positive *z* score is above the mean, and a negative *z* score is below the mean. In essence, *z* scores are synonymous with standard deviation units. Figure 4.7 graphically demonstrates this equivalence, using the offender IQ data and rounding the mean and standard deviations.

To demonstrate the usefulness of *z* scores, let us take an individual from our offender data with an IQ of 106 and transform this raw score into a *z* score.

$$z = \frac{X - \bar{X}}{s} = \frac{106 - 94}{12} = \frac{12}{12} = 1.00$$

A *z* score of 1.00 means that this individual has a score that lies 1 standard deviation above the mean. We saw in Figure 4.2 that .3413 of the total area under the normal curve lies between the mean and +1*s*. Below the mean lies .50 of the total area. To find the total area of the curve corresponding to a *z* score of 1.0 we simply sum those two proportions to get .8431. This strategy is demonstrated graphically in Figure 4.8.

What this means in substantive terms is that an offender with an IQ score of 106 has an IQ higher than 84.13 percent of the offenders in the sample. Con-

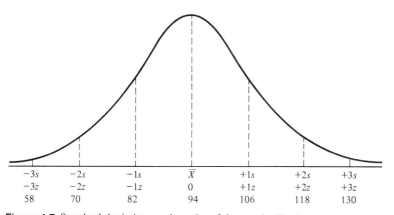

−3*s*	−2*s*	−1*s*	*X̄*	+1*s*	+2*s*	+3*s*
−3*z*	−2*z*	−1*z*	0	+1*z*	+2*z*	+3*z*
58	70	82	94	106	118	130

Figure 4.7 Standard deviations and *z* units of the standardized normal curve and equivalent raw scores from the offender IQ data

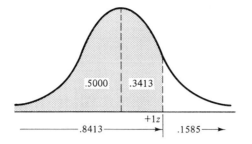

Figure 4.8

versely, his IQ score is lower than 15.85 percent of the sample. In other words, he scores higher than about 316 of the other subjects in the sample and lower than about 60.

Let us now take an individual from our sample of juvenile delinquents who also has an IQ of 106 and compute his z score. From Figure 4.4, distribution C, we see that the mean IQ is 92.2 and the standard deviation is 10.5. We will not round our figures this time.

$$z = \frac{X - \bar{X}}{s} = \frac{106 - 92.2}{10.5} = \frac{13.8}{10.5} = 1.31$$

A z score of 1.31 is not readily converted to an area under the curve by visual inspection. Luckily, there is a table in which areas under the curve for any z score have been precisely determined. This **normal curve table** is presented in Appendix A. Table 4.4 reproduces a small portion of this table for our present use.

The four-digit numbers in the body of the table represent areas of the curve falling between a given z score and the mean. The numbers in the column at the far left are the first two digits of the z score, and the numbers in the top row correspond to the third digit of the z score. A z score of 1.00, for instance, is located at the top left-hand corner of the table (.3413). To find the area corresponding to our computed z score of 1.31, go down the column until you reach the value of 1.3. Then go across that row until you come to the third digit

TABLE 4.4 SECTION OF AREAS UNDER THE NORMAL CURVE TABLE

z	.00	.01	.02	.03	.04	.05	.06
1.0	3413	3438	3461	3485	3508	3531	3554
1.1	3643	3665	3686	3718	3729	3749	3770
1.2	3849	3869	3888	3907	3925	3944	3962
1.3	4032	4049	4066	4083	4099	4115	4131
1.4	4192	4207	4222	4236	4251	4265	4279
1.5	4332	4345	4357	4370	4382	4394	4406
1.6	4452	4463	4474	4485	4495	4505	4515
1.7	4554	4564	4573	4582	4591	4599	4608
1.8	4641	4649	4656	4664	4671	4678	4686
1.9	4713	4719	4727	4732	4738	4744	4750

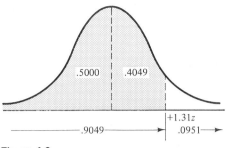

Figure 4.9

of 1.31, which is .01. The value you find there is 4049. You can read this as either a proportion (.4049) or a percentage (40.49 percent) of the area under the normal curve from the mean. The total area under the curve corresponding to a z score of 1.31 is this value plus the area below the mean (.5000 + .4049 = .9049). Our juvenile delinquent with an IQ of 106 has a score that exceeds 90.49 percent of all the other scores in the sample (see Figure 4.9). An important point for you to remember is that the probability of finding a juvenile delinquent with an IQ score of 106 or higher is only about 10 percent (only about 10 percent of the area of the curve contains scores that high or higher).

We now have a basis for comparing similar IQs across two different samples. Although both the juvenile and the adult offender had a similar IQ of 106, the juvenile scores better relative to the other subjects in the sample. We could also compare scores of an individual on different attributes by using z scores. For instance, we might want to know if our delinquent's years of schooling is as high relative to his delinquent peers as his IQ is. In other words, do his years of schooling exceed the mean number of years of schooling for the sample by as many z units as his IQ exceeds the mean IQ?

What if an adult offender scored 79 on an IQ test? How many of his peers would score higher or lower than he did? His z score would be $(79 - 94)/12 = -1.25$. Ignoring the negative sign for the moment, we see that the area corresponding with a z score of 1.25 is .3944. Since the sign is negative, this figure corresponds with 39.44 percent of the area *below* the mean. Note that in the negative case the z score area is subtracted from the .5000 rather than added to it. An offender with an IQ of 79 scores higher than only about 10 percent of other subjects in the sample and lower than about 90 percent (see Figure 4.10).

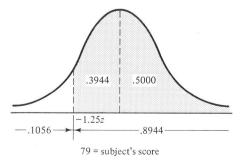

79 = subject's score

Figure 4.10

4.2.4 Finding the Area Under the Curve Between Two Scores

On occasion you may wish to determine the area under the curve between two scores rather than simply the area above or below the mean. For example, suppose that we wanted to determine what proportion or percentage of our adult offenders had IQ scores considered to be in the "normal" range between 90 and 110. The first thing you would do is convert these two raw scores (90 and 110) into z scores.

$$\text{raw score } 90: \quad z = \frac{90 - 94}{12} = \frac{-4}{12} = -0.33$$

$$\text{raw score } 110: \quad z = \frac{110 - 94}{12} = \frac{16}{12} = 1.33$$

Since we have not included scores as low of 0.33 in Figure 4.4 you will have to turn to Appendix A to complete this exercise. The first two digits are 0.3. Tracing along this row until you reach the final digit (.03), you will find an area of .1293, which corresponds to the area below the mean. For our second z score of 1.33, the area is .4082, which corresponds to the area above the mean. To find the total proportion of the area corresponding to IQ scores of 90 and 110, you simply sum the two areas (.1293 + .4082 = .5375). Thus, 53.75 percent of our offenders had IQs in the normal range (see Figure 4.11).

If you wanted to find the area between two positive z scores, say 0.50 and 1.55, you would first find the areas lying between the mean and 0.50 (.1915) and 1.55 (.4394). Having done so you would then subtract the smaller area from the larger (.4394 − .1915 = .2479). The area of the curve between z scores of 0.50 and 1.55 is 24.79 percent. A similar strategy would be followed if both z scores were negative (see Figure 4.12).

In our examples so far we have started with a known score, computed z, and then found the corresponding area of the curve. We will now illustrate the reverse process. Suppose, for instance, we wish to know between what two IQ scores in our offender data do the middle 50 percent of the cases fall. If we start from the mean, a figure of 50 percent means that 25 percent of the cases will be

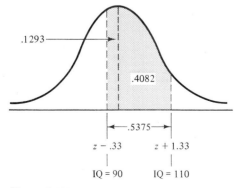

Figure 4.11

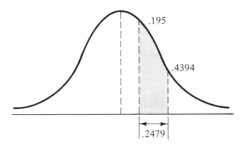

Figure 4.12

below the mean and 25 percent will be above the mean. We turn to Appendix A to find what z score is associated with an area of .2500. The closest value in the table is .2486, which is associated with a z score of 0.67. A z score of 0.67 is 67 percent of 1 standard deviation $(.67)(12) = 8.04$. Adding and subtracting 8 (rounded) from the mean, we find that the middle 50 percent of the cases fall between IQ values of 86 and 102 (see Figure 4.13).

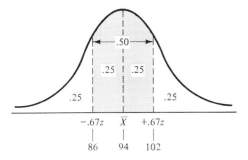

Figure 4.13

THE MEAN AND STANDARD DEVIATION OF A NORMALLY DISTRIBUTED VARIABLE

It was previousely stated that the standard normal curve is a normal curve that has been standardized to a mean of zero and a standard deviation of 1. Now that you understand how z scores are computed we can demonstrate this phenomenon. We will take ten subjects from our adult offender data and compute their z scores on IQ. We will treat these z scores as raw values and calculate their mean and standard deviation. Within rounding errors, the total of the z column will be approximately zero and the sum of the z-squared column will be approximately equal to N (10). They will be only approximations because we are dealing with sample data and not a population. If we chose a further random sample of ten cases we would get slightly different results.

THE MEAN AND STANDARD DEVIATION OF A DISTRIBUTION OF z SCORES

IQ Score	$(X - \bar{X})/s$		z	z^2
69	$69 - 94/12$	$=$	-2.0833	4.3401
82	$82 - 94/12$	$=$	-1.0000	1.0000
89	$89 - 94/12$	$=$	-0.4166	0.1736
90	$90 - 94/12$	$=$	-0.3333	0.1111
93	$93 - 94/12$	$=$	-0.0833	0.0069
96	$96 - 94/12$	$=$	0.1666	0.0277
98	$98 - 94/12$	$=$	0.3333	0.1111
100	$100 - 94/12$	$=$	0.5000	0.2500
110	$110 - 94/12$	$=$	1.3333	1.7777
113	$113 - 94/12$	$=$	1.5833	2.5069
			0.0000	10.3051

The mean ($\bar{z}$) of a distribution of z scores is

$$\bar{z} = \frac{\Sigma z}{N} = \frac{0}{10} = 0$$

The standard deviation (sz) of a distribution of z scores is

$$sz = \sqrt{\frac{\Sigma z^2 - [(\Sigma z)^2/N]}{N}} = \frac{\sqrt{10.3051 - (0)^2/10}}{10}$$

$$= \sqrt{\frac{10.3051 - 0}{10}} = \sqrt{1.03051} = 1.0151$$

4.2.5 The Normal Curve and Probability

Let us sum up some of the things we have learned about the normal curve. First, it is a probability distribution in which the total number of observations under it equals 100 percent. It contains a central area, under which most of the observations are to be found, and increasingly smaller areas on both sides of the central area, where fewer and fewer observations are found. Rather than thinking of the normal curve as a way of describing the proportion of the area above and below the mean, we will now think of it as a distribution of probabilities analogous to the probability histogram in Figure 4.1.

Even the probabilities of such simple events as outcomes of coin tossing can be approximated by the normal curve. In an infinite number of tosses of a fair coin you could expect exactly 50 percent to be heads and 50 percent to be tails. The probability of throwing two heads in succession is $(.5)(.5) = .25$; of three heads, $(.5)(.5)(.5) = .125$; and of four heads, $(.5)(.5)(.5)(.5) = .0625$. Throwing four heads in a row with a fair coin, therefore, is unlikely but possible about six times out of every 100 sets of four tosses.

We can even calculate an approximate standard deviation for binomial events like coin-tossing outcomes. Suppose we flip a fair coin 400 times and observe that it falls heads 220 times and tails 180 times. If only chance is operating we would, of course, expect 200 heads and 200 tails, or something very close to it. We now have to ask ourselves what the probability is of observing the experimental outcome, that is, 220 heads and 180 tails. Before we can determine this figure we have to calculate the standard deviation according to the formula

$$s = \sqrt{N(p)(q)}$$

where p = the proportion of heads

$q = 1 - p$ (i.e., the proportion of tails)

Substituting, we get

$$s = \sqrt{N(p)(q)} = \sqrt{400(.55)(.45)} = \sqrt{400(.2475)} = \sqrt{99} = 9.95$$

We use the z distribution to determine the probability of observing 220 or more heads or 180 or fewer tails in 400 flips of a fair coin. To calculate z we subtract the value we would expect under conditions of pure chance from what we actually observed and then divide by the standard deviation.

$$z = \frac{O - E}{s}$$

where O = observed frequency

E = expected frequency

s = standard deviation

Putting in the numbers, we get

$$z = \frac{220 - 200}{9.95} = \frac{20}{9.95} = 2.01$$

Turning to the table of z scores, we find that a z of 2.01 is equal to .4778. We add .500 to this figure as demanded by the symmetry of the curve to arrive at .9778, and we find that such an outcome could happen by chance in about $(1 - .9778)$ = .0222, or in about 2 percent of an infinite series of successive coin flips of 400 flips each. Do not forget: It is the area of the curve beyond a z score that provides us with probabilities.

The probability of observing a given score or value in a normal distribution of cases for any variable is obtained in exactly the same manner. Such a probability is always given relative to 100 percent, the entire area under the curve. Thus, we treat probability as the number of times a given event could occur out of 100 chances. What is the probability that a randomly selected case in a normal distribution will have a score between minus 1 and plus 1 standard deviations? The answer is about 68/100, or .68. The probability of a randomly selected case having a score between 2 standard deviations on either side of the mean is about 95/100, or 95 percent. It follows that the probability of a randomly selected case having a score greater than 2 standard deviations above or below the mean is 1 − .9544 = .0456 (turn to Figure 4.2 to verify this result for yourself).

To relate this probability to our offender data: If we randomly selected an individual from the sample, the probability that he would have an IQ further than

2 standard deviations above or below the mean is about .05. Stated another way, the chances of finding an offender with an IQ equal to or less than 70 or equal to or greater than 118 are theoretically about 5 in 100. If you turn back to Table 4.3 and count the actual number of observations that are either equal to or less than 70 or equal to or greater than 118, you will find 28 such cases. Twenty-eight is 7.4 percent of the 376 cases in the distribution. Thus, our empirical distribution is quite close to the theoretical expectation. It is important to remember, then, that small deviations from the mean are a lot more common than large deviations from the mean, that very large deviations from the mean are rare, and that positive and negative deviations from the mean occur in roughly identical proportions.

4.3 SUMMARY

Probability is a ratio of an event or outcome to the total number of possible events or outcomes. Probability is a vital concept to the understanding of statistics. We have discussed some basic ideas of probability, such as computing probabilities by using the addition and multiplication rules for independent and dependent events. We will discuss these concepts again as the need arises. We also showed how a theoretical binomial probability distribution curve is generated.

The normal curve is a very useful tool in statistical analysis. There are many different normal curves, the shapes of which are determined by their means and standard deviations. Curves with small standard deviations are leptokurtic, and curves with large standard deviations are platykurtic. Normal curves are perfectly symmetrical, with 50 percent of the area falling on one side of the mean and 50 percent falling on the other side of the mean. One standard deviation on either side of the mean contains 68.26 percent of the area, 2 standard deviations on either side contain 95.4 percent, and 3 standard deviations on either side contain 99.74 percent.

A standardized normal curve is one that has been standardized to a mean of zero and a standard deviation of 1. It is a model by which we compare chance events in an empirical distribution by the use of z scores, which give us the proportion of the normal curve corresponding to a given raw score. The larger the value of the computed z score (either positive or negative) the rarer is the value of the raw score. We find the area corresponding to a z score in the table of z scores in Appendix A. This is an important use of the normal curve and z scores because inferential statistics is concerned with estimating the probabilities of events.

PRACTICE APPLICATION: THE NORMAL CURVE AND z SCORES

A psychologist in the process of assessing various juvenile delinquents for the courts wants to determine the relative standing of selected members on IQ from our sample of 120 juveniles. Distribution C follows:

Distribution C

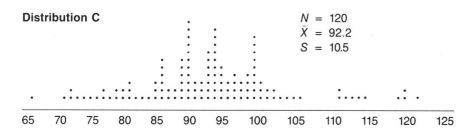

N = 120
$\bar{X}$ = 92.2
S = 10.5

| 65 | 70 | 75 | 80 | 85 | 90 | 95 | 100 | 105 | 110 | 115 | 120 | 125 |

Johnny and LeRoy are particularly troublesome children. Johnny's IQ score is 75 and LeRoy's is 120. Calculate their z scores.

Johnny: $z = \dfrac{75 - 92.5}{10.5} = \dfrac{17.5}{10.5} = -1.67$

LeRoy: $z = \dfrac{120 - 92.5}{10.5} = \dfrac{27.5}{10.5} = 2.62$

Graph their positions on the normal curve:

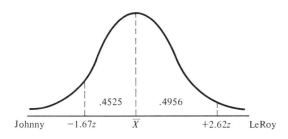

What percentage of the juveniles scored higher and lower than Johnny?

Higher: .4525 + .5000 =   .9525 =   95.25%

Lower: 1 − .9525 =   .0475 =   4.75%

Total: 1.000   100%

What percentage of the juveniles scored higher and lower than LeRoy?

Higher: 1 − .9956 =   .0044 =   0.44%

Lower: .4956 + .5000 =   .9956 =   99.56%

Total: 1.0000   100%

What percentage of the cases fall between Johnny's and LeRoy's scores?

.4525 + .4956 = .9481 = 94.81%

Johnny and Leroy are from a community that is 75 percent white and 25 percent black. If only chance were operating we would expect the sample to consist of 90 whites (120 × .75 = 90) and 30 blacks. We observe that 35 boys in the sample are black. What is the probability that this is a chance occurrence?

Compute the standard deviation:

$$S = \sqrt{N(p)(q)} = \sqrt{120(.75)(.25)} = \sqrt{120(.1875)} = 4.74$$

Compute z:

$$z = \frac{O - E}{s} = \frac{35 - 30}{4.74} = \frac{5}{4.74} = 1.05$$

The area of the curve corresponding to a z of 1.05 is .3531. Adding this figure to the other side of the curve as demanded by symmetry yields .8531. The area of the curve beyond .8531 is $1 - .8351 = .1469$. The probability that we would observe 35 or more blacks in the sample is due to random chance is .1469, or in about 15 times in every 100 similar samples we could expect such a finding on the basis of chance.

REFERENCE

Reiss, I., and Lee, G. (1988). *Family systems in America.* New York: Holt, Rinehart and Winston.

Chapter 5

Sampling and the Sampling Distribution

5.1 SAMPLING

In Chapter 1 we noted that populations of interest to the social scientist are usually much too large to be studied as a whole. Social researchers have to study small subsets of the population, called samples, and from the information derived from these samples they draw conclusions about the population from which the samples were taken. As we have seen, making statements or generalizations about populations from samples is formally called "using statistics to estimate parameters." The present chapter extends this discussion.

To make inferences about population parameters from sample statistics we must make sure that our sample is representative of the population. This is easily accomplished in the physical sciences since one piece of tungsten, for instance, is representative of every other piece of tungsten in the universe. It is less easily accomplished in the behavioral sciences because of the great variability among people on the attributes that we are interested in. Because of this variability we cannot make general statements about the objects of our interest unless we have a relatively large, and more important, a truly representative sample. It would be of no value, for instance, to obtain the height and weight means of a college's basketball and football teams, just because their members were readily available, to estimate the height and weight means of all males at the university. Such a strategy would result in a biased sample that would greatly overestimate the population's height and weight parameters. Obviously, athletes are not physically representative of all males, and the researcher could not generalize beyond that sample.

But how do researchers know if their sample is representative unless they already know what the population parameters are? And if the population parameters are known, why bother to sample? Of course, we can never know the population parameters, so however methodologically correct we are able to be, some degree of uncertainty will always remain. However, we can collect samples that are as representative as possible, which will allow us cautiously to generalize to the population of interest. An exhaustive discussion of sampling techniques more properly belongs in a text on research methodology. However, we will briefly discuss some of the more usual methods of sampling.

5.1.1 Simple Random Sampling

Simple random sampling is the "ideal" method of achieving representativeness, although it does not guarantee it. Simple random sampling is based on probability. A probability sample is one in which the probability of selecting any case in the population is known or is ascertainable prior to selection. *Random* does not mean haphazard or coincidental sampling. Rather, random sampling relies on very precise methods in which every member of a defined population has an equal chance of being included in the sample. For instance, if a random sample consists of 100 divorced women from a dating service known to have 1000 divorced women among its members, each divorced woman should have a .10 probability of being included in the sample.

Examples of nonrandom sampling abound. Magazines and newspapers often invite their readers to send in their answers to questionnaires, for instance. These requests often result in much larger samples than the typical social science researcher is able to collect. Samples of more than 10,000 are not uncommon, for example, *Redbook's* survey of female sexuality and the famous Ann Landers question asking whether women would rather cuddle or have sex. Despite the numerically overwhelming responses to these requests, the results are extremely unreliable because respondents were self-selected, and thus perhaps captured only those respondents who have a certain grievance or who are particularly interested in the topic. The readers of *Redbook* and the Ann Landers column constitute a rather special population, which we cannot assume to be representative of all American females. Furthermore, those readers who are willing to talk about their sex lives are a subset of even these unique populations. This is not to say that the results were inherently uninteresting; they just cannot be generalized beyond their respective samples.

A random sample requires three things: (1) a defined population, for example, all MS patients in Idaho; (2) an exhaustive list of all members of the population; (3) a selection process that assures that every case or group of cases in the population has an equal probability of being selected. The first two requirements constitute a **sampling frame,** that is, a kind of operational definition of the target population. Ideally, the sampling frame and the target population should be identical, but this is rarely possible. No lists are ever completely exhaustive. For instance, if we wanted to poll the citizens of Waterloo, Iowa, probably the best list we could obtain would be the telephone directory. But because we know that some people have unlisted numbers and others do not have a phone, we would have to rely on an incomplete list to conduct our poll. In countries where a telephone is considered a luxury, such a sampling procedure would be useless because we would presumably be polling only the wealthy.

Assuming that a list of the population exists, the selection process can begin. The most usual way of approaching case selection is to begin with a randomly selected number from a table of random numbers (lists of number without any pattern to them). The researcher then selects the case on the list that corresponds to the randomly selected number, repeating this process until the desired sample size is selected. If you are lucky enough to have a sampling frame on magnetic tape in a computer, you can have the computer generate a random sample for you.

This was the procedure I used to select the sample of MS patients included in this book. However, we are not assured of complete representativeness even with this procedure. First, the list from which the sample was taken included only members of the Idaho MS Society, and not all MS patients are members. My sampling frame was thus not fully consistent with the population I wished to target (strictly speaking, this is a problem of research design rather than one of sampling). Second, not all selected cases responded to the questionnaire, although the return rate of 67 percent was exceptional for survey research. What we have, then, is a fairly representative sample of all MS patients in Idaho who are members of the MS society. We run into problems like this all the time in social research. Even the most assiduous attempts to select a truly random sample are not free of research design and sampling problems that are usually beyond the power of the researcher to control.

5.1.2 Stratified Random Sampling

A second kind of probability sampling is **stratified random sampling.** These designs subdivide a heterogeneous population into homogeneous subsets (strata) and randomly select cases from each subset as in simple random sampling. A stratified random sample can be proportional or disproportionate.

Suppose you were interested in determining the mean income in your city of each of four racial groups based on a sample of 400 cases. Further suppose that Orientals made up only 5 percent of the population. If you wanted proportional representation in your sample you would have to select the sample in such a way as to ensure that Orientals constituted 5 percent. So with your proposed sample of 400 cases you would randomly select 20 cases from the Oriental population of your city.

Another type of stratified sampling is disproportionate stratified sampling, used when the researcher wishes to get an equal number of cases from each list regardless of the proportion of cases in each sublist. For instance, the 20 Oriental cases in the preceding example may not be adequate for interstratum comparisons of income, and you might find it necessary to select disproportionately more Orientals in order to make such comparisons. As long as disproportionate substrata are analyzed comparatively, the disproportionate sampling method need not alarm us. However, if the subgroups are to be combined and then analyzed to obtain an income picture of the entire city, we must take the sampling method into consideration. We would have to adjust for the disproportionate number of Orientals by a process known as weighting. This process is a simple one and is found in texts on sampling and research methods.

The offender data in this book is a disproportionate stratified sample. I began by taking every sex offender sentenced in a four-year period in this particular jurisdiction. Since I took every sentenced sex offender in the county, technically I had a population of sex offenders for the given time period. However, I wanted a sample of non-sex offenders to serve as a comparison group. Since only felony cases and male offenders were needed, I determined that this population for the same time period was 2970. The initial number of sex cases was 208, so I divided 2970 by 208 to get approximately 14. I started with a random "seed" number and selected every fourteenth non-sex case thereafter until I reached 208 cases. If the fourteenth case happened to be a female client or the crime happened to be a misdemeanor (both relatively infrequent in the files), I simply selected the next case.

This kind of systematic random sampling is not always wise. By selecting every fourteenth case, I had completely determined the sample to be selected. Any case that was not a multiple of 14 (28, 42, 56, etc.) was systematically excluded, and every case that was a multiple of 14 was included. If cases are processed and filed in some meaningful order, systematic sampling may seriously misrepresent the population. Luckily, the criminal cases in this sample were filed simply in the order that they were adjudicated.

There are many other ways of selecting a sample that we cannot discuss here. All of them in one way or another are attemptss to compensate for the inability to select randomly a representative sample. As the population to which we want to generalize becomes larger and more diverse, the difficulties of selecting a representative sample increase. We could easily, for example, select a truly random sample from the population of coeds at a college. But if the population to which we wanted to generalize was "American woman," our sampling task would be monumental since every woman in America would have to have an equal probability of being selected. Such a sample would require a sampling technique known as multistage cluster sampling, whereby the researcher would sample clusters, or subpopulations, of women living in various areas in the United States.

Whatever the sampling design, whether relatively simple or complex, the basic steps of listing and randomly sampling are always the same. The main obstacle to truly random sampling is the unavailability in many instances of the exhaustive lists we spoke about. In many cases such lists simply don't exist, and if they do exist they may not be freely supplied to researchers. Even if lists exist and are available, we still must confront the problem of nonresponse. We have to live with the obstacles presented to us and do the best that we can, being very careful not to make generalities beyond those warranted by the data.

5.2 THE SAMPLING DISTRIBUTION

Suppose that we have a large amount of information from a random sample: How is it that we are justified in making inferences to the population? For instance, we saw in Chapter 3 that the mean IQ for our offenders was 93.561. If we wanted to estimate the population parameter (the population mean IQ), this would be our best estimate. But, you may protest, we have only a sample; what if we took another sample and found the mean to be 95.5, or a number of samples and found that the mean differed each time? You would be right in saying that we would almost certainly find different means with each sample. Means vary across samples just like scores within them vary from their mean. In fact, I took 60 different random samples of 30 cases each from the IQ data and not once did I find exactly the same mean. How then do I know that my single sample mean is my best estimate?

We are rescued from this apparent dilemma by a theoretical probability distribution known as the **sampling distribution of means**. We can think of the sampling distribution of means as a frequency distribution of all possible sample means of constant sample size that we could draw from the same population. The number of possible samples is almost infinitely large when the population N is large. However, there is a deceptively simple formula for determining the possible number of samples of a given size from a population of a known size:

$$C_n^N = \frac{N!}{n!(N-n)!}$$

where N = size of population

n = sample size

Taking a simple example of $N = 5$ and $n = 3$, the possible number of samples is

$$C_3^5 = \frac{5!}{(3!)(2!)} = \frac{(5)(4)(3)(2)(1)}{[(3)(2)(1)][(2)(1)]} = \frac{120}{12} = 10$$

You can readily see that the possible number of samples from a population of any decent size would soon become huge. If we take a population of only 100 units and drew small samples of size 5, the number of possible samples is 75,287,520!

If we were able to take all possible sample means, sum them and divide by the number of samples, we would have the exact value of the population mean. In other words, "sample means" are treated as the variable in a distribution of sample means. As with all distributions, the distribution of sample means will have a mean itself—a "mean of means." With a large enough sample of sample means, the distribution will center around the population mean, and its shape will approximate the normal distribution. As we see from Figure 5.1, however, the sampling distribution of means is thinner (more leptokurtic) than the population distribution. This result reflects the fact that although the means of the two distributions are identical, the standard deviation of the sampling distribution is smaller than the standard deviation of the population distribution. This result occurs because sample means will differ less from the mean of means than raw scores in an empirical distribution will differ from their mean.

What all this tells us is that we know from the theory of the sampling distribution that we are justified in using sample statistics to estimate parameters. When we are making inferences from samples to populations, then, we are actually dealing with three distinct distributions: the empirical (sample) distribution, the empirical but unknown population distribution, and the theoretical (nonempirical) sampling distribution. As is the case with the normal distribution, the shape, central tendency, and dispersion of the distribution are deduced from the laws of probability.

Figure 5.1 illustrates the relationship among the three distributions. We have a parent population that is empirical, meaning that there actually is a population. We do not usually know the population mean (or any other population parameter) but we can estimate it statistically from a random sample drawn from the population. We know that we can do this with some confidence because of the theory underlying the sampling distribution. There will be a certain amount of error, but we are able to determine it and take it into account in our estimations.

Figure 5.2 is a distribution of sample means consisting of 60 computer-selected random samples of size 30 taken from our IQ data. Random selection means that every unit or case has an equal probability of being selected in each of our 30 samples. So each case has a probability of being selected, determined by the formula n/N, where n = sample size and N = population size. Each case will therefore have a $30/637 = .047$ probability of being included.

We are treating the sample distribution of offender IQs as a population distribution for the purpose of making our point, but you should realize that the popu-

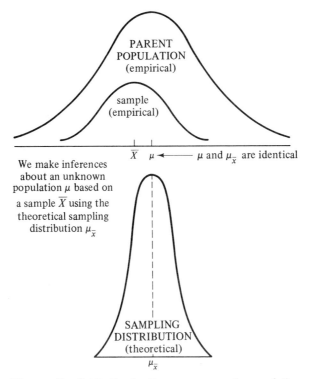

(The sampling distribution has the same mean as the population distribution but a smaller standard deviation)

Figure 5.1 The population, sample, and sampling distributions

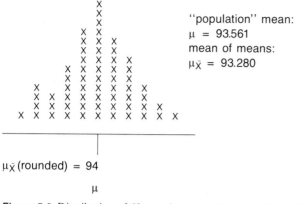

"population" mean:
μ = 93.561
mean of means:
$\mu_{\bar{X}}$ = 93.280

$\mu_{\bar{X}}$ (rounded) = 94

μ

Figure 5.2 Distribution of 60 sample means from samples of ($N = 30$) offender IQ "population"

lation mean is generally unknown and probably unknowable. The "population" mean IQ has been rounded to 94, and each of the sample means were rounded to the nearest whole number for ease of diagraming. Instructions on using the computer to generate random samples from a data set are given in the chapter appendix.

As we see from Figure 5.2, the distribution of sample means cluster around the known "population" mean. The mean of these means (calculated prior to rounding) is 93.28, which only differs from the unrounded "population" mean by .281 (93.561 − 93.28 = .281). If we took more random samples and plotted them on Figure 5.2 we would come even closer to the "true" population mean. Do not forget though: No matter how many samples we took we would still be only approximating the sampling distribution since it is a purely theoretical distribution based on an infinite number of samples.

The beauty and elegance of the sampling distribution is such that even if the population, and hence the samples drawn from it, is not normally distributed, repeated samples will generate means that are approximately normally distributed. Since we have no population distribution we will again have to suspend reality and use a sample distribution to make the point. In Chapter 2 we saw that the sample distribution of MS patients is highly skewed. I had the computer generate 30 random samples of size 30 from this distribution and plotted them in Figure 5.3. You can see that with just 30 samples the distribution of sample means is

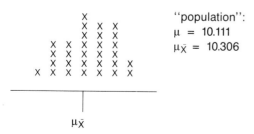

"population":
μ = 10.111
$\mu_{\bar{X}}$ = 10.306

$\mu_{\bar{X}}$

Figure 5.3 Distribution of 30 sample means from samples of size 30 from highly skewed distribution of years since diagnosis for MS patients

beginning to approximate the normal curve. The mean of the means is 10.306, which is only .195 away from the "population" mean of 10.111. Please remember that once again we are only assuming the sample to be a population to illustrate the point.

Of course, we rarely take more than one sample to estimate the population parameters, which means that we will almost certainly be in error in making our estimations. However, statistics is the science of error. The difference between a sample statistic and its corresponding population parameter is known as **sampling error**. Each mean in Figure 5.3 whose value is not 10.111 is in error. Nevertheless, if we use the sample mean as an estimate of the population mean, we will be making an error of less magnitude than if we use any other value. Just as there are fewer and fewer raw scores in a frequency distribution as we move away from the mean toward the tails of the distribution, Figures 5.2 and 5.3 demonstrate that fewer and fewer samples have means that are much larger or much smaller than the population mean in the sampling distribution. In both of these figures, the means are clustered around their "population" means and have peaked at these values. Some sample means missed the mark, but the frequency of the misses became less and less as the magnitude of the difference became larger and larger.

5.2.1 Standard Error of the Sampling Distribution

As with all distributions, the sampling distribution has a standard deviation. As we have already pointed out, the mean of the sampling distribution will be the same as the population mean, but the standard deviation will be smaller than the population standard deviation. The standard deviation of the sampling distribution has a special name: the **standard error**, or sometimes the *standard error of the mean*. The standard error of a sampling distribution is equal to the standard deviation of the parent population divided by the square root of the sample size. The smaller the standard error the more confident we can be that the sample mean is close to the population mean. The standard error is found by Formula 5.1.

$$\sigma_{\bar{x}} = \frac{\sigma}{\sqrt{N}} \tag{5.1}$$

It is important not to confuse the standard deviation with the standard error of the mean. Although both are standard deviations, we must not lose sight of the fact that s is a measure of variability derived from the actual observations of a sample. The standard error of the mean, on the other hand, represents the variability of possible mean values that could be attained from a series of sample means.

From Formula 5.1 we see that the standard error of the sampling distribution is a function of sample size. This should not be too surprising. We mentioned in our discussion of the standard deviation in Chapter 3 that there is less variability in a sample than there is in the parent population. This statement makes sense since the population by definition includes all extreme scores. The smaller the sample the less likely it is to include extreme scores because they are rare relative

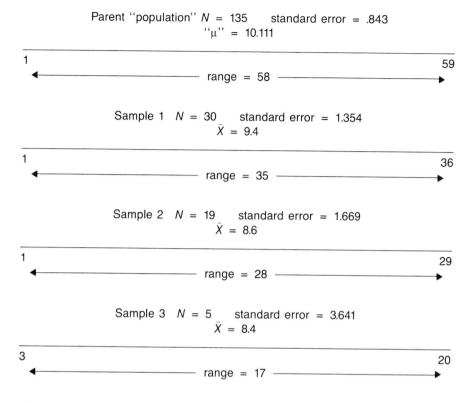

Parent "population" N = 135   standard error = .843
"μ" = 10.111

Figure 5.4

to scores closer to the mean. Figure 5.4 illustrates this concept with three randomly selected samples of size 30, 19, and 5 from our MS data; the number of
years since the diagnosis is the variable. Notice that the range of values included
in the samples (and hence the variability) decreases as the sample size decreases. Also note that the standard error becomes larger as the sample size
decreases. You should realize that although the standard error is a measure of
variability, these last two sentences are not contradictory. The standard error is a
function of both the variance and N. The smaller the N the smaller the number we
divide the variance by, and hence, the larger the standard errors obtained with
small samples. You should also note that the smaller the sample the more error
we make in estimating the population mean from the sample mean.

5.2.2 The Central Limit Theorem

We can summarize much of what we have discussed so far in this chapter by an
important statistical concept known as the **central limit theorem**:

> If repeated random samples of size N are drawn from a population having a mean μ
> and a standard deviation σ, as N becomes large, the sampling distribution of sample
> means will approach normality with a mean μ and a standard deviation $\sigma/\sqrt{N}$.

The central limit theorem is perhaps the most important theorem in statistical theory. It tells us that we can make inferences from samples to populations regardless of the shape of their distributions and regardless of whether the population values are discrete or continuous. Further, it tells us that we can do so with relatively small samples, providing they are randomly selected. The theorem states "as N becomes large," but "large" is usually considered to be any number over 30, although this is a somewhat arbitrary rule of thumb that is sometimes distinguished from the central limit theorem as the "law of large numbers." It should be intuitively reasonable to you that as sample sizes become larger and larger the data will come closer and closer to the population values. The "as N becomes large" statement also removes the constraint of the assumption of normality of the parent population distribution, as we saw from the demonstration in Figure 5.3.

Before we see how the standard error is used to estimate parameters, it is a good idea to distinguish between the symbols used for the different types of distributions (populations, samples, and sampling) we have been discussing (see Table 5.1).

TABLE 5.1   SYMBOLS FOR MEANS AND STANDARD DEVIATIONS FOR THE POPULATION, SAMPLE, AND SAMPLING DISTRIBUTIONS

Distribution	Mean	Standard Deviation
Population	μ	σ
Sample	$\bar{X}$	s
Sampling	$\mu_{\bar{x}}$	$\sigma_{\bar{x}}$

5.2.3 Point and Interval Estimates

There are two kinds of estimates of population parameters from sample statistics: point estimates and interval estimates. A **point estimate** is a single value and an **interval estimate** is a range of values. When we say that the mean IQ of our offenders is 93.561, this is a point estimate of the population parameter. When a pollster says that 60 percent of the population is pro-choice on the issue of abortion, this is a point estimate of the percentage of people in the population who are so inclined. An interval estimate would be of this kind: "The mean IQ of criminal defendants is between 90.5 and 95.5" or "Between 57 percent and 63 percent of the population is pro-choice on the issue of abortion."

A statistic used to estimate a parameter should be unbiased, consistent, and efficient. For instance, a sample mean is an **unbiased estimate** of the population mean if the mean of the sampling distribution (the mean of means) is equal to the population mean. We know from our discussion of the central limit theorem that sample means are unbiased estimates of population means if the sample is randomly selected. However, the sample standard deviation (s) is a biased estimator of the population standard deviation (σ), as we saw in Chapter 3. We also saw that the sample s^2 is considered an unbiased estimator of σ^2 if $N - 1$ is used in its calculation rather than N.

Unbiasedness only means that over the long run the average sampling error is zero. A **consistent estimate** is one in which there is agreement between the value of the sample statistic and its parameter. The larger the sample size the greater the consistency of these values. As sample size increases the standard error decreases (Figure 5.4), meaning that the potential for sampling error decreases. If two random samples are drawn from the same population of size $N = 50$ and $N = 500$, there will be greater consistency in the larger sample.

The efficiency of a statistic refers to its relative superiority as a point estimate compared to alternative estimates. The mean, for instance, is a more **efficient estimate** of central tendency than is the median or the mode because of its greater stability in a normally distributed population. The standard error of the mean is less than the standard errors of the median or mode, making for less sampling error. This concept was demonstrated in Chapter 3.

5.2.4 Confidence Intervals and Alpha Levels

To establish the range of interval estimates we use the standard error. We will establish the interval range for the population mean of offenders by using our sample mean. We will now cease using our sample means as the assumed population mean and again treat it as what it actually is, a sample mean. The first thing we have to do is calculate the standard error. We know that the sample mean IQ is 93.561 and that $N = 376$. Since we do not know the population standard deviation we estimate it with the sample standard deviation, which we know from Figure 4.9 to be 12.18. Putting these numbers into the formula for the standard error, we get

$$\sigma_{\bar{x}} = \frac{s}{\sqrt{N}} = \frac{12.18}{\sqrt{376}} = \frac{12.18}{19.39} = .628$$

We know that the sampling distribution performs the same function for samples that the normal distribution performs for raw scores. With a distribution of raw scores, approximately 68 percent of all scores lie between plus and minus 1 standard deviation, approximately 95 percent lie within plus and minus 2 standard deviations, and approximately 99 percent lie within plus and minus 3 standard deviations. Similarly, the same percentages of sample means lie within the respective standard errors. That is, if an infinite number of sample means were calculated, 68 percent of them will be between plus and minus 1 standard error of the population mean. Assuming our sample IQ mean is the population mean once again, 68 percent of all sample means from this population will be within plus or minus .628 of 93.561. So, 68 percent of the sample means in the sampling distribution will fall within the range 92.933 to 94.189. Ninety-five percent of sampling means in the sampling distribution will fall within plus or minus 2 standard errors of the mean (plus or minus $.628 \times 2 = 1.256$), and 99 percent within $.628 \times 3 = 1.884$ on either side of the mean. This range of values constructed around the point estimate is known as the **confidence interval**. Thus, we are 99 percent confident that the population parameter (μ IQ) lies within the range of 2.58 standard errors on either side of our point estimate ($\bar{X}$ IQ).

An interval estimate is wrong if it does not contain the population parameter. How do we know if it is right or wrong? Actually we never do, although we can state the interval estimates with a known probability that we are wrong. The probability of being wrong is called alpha, also called the confidence level (confidence interval = 1 − alpha). By convention social scientists choose one of two alpha levels: the .05 and .01 levels. At an alpha level of .05, the social scientist is saying that he or she is willing to run the risk of being wrong five times out of 100. At the .01 level the risk of being wrong is one time out of 100. Running the risk of being wrong five times out of 100 is the same as saying that the social scientist is 95 percent confident that the interval contains the parameter. Stated another way, if an infinite number of intervals were constructed at the .05 alpha level, 95 percent of them would contain the population value and 5 percent of them would not.

If we turn to Appendix A we will find that the area under the normal curve that corresponds to the 95 percent confidence level has a z value of 1.96. To refresh your memory, turn to Appendix A and locate the area of the curve above a z score of 1.96. We find this value to be .4750. Doubling this value to take in both sides of the curve, we get .95, or 95 percent. The area beyond this value (1 − .95 = .05) is our alpha level. Table 5.2 presents the areas under the curve and the corresponding alpha levels and z scores for three different confidence levels. Note that the alpha level corresponds to the area beyond the z score—the rare events.

TABLE 5.2   RELATIONSHIP BETWEEN CONFIDENCE LEVELS, ALPHA LEVELS, z
SCORES, AND AREAS UNDER THE NORMAL CURVE

Confidence Level	Alpha Level	z Score	Area from Mean to z Score	Area Times 2	Area Beyond z Score (Alpha)
95.0%	.05	1.96	.4750	.95	.05
99.0%	.01	2.58	.4950	.99	.01
99.9%	.001	3.30	.4995	.999	.001

5.2.5 Calculating Confidence Intervals

If, as we have said, $\bar{X}$ is within 1.96 $\sigma_{\bar{x}}$ of μ 95 percent of the time, if we start at $\bar{X}$ and go 1.96 $\sigma_{\bar{x}}$ in either direction, that interval should include μ (see Figure 5.5). The distribution is the sampling distribution with an unknown μ corresponding to the population μ and an estimated standard error. Sample mean a falls within the interval $\pm 1.96\sigma_{\bar{x}}$, but sample mean b does not.

We are now in a position to calculate confidence intervals for our population mean. We determine the risk we are willing to take that we are wrong by specifying the z score corresponding to a given alpha level in the following formula:

$$ci = \bar{X} \pm z(s/\sqrt{N})\qquad\qquad(5.2)$$

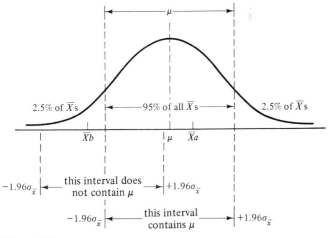

Figure 5.5

where ci = confidence interval

   $\bar{X}$ = sample mean

   s = sample standard deviation

We know that the sample mean and standard deviation for our offender data in Chapter 4 are 93.561 and 12.18, respectively. All that remains is for us to select a level of confidence. We choose the 95 percent level ($z = 1.96$). Therefore, the confidence intervals for the population mean are

$$ci = \bar{X} \pm (z)(s/\sqrt{N}) = (1.96)12.18/\sqrt{376}$$

$$= (1.96)(12.18/19.391) = (1.96)(.628) = 1.231$$

$$ci = 93.561 \pm 1.231$$

lower confidence interval (LCI) = $93.561 - 1.231 = 92.33$

upper confidence interval (UCI) = $93.561 + 1.231 = 94.792$

Thus, we are 95 percent confident that the population mean is somewhere between 92.33 and 94.792. More precisely, if we took an infinite number of random samples from the same population and constructed confidence intervals for each one, the confidence interval would contain μ 95 out of 100 times. If we want more confidence, we substitute the z value for the desired level. If we want to be 99.9 percent confident, meaning we wish only to run the risk of being wrong one time in every 1000, we set z at 3.3.

$$ci = \bar{X} \pm (z)(s/\sqrt{N}) = 93.561(3.30)(.628) = 2.072$$

$$ci = 93.561 \pm 2.072$$

lower confidence interval (LCI) = $93.561 - 2.072 = 91.489$

upper confidence interval (UCI) = $93.561 + 2.072 = 95.633$

Note that as confidence that our our sample mean includes the population mean increases the intervals widen. There is a constant trade-off in statistics between confidence and precision of estimates. You could be absolutely sure, for instance, if you estimated the population mean IQ of offenders to be 80 and 120, but it wouldn't be very useful. Conversely, the narrower the confidence intervals the less confident we are that they include the population mean.

5.2.6 Interval Estimates for Proportions

The procedure for estimating population proportions from sample proportions is similar to that for estimating population means from sample means. Based on the central limit theorem, sample proportions have sampling distributions that are normal in shape. We can thus construct confidence intervals for population proportions based on sample proportions by using the following formula:

$$ci = Ps \pm z\sqrt{\frac{(Pp)(Qp)}{N}} \tag{5.3}$$

where Ps = sample proportion

Pp = population proportion

$Qp = 1 - Pp$

Since we select the value of z depending on how confident we wish to be, and Ps and N are sample values, we are left only with the value we have to estimate (Pp). By definition Pp is an unknown, so what do we do? Again, we simply use the sample proportions as our best estimates.

Suppose that we wanted to estimate the proportion of females with MS in Idaho who were divorced after diagnosis and compare this figure with the proportion of males with MS who were divorced after diagnosis. From our MS sample data we see that the proportion of once-married females who were divorced after diagnosis is .42, and the corresponding proportion for males is .30. We can now place confidence intervals around these proportions, using the 95 percent level of confidence.

Females

$$ci = Ps \pm z\sqrt{\frac{(Ps)(Qs)}{N}} = 1.96\sqrt{\frac{(.42)(.58)}{135}} = 1.96\sqrt{\frac{.2436}{135}}$$

$$= 1.96\sqrt{.00180} = (1.96)(.0425) = .0833$$

$$ci = .42 \pm .0833$$

$$LCI = .42 - .0833 = .3367$$

$$UCI = .42 + .0833 = .5033$$

Males

$$ci = Ps \pm z\sqrt{\frac{(Ps)(Qs)}{N}} = 1.96\sqrt{\frac{(.30)(.70)}{135}} = 1.96\sqrt{\frac{.2100}{135}}$$

$$= 1.96\sqrt{.00155} = (1.96)(.03937) = .0772$$

$$ci = .30 \pm .0772$$

$$LCI = .30 - .0772 = .2228$$

$$UCI = .30 + .0772 = .3722$$

Our best estimate of the proportion of once-married female MS patients who were divorced after diagnosis based on our sample finding is .42. With 95 percent confidence we can say that this estimate is wrong by no more than about .08 (or 8 percent) in either direction. Stated another way, we estimate that between about 34 percent and 50 percent of women in Idaho with MS who get divorced will do so after MS is diagnosed. The corresponding figures for males are between 22 percent and 37 percent.

5.2.7 Estimating Sample Size

One way to narrow the range of the confidence intervals without sacrificing confidence that they contain the population parameter is to increase sample size. As we have seen, the larger the sample the smaller the standard error. For instance, if our offender sample of IQ observations was doubled, all other things being equal, the standard error would be .444 rather than .628. With a standard error of .444 our confidence intervals would be smaller at the 99 percent confidence interval than it is at the 95 percent interval with a standard error of .628. You can verify this result for yourself as an exercise.

The question "How big should my sample be?" depends on three things: (1) the degree of precision desired in estimating the parameter, (2) the desired level of confidence, and (3) some estimate of the parameter standard deviation. The first two requirements are easily met because they are determined by the researcher. The last requirement is problematic, for if we knew the population standard deviation we would also know the mean, and sampling the population to get a value we already know would be redundant. What we have to do in effect is to make an enlightened guess about the unknown population standard deviation. Let us suppose that we wish to estimate the mean IQ for offenders with 95 percent confidence and that we want to be wrong by only 1 IQ point on either side of the population mean. An enlightened "best guess" would have to be derived from previous studies or a pilot study (a small-scale study done to provide a larger study with guidelines) of our own. Let us say that our offender study was a pilot study. In that case we can use the standard deviation derived from it (12.18) to estimate the population standard deviation. Under these conditions we can determine the required sample size by the following formula:

$$N = \left[\frac{(z)(\sigma)}{E} \right]^2 \tag{5.4}$$

where z = desired level of confidence

σ = population standard deviation estimated from sample s

E = desired accuracy (amount of error we are willing to accept)

Formula 5.4 is a byproduct of the theory of the standard error in that the standard error is an estimate of how much an estimated mean will be "off" (E) the value of the population mean. Thus, we could write E, with the 95 confidence level, as

$$E = 1.96 \frac{\sigma}{\sqrt{N}}$$

By algebraically manipulating this formula, we get Formula 5.4. We have said that we want the 95 percent confidence level and that we want to be wrong by no more than 1 IQ point from the population mean. We simply substitute our tolerable error (1) for E and solve for sample size:

$$N = \left[\frac{(z)(\sigma)}{E} \right]^2 = \left[\frac{(1.96)(12.18)}{1} \right]^2 = \left[\frac{23.8728}{1} \right]^2$$

$$= (23.8728)^2 = 570 \text{ (rounded)}$$

We would need a sample of 570 cases if we wanted to have an error of 1 IQ point on either side of the population mean with a confidence level of 95 percent. Verify for yourself that if we are willing to be wrong by 2 IQ points with the same level of confidence, our sample size of 376 is more than adequate.

5.2.8 Estimating Sample Size for Proportions

We can estimate the sample size required to estimate a population proportion from the sample proportion. Again, the researcher determines the confidence level and the amount of error he or she is willing to tolerate. Suppose we wanted a closer estimate of the proportion of women in Idaho who were divorced after MS was diagnosed. We will consider our sample as a pilot study and the 8 percent interval estimates as too large for us to tolerate. We want to be wrong by no more than 3 percent in either direction. What is the sample size required? We can determine this figure by the following formula:

$$N = \frac{z^2 (Ps)(Qs)}{E^2} \tag{5.5}$$

where z^2 = alpha squared

E^2 = tolerable error squared

The researcher sets the alpha level (we choose .05) and the error he or she will tolerate (.03 in either direction). *Ps* and *Qs* are derived from the sample. Putting in the numbers, we have

$$N = \frac{z^2(Ps)(Qs)}{E^2} = \frac{1.96^2(.42)(.58)}{(.03)^2} = \frac{(3.8416)(.2436)}{.0009}$$

$$= \frac{.9358}{.0009} = 1040 \ (\text{rounded})$$

We would need a sample of about 1040 cases to make an estimate of the number of female MS patients in the population who were divorced after diagnosis if we wanted interval estimates no larger than 3 percent with 95 percent confidence.

5.3 SUMMARY

When we estimate population parameters from sample statistics we assume that the sample is representative of the population. A simple random sample is one in which every element in the population has an equal chance of being included. There are other types of samples such as proportionate and nonproportionate stratified samples. Although our statistical tests assume representative samples, you should be aware of the difficulties of collecting such samples in social science.

When making inferences from samples to populations we are actually dealing with three kinds of distributions—sample, population, and sampling distributions. The sampling distribution is a theoretical distribution of an infinite number of sample means of equal size taken from a population. This distribution of sample means has a mean, and we take this "mean of means" to be the mean of the population from which the infinite samples were selected. An interesting observation of the sampling distribution is that even if the underlying distribution of some characteristic is not normally distributed, repeated sampling from this population will result in a sampling distribution of means that is approximately normally distributed.

As with any other distribution, the sampling distribution has a standard deviation. We call the standard deviation of a sampling distribution the standard error. The smaller the standard error the more confident we can be that the sample mean is a good estimate of the population mean.

The central limit theorem is a pivotal concept in inferential statistics. It states that if repeated random samples of size N are drawn from a population, the sampling distribution of sample means will approach normality as N becomes large. "Large" can be defined as 30 or more for populations that are normally distributed.

We can estimate two types of parameters from statistics, point and interval estimates. A point estimate is a single value, and an interval estimate is a range of values. We use sample statistics and the standard error to place confidence intervals around interval estimates. We have shown in this chapter how confidence intervals are placed around means and proportions. Confidence intervals become smaller, and therefore more precise, as sample size increases because the larger the sample the smaller the standard error. We discussed techniques for estimating required sample sizes for given confidence levels and amount of error the researcher is willing to tolerate.

PRACTICE APPLICATION: THE SAMPLING DISTRIBUTION AND ESTIMATION

A university dean collects the annual salaries of the social science faculty, ranging from instructors to full professors. The dean obtains the following list of 30 salaries rounded to the nearest thousand dollars and computes the mean, standard deviation, standard error, and range. Since the dean has included the entire faculty, he or she has the entire population of interest, not a sample.

ANNUAL SALARY IN THOUSANDS OF DOLLARS FOR SOCIAL
SCIENCE FACULTY POPULATION

16	18	25	28	32
18	20	26	29	32
19	24	26	30	35
20	24	27	30	36
23	25	27	31	40
24	25	28	32	40

$\bar{X} = 27.00$ $S = 6.159$ $S.E. = 1.124$ range $= 24$

From this population take ten random samples of various sizes and compute means, standard deviations, and ranges.

Sample	N	$\bar{X}$	s	Range	Sample	N	$\bar{X}$	s	Range
a	8	30.37	2.56	8	f	8	25.50	5.88	16
b	7	27.71	5.22	16	g	9	28.89	4.86	16
c	10	28.70	4.99	16	h	13	25.92	4.17	22
d	4	24.75	6.18	14	i	8	25.62	6.45	14
e	9	24.56	5.43	16	j	7	27.57	6.83	21

The ranges of the samples are smaller than the range in the population. The population range is 24, the smallest sample range is 8, and the largest is 22.

Compute the mean of means.

$$\bar{X} + \bar{X} + \cdots + \bar{X}/N$$

$$= 30.37 + 27.71 + \cdots + 27.57/10 = 26.959$$

The mean of means only differs from the population mean by .041. The mean of means will equal the population mean in the long run, as the central limit theorem says it should.

Compute 95 percent confidence intervals for sample mean a.

SAMPLE A.

$$ci = \bar{X} \pm z(s/\sqrt{N}) = (1.96)2.56/\sqrt{8}$$

$$= (1.96)(2.56/2.828) = (1.96)(0.905) = 1.774$$

$$LCI = 30.37 - 1.774 = 28.596$$

$$UCI = 30.37 + 1.774 = 32.144$$

Mean a misses the population mean at the 95 percent confidence interval. Only means i, h, j, and b fall within 2 standard errors of the mean, as the following graph illustrates. Sample sizes are too small to estimate adequately the population mean.

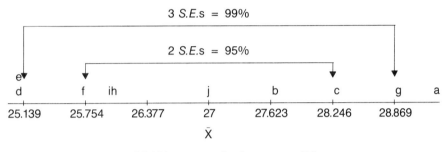

means of means $= 26.959$ standard error $= .623$

Imagine now that our population of social science professors is a random sample of social science professors from all western universities. How big should our sample be if we are willing to tolerate an error of plus or minus $500 in estimating the population mean with 95 percent confidence.

$$N = \left[\frac{(z)(\sigma)}{E} \right]^2 = \left[\frac{(1.96)(6.159)}{.5} \right]^2 = \left[\frac{12.0716}{.5} \right]^2$$

$$= (24.1433)^2 = 583 \text{ (rounded)}$$

APPENDIX: Computer Instructions for Generating Random Sample from a Data Set

```
    SPSSx
SELECT IF (IQ LT 999)
SAMPLE 30 FROM 376
FREQUENCIES GENERAL = IQ
STATISTICS ALL
```

The first command selects only those cases in the data set for which IQ information is available. The next command tells the computer to SAMPLE randomly 30 cases from the 376 for which IQ information is available. We then run a FREQUENCIES to obtain descriptive statistics. The output follows. Notice how very close the mean and standard deviation are to the corresponding values for the entire 376 cases, and how much larger the standard error is.

IQ   SUB IQ SCORE

VALUE LABEL	VALUE	FREQUENCY	PERCENT	VALID PERCENT	CUM PERCENT
	67	1	3.3	3.3	3.3
	68	1	3.3	3.3	6.7
	75	1	3.3	3.3	10.0
	78	1	3.3	3.3	13.3
	83	1	3.3	3.3	16.7
	84	1	3.3	3.3	20.0
	85	2	6.7	6.7	26.7
	86	1	3.3	3.3	30.0
	88	1	3.3	3.3	33.3
	92	4	13.3	13.3	46.7
	95	1	3.3	3.3	50.0
	96	1	3.3	3.3	53.3
	98	3	10.0	10.0	63.3
	100	1	3.3	3.3	66.7
	101	3	10.0	10.0	76.7
	104	2	6.7	6.7	83.3
	106	1	3.3	3.3	86.7
	107	1	3.3	3.3	90.0
	108	1	3.3	3.3	93.3
	110	1	3.3	3.3	96.7
	120	1	3.3	3.3	100.0
	TOTAL	30	100.0	100.0	

MEAN	93.800	STD ERR	2.248	MEDIAN	95.500
MODE	92.000	STD DEV	12.313	VARIANCE	151.614
KURTOSIS	.079	SKEWNESS	− .363	RANGE	53.000
MINIMUM	67.000	MAXIMUM	120.000	SUM	2814.000

Chapter 6

Hypothesis Testing:
Interval/Ratio Data

6.1 PARAMETRIC STATISTICS

Chapters 4 and 5 concentrated mainly on a seemingly endless discussion of theoretical probability curves of all shapes and sizes. We also talked a lot about means, standard deviations, and z scores and how we use sample statistics to estimate population parameters. We have been, and will remain so for most of the rest of the book, heavily dependent on the normal curve of distribution, in which the bulk of observations cluster around their mean and become rarer and rarer as we approach the tails of the curve. We have paid this much attention to curves because most inferential statistics such as z and t, which are discussed in this chapter, assume that samples are drawn from normally distributed populations. For this reason these are known as **parametric statistics.**

Without a complete enumeration of the population we can never know if the population is normally distributed. Yet as we have seen, the sampling distribution of sample means verges on normality with as few as 30 sample means. Parametric tests also assume that the population standard deviation is known. Thus, parametric statistics are based on the assumption of a normally distributed population whose standard deviation is known, and can thus be estimated from sample data. We now turn to the issue of hypothesis testing.

6.2 THE LOGIC OF HYPOTHESIS TESTING

Hypotheses are hunches or educated guesses that the researcher makes about relationships between or among variables. These educated guesses are derived from previous research and theory. If we begin with what we already know (or think we already know) from theory, we can make logical deductions from that knowledge about how two or more variables should be related. For instance, the theory of biological stress tells us that long-term stress will eventually be manifested in elevated blood pressure, and social assimilation theory tells us that adjusting to an alien culture is inherently stressful. From these theories we might deduce that immigrants who are having a great deal of difficulty adjusting to the new culture will have higher blood pressure levels than those who are having less difficulty.

This deduction makes logical sense and would be considered the conclusion in a syllogistic argument (a syllogism is an argument that flows from a "self-evident" premise through a minor premise to a conclusion logically derived from those premises). What serves as the conclusion for the philosopher is really just the beginning for the scientist, however. The logic derived from theory must be put to the test of experience. It may seem strange, but what we do in science is to test the hypothesis of no relationship or no difference. This test of "no difference" is referred to as the **null hypothesis.** The researcher sets up the null hypothesis and subjects it to rigorous testing procedures.

The logic of the null hypothesis is similar to the logic of the criminal trial process in the Anglo-American tradition. The police and the prosecutor have educated guesses concerning the relationship between the crime committed and the accused, namely, that he or she is guilty. The jury is analogous to the scientist's sample in that it is supposed to be representative of the population. The assumption that the accused is not guilty is identical to the null hypothesis. The alternative assumption (the accused is guilty) is put to a stringent test in that his or her guilt must be "proved beyond a reasonable doubt." If the null hypothesis of "not guilty" cannot be rejected, the accused is set free.

The null hypothesis is stated symbolically according to the kind of test being conducted. For population means it is stated as

$$H_0 : \mu_1 = \mu_c \quad \text{or} \quad H_0 : \mu_1 = \mu_2$$

In the first case it states that the population mean (estimated from the sample mean) is equal to some constant (e.g., a known population mean). In the second case it states that the mean of population 1 is equal to the mean of population 2. If we were testing the blood pressure/assimilation hypothesis, we would state the null in prose something like this: "The mean blood pressure level of immigrants having difficulty in assimilation is equal to the mean blood pressure level of immigrants not having difficulty in assimilation." You must always remember that although we are actually working with sample means, we are really testing hypotheses about population means. It is therefore technically incorrect to state the null as $\bar{X}_1 = \bar{X}_2$.

Of course, prosecutors in a criminal trial are really interested in the alternative to the assumption of innocence. If they did not have very good reasons for believing in the accused's guilt they would not have bothered with the indictment in the first place. The assumption of innocence is a cautionary mechanism to maximize the probability that a person who is innocent will not be unjustly punished. Nevertheless, prosecutors believe that the "truth" is contradictory to the assumption of innocence. Likewise, researchers are really interested in the opposite of the null hypothesis, which is called the **alternative** or **research hypothesis.** They are much more interested in any *difference* between blood pressure levels of immigrants having differential success in assimilation, for example. If the sample results indicate that there is indeed a difference between the two blood pressure means, the researchers reject the null hypothesis just as a jury, after examining the evidence, may reject the assumption of the accused's innocence. In both cases, however, the innocent, or null, hypothesis is considered true until the evidence suggests otherwise. The research hypothesis for population means is stated symbolically as

$$H_1 : \mu_1 \neq \mu_c \quad \text{or} \quad H_1 : \mu_1 \neq \mu_2$$

where $\neq$ means "not equal to"

6.3 THE EVIDENCE AND STATISTICAL SIGNIFICANCE

In a court of law the accused is found guilty because the evidence supposedly points to the conclusion that he or she committed the crime "beyond a reasonable doubt." This does not mean beyond all possible doubt, only beyond *reasonable* doubt. What constitutes "reasonable doubt" for the researcher that will allow the rejection of the null hypothesis? In Chapter 4 it was shown that by marking off standard units of distance under the normal curve we were able to determine the percentage of the population that was within and beyond those units. The standard scores used to mark off the standard units of difference are z scores. We also saw that a z score of 1.96 marks an area of the normal curve beyond which rare cases are found; in fact only 5 percent of the cases lie beyond plus or minus 1.96 standard units of the curve. We saw that any individual with a z score of 1.96 on an IQ test scored better than 97.5 percent of the other members of the sample, and that only 2.5 percent scored better. We also saw that the further away an individual's score was from the mean the less probable it was that we would find a similar score.

We can think of differences between means in the same way. Just as there are distributions of raw scores and of sample means (the sampling distribution), there are sampling distributions of mean differences. Such a distribution, like the sampling distribution, is purely theoretical. Let us suppose that we take an infinite number of means from equally sized samples from the same population. We then compute the mean of means and note the difference between each sample mean and the mean of means $\bar{x} - \mu$. Each of these differences is then graphed in a distribution of mean differences. It should not surprise you that such a distribution of mean differences would be approximately normal. The mean of this theoretical distribution of mean differences would be zero since negative and positive differences are expected to cancel one another out in such a symmetrical curve. Differences between means would get larger and larger as they move away from the center and toward the tails, where there would be fewer and fewer of them.

When a mean difference is large enough to be 1.96 standard deviations on either side of the mean of mean differences, we have an event rare enough to constitute "reasonable doubt" that the null hypothesis is true; that is, the observed difference is not the result of simple chance.

To help illustrate this point, let us return to the distribution of 60 sample means in Figure 5.2. We can compare these sample means to the "population" mean of 94 to determine by how much each of them differs from it. For instance, the lowest sample mean value is 89, which is 5 less than 94, and the highest mean value is 99, or 5 more than the mean. These two mean scores represent the extreme departures from the mean of means. Other differences are less extreme, with 13 of the sample means having exactly the same value as the mean of means.

Table 6.1 is a histogram representing the distribution of mean differences between the mean of means and the 60 sample means. Small differences are clustered around the center, and larger differences are at the tails of the distribution. The mean of the mean differences for the distribution of 60 sample mean differences is -0.067, and the standard deviation is 2.177. As with a distribution of raw scores and a sampling distribution of means, the standard deviation of mean differences tells us that about 68 percent of sample mean differences will be between plus and minus 1 standard deviation, or between plus and minus 2.177, and about 95 percent of the mean differences will be within 1.96 standard deviations (plus or minus 4.27) from the mean. The probability of any mean difference falling within plus and minus 1.96 standard deviations is about .95. Conversely, the probability of finding a mean difference greater than plus or minus 1.96 standard deviations is about .05. Only the two extreme means (89 and 99), and thus the two extreme mean differences (-5 and $+5$), fall beyond plus or minus 1.96 standard deviations. You can readily see why the sampling distribution of mean differences provides a sound basis for testing hypotheses about differences between means.

TABLE 6.1 DISTRIBUTION OF SAMPLE MEAN DIFFERENCES FROM THE SAMPLING DISTRIBUTION OF MEANS IN FIGURE 5.2

$\bar{X}$	freq.	$\bar{X} - \mu$ (where $\mu = 94$)		
89	1	-5.00	-5	***
90	4	-4.00	-16	*********
91	3	-3.00	-9	********
92	6	-2.00	-12	***************
93	10	-1.00	-10	*************************
94	13	.00	0	********************************
95	9	1.00	$+9$	**********************
96	7	2.00	$+14$	******************
97	4	3.00	$+12$	**********
98	2	4.00	$+8$	*****
99	1	5.00	$+5$	***
	60		$-4/60 = -.067 =$ mean of mean differences	

Differences between two means that could have occurred as a result of random error only five times in every 100 samples are called *significant* differences, meaning that the difference between them is large enough for us to bet (the rent, if not the mortgage) that it is a real difference rather than one that could be a chance occurrence. The cutoff point for determining significance is called an **alpha level.** As we saw in the last chapter when discussing confidence intervals, an alpha of a given level says that the researcher is willing to be wrong in a certain percentage of every 100 samplings of the population. At the .05 level it is five times in 100, at .01 it is one time in 100, and at .001 it is one time in every 1000. The lower we set the alpha, the more difficult it will be to reject the null simply because we are moving further toward the ends of the decreasing areas of the curve where extremely rare events occur. To summarize, if a statistical test of the null hypothesis fails to achieve significance at a predetermined alpha level, we do not reject the null and the status quo is maintained, just as it is in a court of law when the accused is released.

6.4 ERRORS IN HYPOTHESIS TESTING

Regardless of the strength of the evidence used to reject a null hypothesis, it must be understood that it remains possible that our decision to reject could be wrong. Just as innocent people are sometimes found guilty, true null hypotheses are sometimes rejected. Wrongly rejecting a true null hypothesis is called a **type I (or alpha) error**. We never really know if we have committed a type I error, but we can guard against the likelihood by requiring more stringent rules of evidence before making our decision. In science we do this by setting alpha at a lower level, thus moving the critical rejection region further away from the nonrare cases clustered around the mean. That is, a more conservative test of the null is to set the alpha level at .01. The **critical region** is the area under the sampling distribution that includes unlikely sample outcomes. When we select an alpha level, we are defining "unlikely" as being the selected probability level.

There is a problem with selecting lower alpha levels that should be obvious: As the critical region becomes smaller the noncritical region necessarily becomes larger. What this means is that as we minimize the risk of rejecting a true null, we increase the probability of failing to reject a null hypothesis that is in fact false. Failing to reject a false null hypothesis is known as a **type II (or beta) error**. This kind of error is analogous to setting free an accused person who is in fact guilty. Since the two types of errors are inversely related to one another, it is impossible to minimize the risk of committing both types of errors simultaneously within the same sample. Within a single sample we can only minimize the risk of one type of error at the expense of the other.

Usually, social scientists want to minimize the probability of a type I error without increasing the probability of a type II error. They can do so by replicating the study with other samples. If four different samples allow for the rejection of the null at a given alpha level, researchers will be more confident that the right decision has been made. Increasing sample size will also have the same effect

---

FACTORS AFFECTING CHANCES OF MAKING TYPE I AND TYPE II ERRORS

Type I Error (Rejecting a True Null)
1. Setting alpha too high (e.g., .10, or perhaps even .05 for especially critical studies such as a test of drug safety)
2. Nonrandom sample
3. Small sample

Type II Error (Failing to Reject a False Null)
1. Setting alpha too low (e.g., .01 or .001)
2. Nonrandom sample
3. Small sample

---

since, as we have seen, sampling error is inversely related to sample size. Increased sample size will also minimize the probability of a type II error for a given type I error. Figure 6.1 illustrates possible outcomes (correct decisions and errors) in hypothesis testing compared to possible outcomes for a jury trial.

In this chapter we will deal with hypothesis testing by using the z and t distributions. We will introduce methods that enable us to decide whether to reject or accept hypotheses about means of populations. Whenever we compare means from samples and hypothesized populations means, we almost always observe a difference. Hypothesis or significance testing allows us to decide if the observed difference is large enough to draw the conclusion that the mean of the variable of interest is significantly different from the hypothesized mean of the population from which it was drawn. Hypothesis testing also allows us to determine whether two or more population means differ significantly.

Both the relative sizes of the means of two groups and the size of the variances associated with them contribute to the finding of a significant difference. The greater the absolute difference between the means the more likely you are to

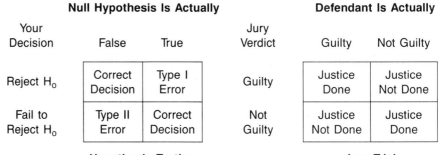

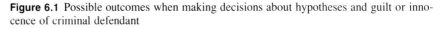

Figure 6.1 Possible outcomes when making decisions about hypotheses and guilt or innocence of criminal defendant

find a significant difference. You are also a lot more likely to find a significant difference when groups have less variability (low standard deviations) within them, that is, when there are large differences between the two groups but relatively small differences among subjects or observations within each separate group.

6.5 ONE SAMPLE *z* TEST

In Chapter 3 we noted that the mean IQ for our sample of felons was 93.56, with a standard deviation of 12.18. We know from numerous testings with millions of subjects over many years that the population mean IQ (in this instance "population" refers to all Americans) is 100, with a standard deviation of 15. We immediately see that our sample mean is 6.44 IQ points below the population mean. The question is whether or not this observed difference could have been obtained by simple chance. Since we are dealing with a sample, we can never be absolutely sure that the difference is a real one, not attributable to chance. However, as we have seen, we can use procedures that allow us to decide if the two means really are different, with a very low probability that we have made an incorrect decision.

We saw in Chapter 4 that we could translate any raw score in a normal distribution into a *z* score by subtracting the mean of the distribution from it and dividing by the standard deviation. Since we can do this computation for a single score or case, it should not surprise you that we can also do so for a group of cases. Any observation, whether it be a single case or a group of cases, minus the population mean from which the observation came and divided by the population standard deviation will equal *z*. To test our hypothesis, rather than having a single raw score from the distribution of scores as the observation, we permit the sample mean to be the observation, and the known population mean to be the value subtracted from it in the numerator. A value known as the **standard error of the difference** (between means) substitutes for the sample standard deviation in the denominator. It is calculated in the same manner as the standard error of the mean. Thus,

$$z = \frac{X - \bar{X}}{s} \quad \text{for a single score} \tag{6.1}$$

becomes

$$z = \frac{\bar{X} - \mu - 0}{\sigma/\sqrt{N}} \quad \text{for groups of scores}$$

where $\bar{X}$ = mean of sample

μ = mean of population (mean of means)

0 = mean of the sampling distribution of mean differences

$\sigma/\sqrt{N}$ = standard error of difference

We will illustrate a test of a hypothesis of the form $\mu_1 = \mu_c$ by comparing our offenders' IQs with IQs from the larger population (i.e., all adult Americans). First, the assumptions of the z test:

Assumptions for the Use of the z Test

1. The subjects are a random sample.
2. Data are interval or ratio level.
3. The population distribution is normal.

We begin the process conservatively by assuming that the sample mean is equal to the population mean. Again, the formal name for the assumption of equality, or "no difference," is the null hypothesis. The opposite assumption, the assumption that the observed difference is real and not due to chance, is known as the research hypothesis. These two assumptions can be stated symbolically as follows:

Null hypothesis $H_0 : \mu_1 = \mu_c = 100$

Research hypothesis $H_1 : \mu_1 \neq \mu_c = 100$

The logic of the normal curve and the z score tells us that we can reject the null hypothesis if we obtain a z score of -1.96 or $+1.96$. Shown graphically in Figure 6.2, we reject the null if our computed z falls within the shaded areas (the critical regions) on either side of the tail. Actually we know at this point that the z score will be negative and will thus be located somewhere to the left of the mean. However, null hypotheses should be formulated prior to data collection to keep us honest. To continue with our criminal trial analogy, assume for now that the direction of the difference is "excluded evidence" and that we are equally interested in rejecting the null at either tail of the curve. When we are equally interested in outcomes at either end of the tail, the .05 rejection region is divided between the two tails of the distribution, as in Figure 6.2.

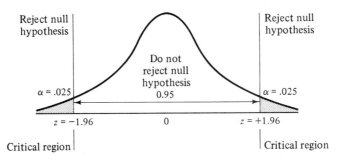

Figure 6.2 Sampling distribution of mean differences and area under the curve and z value for significance test at .05 level

We can now proceed with the test of our hypothesis.

COMPUTING z

American Population $\mu = 100; \sigma = 15)$	Sample of Offenders $(\overline{X} = 93.56; s = 12.18; N = 376)$	
STEP 1	STEP 2	STEP 3

Put in the numbers, subtract μ from $\overline{X}$, and take the square root of 376.   Divide 15 by 19.39.   Divide -6.44 by .774.

$$z = \frac{93.56 - 100 - 0}{15/\sqrt{376}} = \frac{-6.44 - 0}{15/19.39} = \frac{-6.44}{.774} = -8.32$$

$z = -8.32, \ p < .05$

Our computed z of -8.32 greatly exceeds -1.96. It is extremely unlikely that the observed difference between the sample and population means is due to chance. The notation following the z value is shorthand for saying "probability (p) is less than ($<$) the selected alpha level (.05)." If we had attained a z value of less than 1.96, the notation would have been $p > .05$ (greater than .05).

It must be kept in mind that any conclusion the researcher makes must be based on a random sample that is representative of the population. Since our data were obtained from only one jurisdiction, we can only legitimately claim that convicted felons in this jurisdiction have a significantly lower mean IQ than the U.S. population as a whole. Wilson and Herrnstein (1985, p. 159) point out that over a large number of samples over four decades, a 10-point difference between offenders and the general population IQ is rather consistently found. Our sample IQ for offenders has a mean IQ somewhat greater than is typically found among offenders—probably because we have in our sample a disproportionate number of sex offenders, who tend as a group to have a higher mean IQ.

An important thing for you to remember is that although we have rejected the null hypothesis in this example, we have not proven the research hypothesis. We have simply made a decision based on probability that the null is untenable. In other words, whereas the null can be accepted or rejected, the research hypothesis can only be tested; it can never be proven.

6.6 TESTING HYPOTHESES ABOUT TWO POPULATION MEANS

Suppose now that we want to test the null hypothesis that check forgers differ significantly in IQ from all other offenders. To test this hypothesis we randomly select a sample of 150 check forgers and 150 criminal offenders who have committed some other crime. We find that the mean IQ for check forgers is 97.5, with a standard deviation of 10.4, and the other offenders have a mean of 94.4, with a standard deviation of 11.2. The test statistic (z) is computed by dividing

THE RELATIONSHIP BETWEEN SIGNIFICANCE TESTING AND CONFIDENCE INTERVALS

I have found that students sometimes grasp the idea of significance more readily if I build on what they have already learned about confidence intervals. Given a sample mean and an unknown population mean, we can reject the assumption that the $\bar{X}$ is an adequate estimator of μ if μ does not fall within the lower and upper confidence intervals of $\bar{X}$ for a given level of confidence. It was shown in Chapter 5 that the lower and upper confidence intervals at the 99.9 percent level of confidence for the mean of the offender IQ data were 91.485 and 95.637, respectively. Since μ IQ $=$ 100 for the general U.S. population, we would immediately know that μ is not contained within these intervals—we would know that $\bar{X}$ and μ were quite different. Since we denote the level of significance as alpha, and the confidence level as $1 -$ alpha (expressed as a percentage), we would know that $\bar{X}$ and μ were different at least at the .0001 $(1 - .999 = .0001)$ level of significance. Now, if we set z at the value of 8.32 as calculated and multiply by the standard error of .774, we get a confidence interval of 6.44, which is the difference between $\bar{X}$ and μ. Adding 6.44 to the sample mean of 93.56, we get 100, the population mean.

To reiterate, when calculating confidence intervals we have $\bar{X}$ and an unknown μ. Using the central limit theorem and an alpha level arbitrarily selected by the researcher, we can within a known margin of error set boundaries around the mean. When testing hypotheses of the kind just tested, we start with a known μ and a known $\bar{X}$ and the difference between them. By dividing this difference by the standard error of the difference, we arrive at the precise probability (z) of the difference occurring by chance.

the difference between the means by the standard error of the difference. In symbolic form,

$$z = \frac{\mu_1 - \mu_2 - 0}{\sigma_{\bar{x}_1 - \bar{x}_2}} \tag{6.2}$$

where $\sigma_{\bar{x}_1 - \bar{x}_2} =$ the standard error of the difference

The standard error of the difference is defined as

$$\sigma_{\bar{x}_1 - \bar{x}_2} = \sqrt{\frac{s_1^2}{N_1 - 1} + \frac{s_2^2}{N_2 - 1}}$$

Note that we use the sample standard deviation to estimate the population standard deviation.

Since the second term in the numerator of Formula 6.2 always reduces to zero, we will ignore it from now on. Just as we use the sample standard deviations to estimate the population standard deviations, we use the sample means to estimate the population means. The formula for testing the null hypothesis becomes

$$z = \frac{\bar{X}_1 - \bar{X}_2}{\sqrt{\dfrac{S_2^2}{N_1 - 1} + \dfrac{S_2^2}{N_2 - 1}}}$$

The null hypothesis is

$$H_0 : \mu_1 = \mu_2 = \bar{X}_1 = \bar{X}_2$$

The sample outcomes are

check forgers $\bar{X} = 97.5,\ S = 10.4,\ N = 150$

other offenders $\bar{X} = 94.4,\ S = 11.2,\ N = 150$

$$z = \frac{97.5 - 94.4}{\sqrt{\dfrac{10.4^2}{149} + \dfrac{11.2^2}{149}}}$$

STEP 1 Substitute the numbers into the formula. Subtract 94.4 from 97.5. Square the two standard deviation values.

$$z = \frac{3.1}{\sqrt{\dfrac{108.16}{149} + \dfrac{125.44}{149}}}$$

STEP 2 Divide 108.16 by 149 and 125.44 by 149

STEP 3 Add .7259 and .8419 (= 1.5678) and take the square root of this sum (1.252).

$$z = \frac{3.1}{\sqrt{.7259 + .8419}}$$

$$z = \frac{3.1}{1.252}$$

STEP 4 Divide 3.1 by 1.252.

$$z = 2.476,\ p < .05$$

We know that an alpha of .05 corresponds to a z of 1.96. Our computed z is greater than 1.96. Therefore we reject the null hypothesis; check forgers do have significantly higher IQs than other offenders.

6.7 THE *t* TEST

In our use of the z test we have dealt with instances in which the population standard deviation was known. However, when this value is not known or when we have small samples, we can no longer assume that sample variances are close approximations of their population variances. It is extremely rare for the population variance to be known in social science research. Therefore, we have to estimate not only a population mean from a sample but also a standard error. In such instances the use of the z distribution would not be appropriate.

In addition to not knowing a population variance, small samples also render the z distribution inappropriate. As we saw in Chapter 5, the smaller the sample, the larger the standard error tends to be. Fortunately, there is a distribution that we can use both when the population variance is unknown and when we have small samples: the t distribution.

6.7.1 Degrees of Freedom

Before we discuss the t distribution and t test it is necessary to briefly discuss the concept of **degrees of freedom,** which is involved in many of the statistics we will be discussing. Degrees of freedom basically represent restrictions placed on the data. Suppose that we have to select five numbers that must sum to 30. We can choose any five as long a their sum is 30, but only our first four choices are "free" choices since the fifth number is entirely determined by our previous choices. If we select numbers 9, 6, 5, and 4, for example, our fifth number is restricted to 6. Degrees of freedom in the context of the t test refers to the size of the sample(s) minus the number of parameters being estimated. In testing the difference between two population means based on samples taken from those populations, one sample having an N of 150 and the other an N of 201, the degrees of freedom would be 149 and 200, respectively, for a total of 349 df. Now in such a test we have actually estimated four parameters: two population means and two population standard deviations. However, we do not "lose" any df in the estimation of the mean. You might want to convince yourself of this fact by again examining the formula for the mean. We must know the values of all scores of N to calculate the mean, so in this sense they are all free to vary ($df = N$). When estimating s, on the other hand, $N - 1$ values are free to vary. That is, since we know that the sum of the deviations from the mean must always be zero, all deviations except the last one are free to vary.

A more complete explanation of the idea of degrees of freedom requires mathematical proofs. For our purposes we will be content with defining the degrees of freedom generally as some function of the number of observations from which a statistic is computed. Specific methods for determining degrees of freedom with different statistical techniques will be explained as the need arises.

6.7.2 The t Distribution

The t distribution only approximates the normal curve, being more platokurtic (flatter) than the normal curve when df is less than 120. For all practical purposes, when $df > 120$, the t distribution is identical with the normal curve. The t distribution is a continuous distribution, like the normal curve, but unlike the normal curve it is independent of μ and σ and is entirely specified by a single parameter, the degrees of freedom. Since the single factor determining the shape of t is the number of df, and df are defined as $N - 1$ for a single-sample t test or $N - 2$ for a two-sample test, it is easy to see that as the sample size changes, the shape of the curve also changes. Unlike the normal curve, for every value of df we generate a unique t distribution. As sample sizes become larger and larger, the shape of the curve approaches that of the normal curve.

Figure 6.3 illustrates the *t* distribution with 20 and infinite *df* superimposed on the normal curve. Note that the tails of the *t* curve with 20 *df* contain more area than the tails of the normal curve. This means that the area under the sampling distribution is larger for *t* than it is for the normal curve, and so we have to assign higher probabilities to extreme value outcomes for *t* than we do for *z*. Otherwise stated, the smaller the sample, the larger the value of the *t* ratio must be to claim significance. For instance, with two groups of subjects having a combined *N* of 22 (degrees of freedom = $N - 2 = 20$), the alpha = .05 rejection region is 2.086 standard deviations from the mean rather than the 1.96 required by *z*. With $df = 4$, a *t* value of 2.776 or higher is required to reject the null at the .05 level of significance.

The *t* **distribution** is a popular statistic for comparing means between two samples regardless of the sample size. Its popularity probably rests in the observation that as sample size increases the *t* distribution becomes more and more like the normal distribution. If you turn to Appendix B you will note, with degrees of freedom greater than 120, that the critical region for rejection of the null hypothesis is exactly the same (1.96) as it is for *z*.

6.7.3 Computing *t* with Small Samples

To illustrate the computation of *t* with small samples we will use a simple example. Suppose researchers are interested in comparing the mean alienation scores of faculty and maintenance staff at a university. They take a random sample of 12 faculty members and 13 maintenance staff and find that the faculty members have a mean score of 50 and a standard deviation of 19.54, and the maintenance workers have a mean of 57.69 and a standard deviation of 14.23.

Implicit in the research is the assumption that somehow one's occupational status will influence one's alienation score. Put otherwise, the researchers believe that they can predict the level of alienation on the basis of occupation. Thus, the alienation level is viewed as being dependent on occupation. A variable that is considered to be dependent on some other variable is said to be a **dependent variable.** The variable that is thought to influence or predict the values of the dependent variable is known as the **independent variable.** More strongly, the independent variable is assumed to "cause" the dependent variable. In the present case, the independent variable, occupation, is assumed to bring about the effect of variation in alienation scores—the dependent variable.

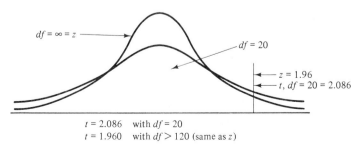

Figure 6.3 *t* Distributions with 20 and infinite *df* and critical regions for rejecting the null hypothesis at alpha = .05

Before we go on to compute t from these data, a short discussion of directional hypotheses is necessary at this point.

6.7.4 Directional Hypotheses: One- and Two-tailed Tests

If the researchers have no theoretical reasons for believing one group would be more alienated than the other, they would conduct what is called a **two-tailed** or a **nondirectional test of the hypothesis**. In a nondirectional hypothesis test we might find a significant difference at either side of the distribution curve. We refer to a nondirectional test as two-tailed because we can reject the null only if the region of rejection falls within either tail of the sampling distribution, that is, in those areas of the curve that each contain 2.5 percent of the total area. These areas on both sides of the distribution correspond to plus or minus 1.96 standard errors of the normal distribution.

In a two-tailed test the researchers are equally interested in sample outcomes that are significantly greater than or less than the population value or in which one population value is significantly greater or less than the value of the other. On the other hand, if there are theoretical reasons for expecting a difference in a particular direction, the researchers will conduct a **one-tailed** or **directional** test. In such cases the researchers are concerned only with sample outcomes in one of the tails in the distribution. In a one-tailed test the rejection region is plus or minus 1.65 z units rather than 1.96. To convince yourself of this, turn to Appendix A, containing areas under the normal curve, and you will find that a z of 1.65 corresponds to .4505. If we are equally interested in sample outcomes on either side of the mean, we have to double this value to get .9010, leaving about 5 percent of the area on either side, or 10 percent overall, that is beyond this range. The .10 level is not usually considered small enough to reject the null. However, if we are only interested in outcomes in one side of the tail, we can add the entire area of the side of the curve in which we have no interest to the area of the side of the curve in which we do have interest. Thus, .5000 + .4505 = .9505. There are now only about 5 percent of outcomes beyond this single-tailed range, so we can reject the null.

What the researchers have done by specifying direction is to locate the five percent of the area that constitutes the rejection region in one tail of the curve. In doing so, they have moved the critical region closer to the mean of the sampling distribution, and thereby increased the probability of rejecting the null. But beware: One-tailed tests should be used only when the direction of the outcome can be theoretically justified prior to conducting the test. It should not be used simply to increase the probability of rejecting the null hypothesis. Figure 6.4 illustrates the differences in rejection regions for two-tailed and one-tailed tests.

We can now return to the computation of t based on our alienation data. (The means and standard deviations follow.) We assume that the researchers have good theoretical reasons for believing that blue-collar workers are more alienated than professionals, and are therefore justified in conducting a one-tailed test. The data previously given are shown again, and the formula for computing t is given in Formula 6.3. The assumptions for the use of the t test are these:

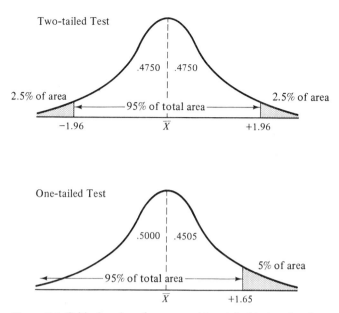

Two-tailed Test

.4750 | .4750

2.5% of area   2.5% of area

95% of total area

−1.96 $\bar{X}$ +1.96

One-tailed Test

.5000 | .4505

5% of area

95% of total area

$\bar{X}$ +1.65

Figure 6.4 Critical regions for one- and two-tailed tests using the *t* test with $N > 120$

Assumptions for Use of the *t* Test

1. A random sample has been taken.
2. Data are interval or ratio level.
3. Populations are normally distributed.
4. Population variances are equal.

Faculty	**Maintenance Staff**
$\bar{X} = 50.0$ $s = 19.54$ $N = 12$	$\bar{X} = 57.69$ $s = 14.23$ $N = 13$

$$t = \frac{\bar{X}_1 - \bar{X}_2}{\sqrt{\dfrac{N_1 s_1^2 + N_2 s_2^2}{N_1 + N_2 - 2}}\sqrt{\dfrac{N_1 + N_2}{(N_1)(N_2)}}} \tag{6.3}$$

Notice that by adding the variances of our two samples together we have pooled the variance for each group after we have computed it by squaring the standard deviations. The $N + N - 2$ notation is the computation for the degrees of freedom, correcting for bias. In prose form, the *t* ratio is equal to the difference between means divided by the standard error of the difference. Putting in the numbers, we obtain

$$t = \frac{50 - 57.69}{\sqrt{\dfrac{(12)(19.54)^2 + (13)(14.23)^2}{12 + 13 - 2}}\sqrt{\dfrac{12 + 13}{(12)(13)}}}$$

STEP 1 Put in the numbers, subtract mean 2 from mean 1, and square the standard deviations.

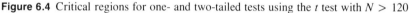

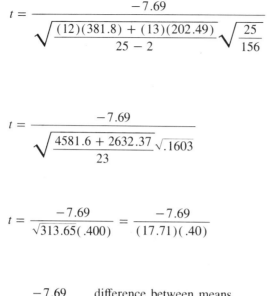

$$t = \frac{-7.69}{\sqrt{\dfrac{(12)(381.8) + (13)(202.49)}{25 - 2}}\sqrt{\dfrac{25}{156}}}$$

STEP 2 Multiply both variances by their respective Ns, perform the multiplication and addition on the right side of the equation, and subtract 2 from 25.

$$t = \frac{-7.69}{\sqrt{\dfrac{4581.6 + 2632.37}{23}}\sqrt{.1603}}$$

STEP 3 Perform the addition on the right side of the equation and then divide that sum by 23. Take the square root of .1603

$$t = \frac{-7.69}{\sqrt{313.65}(.400)} = \frac{-7.69}{(17.71)(.40)}$$

STEP 4 Take the square root of 313.65 and multiply the result by .40 ($=7.084$). Divide -7.69 by 7.084.

$$t = \frac{-7.69}{7.084} = \frac{\text{difference between means}}{\text{standard error of difference}} = -1.085$$

Our computed t value is -1.085. To determine if this value is statistically significant, we turn to the table of t values in Appendix B. Since we have specified which of these two means would be greater, we use the line in the table marked "level of significance for one-tailed test." If we want to run the risk of being wrong five times in 100 we will use the .05 column and read down the extreme left-hand column until we get to the number 23, which is our number of degrees of freedom. Where these two values intersect in the body of the table we find the number 1.714. This means that to claim a significant difference between the means with a probability of .05 or less and using a one-tailed test, the difference between means must be equal to or greater than 1.714 times the value of the standard error of the difference. If our computed t value is equal to or greater than this value, we reject the null hypothesis. However, our calculated t value is only -1.085, which is less than 1.714 (the negative sign is ignored in reading the t table, as it is when reading areas under the curve). We thus conclude that there is no significant difference between the means of these two populations with regard to their alienation scores: Occupation does not predict alienation levels.

6.7.5 t Test for Correlated Means

The t test formulas discussed so far have assumed random samples from independent groups. We sometimes have occasion to test differences between means from nonindependent groups, such as means obtained from matched pairs of subjects or from the same individuals tested twice. If we match individuals on IQ scores obtained from one test, for instance, and then compare group IQ means from a second test, we are not likely to see a very large difference between the means. Similarly, if we test individuals at time 1 and time 2, an individual who scored high at time 1 is likely also to score high at time 2. In other words, the two means being compared have a built-in correlation. The correlated *t* test provides a basis for testing correlated groups because it has a factor in its formula that corrects for the built-in correlation.

Suppose we ask 10 social workers on July 10 to rate a hypothetical family's need for subsidized housing. The ratings are based on a scale of zero (no need) to 20 (extreme need). We then go back to the same social workers on December 10 and present them with the same case. Since December 10 is close to Christmas, we expect them to be more charitable this time around. The data for the two testing times and the statistical procedure for testing our assumption are presented in Table 6.2.

In Table 6.2 we have arrayed the scores of each social worker taken at time 1 and time 2 and calculated the means. We have then taken the difference between time 1 and time 2 and calculated the mean difference ($\bar{D} = 1.0$). We then squared each difference and summed to arrive at the sum of the squared differences. Having made the calculations, we substitute the appropriate values into Formula 6.4 for the *t* test for correlated means. Since in this problem the same subjects are tested twice, be aware that $N = 10$, not 20.

$$t = \frac{\Sigma D}{\sqrt{\dfrac{N \Sigma D^2 - (\Sigma D)^2}{N - 1}}} = \frac{10}{\sqrt{\dfrac{(10)(22) - (10)^2}{10 - 1}}} \tag{6.4}$$

$$= \frac{10}{\sqrt{\dfrac{220 - 100}{9}}} = \frac{10}{\sqrt{\dfrac{120}{9}}} = \frac{10}{\sqrt{13.333}} = \frac{10}{3.651} = 2.739$$

$$t = 2.739, \; df = 9, \; p < .05$$

TABLE 6.2 DATA ON SOCIAL WORKER RATINGS AND SUMMARY OF PROCEDURES FOR *t* TEST OF CORRELATED MEANS

Social Worker	Time 1	Time 2	Difference (D)	D^2
1	17	19	2	4
2	16	17	1	1
3	14	15	1	1
4	13	12	-1	1
5	12	15	3	9
6	17	19	2	4
7	16	16	0	0
8	9	9	0	0
9	9	10	1	1
10	13	14	1	1
$N = 10$	$\Sigma X_1 = 136$	$\Sigma X_2 = 146$	$\Sigma D = 10$	$\Sigma D^2 = 22$
	$\bar{X}_1 = 13.6$	$\bar{X}_2 = 14.6$	$\bar{D} = 1.0$	

Our computed $t = 2.739$. With 9 df, critical $t = 2.262$, with alpha set at .05. Reject the null; the mean at time 2 is significantly greater than the mean at time 1.

If we had used the t test for independent samples with these data do you think we would have found a significant difference between the means? Your emerging statistical intuition will tell you that with a difference of only 1 rating point between the mean at time 1 and the mean at time 2, you would not be likely to reject the null by using Formula 6.3. In fact, the value of t for these data from Formula 6.3 is only 0.65. You would expect to find such a difference by chance alone in about half of an infinite number of similar samplings. (Perhaps you can be tempted to verify this result for yourself as an exercise.) The correction factor built into Formula 6.4 assures that you are more likely to pick up a difference, if one exists. Hence you are less likely to make a type II error.

6.7.6 The Effect of Sample Variability on Significance Testing

Figure 6.5 illustrates the effects of sample variability in rejecting or failing to reject the null hypothesis with the same observed mean difference. In the first example there is small variability in both samples. If we compute the standard

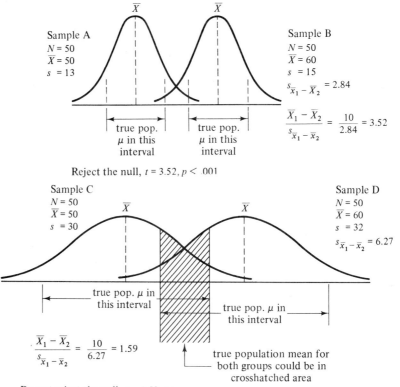

Sample A
$N = 50$
$\overline{X} = 50$
$s = 13$

Sample B
$N = 50$
$\overline{X} = 60$
$s = 15$

$s_{\overline{X}_1 - \overline{X}_2} = 2.84$

$\dfrac{\overline{X}_1 - \overline{X}_2}{s_{\overline{x}_1 - \overline{x}_2}} = \dfrac{10}{2.84} = 3.52$

true pop. μ in this interval

true pop. μ in this interval

Reject the null, $t = 3.52, p < .001$

Sample C
$N = 50$
$\overline{X} = 50$
$s = 30$

Sample D
$N = 50$
$\overline{X} = 60$
$s = 32$

$s_{\overline{x}_1 - \overline{x}_2} = 6.27$

true pop. μ in this interval

true pop. μ in this interval

$\dfrac{\overline{X}_1 - \overline{X}_2}{s_{\overline{x}_1 - \overline{x}_2}} = \dfrac{10}{6.27} = 1.59$

true population mean for both groups could be in crosshatched area

Do not reject the null, $t - 1.59$, n.s.

Figure 6.5 Illustrating the effects of small and large variability in the rejection or retention of the null hypothesis

error of the difference between the means of sample A and B we get 2.84. Dividing the difference between means (10) by the computed standard error, we obtain a significant *t* ratio of 3.52. Now consider samples C and D. Although the means are the same as samples A and B, the variability is much greater. Computing the standard error of the difference between these two means, we obtain 6.27 for a *t* ratio of 1.59, which is not large enough to allow us to reject the null. The overlap of variability for samples C and D is shown in the crosshatched area of Figure 6.5. Clearly, both samples could have come from populations with identical means. Therefore, we cannot reject the null hypothesis of no difference.

6.7.7 Large-Sample *t* Test: A Computer Example

Now that you understand the logic underlying the two-sample *t* test, we can present a further example from our sex offender data. Suppose that we want to find out if sex offenders or non-sex offenders are punished more severely in this jurisdiction. Sentence severity is rendered in terms of days in prison. Thus, each offender group has a mean number of days of imprisonment. Our null hypothesis states that there is no significant difference between the sentence severity means of the two groups.

However, there are sound theoretical reasons for us to believe that sex offenders are punished more severely than non-sex offenders. In this case, since we have predicted direction, we will use a one-tailed test. Our research hypothesis states that sex offenders receive significantly harsher penalties than do non-sex offenders. Notice that we have designated offense type (sex offense/non-sex offense) as our independent variable assumed to affect sentence severity, the dependent variable. The computer commands necessary to produce the findings presented in Table 6.3 are given in the chapter appendix.

Interpreting the Printout   The output in Table 6.3 compares the sentence severity means of group 1 (non-sex offenders; $N = 206$) and group 2 (sex offenders; $N = 431$). The first piece of information tells us that the mean severity of sentence for non-sex offenders is 324.13, and the mean for sex offenders is 572.26. The difference between the means of the two groups is a substantial one of 248.1 sentence severity points. We shall see later that this difference between

TABLE 6.3   COMPUTER PRINTOUT FOR SAS T-TEST

VARIABLE: SENSEV   SUBJECTS SENTENCE SEVERITY SCORE

GROUP	N	MEAN	STD DEV	STD ERROR
1. (Non-sex off.)	206	324.13592233	569.99745911	39.7136047
2. (Sex offender)	431	572.26450116	779.57057626	37.5505933

VARIANCES	T	DF	PROB > |T|
UNEQUAL	−4.5399	532.5	0.0001
EQUAL	−4.0764	635.0	0.0001

FOR HO: VARIANCES ARE EQUAL, F' = 1.87 WITH 430 AND 205 DF
        PROB > F' = 0.0001

means is called the unstandardized beta in bivariate regression when we have a dichotomous independent variable, as we have here.

Next we look at standard deviations. Their most overwhelming feature is that they are both larger than their respective means. Obviously one standard deviation below the mean in both cases is going to put us into negative sentence severity scores. We know it is not possible for an offender to have a negative sentence severity score; thus our curves for these two groups are clearly very positively skewed. Because these standard deviations are larger than their respective means, we conclude that these are not normal curves. Insofar as theoretical interpretation of the result is concerned, you should not be unduly alarmed about this finding. A great deal of sentencing variation is to be expected when dealing with a heterogeneous sample of criminals who have committed crimes ranging from receiving stolen property to murder.

Clearly there is a difference in sentence severity means between these two groups of offenders, but is the difference significant? We know immediately that our directional hypothesis corresponds to what is going on statistically. That is, we hypothesized that sex offenders were going to get more severe sentences than non-sex offenders, and they do. In other words, the independent variable does help us make predictions regarding the dependent variable, but only if the difference is significant.

Next we consider the "STD ERROR," or the standard error of the mean. Again, this is the standard deviation divided by the square root of N, computed for each of our two categories. As we saw in Chapter 5, we can use the standard error to place confidence intervals around the means of our two offender groups.

Next in the listing we encounter VARIANCES. You will recall from Chapter 3 that variance is a measure of how the scores are dispersed around the mean. The larger the spread of scores around the mean the larger the variance. The computer calculates two t tests based on EQUAL and UNEQUAL variance. Generally speaking, the t test assumes equality of variances, or as the assumption is more formally known, **homogeneity of variance**. This assumption makes sense because if two groups are sampled from the same population, we should expect only random variance difference. Although homogeneity of variance is an assumption of the t test, the t test is quite robust. **Robustness** refers to the ability of a test to withstand violations of its assumptions without seriously impairing its interpretation.

At this point we must make a decision about which of these two tests we are going to use. To help us make this decision SAS prints out an F value (as does SPSSx). We will discuss the F test in greater detail in the next chapter. For now just think of it as simply another test of the significance of difference. In this case it is a test of the significance of difference between sample variances. The part of the printout that addresses the issue of whether or not the two group variances differ reads, FOR HO: VARIANCES ARE EQUAL, $F' = 1.87$ WITH 430 AND 205 DF PROB $> F' = 0.0001$. This means that under the null hypothesis that the variances are equal, F with 430 and 205 degrees of freedom (the degrees of freedom associated with each group) was calculated to be 1.87, and the probability that the variances are equal is .0001, or one chance in 10,000. What this statement means practically is that when the F value falls below .05 we must use the unequal variance test to determine whether or not *t* is significant. To obtain the *F* value, we square the standard deviations for each of the groups to get the variance and then divide the larger variance by the smaller variance. Presented symbolically,

$$F = \frac{s^2(\text{larger variance})}{s^2(\text{smaller variance})} = \frac{779.6^2}{570^2} = \frac{607776.2}{324900.0} = 1.87$$

Thus in our example, the larger variance is 1.87 times greater than the smaller variance.

Since our *F* value is significant, we have **heterogeneity of variance** and must use the *t* value based on unequal variance. This *t* value is given as -4.5399, which is significant at the .0001 level with degrees of freedom equal to 532.5. The nice thing about these computer listings is that they give us the exact probability of the *t* test and we do not have to use a table. Thus we conclude that there is a significant difference between the sentence severity score of sex offenders and non-sex offenders. We accept our directional hypothesis: Sex offenders receive significantly more severe sentences.

We should point out that these computer printouts give us the two-tailed level of significance. If we are conducting a directional hypothesis we would simply divide the given probability value by 2. It makes no difference in the present example, but if the probability level was, say, .0650, knowing this value would prevent you from correctly rejecting a false null since .0650/2 = .0325.

6.7.8 Calculating *t* with Unequal Variances

How is it that we can obtain two different *t* values based on the same data? The answer is that two different formulas are used. The first formula is Formula 6.2, used to calculate *t* for our alienation example. We calculated our example under the assumption of equal variances, an assumption that allowed us to pool the variances of both samples and treat them as a single variance. If the variances are unequal we cannot pool them, and they must be considered separately (the SPSSx program uses the terms *pooled* and *separate* rather than *equal* or *unequal* in its *t* test printout). Since we treat unequal variances separately, we require a different formula, Formula 6.5. Compare this formula with Formula 6.2 for pooled variance. We will demonstrate the use of the separate variance formula by using the sentence severity group data.

$$t = \frac{\bar{X}_1 - \bar{X}_2}{\sqrt{\dfrac{s_1^2}{N_1 - 1} + \dfrac{s_2^2}{N_2 - 1}}}$$

$$= \frac{324.1 - 572.2}{\sqrt{\dfrac{570.0^2}{205} + \dfrac{779.6^2}{430}}} = \frac{-248.1}{\sqrt{\dfrac{324900}{205} + \dfrac{607776.2}{430}}} \qquad (6.5)$$

$$= \frac{-248.1}{\sqrt{1584.9 + 1413.4}} = \frac{-248.1}{\sqrt{2998.3}} = \frac{-248.1}{54.76} = -4.53$$

$t = -4.53, \ p < .0001$

Our computed t of -4.53 matches the printout. Notice that the computer also adjusts the degrees of freedom when the variances are unequal. The formula used to accomplish this computation is formidable, and it is not really necessary for you to know at this stage in your statistical education. Do note that if we had based our decision on the assumption of equal variances, we would have had extra protection against rejecting a true null hypothesis, as reflected by the smaller t value. When the larger sample is associated with the larger variance, as is the case here, the t test is conservative with respect to committing type I errors. In other words, the deck is stacked in favor of the null hypothesis in such instances.

6.7.9 A Note on the Significance Test Controversy

It is probably true that the majority of social and behavioral researchers support the use of significance testing as an indispensable part of the scientific research process. However, a substantial (significant?) minority questions the utility of significance testing. The most telling point put forth by the latter group is that these tests of significance rest on the assumption of random sampling. We rarely achieve a truly random sample of nontrivial populations in the social and behavioral sciences. Further, if we were able to overcome all of the obstacles to obtaining a random sample mentioned in Chapter 5, typically high nonresponse rates will turn what started out as a simple random sample into a nonrandom sample because of self-selection on the part of the respondents (Henkle, 1976, pp. 80–81).

Does this mean that we should discard significance testing? Henkle (1976), a leading figure in the controversy, argues against the process of significance testing. Nevertheless, he supplies some arguments against his position that convince me that significance testing must remain an integral part of our research: They do provide some assurance that chance has been ruled out as an explanation of research results, they provide a standard or criterion for evaluating one's findings and the findings of others, and "The adoption of conventional probability levels, such as the .01 and .05, provides a uniform and easily applied standard for determining, if nothing else, which results do not seem to merit further consideration" (p. 87).

The point should be strongly made that statistical significance is not the same as substantive or theoretical significance. Statistical significance tells us when some difference is large enough to be consistently found. A statistically significant finding may be of little or no theoretical importance. With a large enough sample, even small differences, if they exist, will be found. But, as one statistician put it, "Like an old penny on the floor, people may be able to find it but are unwilling to pick it up." To avoid the confusion over statistical and theoretical significance, the term *statistically reliable,* or perhaps *statistically dependable,* would be a better one to use. However, we are not about to tamper with the time-honored terminology of statistics.

One strategy to determine if a statistically significant finding is worth picking up is always to compute a measure of association in conjunction with every test of significance. We will discuss the concept of association at great length in Chapter 10. It is enough to say now that a measure of association quantifies the degree to which two variables are related or associated. These measures range within fixed limits of 0.0 to 1.0 or -1.0 to $+1.0$; the closer the measure to -1.0 or $+1.0$ the closer the two variables are related to one another. The measure of association typically calculated in conjunction with difference between means tests is eta (discussed in the next chapter).

In short, although significance testing is a valuable tool, you should constantly be aware of the shortcomings of your sampling procedures, of the distinction between statistical and theoretical significance, and of the need to compute a measure of association with each test. Do not generalize beyond the population from which the sample was drawn. For instance, do not make assumptions about all Democrats from a sample of Democrats drawn from Toledo, Ohio. This is not to say that a dozen small, well-designed studies of single communities around the country will not tell you a great deal about Democrats in general when the studies are viewed in their entirety.

6.8 SUMMARY

Hypothesis testing is a process of testing propositions derived from theory according to rigorous rules. We begin with a hypothesis about parameters in one or more populations and test it with sample statistics. The hypothesis to be tested is the null hypothesis of equality, or "no difference." We reject the null hypothesis only if our computed statistics achieve a given level of significance. A level of statistical significance is known as an alpha level, conventional alpha levels being .05 and .01. These levels correspond with areas under the sampling distribution, which are known as critical regions.

Two types of inversely related errors—type I (alpha) and type II (beta)—were identified. A type I error is the wrongful rejection of a true null hypothesis, and a type II error is the failure to reject a false null hypothesis. Scientists try to minimize the probability of a type I error by moving the rejection region closer to the tail of the sampling distribution, a strategy that simultaneously increases the risk of a type II error. Increasing sample size is one method of decreasing the probability of making either type of error.

We use the z distribution to test the hypothesis that some population mean estimated by a sample mean is equal to some constant (a known mean) or that two population means estimated from sample means are equal. When sample Ns are 120 or fewer we use the t distribution. The t distribution is more platykurtic than the z distribution, but it is identical with it when df are greater than 120.

Tests of hypotheses can be either nondirectional or directional. A nondirectional hypothesis is one in which the direction of any difference between means is not predicted from prior theoretical knowledge and in which the researcher is equally interested in outcomes in either tail of the distribution. This type of test is also known as a two-tailed test. A directional, or one-tailed test, is conducted when there are good theoretical reasons for expecting differences to occur only in one tail of the distribution. The effect of a one-tailed test is to move the rejection region closer to the mean. At the .05 level a one-tailed test will reject the hypothesis at z (or t if N is equal to or greater than 120) $= 1.65$, rather than the 1.96 required for a two-tailed test.

Depending on whether or not there are equal variances in the two groups, t tests are computed differently. Equality of variance is computed by obtaining the ratio of the larger variance to the smaller variance. If the variances are determined to be equal with the F ratio, t is computed by pooling the variances. If the variances are not equal, t is computed by the separate variance formula.

PRACTICE APPLICATION: t TEST

Researchers are interested in determining whether or not differential socialization of males and females leads to a differential acceptance of their bodies. They ask 125 females and 85 males to express their level of satisfaction with their bodies on a five-point scale ranging from zero for complete acceptance to 5 for complete lack of acceptance. The null hypothesis is that there is no difference between males and females in the acceptance of their bodies. The researcher obtains the following data:

$$\text{female:} \quad N = 125 \quad \bar{X}\,2.75 \quad s = 1.40$$

$$\text{male:} \quad N = 85 \quad \bar{X}\,1.50 \quad s = 1.30$$

Are variances equal?

variance for females $= 1.40^2 = 1.96$ males $= 1.30^2 = 1.69$

F ratio $= 1.96/1.69 = 1.16$ F critical with 124 and 84 $df = 1.42$

Computed F (1.16) does not exceed F critical (1.42): The variances are equal. Use the t test formula for equal variances.

$$H_0: \mu_1 = \mu_2 \qquad H_1: \mu_1 \neq \mu_2$$

alpha $= .05$

$$t = \frac{\bar{X}_1 - \bar{X}_2}{\sqrt{\dfrac{N_1 S_1^2 + N_2 S_2^2}{N_1 + N_2 - 2}}\sqrt{\dfrac{N_1 + N_2}{(N_1)(N_2)}}}$$

$$= \frac{2.75 - 1.50}{\sqrt{\dfrac{(125)(1.96) + (85)(1.69)}{125 + 85 - 2}}\sqrt{\dfrac{125 + 85}{(125)(85)}}}$$

$$= \frac{1.25}{\sqrt{\dfrac{245 + 143.65}{208}}\sqrt{\dfrac{210}{10625}}}$$

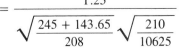

$$t = \frac{1.25}{\sqrt{1.8685}\,\sqrt{.01976}} = \frac{1.25}{(1.3669)(.1406)} = \frac{1.25}{.1922} = 6.5$$

The critical value of t in the t table with df above 120 (at infinity) at the .05 critical value is 1.96. Thus if our computed t is equal to or larger than 1.96, we reject the null hypothesis and accept the research hypothesis. Since 6.5 is larger than 1.96 we reject the null. Males are more accepting of their bodies than females. Something about male and female socialization clearly leads males to feel more accepting of their bodies than females.

APPENDIX: Computer Instructions for *t* Test

Command 6.1

```
      SAS                              SPSSx
PROC TTEST:           T-TEST GROUPS = GROUP/VARIABLES = SENSEV
CLASS GROUP;
VAR SENSEV;
```

PROC TTEST in SAS and T-TEST in SPSSx informs the computer of the procedure you wish to run. The independent variable, GROUP, is specified by CLASS (SAS) or GROUPS (SPSSx), and the dependent variable, SENSEV, by VAR (SAS) or VARIABLES (SPSSx).

REFERENCES

Henkle, R. (1976). *Tests of significance.* Beverly Hills, CA: Sage.

Wilson, J., and Herrnstein, R. (1985). *Crime and human nature.* New York: Simon & Schuster.

Chapter 7

One-Way Analysis of Variance

The z and t tests allow us to compare differences between two group means. **Analysis of variance (ANOVA)** is an extension of the t test and allows us to compare more than two means simultaneously to determine whether any differences among two or more of them are greater than would be expected by chance. There are many forms of ANOVA, ranging from the relatively simple to the complex. In this chapter we will examine the most basic form of ANOVA, one-way analysis of variance. In one-way ANOVA we are interested in the mean values of an interval- or ratio-level dependent variable within different categories (usually three or more) of an independent variable. A two-way ANOVA examines the combined effect of two independent variables on the dependent variable.

Assumptions of Analysis of Variance

1. Independent random samples
2. Interval or ratio level of measurement
3. Independent subjects in each group (i.e., not the same subjects tested twice and not matched subjects)
4. Homogeneity of variance
5. Normal sampling distribution

Thus, in ANOVA we are testing the equality of means under the assumption that all category, group, or sample means come from a random sample of independent subjects from the same population. If we are testing the equality of three category means, the null hypothesis would be presented symbolically as

$$H_0 : \mu_1 = \mu_2 = \mu_3$$

The research hypothesis would be that at least two of the means differ.

7.1 THE BASIC LOGIC OF ANOVA

ANOVA is based on a comparison of two sources of variance in the sample groups: between- and within-group variance. The between-group variance is often referred to as the explained variance because it is accounted for by the grouped or categorized variable. The within-group variance is often referred to as the unexplained variance because it is that proportion of the variance left unexplained by the groups. The first of these sources of variance is an estimate of the variance between the group means (it would be more grammatically correct to say *among* the groups, but *between* is the convention). If there is no difference between the means other than that attributable to chance, the null hypothesis is true. The second source of variability is due to differences among the individual observations within the groups. Thus, in ANOVA we are examining a ratio of within-group variance to between-group variance. The null hypothesis testing the equivalence of these two sources of variance is tested with the F distribution (the F is capitalized because it is named after its founder, the British statistician Ronald Fisher). The logic of ANOVA is that if the variance between groups is significantly greater than the variance within the groups, the populations from which the groups came can also be considered to be different with regard to the dependent variable.

Refer back to Formula 6.2 for the t test. The difference between two group means constitutes the numerator, and the denominator is the standard error of the difference of means, which is a measure of the differences within the two groups being compared. The t ratio is a measure of the difference between the means of the groups being compared relative to the combined estimate of the variance within each group (the standard error of the difference). The larger the t ratio, the greater the probability of rejecting the null hypothesis. The logic of ANOVA is analogous. The difference is that t focuses on means whereas ANOVA focuses on variances, although, of course, means and variances are used in the calculation of both statistics. The comparison is made for you symbolically, and both formulas describe a ratio of between- and within-group differences.

$$t = \frac{\text{difference of means}}{\text{standard error of difference}} \qquad F = \frac{\text{between-group variance}}{\text{within-group variance}}$$

7.1.1 The Idea of Variance

Variance or *variability* refers to the extent to which individuals, objects, or scores differ from the grand mean of a sample on a given characteristic or attribute. The objective of social science is to determine the source of this variability. We ask questions like "What is it that 'causes' or accounts for the observed differences between this group of people and that group of people or this individual or that individual?"

The sample distributions in Figure 7.1 may make the logic of accounting for variance understandable. There is considerable variation in both samples; the scores range from 30 to 54 in sample A, and from 12 to 70 in sample B.

Although the pattern of variation in both samples is quite different, their grand means are identical at 42. It is the pattern of dispersion or variation around the grand mean that provides the basis for assessing the significance of group mean differences by examining the pattern of variation within and between the sample groups. *Between-group* variance refers to the variation of group means about the grand mean. Which of these two samples shows greater variation of group means from their respective grand means? From simple observation of the figure the obvious answer is sample A.

Within-group variance refers to the variance of each raw score from its group mean. Which of the two samples has greater within-group variance? Obviously, it is sample B. In sample A the maximum difference within any group (among the individual group members) is 4, whereas in sample B the maximum difference is 43. Clearly, the variance attributable to theoretically meaningful categories of the independent variable (between-group variance) in sample A is larger than the variance attributable to individual differences (within-group variance). In sample B we observe the opposite situation, in which between-group variance, although fairly substantial, is much less than the variance within the groups. The distribution curves of each subsample further help you to visualize the difference between between- and within-group variance. Notice that the leptokurtic curves in sample A have no significant overlap. The platykurtic curves in sample B reflect the greater variability of the scores within them, and there is a great amount of overlap.

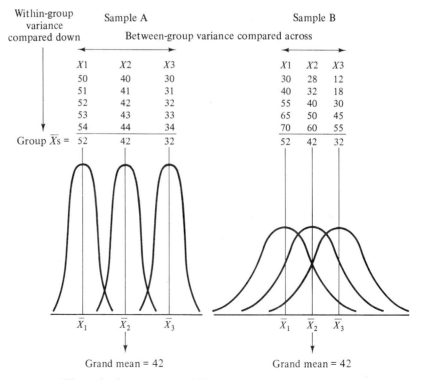

Within-group variance compared down

Sample A

Between-group variance compared across

Sample B

	$X1$	$X2$	$X3$		$X1$	$X2$	$X3$
	50	40	30		30	28	12
	51	41	31		40	32	18
	52	42	32		55	40	30
	53	43	33		65	50	45
	54	44	34		70	60	55
Group $\overline{X}$s =	52	42	32		52	42	32

$\overline{X}_1$ $\overline{X}_2$ $\overline{X}_3$ $\overline{X}_1$ $\overline{X}_2$ $\overline{X}_3$

Grand mean = 42   Grand mean = 42

Figure 7.1 Illustrating between- and within-group variance

If the raw scores in Figure 7.1 represented scores on some kind of test and subjects were categorized according to high, medium, and low socioeconomic class, what might we conclude from these two samples? In sample A we would conclude that an individual's social class is more important than any personal attributes in accounting for his or her score on this particular test. In other words, the variance observed between social class groups is greater than the variance within social class groups. We would conclude the opposite from sample B; that is, individual differences are much more important in determining test scores than is the social class into which the individuals are grouped. Sample B shows greater within-group variance. Remember this distinction of between- and within-group variance.

7.1.2 The Advantage of ANOVA over Multiple Tests

You might wonder why we do not simply calculate separate t tests between all possible pairs of groups. The main problem with this strategy is that it is inefficient and it could be misleading. The number of pairwise group comparisons is determined by the formula $N(N - 1)/2$. If we were comparing four group means we would have to run $(4)(3)/2 = 6$ separate t tests. With ANOVA we have to perform only one test. Furthermore, if we run six separate t tests they would not all be independent comparisons and the resulting probabilities would overlap, thus increasing the probability of making a type I error. Remember, if we are looking for a difference that is statistically significant at the .05 level, we would falsely reject a true null hypothesis in the long run in one out of every 20 comparisons. The more separate tests we conduct, the more likely it becomes that we will claim that some difference is real when it is actually due to chance. For instance, with six separate t tests, each with an alpha of .05, the actual combined alpha would be

$$\text{actual alpha} = 1 - (1 - \alpha)(1 - \alpha)(1 - \alpha)(1 - \alpha)(1 - \alpha)(1 - \alpha)$$

$$= 1 - (.95)(.95)(.95)(.95)(.95)(.95)$$

$$= 1 - .73509 = .2649$$

From the preceding we see that the probability of one or more type I errors in using a series of t tests where each is set at .05 is about .2649. In short, the more tests we perform the more we increase the risk of rejecting a true null hypothesis. So in addition to being a more parsimonious test, the problem of overlapping probabilities is avoided when ANOVA is used to compare multiple means.

7.1.3 The *F* Distribution

The variance ratios in ANOVA are tested for significance with the **F distribution**, a family of distributions that like the t distribution vary in shape according to the number of degrees of freedom used in calculation. The F distribution begins to look something like the normal curve as df increases, but it always remains positively skewed (we cannot have a negative F value although we can have a negative t value). Unlike other distributions, the F distribution is described

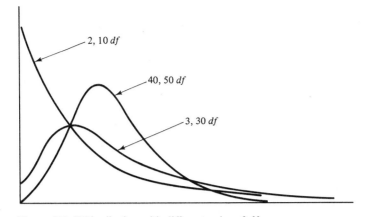

Figure 7.2 *F* Distribution with different pairs of *df*

by two types of *df*: the degrees of freedom between groups (*dfb*) and the degrees of freedom within groups (*dfw*). The former (*dfb*) are determined by $k - 1$, where $k = $ the number of groups or categories. If we are examining four different groups, *dfb* would be $4 - 1 = 3$ because three group means are free to vary whereas the fourth is determined. The within-group degrees of freedom (*dfw*) are determined by $N - k$, where $N = $ the total number of cases in all groups. If we were examining four groups of 25 members each, *dfw* would be $100 - 4 = 96$. Figure 7.2 illustrates *F* distributions with various degrees of freedom.

7.2 AN EXAMPLE OF ANOVA

Suppose a researcher wants to study the effects of class standing in college on levels of general knowledge. He or she randomly elects six sophomores, six juniors, and six seniors and administers a general knowledge test. The H_0 is that the means of the three groups will not differ among themselves, and the H_1 is that at least two group means will be significantly different. To determine if there is any effect of class standing on general knowledge it is necessary to sum the scores of each member in each group and divide by the number of members in the group to arrive at a group mean. The three group means have been calculated for you in Table 7.1. The means represent the average performance in each group and the basis of the calculation of the between-group variance. Next, we determine the overall average performance, that is, the sum of the performances of all subjects divided by the total sample size. The total mean serves as the basis for calculating the total variance. If the between-group variance exceeds the within-group variance by a specified amount, we will be in a position to reject the null hypothesis.

The computation of ANOVA uses the sum of squares (*SS*), which we examined in Chapter 3. Recall that symbolically *SS* is expressed as

$$SS = \Sigma(X - \bar{X})^2$$

In ANOVA we have separate group means as well as a total mean. To avoid confusion about which mean has to be included in the formula for determining the **total sum of squares** (SS_{total}), the formula for SS_{total} is written in ANOVA as in Formula 7.1

$$SS_{total} = \Sigma(X - \bar{X}t)^2 \qquad (7.1)$$

where $\bar{X}_t$ = total mean

From the data in Table 7.1 we will now calculate SS_{total} exactly as we did according to the definitional formula for SS in Chapter 3.

TABLE 7.1   PRELIMINARY ANOVA COMPUTATIONS

	Sophomores	Juniors	Seniors
	73	72	83
	75	78	86
	77	74	89
	75	80	85
	78	83	90
	75	80	95
	456	467	528
Group $\bar{X}$s	75.5	77.83	88.0

Total mean ($\bar{X}t$) = 456 + 467 + 528 = 1448/18 = 80.444

STEP 1.   Calculate SS_{total} by subtracting the total mean from each of the 18 individual scores, squaring each difference, and then summing.

$$SS_{total} = \Sigma(X_1 - \bar{X}_t)^2 + (X_2 - \bar{X}_t)^2 + \cdots + (X_{18} - \bar{X}_t)^2$$

$$SS_{total} = (73 - 80.444)^2 + (75 - 80.444)^2 + \cdots + (95 - 80.444)^2$$

$$= 55.41 + 29.64 + \cdots + 211.88$$

$$SS_{total} = 722.5$$

We now have the total sum of squares. SS_{total} is the sum of the variation in the entire sample; therefore, it is 100 percent of the variance in the data set. Now we have to partition the SS_{total} into the between-group SS ($SS_{between}$) and the within-group SS (SS_{within}). $SS_{between} + SS_{within} = SS_{total}$.

STEP 2.   Calculate $SS_{between}$. The definitional formula for $SS_{between}$ is Formula 7.2

$$SS_{between} = \Sigma N(\bar{X}g - \bar{X}t)^2 \qquad (7.2)$$

where N = group N

$\bar{X}g$ = group mean

$\bar{X}t$ = total mean

Substituting

$$SS_{between} = 6(75.5 - 80.444)^2 + 6(77.83 - 80.444)^2 + 6(88.0 - 80.444)^2$$

$$= 146.66 + 342.56 + 342.56$$

$$SS_{between} = 530.2$$

$SS_{between}$ is the amount of variation in the data set accounted for by the grouping (class level). The next task is to determine the amount of variation left unaccounted for by the grouping (SS_{within}). Since $SS_{total} = SS_{between} + SS_{within}$, we could determine SS_{within} at this point by simply subtracting $SS_{between}$ from SS_{total} ($SS_{within} = 722.5 - 530.2 = 192.3$). However, because such a short-cut would not help you understand the logic of ANOVA, we will therefore proceed to calculate SS_{within}. The definitional formula for SS_{within} is Formula 7.3.

$$SS_{within} = \Sigma\Sigma(X - \bar{X}g)^2 \qquad (7.3)$$

This formula instructs you to subtract each score of each group from its respective group mean, square the difference, and then sum. After this has been done for each group, sum the sums.

SS_{within} for Sophomores

$$(73 - 75.5)^2 + (75 - 75.5)^2 + \cdots + (75 - 75.5)^2 = 15.5$$

SS_{within} for Juniors

$$(72 - 77.83)^2 + (78 - 77.83)^2 + \cdots + (80 - 77.83)^2 = 84.8$$

SS_{within} for Seniors

$$(83 - 88)^2 + (86 - 88)^2 + \cdots + (95 - 88)^2 = 92.0$$

$$\text{total } SS_{within} = 15.5 + 84.8 + 92.0 = 192.3$$

$$SS_{between} + SS_{within} = SS_{total}$$

$$520.2 + 192.3 = 722.5$$

We have just suffered through the long and tedious method of calculating the total variance and its two sources by the definitional formulas for ANOVA. This step was necessary for you to understand ANOVA. Happily, there are short-cut "computational" formulas for ANOVA that you can use once you have grasped the logic behind the computations. Besides being quicker to calculate, these formulas minimize the opportunities for error because there are fewer operations to perform. The computational formula for SS_{total} is Formula 7.4

$$SS_{total} = \Sigma Xt^2 - \frac{(\Sigma Xt)^2}{Nt} \qquad (7.4)$$

This formula requires you to calculate the sum of the squared individual scores and then the sum of the individual scores squared. We will now do so with the same data we used in Table 7.1, which are reproduced in Table 7.2.

TABLE 7.2 PRELIMINARY ANOVA COMPUTATIONS

Sophomores		Juniors		Seniors	
X	X^2	X	X^2	X	X^2
73	5329	72	5184	83	6889
75	5625	78	6084	86	7396
77	5929	74	5476	89	7921
75	5625	80	6400	85	7225
78	6084	83	6889	90	8100
75	5625	80	6400	95	9025
453	34217	467	36433	528	46556
$\bar{X}$s 75.5		77.83		88.0	

STEP 1.   Compute ΣX^2 and $(\Sigma X)^2$.

$\Sigma X = 453 + 467 + 528 = 1448$ grand mean $= \bar{X}t = 1448/18 = 80.444$

$(\Sigma X)^2 = 1448^2 = 2096704$

$\Sigma Xt^2 = 34217 + 36433 + 46556 = 117206$

STEP 2.   Substitute these values in Formula 7.4 to obtain SS_{total}

$$\Sigma Xt^2 - \frac{(\Sigma Xt)^2}{Nt} = 117206 - \frac{2096704}{18}$$

$$= 117206 - 116483.5 = 722.5$$

$$\boxed{SS_{total} = 722.5}$$

STEP 3.   Partition SS_{total} into $SS_{between}$ and SS_{within}, starting with $SS_{between}$.

$$SS_{between} = \left[\Sigma \frac{(\Sigma Xg)^2}{Ni} \right] - \frac{(\Sigma Xt)^2}{Nt} \tag{7.5}$$

The formula instructs you to subtract the sum of the X scores squared of the total sample from the sum of the sums of each individual group squared divided by the number of observations in each group. Substituting,

$$= \left[\frac{453^2}{6} + \frac{467^2}{6} + \frac{528^2}{6} \right] - \frac{2096704}{18}$$

$$= (34201.5 + 36348.2 + 46464) - 116483.5$$

$$= 117013.7 - 116483.5 = 530.2$$

$$\boxed{SS_{between} = 530.2}$$

STEP 4.   Calculate SS_{within}.

$$SS_{within} = \Sigma \left[\Sigma Xg^2 - \frac{(\Sigma Xg)^2}{Ni} \right] \tag{7.6}$$

This formula instructs you to sum the values obtained by subtracting the sum of the observations in each individual group squared and divided by the number of observations in the group from the sum of the squared observations in each group. Substituting,

$$= \left[34217 - \frac{453^2}{6} \right] + \left[36433 - \frac{467^2}{6} \right] + \left[46556 - \frac{528^2}{6} \right]$$

$$= (34217 - 34201.5) + (36433 - 36348.2) + (46556 - 46464)$$

$$= 15.5 + 84.8 + 92 = 192.3$$

$$\boxed{SS_{within} = 192.3}$$

$$SS_{between} + SS_{within} = SS_{total}$$

$$530.2 + 192.3 = 722.5$$

7.3 DETERMINING STATISTICAL SIGNIFICANCE: MEAN SQUARE AND THE F RATIO

The next step is to determine if our finding is statistically significant. What we have at this point are two sum of squares values, but we have said that ANOVA is based on variance ratios. In Chapter 3 we defined variance as the sum of squares divided by N (or $N - 1$ for samples). We cannot do so here because we have partitioned the sums of squares. Rather we must divide each of the SSs by their respective degrees of freedom to arrive at a value called **mean square** (MS), which is an estimate of the population variance. We previously defined the degrees of freedom for $SS_{between}$ as $k - 1$, and for SS_{within} as $N - k$. We have three categories of the dependent variable and 18 observations. The degrees of freedom for $SS_{between}$ are therefore $3 - 1 = 2$, and for SS_{within} they are $18 - 3 = 15$. The mean square values are calculated from Formula 7.7.

$$\text{mean square between} = \frac{SS_{between}}{df} = \frac{530.2}{2} = 265.1 \tag{7.7}$$

$$\text{mean square within} = \frac{SS_{within}}{df} = \frac{192.3}{15} = 12.82$$

We are now in a position to test for significance with the F distribution. The **F ratio** is determined by the ratio of the mean square within to the mean square between, as in Formula 7.8. If there are no differences among the groups, the between-group and within-group variances will be approximately equal, and the value of F will be about 1. The more the between-group variance exceeds the within-group variance the greater the probability that the groups represent different populations.

$$F = \frac{MS_{\text{between}}}{MS_{\text{within}}} = \frac{265.1}{12.83} = 20.66 \tag{7.8}$$

This F value of 20.66 means that the between-group variance is 20.66 times larger than the within-group variance. We now have to make our decision regarding H_0 by comparing our computed F with the critical F found in the F distribution table in Appendix C. As with the other distributions we have examined, the value of critical F depends on the selected alpha level and the degrees of freedom. However, there are two sets of degrees of freedom in the F distribution corresponding to the denominators of the mean square formula (in the present example, $df = 2$ and 15).

Many students have more difficulty in reading the F distribution table than any other because it involves two sets of degrees of freedom and because there are separate tables for the .05 and .01 alpha levels. The reproduction of a small portion of the F distribution table for alpha $= .05$ in Figure 7.3 should help. Note that the degrees of freedom between (the numerator) run across the top of the table, and the degrees of freedom within (the denominator) run down the side.

Start at the top of the table and find the degrees of freedom between $(dfb = 2)$; then trace the column down until you come to degrees of freedom within $(dfw = 15)$. At the intersection of these two values is the minimum value of F necessary to reject the null. This value is 3.68 at the .05 level (the corresponding value at the .01 level is 6.36). Our computed F of 20.66 greatly exceeds both of these values. We may reject the H_0 and accept the research hypothesis: There is a real difference in the levels of general knowledge among the three groups. Figure 7.4 shows the critical regions in the F distribution for

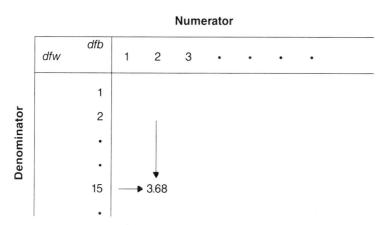

Figure 7.3 Reading the F distribution table with 2 and 15 df, alpha $= .05$

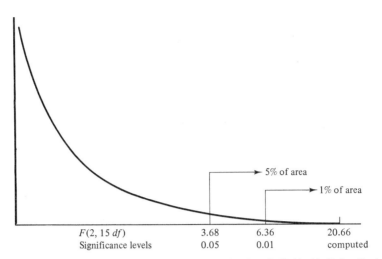

Figure 7.4 Rejection regions at .05 and .01 with 2 and 15 df with F distribution

rejection of the null at the .05 and .01 levels of confidence compared to our computed F.

7.4 MULTIPLE COMPARISONS: THE TUKEY HSD TEST

The ANOVA procedure tells us whether any two means differ significantly from one another. Since we have rejected the null hypothesis, we know that at least two means differ significantly, but we don't know which two, or even if all three means differ from one another. There are a number of ways by which you can determine which means differ. I prefer **Tukey's honestly significant difference** (HSD) test when sample sizes are equal. The Scheffe multiple comparison method is used when we have an unbalanced design (unequal groups). We will discuss the Scheffe method later in the context of a computer example. The HSD method locates the minimum true value by which two means must "honestly" differ to attain statistical significance.

The first step in calculating HSD is to select the alpha level; we will select 0.05. The next step is to turn to Appendix D to determine the appropriate value of q at the .05 level necessary to reject the null hypothesis. This q is the studentized range statistic, defined as the ratio of the difference in a pair of means to the standard error of the mean. Although this is exactly the method used by the t test, HSD adjusts for the fact that the likelihood of a type I error increases as the number of means being compared increases. As with the F table, we enter the q table with two sets of degrees of freedom. The first df value is found across the rows of the table and corresponds to the number of groups being compared. In our case, three group means are being compared. The second df value is found in the columns of the table and corresponds to the degrees of freedom used in calculating MS_{within}. Therefore, we enter the table with 15 df and three means and find the q value to be 3.67. We can now put in our values to determine HSD from Formula 7.9.

$$HSD = q\alpha \sqrt{\frac{MS_{within}}{Ni}} \tag{7.9}$$

where $q\alpha$ = percentage points of studentized range at given alpha

Ni = number of observations on which each of the means is based.

We have already determined MS_{within} to be 12.82, and each means is based on six observations; therefore

$$HSD = 3.67\sqrt{\frac{12.82}{6}} = 3.67\sqrt{2.137} = (3.67)(1.462) = 5.365$$

The computed HSD value of 5.365 means that this is the minimum difference between a pair of means in our sample that could be considered significantly different. Our sophomore mean is 75.5 and our junior mean is 77.83. The difference between these two means is 2.33. These two means do not differ significantly. The mean difference between the seniors and the sophomores is $88.0 - 75.5 = 12.5$, and between the seniors and the juniors it is $88.0 - 77.83 = 10.17$. Both of these differences exceed the HSD value of 5.365. We conclude that we do not have evidence to support a significant increase in general knowledge between sophomores and juniors, but we do have evidence to the effect that seniors have significantly greater general knowledge than either sophomores or juniors.

7.4.1 Computing Eta Squared

As I frequently emphasize, it is always advisable to compute a measure of association to accompany a test of significance. Any difference between and among means can be statistically significant if we have a large enough sample. It is for this reason that we should always report a measure of association if the null hypothesis is rejected. Having rejected the null hypothesis that class standing is unrelated to the level of general knowledge, we now ask ourselves how strong this relationship is. The measure of association traditionally associated with ANOVA is **eta squared**, which is defined as the ratio of $SS_{between}$ and SS_{total} as in Formula 7.10. Eta squared is always a positive number that ranges between zero and $+1$.

$$\eta^2 = \frac{SS_{between}}{SS_{total}} = \frac{\text{explained variance}}{\text{total variance}} = \frac{530.2}{722.5} = .7338 \tag{7.10}$$

Eta squared is interpreted as the amount of variance in the dependent variable that is explained by the independent variable. When we talk about variance explained, we mean this in a statistical rather than a causal sense. Class standing does not "cause" variation in general knowledge; it does statistically explain, or account for, about 73.4 percent of the variance in general knowledge: $1 - \eta^2 =$ the amount of variance left unexplained by the independent variable, or 26.6 percent.

7.4.2 Eta Squared and the *t* Test

Eta squared is also an appropriate measure of variance explained for the *t* test. Unfortunately, neither SAS or SPSSx compute eta in the *t* test program. As an alternative to the *t* test, it is perfectly permissible to apply ANOVA to only two groups. If we apply ANOVA to the sentence severity problem in Chapter 6, the relationship between the *t* ratio and the *F* ratio is apparent. The ratio of MS_{within} to $MS_{between}$ for this problem is 16.617. When $df = 1$ for between groups, the square root of $F = t(\sqrt{16.617} = 4.076)$, which is exactly the *t* ratio computed in Table 6.3. Thus, we can think of *t* squared in ANOVA terms as $SS_{between}$, and *t* squared plus the degrees of freedom as SS_{total}. The ratio of these two values gives us eta squared (see Formula 7.11).

$$\eta^2 = \frac{t^2}{t^2 + df} \tag{7.11}$$

Turning back to the *t* test results in Table 6.3, we find the value of *t* calculated (unequal variances) to be -4.5399, $df = 532.5$. Therefore,

$$\eta^2 = \frac{-4.5399^2}{-4.5399^2 + 532.5} = \frac{20.61}{20.61 + 532.5} = \frac{20.61}{553.11} = .03726$$

We find that about 3.7 percent of the variance in sentence severity is explained by the offender group. If we compute eta squared based on the assumption of equal variances, we obtain a smaller eta squared value.

$$\eta^2 = \frac{-4.0764}{-4.0764 + 635} = \frac{16.62}{16.62 + 635} = \frac{16.62}{651.62} = .0255$$

If we take the square root of eta squared we obtain eta, known also as the correlation ratio. The square root of .0255 is .16. This is a measure of the degree of association or correlation between the type of offender and sentence severity. Since interval-level statistics assume equal variance, this value of eta will be identical to the correlation coefficient (r) between these two variables (offender type and sentence severity) and the standardized beta (β), both to be discussed later.

7.4.3 The ANOVA Table

The final task is to present your results in an ANOVA summary table. Such a table customarily includes the sum of squares between and within, degrees of freedom, mean square, *F* ratio, and significance level. Table 7.3 also includes eta squared and multiple comparison tests (HSD).

7.5 A COMPUTER EXAMPLE OF ONE-WAY ANOVA

This example of one-way ANOVA is based on our Supreme Court data. We test the hypothesis that a series of fictitious proposals involving various social issues

TABLE 7.3   ANOVA SUMMARY TABLE

Sources of Variance	SS	df	Mean Square	F	Sig.	Eta^2
Between groups	530.2	2	265.1	20.66	< .001	.734
Within groups	192.3	15	12.82			
Total	722.5	17				

Multiple Comparison of Means

$\bar{X}$s   sophomore = 75.5, junior = 77.83, n.s.
sophomore = 75.5, senior = 88.00, $p < .05$
junior = 77.83, senior = 88.00, $p < .05$

would be more likely to generate support if they came from the Supreme Court than if they came from either Congress or an unattributed source. Questionnaires were distributed among a convention of recreational vehicle owners, who were mostly retirees. All questionnaires were similar except that one-third listed the Supreme Court as the source of the proposals, one-third listed Congress as the source, and one-third had no source. This methodology is similar to the experimental method in which the independent variable is systematically varied among randomly chosen subjects.

The subjects' scores on each of nine proposals (strongly disagree = 0, disagree = 1, undecided = 2, agree = 3, strongly agree = 5) were added to yield a composite variable we will call "total." Therefore, TOTAL is the dependent variable and SUP (the source of the hypothetical proposals) is the independent variable.

For this example we will use SAS. Since the design is unbalanced, meaning we have unequal Ns in the three groups, we have to use the **Scheffe test** for multiple comparisons. The commands to run this ANOVA are given in command 7.1 (see Table 7.4).

7.5.1 Interpreting the Printout

The top line of the printout gives the MODEL degrees of freedom (df) and the model SUM OF SQUARES and MEAN SQUARE. The term *model* is more conventionally termed the *main effects* and represents the variance accounted for by all of the independent variables (in this case just SUP, or the source of attribution of the proposals). This is the between-group SS. The next line gives the ERROR SS (within-group sum of squares) and the associated df and mean squares.

We should pause here momentarily to explain what the term *error* does and does not mean. *Error* should not be viewed as synonymous with *mistake*. In statistics *error* simply means variation in the dependent variable that cannot be accounted for by the independent variable or variables. In the context of the present example, the SS_{within} is the variance in proposal agreement scores that

TABLE 7.4 SAS COMPUTER PRINTOUT FOR ANOVA (GLM) JOB

```
                       GENERAL LINEAR MODELS PROCEDURE
                          CLASS LEVEL INFORMATION
                  CLASS          LEVELS          VALUES
                  SUP              3              1 2 3
              NUMBER OF OBSERVATIONS IN DATA SET = 150
                                SAS
                    GENERAL LINEAR MODELS PROCEDURE
```

DEPENDENT VARIABLE: TOTAL

SOURCE	DF	SUM OF SQUARES	MEAN SQUARE
MODEL	2	414.43567031	207.21783515
ERROR	147	2719.62432969	18.50084578
CORRECTED TOTAL	149	3134.06000000	
MODEL F =	11.20		PR > F = 0.0001
R-SQUARE	C.V.	ROOT MSE	TOTAL MEAN
0.132236	23.7115	4.30126095	18.14000000

SOURCE	DF	TYPE I SS	F VALUE	PR > F
SUP	2	414.43567031	11.20	0.0001

SOURCE	DF	TYPE III SS	F VALUE	PR > F
SUP	2	414.43567031	11.20	0.0001

```
                    GENERAL LINEAR MODELS PROCEDURE
```

SCHEFFE'S TEST FOR VARIABLE: TOTAL

ALPHA = 0.05   CONFIDENCE = 0.95   DF = 147   MSE = 18.5008
CRITICAL VALUE OF F = 3.05762

COMPARISONS SIGNIFICANT AT THE 0.05 LEVEL ARE INDICATED BY '***'

SUP COMPARISON	SIMULTANEOUS LOWER CONFIDENCE LIMIT	DIFFERENCE BETWEEN MEANS	SIMULTANEOUS UPPER CONFIDENCE LIMIT	
1 −2	1.2192	3.4132	5.6071	***
1 −3	1.4033	3.4330	5.4626	***
2 −1	−5.6071	−3.4132	−1.2192	***
2 −3	−2.2080	0.0198	2.2476	
3 −1	−5.4626	−3.4330	−1.4033	***
3 −2	−2.2476	−0.0198	2.2080	

(Group 1) Supreme Court $\bar{X} = 20.26$.

(Group 2) Congress $\bar{X} = 16.85$.

(Group 3) Unattributed $\bar{X} = 16.83$.

cannot be accounted for by the three sources of the proposals (the categorized dependent variable). Later on we shall discuss *reduction in error,* which means that we have been able to reduce variability or scatter of a set of scores around some value or values in a distribution by a specific amount. When we discuss correlation and regression we will use the term *residual* rather than *error.*

In the next line of the printout is found the CORRECTED TOTAL, or simply, SS_{total}. We see in the next line that the MODEL F ratio is 11.2 and that it is highly significant at .0001. The R-SQUARE is analogous to eta squared, and it represents the proportion of variance in the dependent variable accounted for by the independent variable. In this example *r* squared is .132236, indicating that the source of the hypothetical proposals accounts for about 13.2 percent of the variance in the dependent variable. C.V. is the coefficient of variation, used to assess relative variation rather than absolute variation. It is useful for comparing two distributions having different means or for comparing two distributions when the dependent variable is measured in different units. C.V. is calculated by multiplying the ROOT MSE (the square root of the mean square error) by 100 and dividing by the TOTAL MEAN (grand mean). Performing this operation, we get $[(4.3)(100)]/18.14 = 23.7$. C.V. thus expresses the standard deviation (ROOT MSE) as a percentage of the mean.

7.5.2 The Scheffe Test

The next section of the output relates to the Scheffe test. It lists the alpha and confidence levels, the *df,* the mean square error, and the critical value of the *F* ratio, which is used as part of the formula for all possible pairwise mean contrasts. As indicated earlier, the HSD test is preferable if we have equal group sizes. In social research, however, we rarely obtain equal group sizes, and the researcher needs a method of making comparisons that takes into account unequal sample sizes. As you will see from Formula 7.12, unlike the HSD test, the Scheffe test requires a calculation each time contrasts are made of means with different *N*s. To illustrate the Scheffe test I will contrast only the means for the Supreme Court sample and the Congress sample.

$$\text{Scheffe range} = \left[\sqrt{(K-1)(F \text{ crit})} \right] \left[\sqrt{\frac{1}{N_1} + \frac{1}{N_2}(MSW)} \right] \quad (7.12)$$

where $K - 1 = $ the number of categories minus 1

F crit $ = $ the critical F ratio supplied by the printout

$N_1 = $ the number of cases in sample 1 ($N = 57$)

$N_2 = $ the number of cases in sample 2 ($N = 40$)

$MSW = $ mean square within (given as MSE by the printout)

Substituting,

$$\text{Scheffe range} = \left[\sqrt{(2)(3.05762)} \right] \left[\sqrt{(1/57 + 1/40)(18.5)} \right]$$

$$= \left[\sqrt{6.11524} \right] \left[\sqrt{(.04254)(18.5)} \right]$$

$$= (2.473)(.8871) = 2.194$$

Thus, the minimum distance between the Supreme Court and Congress conditions must be 2.194 or more. We note that the SUP COMPARISON on the first line indicates that the mean of the Congress condition is subtracted from the mean of the Supreme Court condition $(1 - 2)$ to yield a DIFFERENCE BETWEEN MEANS of 3.41, which exceeds the minimum required distance. The output also supplies the lower and upper confidence limits for the mean differences. The difference between the means of the Supreme Court condition and the unattributed condition (3.433) is also significant. The difference between the Congress and the unattributed condition (.0198) is not significant. It appears that respondents are more likely to agree with proposals when they think they come from the Supreme Court than when they come from Congress or from some unattributed source. We will discuss ANOVA further in Chapter 8 when we explore two-way ANOVA (ANOVA with two independent variables).

7.6 SUMMARY

ANOVA is a statistic used for comparing the significance of difference among multiple means. It is based on the comparison of two sources of variance: between- and within-group variance. Between-group variance is the variance attributed to categories of the independent variable, and within-group variance is attributable to individual differences. Within-group variance is also known as error or residual variance.

The statistical significance of ANOVA results is determined by the use of the F ratio, the ratio of the mean square within to the mean square between. $MS_{between}$ and MS_{within} are determined by dividing the respective sources of variance by their respective df. We then enter the F distribution table with $df_{between}$ and df_{within} to determine if the computed F matches or exceeds the tabular value.

ANOVA only tells us if two or more means differ, not which ones. One of the ways to determine which pair or pairs of means differ is the Tukey honestly significant difference test. This test is used when the researcher has equal sample sizes. When the researcher does not have equal sample sizes, the Scheffe test must be used.

Eta squared is defined as the ratio of $SS_{between}$ to SS_{total} and is a measure of the amount of variance in the dependent variable explained by the independent variable. Eta squared can also be directly computed from the t test.

PRACTICE APPLICATION: ONE-WAY ANOVA

A statistics instructor randomly divides the class of nine into three groups to test the hypothesis that a combination of instructional methods is a superior method of teaching statistics. Group 1 has lectures, a textbook, and a student workbook. Group 2 has lectures and a textbook, and group 3 has lectures only. After one month of instruction each group is given identical tests containing ten questions. The following number of correct answers is obtained by each group. Are these differences statistically significant? Use the computational formula.

GROUP SCORES OF STATISTICS STUDENTS

	Group 1		Group 2		Group 3	
	X	X^2	X	X^2	X	X^2
	9	81	4	16	2	4
	6	36	3	9	5	25
	7	49	3	9	2	4
	22	166	10	34	9	33
$\bar{X}$	7.33		3.33		3.0	$\bar{X}t = 4.56$

$\Sigma X^2 = 233 \qquad (\Sigma X)^2 = 1681$

Compute SS_{total}.

$$SS_{total} = \Sigma Xt^2 - \frac{(\Sigma Xt)^2}{Nt} = 233 - \frac{1681}{9} = 233 - 186.8$$

$$= 46.2$$

$SS_{total} = 46.2$

Partition SS_{total} into $SS_{between}$ and SS_{within}.

$$SS_{between} = \left[\Sigma \frac{(\Sigma Xi)^2}{Ni} \right] - \frac{(\Sigma Xt)^2}{Nt}$$

$$= \left[\frac{(22)^2}{3} + \frac{(10)^2}{3} + \frac{(9)^2}{3} \right] - \frac{1681}{9}$$

$$= (161.33 + 33.33 + 27.0) - 186.8 = 221.66 - 186.8 = 34.86$$

$SS_{between} = 34.86$

$$SS_{within} = \Sigma \left[\Sigma Xi^2 - \frac{(\Sigma Xi)^2}{Ni} \right]$$

$$= \left[166 - \frac{22^2}{3} \right] + \left[34 - \frac{10^2}{3} \right] + \left[33 - \frac{9^2}{3} \right]$$

$$= (166 - 161.33) + (34 - 33.33) + (33 - 27)$$

$$= 4.67 + 0.67 + 6.0 = 11.34$$

$$\boxed{SS_{within} = 11.34}$$

$$SS_{between} + SS_{within} = SS_{total}$$

$$34.86 + 11.34 = 46.2$$

Compute mean squares.

$$MS_{between} = \frac{SS_{between}}{df} = \frac{34.86}{2} = 17.43$$

$$MS_{within} = \frac{SS_{within}}{df} = \frac{11.34}{6} = 1.89$$

Compute the F ratio.

$$F = \frac{MS_{between}}{MS_{within}} = \frac{17.43}{1.89} = 9.22$$

With 2 and 6 df, the tabular critical value is 5.14 at $\alpha = .05$. Computed F exceeds this value. Reject the null; the combinational method is significantly better.

Compute eta squared.

$$\eta^2 = \frac{SS_{between}}{SS_{total}} = \frac{34.86}{46.2} = .754$$

The type of instruction used explains 75.4 percent of the variance in test scores.

Which pairs of means differ? Compute Tukey's HSD.

$Df_{within} = N - k = 6$. We are comparing three groups. The studentized range value for $df = 6$, and $k = 3$ is 4.34.

$$HSD = \sqrt{\frac{MS_{within}}{Ni}} = 4.34\frac{1.89}{\sqrt{3}} = 4.34\sqrt{.63}$$

$$= (4.34)(.794) = 3.446$$

The minimum difference between groups for significance at .05 = 3.446. Group 1 ($\bar{X} = 7.33$) differs from group 2 ($\bar{X} = 3.33$) by 4 points, and from group 3 ($\bar{X} = 3.0$) by 4.33 points. Group 1 differs significantly from groups 2 and 3. Groups 2 and 3 do not differ significantly.

APPENDIX: Computer Instructions for One-Way ANOVA

Command 7.1

SPSSx	SAS
ONEWAY TOTAL BY SUP (1,3)/	PROC GLM;
RANGES = SCHEFFE/	CLASS SUP;
	MODEL TOTAL = SUP;
	MEANS SUP/SCHEFFE;

Since this is an unbalanced model (unequal group sizes) we have to use the SAS PROC GLM (general linear model) rather than ANOVA. Don't let the SAS name change confuse you; we are still performing ANOVA. SPSSx retains the ANOVA command regardless of whether or not the design is balanced. However, if we wish to include a test of significance between each sample in the analysis, we have to use the SPSSx ONEWAY (one-way analysis of variance) program. Also because of our unbalanced design we have to use the Scheffe multiple comparison test rather than HSD. The CLASS SUP command tells the computer that the independent variable is SUP. There are three conditions of SUP: Supreme Court, Congress, and unattributed. The MODEL TOTAL = SUP indicates that the variance in the variable called total is to be found divided among the three categories of SUP. The SCHEFFE command says that you want to determine significance levels among all pairs of groups.

Chapter 8

Two-Way Analysis of Variance

One-way ANOVA examines the effects of a single independent variable on a continuous dependent variable. **Two-way ANOVA** examines the effects of two independent variables on the dependent variable. In experimental research the researcher randomly assigns subjects to experimental and control groups and then manipulates the independent variable. Since subjects are randomly assigned, the researcher is reasonably assured that any post-test difference in the dependent variable is accounted for by the independent variable. The random assignment of subjects into one of the two groups essentially means that all potentially confounding additional variables are evenly distributed across both samples. In experimental research, a one-way ANOVA is sufficient to test the null hypothesis. In nonexperimental research, however, we cannot be confident that all subjects are fairly similar in terms of other variables that may influence scores on the dependent variable. This being the case, researchers have to attempt to eliminate the influence of additional variables by statistical control. This is done by incorporating one or more additional variables that are theoretically meaningful into an ANOVA. We will focus on two-way ANOVA in this chapter.

For our illustration of two-way ANOVA we will add the variable of gender to that of class standing (Chapter 7) and see what effect it has on our previous findings. In addition to class standing, we are also interested in determining if gender has any effect on levels of general knowledge and whether the effects (if any) of class standing on general knowledge are the same regardless of sex. With three levels of class standing and two sexes, we have $3 \times 2 = 6$ different combinations or conditions. This type of analysis is known as a 2×3 factorial design. Table 8.1 presents the raw data within each of the six conditions. We have calculated the cell, column, row, and grand means.

TABLE 8.1   PRELIMINARY CALCULATIONS FOR ANOVA OF GENERAL KNOWLEDGE
BY CLASS STANDING AND SEX

	Factor 1: Class Standing			
	Soph.	Jun.	Sen.	Row totals and means
Male	73	72	83	
	75	78	86	
	77	74	89	
	225	224	258	707
Factor 2: Sex	$\bar{X} = 75$	$\bar{X} = 74.7$	$\bar{X} = 86$	$\bar{X} = 78.6$
Female	75	80	85	
	78	83	90	
	75	80	95	
	228	243	270	741
	$\bar{X} = 76$	$\bar{X} = 81$	$\bar{X} = 90$	$\bar{X} = 82.3$
Column totals	453	467	528	
Column means	$\bar{X} = 75.5$	$\bar{X} = 77.8$	$\bar{X} = 88$	$\bar{X} = 80.44$ (grand mean)

In one-way ANOVA we partitioned SS_{total} into two parts: between- and within-group components. Symbolically

$$SS_{total} = SS_{between} + SS_{within}$$

In a two-way ANOVA things get a little more complicated because we now have two classification schemes, class standing (a) and sex (b). Each individual is classified according to both of these variables. We will thus have two between-group contrasts to examine: between-group class standing (SSa) and between-group sex (SSb). Additionally, the effects of class standing on general knowledge may differ across categories of the sex variable. That is, these two variables may interact in a way that we might not predict solely from knowledge of the two variables examined separately. This means that we have yet another source of variance. In a two-way ANOVA, then, SS_{total} is partitioned four ways: SSa and SSb being separate **main effects** of the two variables; $SSab$, the **interaction** effects; and SS_{within}. Symbolically,

$$SS_{total} = SS_{between(a)} + SS_{between(b)} + SSab_{interaction} + SS_{within}$$

The first step is to compute the total sum of squares as we did before. Obviously, SS_{total} will not differ simply because we have now taken note of the sex of our respondents. Therefore, we will just turn back to Chapter 7 and find that $SS_{total} = 722.5$.

STEP 1.   Calculate SS_{total}.

$$SS_{total} = 722.5$$

Our next step is to calculate $SS_{between}$. However, $SS_{between}$ now has three components: SSa (class standing), SSb (sex), and $SSab$ (the interaction of class standing and sex). We will use the designation $SS_{explained}$ **(explained sum of squares)** to avoid confusion about which component we mean. The computational formula will be used again for ease of calculation and to minimize subtraction and rounding errors.

STEP 2.   Compute $SS_{explained}$ ($SSa + SSb + SSab$) by the formula.

$$SS_{explained} = \Sigma \left[\frac{(\Sigma Xc)^2}{Nc} \right] - \left[\frac{(\Sigma Xt)^2}{Nt} \right]$$

where c = cell totals

t = grand total

In prose, this formula instructs you to sum the values obtained by subtracting the sum of the observations in each individual cell squared and divided by the number of observations in the cell from the sum of the squared observations in the entire sample divided by the total number of observations in the sample. Putting in the numbers,

$$= \left(\frac{225^2}{3} + \frac{228^2}{3} + \frac{224^2}{3} + \frac{243^2}{3} + \frac{258^2}{3} + \frac{270^2}{3} \right) - \frac{2096704}{18}$$

$$= 16875 + 17328 + 16725.3 + 19683 + 22188 + 24300 - 116483.5 = 615.8$$

$$SS_{explained} = 615.8$$

STEP 3.   Partition SSt into components beginning with SSa (class standing). Note that this computation is exactly the same as $SS_{between}$ in the one-way ANOVA.

$$SSa = \left[\Sigma \frac{(\Sigma Xa)^2}{Na} \right] - \frac{(\Sigma Xt)^2}{Nt}$$

$$= \frac{453^2}{6} + \frac{467^2}{6} + \frac{528^2}{6} - \frac{1448^2}{18}$$

$$= 34201.5 + 36348.2 + 46463 - 116483.5 = 530.2$$

$$SSa = 530.2$$

STEP 4.   Compute SSb (sex). Note that in the computation of SSb we use the sum of squares summed across the rows.

$$SSa = \left[\Sigma \frac{(\Sigma Xb)^2}{Nb} \right] - \frac{(\Sigma Xt)^2}{Nt}$$

$$= \frac{707^2}{9} + \frac{741^2}{9} - \frac{1448^2}{18}$$

$$= 55538.8 + 61009 - 116483.5 = 64.3$$

$$\boxed{SSb = 64.3}$$

STEP 5.   Compute main effects (combined effects of class standing and sex).

$$SSm = SSa + SSb$$

$$= 530.2 + 64.3 = 594.5$$

$$\boxed{SSm = 594.5}$$

Compute $SSab$ (class standing $\times$ sex interaction).

$$SSab = SS_{explained} - SSm = 615.8 - 594.5 = 21.3$$

$$\boxed{SSab = 21.3}$$

STEP 6.   Compute SS_{within}.

$$SS_{within} = SS_{total} - SS_{explained} = 722.5 - 615.8 = 106.7$$

$$\boxed{SS_{within} = 106.7}$$

Notice in this example that $SSa + SSb + SSab = SS_{explained}$, and that $SS_{explained} + SS_{within} = SS_{total}$. This nice additive property, whereby $SS_{rows} + SS_{columns} + SS_{rows-by-columns} + SS_{within} = SS_{total}$, holds true only for the "classical" ANOVA case, where we have equal cell numbers. When we have unequal cell Ns, as is almost always the case in nonexperimental research, SS_{total} no longer defines completely separate (nonoverlapping) sources of variation.

8.1 DETERMINING STATISTICAL SIGNIFICANCE

Having partitioned the SS into their various components, we now have to determine, using the F ratio, if the observed effects are significant. As we have seen, the F ratio is easily calculated by dividing the SSs by their respective degrees of freedom to obtain the mean square and then calculating the ratio of the between-group mean square to the within-group mean square. We know that degrees of freedom in ANOVA are $N - 1$ for SS_{total} and $k - 1$ for a given condition. Determining the degrees of freedom for interaction effects is not quite so simple. Calculating $SSab$ involves row and column means, or marginals, as we would call them in tabular analysis. As we know, degrees of freedom are the number of values free to vary. When we calculated $SSab$ we did so by using the grand mean and the row and column means. To determine the degrees of freedom, we ask ourselves how many cell means are free to vary, given the grand mean and all marginal means (row and column means). Table 8.2 reproduces the grand mean and the row and column means for the present ANOVA problem. I have placed two cell means arbitrarily. Any two cells not in the same column will do. Notice that if we fill cell A we need not fill the tied cell D since knowing the value of cell A and the column mean renders D no longer free to vary. Convince yourself that once any two cell means not in the same column in a 3 × 2 table are known the values of the other cells are automatically determined (not free to vary).

TABLE 8.2   DETERMINING $dfSSab$

	A	B	C	Row $\bar{X}$s
	75			78.6
	D	E	F	82.3
			90	
Col. $\bar{X}$s	75.5	77.8	88	80.4

Therefore, $dfSSab$ are always determined by the number of rows minus 1 multiplied by the number of columns minus 1 $(r - 1)(c - 1)$. In a 3 × 2 table such as ours, $dfSSab = (2 - 1 = 1)(3 - 1 = 2)$, and $(1)(2) = 2$. A 2 × 2 design would have 1 df, and a 3 × 4 would have 6 df.

8.1.1 Significance Levels

The $SS_{between}$ for class standing in this two-way ANOVA are exactly the same as they were in the one-way ANOVA. However, the F ratio will not be the same because the addition of a second variable has changed SS_{within}. The F ratio for class standing is now

$$MS_{between} = \frac{SS_{between}}{df} = \frac{520.2}{2} = 265.1$$

$$MS_{within} = \frac{SS_{within}}{df} = \frac{106.7}{12} = 8.89$$

$$F = \frac{MS_{between}}{MS_{within}} = \frac{256.1}{8.89} = 29.82, \ p < .0001$$

We now compute F for the sex condition:

$$MS_{between} = \frac{SS_{between}}{df} = \frac{64.3}{1} = 64.3$$

$$MS_{within} = \frac{SS_{within}}{df} = \frac{106.7}{12} = 8.89$$

$$F = \frac{MS_{between}}{MS_{within}} = \frac{64.3}{8.89} = 7.23, \ p < .02$$

We now compute F for the interaction of class standing and sex:

$$MS_{ab \ interaction} = \frac{SS_{ab \ interaction}}{df} = \frac{21.3}{2} = 10.6$$

$$MS_{within} = \frac{SS_{within}}{df} = \frac{106.7}{12} = 8.89$$

$$F = \frac{MS_{ab \ interaction}}{MS_{within}} = \frac{10.6}{8.89} = 1.20, \ \text{n.s.}$$

The F ratios for the separate main effects are both statistically significant. We now determine the F ratio for the combined main effects of our two independent variables. The main effects are equal to the sum of the class standing SS plus the sex SS (530.2 + 64.3 = 594.5). The main effects SS is then divided by the degrees of freedom used in calculating both separate effects to obtain the mean square value. Since df is calculated by $(k - 1)$ and there were three categories of class standing, the df associated with this variable are $3 - 1 = 2$. Likewise, the df for the sex variables are $2 - 1 = 1$. Therefore, the df used to calculate the mean square for the main effects is $2 + 1 = 3$. The mean square obtained by dividing the main effects by its associated df is $594.5/3 = 198.2$. Dividing this value by the mean square of the within-group mean square ($106.7/12 = 8.89$), we get an F ratio of 22.29 ($198.2/8.89 = 22.29$). Again, this means that the between-group variation is 22.29 times larger than the within-group variation. The critical region for rejecting H at the .05 level with 3 and 12 df is 3.49, and at the .01 level it is 5.95. Our computed F exceeds both of these values by a wide margin. Table 8.3 summarizes the partitioning of variance for each condition and gives their F ratios.

TABLE 8.3 ANOVA SUMMARY TABLE

Source of Variance	SS	DF	Mean Square	F ratio	Sig.
Main effects	594.5	3	198.2	22.29	.000
Class standing	530.2	2	265.1	29.82	.000
Sex	64.3	1	64.3	7.23	.020
Two-way interaction	21.3	2	10.6	1.20	.333
Explained (main + interaction effects)	615.8	5	123.2	13.85	.000
Error (within group)	106.7	12	8.89		
Total (between + within + interaction + error)	722.5	17	42.5		

8.1.2 Tukey Test

Now that we have these summary results we can determine which means differ significantly by using the HSD test. Since we have six pairs of means to contrast, it is a good idea to set up a table of mean differences for instant comparison (see Table 8.4). Before we examine the table we will compute HSD for both the .05 and the .01 levels of significance. We enter the table with 3 and 12 *df* to determine these values and find them to be 3.77 and 5.04, respectively.

$$\text{HDS at } .05 = 3.77\sqrt{\frac{8.89}{3}} = 3.77\sqrt{2.96} = (3.77)(1.72) = 6.48$$

$$\text{HDS at } .01 = 5.04\sqrt{\frac{8.89}{3}} = 5.04\sqrt{2.96} = (5.04)(1.72) = 8.67$$

TABLE 8.4   TABLE OF DIFFERENCES BETWEEN PAIRS OF MEANS

	$\bar{X}ms$	$\bar{X}fs$	$\bar{X}mj$	$\bar{X}fj$	$\bar{X}mn$	$\bar{X}fn$
$\bar{X}ms = 75.0$	—	1.0	0.3	6.0	11.0*	15.0*
$\bar{X}fs = 76.0$		—	1.3	5.0	10.0*	14.0*
$\bar{X}mj = 74.7$			—	6.3	11.3*	15.3*
$\bar{X}fj = 81.0$				—	5.0	9.0*
$\bar{X}mn = 86.0$					—	4.0
$\bar{X}fn = 90.0$						

where m = male, f = female, s = sophomore, j = junior, n = senior

*$p < 0.01$ (i.e., all mean differences > 8.67).

8.1.3 Eta Squared

Having rejected the null hypothesis that class standing and sex are unrelated to the level of general knowledge, we now determine the percentage of variance explained by these variables both separately and jointly. To calculate eta for the effects of class standing on general knowledge, we simply divide the *SS* associated with class standing (530.2) by the total *SS* (722.5):

$$\eta^2 \text{ for class standing} = \frac{SSb}{SSt} = \frac{530.2}{722.5} = .734$$

Of course, this is the value we calculated in our one-way ANOVA. Eta², or eta squared for sex is obtained by dividing the *SS* associated with sex (64.3) by the SS_{total} (722.5):

$$\eta^2 \text{ for sex} = \frac{SSb}{SSt} = \frac{64.3}{722.5} = .089$$

Eta² for the model (the variance explained by both class standing and sex together) is obtained by dividing the main effects *SS* (594.5) by total *SS* (722.5):

$$\eta^2 \text{ for main effects} = \frac{SSm}{SSt} = \frac{594.5}{722.5} = .823$$

This value is called MULTIPLE R SQUARED in the SPSSx computer printout. Note that eta² class standing + eta² sex = eta² main effects (.734 + .089 = .823). Thus, class standing and sex combined explain 82.3 percent of the variance in general knowledge.

The variance explained by the interaction of *a* and *b* (21.3/722.5 = .029) is not added to the main effects variance because it is already accounted for by the two separate independent variables.

8.2 THE CONCEPT OF INTERACTION

Whenever we examine the effects of two or more independent variables on a dependent variable we must alert ourselves to the possibility of interaction effects. Interaction occurs when the effects of one independent variable differ significantly over levels of a second independent variable. Another way of putting it is to say that variation due to interaction effects is the variation in the dependent variable that is not attributable to either of the main effects or treated as error (within-group) variance. In our class standing/sex example we did not observe a significant interaction effect ($F = 0.333$). The insignificant F ratio tells us that the effects of class standing were identical, within the bounds of random error, over both levels of the sex variable. If the interaction effect had been significant we could not interpret the main effects in any meaningful way without first understanding the nature of the interaction effects.

Why can we not interpret main effects if we observe significant interaction? Let us suppose that although females increase their general knowledge as their class standing increases, males actually decrease theirs (an extremely improbable situation but useful to make our point). Since ANOVA combines the data from males and females to determine the effects of class standing, the increase in general knowledge among females would be largely canceled by the decrease among males. That is, the "average" effect of class standing would be about the same over the three conditions of the variable. Such a situation would suggest to us that we should run separate one-way ANOVAs for the males and females if we want to understand the effects of class standing on general knowledge.

Since the concept of interaction is somewhat difficult to grasp, a simple example in which there are no main effects but substantial interaction may help. Suppose we have ten males and ten females taking a test. One section of the test favors verbal abilities and the other favors performance (visual/spatial) abilities, but test results are rendered in terms of a composite (as in full-scale IQ, which is the mean of a person's performance + verbal IQ scores). However, since we have a test representing two kinds of abilities, we would like to know if males and females differ on them. To find out we break down the scores by subtests and perform a two-way ANOVA. Table 8.5 provides hypothetical data for such a test.

TABLE 8.5 DEMONSTRATING TWO-WAY ANOVA WITH NO MAIN EFFECTS AND SIGNIFICANT INTERACTION

	Subtest scores and computations			
	Verbal		Performance	
M	84	7056	110	12100
a	76	5776	102	10404
l	85	7225	98	9604
e	75	5625	90	8100
	80	6400	100	10000
	400	32082	500	50208
	$\bar{X} = 80$		$\bar{X} = 100$	
F	105	11025	85	7225
e	95	9025	75	5625
m	100	10000	70	4900
a	99	9801	90	8100
l	101	10201	80	6400
e				
	500	50052	400	32250
	$\bar{X} = 100$		$\bar{X} = 80$	

Summary table of means

	Verb.	Perf.	Row $\bar{X}$s
Male	80	100	90
Female	100	80	90
Col. $\bar{X}$s	90	90	90

$\Sigma X = 400 + 500 + 400 + 500 = 1800$

$\Sigma(X)^2 = (1800)^2 = 3240000$

$\Sigma X^2 = 32082 + 50208 + 50052 + 32250 = 164592$

It is obvious from the summary of means table in Table 8.5 that there are no main effects for sex over composite test scores. The mean test score is identical for both males and females at 90. Neither are there any main effects for test type averaged over tests; both tests resulted in an average score of 90. There is, however, substantial interaction. Females scored 20 percent better than males on the verbal test, and males scored 20 percent better on the performance test. Although we cannot calculate any main effects, it will be useful to calculate the interaction effects. We will now do so, beginning with SS_{total}.

$$SSt = \Sigma X^2 - \frac{(\Sigma Xt)^2}{Nt} = 164592 - \frac{3240000}{20} = 2592$$

Since we know there are no main effects for either sex or subtest type, we can simply calculate SSw.

$$SSw = \Sigma \left[\Sigma Xi^2 - \frac{(\Sigma Xi)^2}{Ni} \right]$$

$$= (32082 - \frac{400^2}{5}) + (50208 - \frac{500^2}{5}) + (50052 - \frac{500^2}{5}) + (32250 - \frac{400^2}{5})$$

$$= (32082 - 32000) + (50208 - 50000) + (50052 - 50000) + (32250 - 32000)$$

$$= 82 + 208 + 52 + 250 = 592$$

Since $SSt = 2592$ and $SSw = 592$, $SSab = 2000$.

We can now compute mean square for SSw and $SSab$:

$$MSw = \frac{SSw}{df} \quad \text{where } dfw = N - k = 20 - 4 = 16 = 592/16 = 37$$

$$MSab = \frac{SSab}{df} \quad \text{where } dfab = (r - 1)(c - 1) = (2 - 1)(2 - 1) = 1$$

$$= 2000/1 = 2000$$

We can now compute the F ratio for interaction effects:

$$F = \frac{MSab}{MSw} = \frac{2000}{37} = 54.054, \; p < .0001$$

We can conclude from the preceding that although test scores did not differ by sex nor by type of subtest, the interaction between sex and subtest type was highly significant: Males showed greater performance ability and females showed greater verbal ability.

Some texts talk about the interaction effect being the "joint" effect of the two independent variables. This term can lead to confusion because in one sense they are and in another they are not. The interaction effect is the joint effect in our example of class standing and sex in the sense that it represents the joint influence of class standing and sex *after* the main effects of class standing and sex operating independently have been accounted for. The interaction effect certainly is not the joint (combined) effect in an additive sense, as our discussion of eta squared demonstrated.

8.2.1 An Example of a Significant Interaction Effect from the Computer

The following serves both as a discussion of interaction effects and as a guide to interpreting two-way ANOVA computer output with SPSSx. Suppose we wish to determine the effects of victim/offender relationship and probation officer ideology on probation officers' recommendations for the sentencing of sex offenders. There are eight categories of the victim/offender relationship in our offender data.

Deciding that this number is too many, we collapse the eight categories into three more general conditions by using the recode command. These conditions are (1) In family (relatives of the victim), (2) acquaintances (neighbors, ex-girl-friends, etc.), and (3) strangers. We then divide the officers into two ideological groups by using questionnaire scores. Then we request a two-way ANOVA with command 8.1. The output produced by this command is shown in Table 8.6.

TABLE 8.6 A COMPUTER EXAMPLE OF TWO-WAY ANOVA

```
                               ***CELL MEANS***
                  POREC        RECOMMENDATION OF PROBATION OFFICER
                BY RELAT       RELATIONSHIP OF SUB TO VICTIM
                  PONAM        NAME OF OFFICER (Officer Ideology)

TOTAL POPULATION
    520.99
  (   351)
RELAT
       1         2         3
    311.30    410.27    926.05
  (   92)  (   166)  (    93)
PONAM
       1         2
    362.98    735.21
  (   202)  (   149)
         PONAM
                  1         2
RELAT
      1     287.74    340.61
          (   51)   (   41)
      2     318.73    580.72
          (  108)   (   58)
      3     563.33   1238.00
          (   43)   (   50)

                  ***ANALYSIS OF VARIANCE***

                  POREC        RECOMMENDATION OF PROBATION OFFICER
                BY RELAT         RELATIONSHIP OF SUB TO VICTIM
                  PONAM        NAME OF OFFICER (Officer Ideology)
```

SOURCE OF VARIATION	SUM OF SQUARES	DF	MEAN SQUARE	F	SIGNIF OF F
MAIN EFFECTS	29858903.689	3	9952967.896	22.218	0.000
RELAT	17977288.719	2	8988644.359	20.065	0.000
PONAM	8519771.725	1	8519771.725	19.019	0.000
2-WAY INTERACTIONS	4656985.602	2	2328492.801	5.198	0.006
RELAT PONAM	4656985.602	2	2328492.801	5.198	0.006
EXPLAINED	34515889.291	5	6903177.858	15.410	0.000
RESIDUAL	154549331.683	345	447969.077		
TOTAL	189065220.974	350	540186.346		

```
     431 CASES WERE PROCESSED.    80 CASES (18.6 PCT) WERE MISSING.
```

Interpreting the Printout   To start at the top of the table, the grand mean recommendation severity for all 351 sex offenders is 520.99. Following are the mean recommendation scores for the family (311.30), acquaintance (410.27), and stranger (926.05) categories. The next line gives us the mean recommendations for the liberal (362.98) and conservative (735.21) officers. This line is followed by six different categories listing the mean recommendations of liberal and conservative officers broken down by victim/offender relationship category.

Turning to the ANOVA results, we note that the separate main effects of RELAT and PONAM are both significant. Note in this example that the SSs associated with each of the separate main effects do not sum to the value labeled MAIN EFFECTS (we don't have an orthogonal design). Although the separate effects of victim/offender relationship and probation officer ideology are clearly significant, we cannot get an accurate picture unless we explore the interaction effects further. We will do so after we have explained the rest of the computer output. Note that SPSSx uses the term RESIDUAL rather than "error" to denote SS_{within}.

Below the ANOVA results in a SPSSx printout is what is known as a *multiple classification analysis* (MCA). MCA is a technique of standardization that tells us the net effects on the dependent variable of each of the independent variables in the model when the effects of each independent variable on the other are controlled for. The SPSSx manual (Nie et al., 1975, p. 409) states, "The MCA table can be viewed as a method of displaying the results of analysis of variance especially when there are no significant interaction effects." The present example was purposely chosen to demonstrate interaction, so we cannot use it to illustrate the MCA results.

Since it is important to gain some understanding of MCA, I will use a further example, substituting the victim's sex as the second independent variable for probation officer ideology. The ANOVA and MCA results are shown in Table 8.7. As you can see, there are no RELAT/VSEX interaction effects ($F = 1.625$). We will discuss only the MCA results. Note that unlike the POREC/PONAM example, we do not have any missing cases this time. Therefore, the grand mean (512.16) for POREC is different from that given in Table 8.6.

In the MCA table are the grand mean, the various categories of both of our independent variables, and the Ns for those categories. The UNADJUSTED DEV'N column shows the amount of deviation of each category mean from the grand mean before any adjustments are made for the presence of another variable. For instance, the in-family mean is 229.53 less than the grand mean (512.16 − 229.53 = 282.63). ETA is the zero-order correlation between the two variables. We note that eta for recommendation and victim/offender relationship is .39, and between victim's sex and recommendation it is .07. As I pointed out in Chapter 7, eta is simply the square root of eta squared. Therefore, the variance in recommendations accounted for by RELAT is 15.21 percent, and the variance accounted for by victim's sex is $.07^2 = .005$ percent.

The column ADJUSTED FOR INDEPENDENTS DEV'N contains the recommendation means after adjusting for the effects of the second independent variable. The adjusted means for the different categories are the means of those categories that we should observe if the offenders in those categories had the

TABLE 8.7   TWO-WAY ANOVA WITH MULTIPLE CLASSIFICATION ANALYSIS (SPSSx)

ANALYSIS OF VARIANCE

	POREC	RECOMMENDATION OF PROBATION OFFICER
	BY RELAT	RELATIONSHIP OF SUB TO VICTIM
	VSEX	SEX OF VICTIM

SOURCE OF VARIATION	SUM OF SQUARES	DF	MEAN SQUARE	F	SIG OF F
MAIN EFFECTS	32632688	3	10877562.563	25.364	.000
RELAT	31663046	2	15831523.171	36.916	.000
VSEX	192808	1	192807.602	.450	.503
2-WAY INTERACTIONS	1394094	2	697046.904	1.625	.198
RELAT VSEX	1394094	2	697046.904	1.625	.198
EXPLAINED	34026781	5	6805356.229	15.869	.000
RESIDUAL	182261490	425	428850.564		
TOTAL	216288271	430	502995.980		

MULTIPLE CLASSIFICATION ANALYSIS

	POREC	RECOMMENDATION OF PROBATION OFFICER
	BY RELAT	RELATIONSHIP OF SUB TO VICTIM
	VSEX	SEX OF VICTIM

GRAND MEAN = 512.16

VARIABLE + CATEGORY	N	UNADJUSTED DEV'N	ETA	ADJUSTED FOR INDEPENDENTS DEV'N	BETA
RELAT					
1 IN FAMILY	112	−229.53		−227.18	
2 ACQUAINTANCE	204	−127.35		−126.81	
3 STRANGER	115	449.45		446.21	
			.39		.38
VSEX					
1 FEMALE	368	−19.63		−8.79	
2 MALE	63	114.64		51.37	
			.07		.03
MULTIPLE R SQUARED					.151
MULTIPLE R					.388

same distribution on the control variable as the entire sample. This is analogous to adjusting mortality rates for age or adjusting annual income for inflation. For instance, the adjusted in-family mean of −227.18 is the mean of the in-family category after adjusting for the effect of victim's sex. A comparison of the unadjusted and adjusted means for each victim/offender relationship category shows that victim's sex has almost no effect.

We now turn to the MCA for the effects of victim's sex, adjusting for victim/offender relationship; the adjusted mean of 51.37 indicates that the mean recommendation for offenders convicted of assaulting male victims is 51.37 points greater than the grand mean after adjusting for the effects of victim/ offender relationship.

The next statistic in the MCA table is beta. We will be discussing beta in greater length in the chapters on regression. For now, think of it as being another measure of the strength of the relationship between two variables. In a

MCA analysis, beta is actually partial beta, or the strength of association between two variables after the effects of a third variable have been adjusted for. The partial beta is thus a measure of the strength of the association between POREC and RELAT after adjusting for the effects of VSEX. We can compare eta, which is equivalent to the bivariate zero-order beta in MCA, to the partial beta to observe the influence of the control variable. We see that the strength of the relationship between POREC and RELAT decreases slightly after adjusting for VSEX (eta = .39; beta = .38).

The MULTIPLE R SQUARED and the MULTIPLE R will also be discussed in later chapters. For now, multiple R is a measure of the strength of the association between POREC and the two independent variables combined. The multiple R squared is simply the square of multiple R, and it represents the percentage of the variance in probation officers' recommendations accounted for by the additive effects of RELAT and VSEX. The multiple R squared value is .151, indicating that 15.1 percent of the variance in probation officers' recommendations is accounted for by the additive effects of both independent variables.

8.2.2 A Further Look at Interaction

The concept of interaction is synonymous with parallelism in the sense that lines drawn between means of the dependent variable (Y) across values of the first independent variable (X) for fixed values of the second independent variable (V) are parallel. If the lines linking the values of Y on X remain generally parallel regardless of the value of V, there is no X-by-V interaction. If there is significant X-by-V interaction, the lines will not be parallel. We will now plot the recommendation means for each victim/offender category for both the liberal and conservative officers in Figure 8.1.

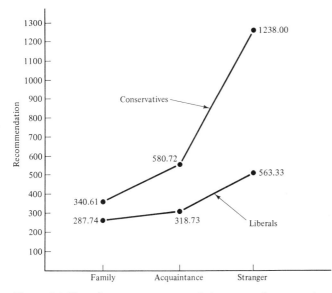

Figure 8.1 Plot of sentence recommendation means for categories of victim/offender relationship by probation officer ideology

Having plotted the means across categories of victim/offender relationships in Figure 8.1, we see that the lines drawn between the means for the liberal and conservative officers are not parallel. Although there is clearly a linear relationship between recommendation severity and victim/offender relationship for both sets of officers, the severity of the effects depends quite a lot on the probation officers' ideology. This type of interaction is not so interpretively difficult as one in which the levels of the second independent variable produce opposite results. For example, if the plot of means for the liberal officers remained the same as seen in Figure 8.1, but the ranking of the conservative officers' recommendation means were stranger, acquaintance, and family, we would have the crossover effect illustrated in cell D of Figure 8.2. Such a distribution of means would render the main effects totally uninterpretable.

The preceding results suggest that we could get a more accurate picture of recommendation severity and victim/offender relationship if we examined it within separate categories of probation officers' ideology. We ran three separate ANOVAs with our data to demonstrate: one with conservative officers only; one with liberal officers only; and one combining the officers, that is, without taking ideology into account. This exercise produced the results shown in Table 8.8.

Table 8.8 shows that if we compute a one-way ANOVA for recommendation means for categories of the victim/offender relationship, ignoring probation officers' ideology, we obtain a significant F ratio and account for 15 percent of the variance. We also see from the table that the effects of victim/offender relationship on officers' recommendations are more than four times as great for offenders processed by conservative officers (16.8 percent of the variance) as for offenders processed by liberal officers (4 percent). We now have a more complete picture.

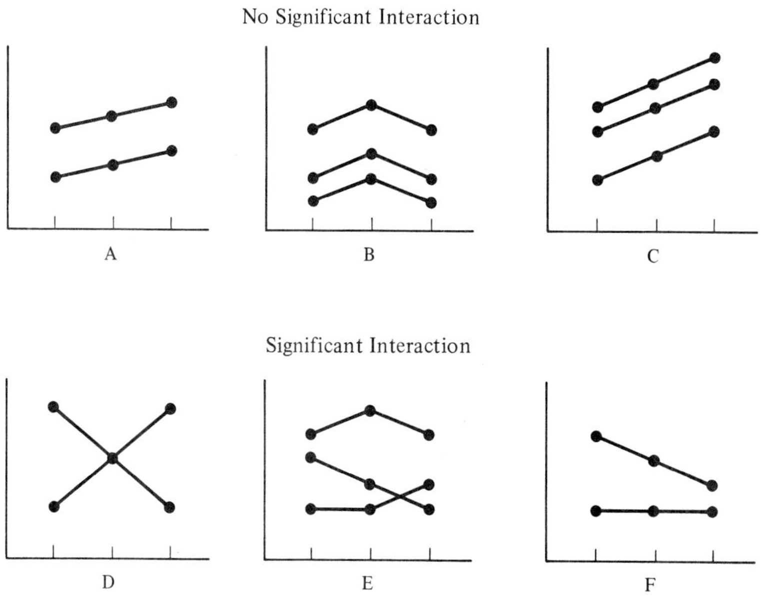

No Significant Interaction

Significant Interaction

Figure 8.2 Illustrating interaction

TABLE 8.8   SEPARATE ANOVA RESULTS FOR COMBINED CATEGORIES OF OFFICERS, LIBERALS, AND CONSERVATIVES, FOR EFFECTS OF VICTIM/ OFFENDER RELATIONSHIP ON SENTENCING RECOMMENDATION

Condition	F	Sig.	eta^2	N
Combined	37.765	.0000	.150	351
Liberals	4.163	.0169	.040	202
Conservatives	14.701	.0000	.168	149

The process of computing two separate ANOVAs when interaction is detected is called *elaboration,* which is discussed in great detail in Chapter 11. The two separate ANOVAs give us essentially the same results as the ANOVA with both sets of officers combined, in the sense that the relationship between officers' recommendations and victim/offender remains significant across both categories of probation officers' ideology. However, we have also specified that the relationship is particularly strong in the conservative officer category. (Why is the F ratio stronger in the combined condition than it is in the conservative condition, whereas the eta squared value is smaller? Think back to the previous discussion of the effect of sample size on significance levels.)

8.2.3 Illustrating Interaction

In Figure 8.2, there are six graphs with plotted means. The top three illustrate cases in which there is no interaction (parallel lines) and the bottom three illustrate interaction effects (nonparallel lines).

8.3 OTHER FACTORIAL DESIGNS AND HIGHER-ORDER INTERACTIONS

We have discussed one-way and two-way ANOVAs as 3×2 factorial designs. There are many other designs that could be used. For example, if we added race to class standing and sex for our general knowledge design, we would have a $3 \times 2 \times 2$ design (three levels of class standing, two levels of sex, and two levels of race). The number of factors and of their levels can be increased up to the computer program's limitation for handling interaction levels (five interaction levels).

However, too many factors and levels tend to get quite messy in terms of interpretation. Consider a $3 \times 2 \times 2$ design for class standing, sex, and race. You would have main effects for the three levels of class standing, for the two levels of sex, and for the two levels of race. You would also have the following interactions to interpret:

1. Class standing $\times$ sex
2. Class standing $\times$ race
3. Sex $\times$ race
4. Class standing $\times$ sex $\times$ race

As more independent variables are added the interactions become more and more complicated. If we added just one more variable to get a $3 \times 2 \times 2 \times 2$ design, we would have ten interaction effects to interpret. There are easier ways to handle and conceptualize the effects of independent variables on an interval or ratio variable. These techniques—multiple regression and dummy variable regression—will be discussed in Chapters 13 and 14, respectively.

8.4 SUMMARY

Two-way analysis of variance is an extension of one-way ANOVA to include the effects of a second independent variable. In a two-way ANOVA the SS_{total} is partitioned four ways—$SS_{between}(a) + SS_{between}(b) + SSab + SS_{within}$.

$SSab$, or interaction, is a very important concept. If the effects of one independent variable differ significantly over levels of the second independent variable, interaction occurs. Interaction renders the interpretation of the main effects problematic. If the interaction effects are significant, you must dig further into the data to understand what is going on. One way to do so is to plot a table of means.

There are many other possible factorial designs in ANOVA. These higher-order designs include multiple tests for interaction and can be quite messy in terms of interpretation.

PRACTICE APPLICATION:
TWO-WAY ANALYSIS OF VARIANCE

Researchers are interested in the problem of maintaining self-esteem among multiple sclerosis patients. They hypothesize that patients who have to use some form of walking aid or who are bedridden will have lower levels of self-esteem than those who have no ambulatory restrictions. They are also interested in whether or not the patients' attitude about the disease affects self-esteem. Attitude about the disease is a three-category variable: denial, acceptance, and integration. These attitude "stages" closely follow the Kubler-Ross stages of death and dying. The table is set out in 3×2 factorial design, and means are calculated.

Set up the table of raw scores and means.

$$\Sigma X = 672 \qquad \Sigma X^2 = 25944 \qquad (\Sigma X)^2 = 451584$$

STEP 1.   Compute SS_{total}.

$$SS_{total} = \Sigma Xt^2 - \frac{(\Sigma Xt)^2}{Nt} = 25944 - \frac{451584}{18}$$

$$= 25944 - 25088 = 856$$

$$\boxed{SS_{total} = 856}$$

Activity Restriction (B)	Attitude Stage (A)						Row Means and Totals
	Denial		Acceptance		Integration		
	X	X^2	X	X^2	X	X^2	
Fully ambulatory	42	1764	31	961	44	1936	
	40	1600	45	2025	50	2500	
	35	1225	37	1369	40	1600	
	117		113		134		364
	$\bar{X} = 39.0$		$\bar{X} = 37.67$		$\bar{X} = 44.67$		40.45
Restricted	32	1024	31	961	42	1764	
	23	529	43	1849	36	1296	
	38	1444	24	576	39	1521	
	93		98		117		308
	$\bar{X} = 31.0$		$\bar{X} = 32.67$		$\bar{X} = 39.0$		34.22
Column Totals	210		211		251		
X^2 totals		7586		7741		10617	
Column means	$\bar{X} = 35.0$		$\bar{X} = 35.17$		$\bar{X} = 41.83$		$\bar{X} = 37.33$

STEP 2.   Compute $SS_{explained}$ $(SSa + SSb + SSab)$.

$$SS_{explained} = \Sigma \left[\frac{(\Sigma Xc)^2}{Nc} \right] - \frac{(\Sigma Xt)^2}{Nt}$$

$$= \left[\frac{117^2}{3} + \frac{93^2}{3} + \frac{113^2}{3} + \frac{98^2}{3} + \frac{134^2}{3} + \frac{117^2}{3} \right] - \frac{451584}{18}$$

$$= (4563 + 2883 + 4256.3 + 3201.3 + 5985.3 + 4563) - 25088$$

$$= 363.9$$

$$\boxed{SS_{explained} = 363.9}$$

STEP 3.   Partition SSt into components beginning with SSa (attitude stage).

$$SSa = \left[\Sigma \frac{(\Sigma Xa)^2}{Na} \right] - \frac{(\Sigma Xt)^2}{Nt}$$

$$= \left[\frac{210^2}{6} + \frac{211^2}{6} + \frac{251^2}{6} \right] - \frac{451584}{18}$$

$$= [7350 + 7420.2 + 10500.2] - 25088 = 182.4$$

$$\boxed{SSa = 182.4}$$

STEP 4.   Compute SSb (activity restriction).

$$SSa = \left[\Sigma \frac{(\Sigma Xb)^2}{Nb} \right] - \frac{(\Sigma Xt)^2}{Nt}$$

$$= \left[\frac{707^2}{9} + \frac{741^2}{9} \right] - \frac{451584}{18}$$

$$= [14721.8 + 10540.4] - 25088 = 174.2$$

$$\boxed{SSb = 174.2}$$

STEP 5.   Compute main effects (combined effects of class standing and sex).

$$SSm = SSa + SSb = 182.4 + 174.2 = 356.6$$

$$\boxed{SSm = 356.6}$$

STEP 6.   Compute $SSab$ (attitude stage $\times$ activity restriction).

$$SSab = SS_{explained} - SSm = 363.9 - 356.6 = 7.3$$

$$\boxed{SSab = 7.3}$$

STEP 7.   Compute SS_{within}.

$$SS_{within} = SS_{total} - SS_{explained} = 856 - 363.9 = 492.1$$

$$\boxed{SS_{within} = 492.1}$$

STEP 8.   Compute mean square MS ($df = k - 1$) for explained, attitude stage, activity restriction, interaction, and within.

$$MS_{explained} = SS_{explained}/df = 363.9/5 = 72.78$$

$$MS_{main} = SS_{main}/df = 356.6/3 = 118.87$$

$$MS_{attitude} = SSa/df = 184.1/2 = 92.1$$

$$MS_{restriction} = SSb/df = 174.2/1 = 174.2$$

$$MS_{interaction} = SSab/df = 7.3/2 = 3.65$$

$$MS_{within} = SS_{within/df} = 492.1/12 = 41.0$$

STEP 9.   Compute F ratios with 0.05 significance level.

explained effects $= MS_{explained}/MS_{within} = 72.78/41.0 = 1.77$
with 5.12 df, F is not significant
(F critical at .05 $= 3.11$)
combined (main) effects $= MS_{main}/MS_{within} = 118.87/41.0 = 2.9$
with 3.12 df, F is not significant
(F critical at .05 $= 3.49$)

attitude effects $= MS_{att}/MS_{within} = 92.1/41.0 = 2.25$
with 2.12 df, F is not significant
(F critical at .05 $= 3.88$)

restriction effects $= MS_{res}/MS_{within} = 174.2/41.0 = 4.25$
with 1.12 df, F is not significant
(F critical at .05 $= 4.75$)

interaction effects $= MS_{int}/MS_{error} = 7.3/41.0 = .178$
with 2.12 df, F is not significant
(F critical at .05 $= 3.88$)

STEP 10.   Compute eta^2.

explained effects eta$^2 = SSex/SSt = 363.9/856.0 = .425$

attitude effects eta$^2 = SSa/SSt = 182.4/856.0 = .213$

restriction effects eta$^2 = SSb/SSt = 174.2/856.0 = .203$

Although we have accounted for a large proportion of the variance in self-esteem levels and we observed no interaction, none of our F ratios was significant. We must fail to reject the null hypothesis that there is no difference in self-esteem based on attitude and activity restriction. An increase in sample size is called for here. Since the overall F test is not significant, it would be pointless to compute HSD.

APPENDIX: Computer Instructions

Computer Command 8.1

SPSSx

```
RECODE PONAM (02,03,05,06,07,10,11,14,20,21,29,30=1)(0,1,04,08,09,
              12,15,16,17,19,28=2)(ELSE=3)
RECODE RELAT (1,2,3=1)(4,5,6,7=2)(8=3)
SELECT IF (GROUP EQ 2)
ANOVA POREC BY RELAT (1,3) PONAM (1,2)
STATISTICS ALL
```

SAS

```
IF GROUP = 2;
IF PONAM = 02 OR PONAM = 03 OR PONAM = 05 OR PONAM = 06 OR PONAM = 07
OR PONAM = 10 OR PONAM = 11 OR PONAM = 14 OR PONAM = 20 OR
PONAM = 21 OR PONAM = 29 OR PONAM = 30 THEN PONAM = 1;
ELSE IF PONAM = 01 OR PONAM = 04 OR PONAM = 08 OR PONAM = 09
OR PONAM = 12 OR PONAM = 15 OR PONAM = 16 OR PONAM = 17 OR PONAM = 19
OR PONAM = 28 THEN PONAM = 2;
ELSE IF PONAM = 13 OR PONAM = 18 OR PONAM = 22 OR PONAM = 23
OR PONAM = 24 OR PONAM = 25 OR PONAM = 26 OR PONAM = 27 OR PONAM = 31
THEN PONAM = ;
IF RELAT < = 3 THEN RELAT = 1;
IF RELAT = > 4 AND RELAT < = 7 THEN RELAT = 2;
IF RELAT = 8 THEN RELAT = 3;
IF RELAT = > 9 THEN RELAT = ;
PROC GLM;
CLASS RELAT PONAM;
MODEL POREC = RELAT*PONAM RELAT PONAM;
MEANS RELAT PONAM RELAT*PONAM;
```

All the probation officers recoded into group 1 by "name of officer" (PONAM) are conservative officers, and all those recoded into group 2 are liberal officers. The remaining officers in group 3 are those who were not employed at the probation department at the time we administered the conservative/liberal questionnaire. Thus, we have lost a number of cases, leaving us with 351 cases for analysis. We have recoded the RELAT variable into the three categories described in the text, and we have selected only the sex offenders. RELAT (1,3) indicates groups 1 through 3 are the RELAT groups to be analyzed, and PONAM (1,2) indicates groups 1 and 2 of the officer ideology variable are to be included. SAS requires you to specify the analysis of interaction effects and request category means. SPSSx gives you this information routinely.

REFERENCE AND SUGGESTED READING

Iversen, R., and Norpoth, H. (1976). *Analysis of variance.* Beverly Hills, CA: Sage. An excellent introduction to more advanced topics in ANOVA

Nie, N., Hadlaihull, C., Jenkins, J., Steinbrenner, K., and Brent, D. (1975). *SPSS statistical package for the social sciences.* New York: McGraw-Hill. This earlier edition of the SPSS manual has better explanations of computer output than later editions of SPSSx.

Chapter 9

Hypothesis Testing with Categorical Data: Chi-Square

One of the most useful and popular tools in social science research is crosstabulation, or joint contingency analysis, using a statistic known as chi-square. The **chi-square test of independence** is a test of significance that is used for discrete data in the form of frequencies, percentages, or proportions. Chi-square is one of a number of tests of significance and measures of association known as *nonparametric* statistics. This terminology should not imply that the populations from which the data are gathered do not have parameters—which is a logical impossibility. The term simply means that unlike their parametrical counterparts, such as *z, t,* and *F,* nonparametric statistics do not require any assumptions to be made regarding the underlying population. These assumptions, you will recall, are that the population is normally distributed or has a known standard deviation. In other words, nonparametric tests are less restrictive than parametric tests. The trade-off for this characteristic is that they are less powerful than their parametric counterparts, which means that when using such tests we are less likely to reject a null hypothesis that should be rejected. Nevertheless, if our data do not meet the stringent demands of parametric tests, nonparametric tests are useful substitutes.

This observation should not lead to dismissal of nonparametric tests as simply "poor relatives" of parametric tests. In fact, a popular science magazine listed the development of chi-square as one of the 20 most important advances in science of the twentieth century (Hacking, 1984, p. 69).

A 2 × 2 chi-square analysis is perhaps the most fundamental statistical technique. Many of the variables with which social science deals are in two values: yes/no, agree/disagree, male/female, for/against, and so on. And two variables is the minimum number we can test for relatedness. Thus, joint contingency analysis deals with the minimum number of variables that can be related (2), each of which has the minimum number of values that a variable can have (2). What could be more basic? In such an analysis, variables measured at the nominal and ordinal levels are displayed in rows and columns in a table to determine their joint frequency. Let us take a very simple example to illustrate joint frequency.

9.1 TABLE CONSTRUCTION

Suppose we are interested in determining whether men and women differ in their stated willingness to vote for a woman for president of the United States regardless of her political party. We collect data from ten men and ten women and ask them this question. Having done so, we have two nominal-level variables called *sex* and *vote,* each having two attributes, male/female, and yes/no. The research hypothesis states that willingness to vote for a female candidate is dependent on gender. Our null hypothesis assumes that these two variables are independent of one another, meaning that willingness to vote for a female candidate and gender of voter are unrelated variables: Men are just as likely as women to report that they would vote for a female candidate. Otherwise put, independence means that the classification of a case into one category (in this case, sex), does not affect the probability that the case will fall into a particular category of the other variable (willingness to vote for a woman). Having selected our sample we discover the distribution in Table 9.1.

TABLE 9.1   TALLY OF MALES AND FEMALES WHO WOULD AND WHO WOULD NOT VOTE FOR A FEMALE CANDIDATE FOR PRESIDENT

Men	Women
no	yes
no	no
yes	yes
no	yes
no	yes
yes	no
no	yes
yes	no
no	no
yes	yes

We count up our responses and discover that four men would vote for a female candidate and six men would not, and that six women would and four would not. We can now put these figures into a bivariate table showing their joint distribution on the two variables.

There are a few rules of thumb for constructing a table. Conventionally, the independent variable is placed at the top of the table and summed downward in the columns, and the dependent variable is placed at the side and summed across the rows. The sums of each row and column are reported and placed in the **mar-**

TABLE 9.2   VOTE BY SEX

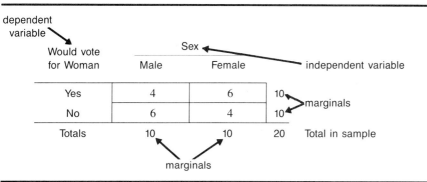

ginals, and the total number of cases is also reported. Let us put our data into a bivariate table, Table 9.2.

We now have four mutually exclusive categories or cells informing us of the joint distribution of the two variables: men who would vote for a woman ($n = 4$), men who would not ($n = 6$), women who would ($n = 6$), and women who would not ($n = 4$). We have labeled the categories of both variables and reported the marginals. All marginals happen to be equal in size in this example, and the two sets of marginals sum to 20. (If your row marginals do not sum to the same figure as your column marginals you have made an error in addition.) Sex is listed as the independent variable since being male or female can conceivably influence one's willingness to vote for a female, but willingness to vote for a female obviously cannot influence one's sex.

9.1.1 Putting Percentages in Tables

It is always useful to report percentages in the tables. What percentage of men would vote for a female? There are four men out of a total of ten who would. Therefore $4/10 = .4 \times 100 = 40$ percent. Similarly, $6/10 = .6 \times 100 = 60$ percent of the women in the sample would do so. After computing all the cell percentages we arrive at a table such as Table 9.3.

TABLE 9.3   PUTTING PERCENTAGES IN TABLE AND RULES FOR COMPARING

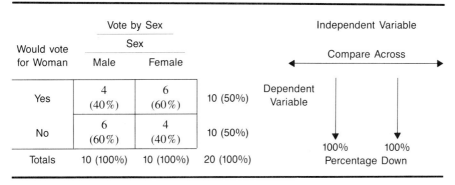

When putting percentages in tables the basic rule is to compute percentages in the direction of the independent variable (down the columns). This rule makes sense since we want to compare the distribution on the dependent variable within our categories of the independent variable. In the present example, we see that four males and six females (the independent variable) would vote for a female for president (the affirmative category of the dependent variable). Thus, we percentage down and compare across. Column percentages will, within rounding error, always sum to 100 percent; that is, each column represents 100 percent of each category of the independent variable.

We report percentages because they standardize the distribution, making interpretation easier. The interpretation of our sex/vote table is fairly easy because of the equal marginal values and the fairly equal cell frequencies. We can see almost instantly that sex is somehow related to willingness to vote for a female candidate for president of the United States. If we had highly unequal cell frequencies, the interpretation would be ambiguous if we did not report cell percentages along with raw numbers.

Assumptions for the Use of Chi-Square

1. We have independent random samples.
2. The data are nominal or ordinal-level.
3. No expected cell frequency is less than 5.

We now wish to determine if this difference between the sexes in their willingness to vote for a woman could have occurred simply by chance. That is, we wish to determine if willingness to vote is *independent* of gender. There are two possibilities: (1) The observed difference in willingness to vote in our sample is also true in the population from which the sample was drawn. (2) There is no gender-based difference in willingness to vote in the general population; the observed difference is simply a function of random chance. The null hypothesis specific to this issue is expressed symbolically as

$$H_0 : Pm = Pf$$

where Pm = probability of males willing to vote

Pf = probability of females willing to vote

We are testing the hypothesis that the same proportion of males and females would be willing to vote for a female candidate. Put another way, we are testing the hypothesis that the *observed* frequencies in the table equal the frequencies we would *expect* under conditions of random chance. To test the present null hypothesis we compute chi-square, the formula for which is

$$\chi^2 = \sum \frac{(O - E)^2}{E} \tag{9.1}$$

where O = observed cell frequency

E = expected cell frequency if null hypothesis is true

Stated in prose form, chi-square equals the sum of the observed frequencies minus the expected frequencies squared, divided by the expected frequency. We already know the observed frequencies. The expected frequencies are computed by Formula 9.2.

$$E = \frac{(\text{column marginal})(\text{row marginal})}{N} \tag{9.2}$$

This formula says that to get the expected frequency for each cell we multiply the relevant column marginal by the relevant row marginal and then divide that value by N (the total number of cases in the sample). As we compute each expected frequency, we place it in the appropriate cell of an expected frequency table. Given the equal marginals in our example, it does not really rquire any computations to determine what the expected cell frequencies would be if chance alone were operating. For an N of 20 with equal marginals we would expect five cases in each of the four cells. I presented this extremely simplified set of data so that you might intuitively grasp the idea that given a sample of ten individuals of one type and ten individuals of another type, and given that ten individuals, regardless of sex, would vote for a woman and ten would not, we would expect five cases in each cell if chance alone was operating.

How would we expect the frequencies to be distributed in the more difficult example in Table 9.4 if there were no sex difference in the willingness to vote for a woman? We would expect the percentage of men willing to vote for a female to be equal to the percentage of women who would do so, and both percentages to be equal to the percentage of the whole sample, regardless of sex, who would vote for a female. We see from Table 9.4 that the overall percentage of those who would vote for a woman is 54.2 percent (128/236). Thus, 54.2 percent of the

TABLE 9.4   WILLINGNESS TO VOTE FOR WOMAN BY SEX

Would vote for Woman	Sex		
	Male	Female	
Yes	A 47 (40.5%)	B 81 (67.5%)	128 (54.2%)
No	C 69 (59.5%)	D 39 (32.5%)	108 (45.8%)
Totals	116 (100%)	120 (100%)	236

expected frequency for A = 116 × 128/236 = 14848/236 = 62.9

expected frequency for B = 120 × 128/236 = 15360/236 = 65.1

expected frequency for C = 116 × 108/236 = 12528/236 = 53.1

expected frequency for D = 120 × 108/236 = 12960/236 = 54.9

males and 54.2 percent of the females would be expected to report a willingness to vote for a woman if sex did not influence a person's willingness. In other words, we would expect $116 \times 54.2/100 = 62.9$ males and $120 \times 54.2/100 = 65.1$ females reporting a willingness to vote for a female candidate. The same strategy is used for calculating percentages for those unwilling. Note that

$$\frac{116 \times 54.2}{100} = \frac{116 \times 128}{236} = \frac{\text{column marginal} \times \text{row marginal}}{N}$$

This discussion demonstrates the logic behind calculating expected frequencies. In practice, however, expected frequencies are more easily computed from raw numbers than from percentages. Let us do these calculations from Table 9.4. We have labeled the cells A, B, C, and D, and we will calculate the expected frequencies one cell at a time.

We place the computed expected frequencies into a table of expected frequencies (Table 9.5). Note that although the cell frequencies have changed, the row and marginal frequencies are exactly the same. If they are not, there has been an error in calculation.

We now have to calculate chi-square by subtracting the expected frequency from the observed frequency for each individual cell, square that value, and divide the result by the expected frequency. When we have done this for each cell, we sum the resulting values to get the chi-square value.

$$
\begin{aligned}
\chi^2 &= \frac{(47 - 62.9)^2}{62.9} + \frac{(81 - 65.1)^2}{65.1} + \frac{(69 - 53.1)^2}{53.1} + \frac{(39 - 54.9)^2}{54.9} \\
&= \frac{252.81}{62.9} + \frac{252.81}{65.1} + \frac{252.81}{53.1} + \frac{252.81}{54.9} \\
&= 4.02 \qquad + 3.88 \qquad + 4.76 \qquad + 4.60 \\
&= 17.26
\end{aligned}
$$

To determine if this value is significant, we must first determine the degrees of freedom. We defined degrees of freedom in Chapter 6 as the number of values free to vary. In the case of tabular analysis we are estimating expected cell frequencies from a given set of marginals, and df equals the number of rows minus 1 multiplied by the number of columns minus 1.

TABLE 9.5 TABLE OF EXPECTED FREQUENCIES

Would vote for Woman	Sex		
	Male	Female	
Yes	A 62.9	B 65.1	128
No	C 53.1	D 54.9	108
Totals	116	120	236

TABLE 9.6   DEGREES OF FREEDOM IN TABULAR ANALYSIS

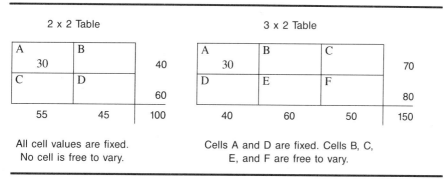

$$df = (R - 1)(C - 1)$$

For a 2 × 2 table, df would be $(2 - 1)(2 - 1) = (1)(1) = 1$, and for a 3 × 3 table, df would be 4. Table 9.6 illustrates the idea of df in the case of tabular analysis. In the 2 × 2 table we see that for a given set of marginals, once we know the value of one cell the rest are no longer free to vary. If we know cell A = 30, we know that cell B has to be 10, that cell C has to be 25, and that cell D has to be 35. In the 3 × 2 table, however, knowing that cell A is 30 will tell us only that cell D has to be 10. We need one more cell value to render the remaining cells fixed. Convince yourself of this truth by adding a cell frequency to any cell other than D (which is not free to vary, given A) and watch the remainder fall nicely into place.

For our 2 × 2 table, then, $df = 1$. We now have to turn to Appendix E where we find the chi-square distribution table to determine if our computed chi-square value of 17.26 is statistically significant. We look at the column labeled df to find the place where $df = 1$ (this is the very first row for our example). We then trace across the row until we get to the spot designated by .05. If our computed value exceeds the value of 3.841, we can say that our chi-square value is significant at the .05 level, meaning that if we took an infinite number of samples of the same composition and size, we could expect to find such a result by chance alone five times in every 100 samplings. Our computed chi-square greatly exceeds this value, so we are fairly confident that our sample was not drawn from a population in which our two variables are unrelated. The 3.841 value for chi-square is known as the critical value, meaning that it is the minimum value of chi-square that is necessary to reject the null hypothesis that the variables are independent of one another at the .05 probability level.

We can be even more confident than at the .05 level because our computed value exceeds even the .01 level of confidence (6.635), which means that we could expect a similar result by chance only once in every 100 samplings. Therefore, we are extremely confident that the relationship between sex and willingness to vote for a female found among the respondents in our sample is also true within the general population from which it was drawn. In other words, females

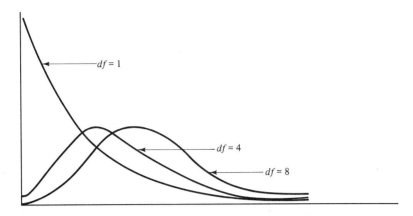

Figure 9.1 Chi-square distribution at 1, 4, and 8 degrees of freedom

are significantly more likely than males to report that they would vote for a female candidate. Thus, we reject the null hypothesis.

If we wish to go a little further to determine whether our computed value is a function more of female willingness to vote for a female or male unwillingness, we merely have to examine the relative magnitude of the four components for the major departures from independence. Male unwillingness (cell C) departs most from independence, with a component value of 4.76, whereas female willingness (cell B) departs least from independence, with a value of 3.88. Thus our computed value of chi-square is a function more of male unwillingness than female willingness.

9.2 THE CHI-SQUARE DISTRIBUTION

As is the case with the t and F distributions, the shape of the **chi-square distribution** is entirely determined by the degrees of freedom, and each df value describes a unique distribution. Figure 9.1 gives examples of the chi-square distribution at 1, 4, and 8 degrees of freedom. Note that the chi-square distribution is not symmetric and that it is skewed to the right. This does not mean that we are performing a one-tailed or directional test. Chi-square testing yields only positive results because it is arrived at by squaring the differences between observed and expected frequencies. The chi-square distribution becomes more and more symmetrical as the degrees of freedom increase, and it begins to look like the normal curve with df greater than 30.

We saw earlier that the t distribution becomes identical in shape to the z distribution when $df > 120$. To give you a further appreciation of the symmetry of statistics, it is also true that the chi-square critical value of 3.841, with $df = 1$, is equal to the square of the critical z value of 1.96. Put otherwise, z squared is equal to chi-square under these conditions. Thus, our computed chi-square of 17.26 is equivalent to a z value of 4.15. In fact, all the distributions we have examined are related in the following fashion:

$$z = t_{\infty df} \qquad = \sqrt{F_{1,\infty df}} \qquad = \sqrt{\chi^2_{1\,df}}$$

($z = t$ with infinite df, which equals the square root of F with 1 and infinite df, which equals the square root of χ^2 with 1 df)

9.2.1 Yate's Correction for Continuity

As we indicated earlier, if we have fewer than five cases in any of the cells in a table of expected frequencies (not observed frequencies), we violate one of the assumptions of chi-square. If such a condition exists we "correct" the chi-square value by using **Yate's correction for continuity**, given by Formula 9.3.

$$\chi_c^2 = \sum \frac{([O - E] - .5)^2}{E} \qquad (9.3)$$

As is readily seen, this correction for continuity has the effect of reducing the value of chi-square since it reduces the absolute value of $O - E$ for each cell by 0.5. Some statisticians recommend using Yates's correction for any 2×2 table, whereas others believe that it overcorrects. The decision whether or not to use the correction for continuity with any 2×2 table depends on how conservative the researcher wishes to be when testing hypotheses. Computer printouts for 2×2 tables give both the corrected and uncorrected chi-square values. As is the case with all correction factors, this correction becomes less meaningful as the sample size becomes larger.

9.2.2 Phi

Although we will be discussing the concept of association more fully in the next chapter, it is appropriate to introduce one such measure at this point because it is based on chi-square with 2×2 tables, and also because I wish to use it to illustrate a point about chi-square and sample size later in the chapter. As you already know, measures of association usually range between -1 and $+1$, indicating a direction to a relationship. However, **phi** is always positive, ranging between zero and $+1.0$. Phi is appropriate only for 2×2 tables or $2 \times k$ tables (2×3, 2×4, etc.) because with larger tables it can exceed unity under certain circumstances. The formula for computing phi directly from the computed value of chi-square is

$$\phi = \sqrt{\frac{\chi^2}{N}} \qquad (9.4)$$

In prose, phi is equal to the square root of chi-square divided by N. Applying phi to our data on sex and willingness to vote for a female presidential candidate, we obtain

$$\phi = \sqrt{\frac{17.26}{236}} = \sqrt{.073} = .27$$

We can interpret this value in variance-explained terms if we square it. To get the percentage of variance explained by gender in willingness to vote for a female, we simply square the computed phi to get phi squared $= .073$. The proportion of variance in willingness to vote for a female for president accounted for by sex is only 7.3 percent. It is statistically significant because the chi-square on which it is based is significant. Is it substantively significant? Well, it depends on the context of the inquiry. I submit that if this were a real research finding it might be considered substantively significant. Interpreting the finding might prove difficult though. Some may take it as being indicative of male chauvinism because most males would not vote for a female presidential candidate. Since the question posed was would the respondent vote for a female candidate regardless of party affiliation, others might say that those who would do so are putting sexual politics above party politics. Statistics only inform us of the situation as it exists; the researcher must interpret them—carefully.

To take the statistical versus substantive discussion a little further, suppose that we had found the same results by using liking for quiche as the dependent variable and sex as the independent variable. To me, as well as to most of you, I suspect, the substantive significance of such a finding would be profoundly uninteresting. Even a perfect relationship would fail to excite us. On the other hand, if you were a caterer with a great deal of surplus quiche to get rid of, and if you were to be catering events at (1) the Ada County Gun Club and (2) the Boise Ladies Knitting Circle, where would you try to unload it? It may also be of some theoretical importance to the sex-role researcher if he or she is convinced that such a finding is a valid indicator of attempts on the part of males who believe that "real men don't eat quiche" to emphasize their masculinity. Substantive significance, I emphasize, depends more on the context of the inquiry than on the magnitude and significance of the computed statistics.

9.2.3 Chi-Square and Goodness of Fit

We can use the chi-square distribution when we have prior knowledge of expected values. Mendel's law of genetics, for example, tells us that cross-breeding of organisms with certain characteristics will yield combinations of those characteristics in a 9:3:3 ratio. The **chi-square goodness-of-fit test** can be used to test whether or not a given genetic experiment yields an observed distribution that "fits" the theoretical expected distribution.

Suppose we know that the racial composition of a given community is 88 percent white, 10 percent black, and 2 percent Hispanic, and we examine violent crime victimization in the community. Our a priori expectation is that in a sample of victims we would observe the races represented in proportion to their numbers in the population. That is, if the race variable were irrelevant to victimization, we would expect 88 percent of the victims to be white, 10 percent to be black, and 2 percent to be Hispanic. However, if race is not independent of the probability of becoming a victim, we will observe some other percentage breakdown.

From our offender data we observe that out of 478 victims of violent crime, 67.4 percent are white, 28 percent are black, and 4.6 percent are Hispanic. The research question is "Is violent victimization in the community in proportion to racial composition in the community, or are people of different races significantly more likely to be victimized?" Stated more formally, "Does the proportion of

TABLE 9.7   OBSERVED AND A PRIORI EXPECTED DISTRIBUTION OF VIOLENT
              CRIME VICTIMS

	Observed		
White	Black	Hispanic	Total
322 (67.4%)	134 (28.0%)	22 (4.6%)	478 (100%)

Expected (based on knowledge of racial composition of community)

Whites	$478 \times .88 = 420.6$
Blacks	$478 \times .10 = 47.8$
Hispanic	$478 \times .02 = 9.6$
Total	478.0

victims of violent crime fit the racial composition of this jurisdiction?'' The null
hypothesis is that the observed ratio equals the 88:10:2 expected ratio. The data
are set up as in Table 9.7.

It is immediately obvious that whites are underrepresented among victims of
violent crimes and that blacks and Hispanics are overrepresented. To determine if
these observed differences could be attributed to chance, we use the chi-square
distribution. We have to enter the chi-square table with 2 df because we have
three categories that have to sum to 478. Two of these categories can vary, but
the size of the third is fixed (not free to vary) by the size of the other two.

$$\chi^2 \Sigma \frac{(O - E)^2}{E} = \overset{\textbf{Whites}}{\frac{(322 - 420.6)^2}{420.6}} + \overset{\textbf{Blacks}}{\frac{(134 - 47.8)^2}{47.8}} + \overset{\textbf{Hispanics}}{\frac{(22 - 9.6)^2}{9.6}}$$

$$= \frac{9721.96}{420.6} + \frac{7430.44}{47.8} + \frac{153.76}{9.6}$$

$$= 23.11 + 155.45 + 16.02$$

$$\chi^2 = 194.58, \ df = 2, \ p < .00001$$

We reject the null hypothesis; observed violent crime victimization does not
fit the expected ratio based on knowledge of the racial composition of the community. Violent crime victimization depends on race. Blacks and Hispanics, particularly blacks, are victims of violent crime significantly more often than their
proportions in the community would lead us to suspect.

Chi-square can also be used to test the significance of difference between
observed values and values that are expected according to some theoretical distribution. Suppose we want to find out if the number of delinquents in each of a

number of IQ levels matches, fits, or conforms to population norms. Specifically, we wish to find out if the observed number of delinquents in each IQ category conforms to the expected frequencies for the U.S. population taken as a whole. Psychologists have determined that about 9 percent of the population falls into the borderline IQ level, about 16 percent into the dull normal level, 50 percent into the normal level, and 25 percent into the bright normal and above level. Given this theoretical distribution, we expect that 53 of our delinquents (9 percent of 587 = 53) will be in the borderline category, 94 in the dull normal category, 293 in the normal category, and 147 in the above-normal category. We can then compare the IQs of our delinquents for goodness of fit with the population distribution. We plot the delinquent IQ levels in a table next to the distribution we would expect if the delinquents were no different from the general population norms on IQ, as in Table 9.8.

Since the computed chi-square exceeds the critical value at the .00001 level of significance, we can conclude that the distribution of delinquents across the various IQ levels differs markedly from what we would expect; there is a lack of fit between the observed distribution and the theoretically expected distribution. Had the chi-square been nonsignificant, we would have concluded that there was a "good fit" between the observed and expected distributions.

TABLE 9.8   GOODNESS OF FIT CHI-SQUARE TEST FOR DELINQUENT IQ

IQ Level	Obs.	Exp.	$(O-E)$	$(O-E)^2$	$(O-E)^2/E$
Low–79	84	53	31	961	18.13
80–90	136	94	42	1764	18.77
91–110	305	293	12	144	.49
111–high	62	147	−85	7225	49.15
	587	587			86.54

$\chi^2 = 86.54$, $df = 3$, $p < .00001$

9.2.4 A Computer Example of Chi-Square

We will now compute chi-square from data arranged in a 3 × 2 table. From our love deprivation/violence data we generate the hypothesis that birth rank (first/middle/last born) is associated with whether a juvenile has ever committed a violent offense (no/yes). The distribution is presented in Table 9.9. In addition to chi-square you will see a lot of other statistical information in the printout. Most of these statistics will be discussed in subsequent chapters, but for now we will ignore them. They are left in the table so that you can see what the complete chi-square output looks like. To get the birth-ranking/violence statistics from the computer, command 9.1 in the chapter appendix is required.

TABLE 9.9 3 × 2 CHI-SQUARE TABLE (SPSSx PRINTOUT)

```
   CROSSTABULATION OF VIOLENT OFFENSE SCORE BY POS FAMILY POSITION
                    POS
          COUNT   I
         ROW PCT I FIRST     MIDDLE     LAST      ROW
         COL PCT I           I          I       I TOTAL
                 I         1I         2I       3I
VOIL  ---------------------------------------------------
       (NO)  1 I   101   I    82  I  56   I    239
               I   42.3  I  34.3  I  23.4 I   40.9
               I   54.3  I  30.8  I  42.1 I
            ---------------------------------------
       (YES) 2 I    85   I   184  I  77   I    346
               I   24.6  I  53.2  I  22.3 I   59.1
               I   45.7  I  69.2  I  57.9 I
            ---------------------------------------
          COLUMN     186       266      133        585
           TOTAL     31.8      45.5     22.7      100.0
```

CHI-SQUARE	D.F.	SIGNIFICANCE	MIN E.F.	CELLS WITH E.F.<5
25.07277	2	0.0000	54.337	NONE

STATISTIC	SYMMETRIC	WITH VIOL DEPENDENT	WITH POS DEPENDENT
LAMBDA	0.06272	0.06695	0.05956
UNCERTAINTY COEFFICIENT	0.02478	0.03179	0.02030
SOMERS' D	0.11068	0.09710	0.12868
ETA		0.20703	0.11078

STATISTIC	VALUE	SIGNIFICANCE
CRAMER'S V	0.20703	
CONTINGENCY COEFFICIENT	0.20273	
KENDALL'S TAU B	0.11178	0.0022
KENDALL'S TAU C	0.12437	0.0022
PEARSON'S R	0.11078	0.0037
GAMMA	0.19450	
NUMBER OF MISSING OBSERVATIONS =	2	

Let us compute chi-square for ourselves from these data.

expected frequency for A = $186 \times 239/585 = 44454/585 = 75.99$

expected frequency for B = $266 \times 239/585 = 63574/585 = 108.67$

expected frequency for C = $133 \times 239/585 = 31787/585 = 54.34$

expected frequency for D = $186 \times 346/585 = 64356/585 = 110.01$

expected frequency for E = $266 \times 346/585 = 92036/585 = 157.33$

expected frequency for F = $133 \times 346/585 = 46081/585 = 78.66$

We now have to calculate chi-square by subtracting the expected frequency from the observed frequency for each individual cell, square that value, and divide the result by the expected frequency as before.

$$\chi^2 = \underset{A}{\frac{(101 - 75.99)^2}{75.99}} + \underset{B}{\frac{(82 - 108.67)^2}{108.67}} + \underset{C}{\frac{(56 - 54.34)^2}{54.34}}$$

$$\underset{D}{\frac{(85 - 110.01)^2}{110.01}} + \underset{E}{\frac{(184 - 157.33)^2}{157.33}} + \underset{F}{\frac{(77 - 78.66)^2}{78.66}}$$

$$= \underset{A}{\frac{625.50}{75.99}} + \underset{B}{\frac{711.29}{108.67}} + \underset{C}{\frac{2.76}{54.34}} + \underset{D}{\frac{625.50}{110.01}} + \underset{E}{\frac{711.29}{157.33}} + \underset{F}{\frac{2.76}{78.66}}$$

$$= \underset{A}{8.23} + \underset{B}{6.54} + \underset{C}{.051} + \underset{D}{5.69} + \underset{E}{4.52} + \underset{F}{.035} = 25.07$$

Our chi-square matches the computer's. There is a significant relationship between birth order and the commission of a violent crime. It is highly unlikely that our data come from a population in which the probability of committing a violent crime is the same for each birth-order group. We see that 239 (40.9 percent) of our 585 juvenile delinquents had not been convicted of a violent crime and that 346 (59.1 percent) had. Firstborn children were the least likely to have committed a violent crime (45.7 percent), and middle-born children were the most likely (69.2 percent). This result fits the general pattern of what psychologists know about birth rankings and crime.

We can use this table to reinforce the discussion of probability in Chapter 4. What is the probability that a delinquent drawn at random from the sample will be firstborn and will have committed at least one violent crime? These two events (birth order and violent crime) are not independent events, as we have seen. We must use the multiplication rule for dependent events, which, you recall, is given as $P(AB) = P(A) \times P(B/A)$. The probability that a delinquent drawn from the sample at random will be firstborn is obtained by dividing the number of delinquents who are firstborn by the total number of delinquents in the sample. Therefore, $P(A) = 186/585 = .318$. The probability of having committed a violent crime given firstborn status is obtained by dividing the number of firstborns who have committed a violent crime by the total number of firstborns. Therefore, $P(B/A) = 85/186 = .457$. Multiplying the probability of A by the probability of B given A gives us $(.318)(.457) = .145$.

Can you think of a faster way to obtain this result? Of course you can. You can simply divide the lower left-hand cell by the total sample size $(85/585 = .145)$. This is the application of the general probability rule:

$$P = \frac{\text{number of ways an event can occur}}{\text{total number of possible outcomes}}$$

As you can plainly see, determining probabilities is a lot simpler and more direct if the data are set up in contingency tables. Now that we know this we can extend our understanding of probability by discussing the odds ratio.

9.3 THE ODDS RATIO

A statistic known as the **odds ratio** is a very useful additional measure that can be computed from the chi-square table. The odds ratio is associated with an advanced method of contingency table analysis known as log-linear analysis. It is for this reason that the odds ratio measure is rarely addressed in elementary statistics texts. However, it is a simple statistic to compute, and it provides valuable additional information concerning the relationship between two variables. Moreover, if we were attempting to explain our findings to those without any statistical training, it is much easier to talk about odds for or against than to confuse them with chi-square values, levels of significance, and measures of association. We all understand odds.

As all gamblers know, the "odds" is simply the ratio of the probability of an event occurring versus the probability of it not occurring. What we are concerned with here is the ratio between the frequency of being in one table category and the frequency of not being in that category. To illustrate the computation of the odds ratio and its meaning, we will reproduce our crosstabulation of sex and willingness to vote for a female presidential candidate in Table 9.10.

From this table, what are the odds that a person, regardless of sex, would vote for a female? We determine this figure by computing the marginal odds: $128/108 = 1.18$. That is, about 1.2 persons report that they would vote for a female for every one person who would not. The **conditional odds** are the chances of voting for a female given that one is a male or a female. The odds on voting for a female for males are $47/69 = .68$, and for females they are $81/39 = 2.08$. The odds ratio provides a summary statistic that is the ratio of the two conditional odds. Algebraically we get

$$\frac{A/C}{B/D} = \frac{A}{C} \times \frac{D}{B} = \frac{(A)(D)}{(B)(C)}$$

TABLE 9.10   WILLINGNESS TO VOTE FOR A FEMALE BY SEX

Would vote for Woman	Sex		
	Male	Female	
Yes	A 47 (40.5%)	B 81 (67.5%)	128 (54.2%)
No	C 69 (59.5%)	D 39 (32.5%)	108 (45.8%)
Totals	116 (100%)	120 (100%)	236 (100%)

That is, to obtain the sex/would vote for female odds ratio, we multiply the frequency of cell A by the frequency in cell D and divide the product by the frequency of cell B multiplied by the frequency of cell C. Putting in the numbers, we get

$$\text{odds ratio} = \frac{(47)(39)}{(81)(69)} = .328$$

This value indicates that males are about one-third less likely than females to report a willingness to vote for a female. We could make this example more intuitively understandable by stating it in reverse, that is, reverse the numerator and the denominator:

$$\text{odds ratio} = \frac{(B)(C)}{(A)(D)} = \frac{(81)(69)}{(47)(39)} = \frac{5589}{1833} = 3.049$$

Now we can say that females are just over three times more likely to report that they would vote for a female than would males.

A further rather neat property of the odds ratio is that it can be easily converted into the traditional measure of association for 2×2 tables, Yule's Q. Again, the concept of association will be developed at greater length in the next chapter. Just slightly out of context at this point, the traditional method of computing Yule's Q will be presented so that you can see its relationship to the odds ratio. The simple formula for Q, Formula 9.5, uses only cell frequencies in its computation, ignoring marginal frequencies. The formula simply instructs us to subtract the product of cells B and C from the product of cells A and D and divide the difference by the sum of the products of cells A and D and B and C.

$$Q = \frac{AD - BC}{AD + BC} \tag{9.5}$$

Part of Table 9.10 follows to facilitate the computation of Q.

Would vote for Woman	Sex	
	Male	Female
Yes	A 47	B 81
No	C 69	D 39

$$Q = \frac{AD - BC}{AB + BC} = \frac{(47)(39) - (81)(69)}{(47)(39) + (81)(69)} = \frac{1833 - 5589}{1833 + 5589}$$

$$= \frac{-3756}{7422} = -506$$

We may interpret the computed value of Q for the present as indicating a moderately strong relationship between our two variables. Now let us see how Q is related to the odds ratio. To obtain Yule's Q directly from the odds ratio, we use Formula 9.6.

$$Q = \frac{\text{odds ratio} - 1}{\text{odds ratio} + 1} \qquad\qquad (9.6)$$

Yule's Q for both of our computed odds ratios:

Example A

$$\frac{.328 - 1}{.328 + 1} = \frac{-.672}{1.382} = -.506$$

Example B

$$\frac{3.049 - 1}{3.049 + 1} = \frac{2.049}{4.049} = .506$$

Please note that odds ratios take on only positive values. Odds ratios of less than 1, as in example A, indicate a negative or inverse relationship, whereas odds ratios of more than 1, as in example B, indicate a positive relationship. Of course, this is also indicated by the directions of the respective Yule's Q values. The direction of Q is arbitrary in our example because the categorization of variables measured at the nominal level is arbitrary. That is, females who reported that they would not vote for a woman could have been substituted in cell A for males who would—there is no "natural" ordering of gender or willingness to vote for a female.

9.4 CHI-SQUARE AND SAMPLE SIZE

The chi-square statistic, as we have pointed out, is very sensitive to sample size. In fact, it is directly proportional to sample size in a 2×2 table. If we were to double the frequencies in each of the cells in our sex/would vote example, the computed chi-square value would be double that which we obtained. As an exercise, you might want to double the frequencies and calculate chi-square and phi. Did you double your chi-square value? What happened to phi?

To illustrate this point, we will compute a chi-square based on $N = 20$. We will then multiply each cell frequency by 10 and recompute chi-square ($N = 200$). We will again multiply each cell frequency by 10 and recompute ($N = 2000$). Although the percentage differences in the cells remain exactly the same, note what happens to chi-square in Figure 9.2.

Note that the values of chi-square increase in direct proportion to the increase in cell frequencies. Multiplying the cell frequencies by 10 results in a chi-square value increased by a factor of 10. Also note that however much we increase the cell frequencies, if they remain similarly distributed the increase will not affect the value of phi. Therefore, observed cell differences in a large sample are more likely to be statistically significant than are the same differences observed in a small sample simply because the larger the sample the more likely we are to capture the situation as it exists in the population from which it was drawn. Sample size, however, does not affect the size of the association if the distribution of the cases in the table remains the same.

4	6
6	4

$\chi^2 = 0.8$, n.s., $\phi = .20$

40	60
60	40

$\chi^2 = 8.0$, $p < .005$, $\phi = .20$

400	600
600	400

$\chi^2 = 80.0$, $p < .00001$, $\phi = .20$

Figure 9.2 The effects of sample size on chi-square with constant cell percentages

9.4.1 How Big Should a Sample Be?

Sample size is often determined by a number of considerations that are not statistical. The issue we are interested in exploring and the time and finances we have available may all place restrictions on sample size. We could use the formula for determining sample size presented in Chapter 5 for proportions, but a simple rule of thumb is to aim for a minimum of ten cases per cell and add ten cases for every four cells. Thus, a 2 × 2 table would require a sample size of 50 (4 cells × 10 cases + 10 cases = 50). A 3 × 2 table would require 6 cells × 10 cases + 15 cases = 75 cases. A 4 × 4 table would require 16 cells × 10 cases + 40 cases (4 sets of 4 cells) = 200 cases. It is easy to see that the more involved the study is, the larger the sample size must be.

The issue of sample size becomes even more crucial in multivariate analysis, which goes beyond the examination of the joint distribution of two variables to examine their joint distribution within categories of a third (or even fourth or fifth) variable. As we shall see, such a strategy soon depletes even large samples.

9.5 KRUSKAL-WALLIS ONE-WAY ANALYSIS OF VARIANCE

The **Kruskal-Wallis one-way ANOVA** test (H) is a nonparametric version of the parametric ANOVA discussed in Chapter 7. It is suitable for data measured at the ordinal level and permits a test of significance by using the chi-square distribution among groups ranked according to some ordinal attribute. The Kruskal-Wallis test can be used to compare two groups, but its special utility is that it can be used to test the significance of difference between more than two rank-ordered groups.

Suppose we ask five randomly selected political science professors from each of three different countries to rank their perceptions of civil liberties in their country on a scale of zero through 100. The responses of these 15 professors are

Country 1   75, 74, 52, 74, 55

Country 2   65, 80, 70, 90, 80

Country 3   74, 92, 85, 82, 95

Rather than working with raw scores, H substitutes the rankings of the items in each group. Thus, the last score (95) would be ranked number 1, and the middle score of country 1 (52) would be ranked 15. Table 9.11 sets up these scores by rank. Note that there is a tie for the sixth rank, where there are two scores of 80. To break the tie we assign those scores the mean of the two ranks they would have occupied if no tie existed ($6 + 7/2 = 6.5$). Similarly, we have a three-way tie on a score of 74 for ranks 9, 10, and 11. We assign the mean of the three ranks to these three scores ($9 + 10 + 11/3 = 10$). After we arrange the ranks we sum the ranks for each country.

When we have summed the ranks, we then substitute these values into Formula 9.7 to compute H. The null hypothesis is that the samples come from the same population, and thus the ranked perceptions regarding civil liberties are identical.

$H_0 : H = 0$

$$H = \frac{12}{N(N + 1)} \left[\frac{S_1^2}{N_1} + \frac{S_2^2}{N_2} + \frac{S_3^2}{N_3} \right] - 3(N + 1) \qquad (9.7)$$

Where the numbers 12 and 3 are constants,

$S_1^2 =$ sum of rank from country 1 squared, etc.

Putting in the numbers, we get

$$H = \frac{12}{15(16)} \left[\frac{22^2}{5} + \frac{41^2}{5} + \frac{57^2}{5} \right] - 3(16)$$

$$= \frac{12}{240} \left[\frac{484}{5} + \frac{1681}{5} + \frac{3249}{5} \right] - 48$$

TABLE 9.11 PROFESSORS' RANKINGS OF CIVIL LIBERTIES

Country 1		Country 2		Country 3	
x	Rank	x	Rank	x	Rank
95	1	90	3	75	8
92	2	80	6.5	74	10
85	4	80	6.5	74	10
82	5	70	12	55	14
74	10	65	13	52	15
	22		41		57

$$= (.05)(96.8 + 336.2 + 649.8) - 48$$

$$= (.05)(1082.8) - 48 = 54.14 - 48 = 6.14$$

We test H for significance when sample sizes are greater than five with the chi-square distribution, entering the chi-square table with $k - 1$ degrees of freedom. Since we have three categories, $df = 2$. The critical chi-square value with 2 degrees of freedom is 5.991 at the .05 level of confidence. Our computed H (6.14) exceeds this critical value; we can therefore reject the null hypothesis.

9.5.1 Computing Eta Squared From H

The measure of association that can be directly computed from H is the now familiar eta squared. The simple formula for this computation is

$$\eta^2 = \frac{H}{N - 1} = \frac{6.14}{14} = .439 \tag{9.8}$$

Thus, perceptions of civil liberties are rather strongly related to the country from which the professor comes, with country of origin accounting for 43.9 percent of the variance.

9.6 SUMMARY

Chi-square is a popular and much-used statistical technique for testing statistical independence and goodness of fit with tabular data. A test for independence is essentially testing whether or not the distribution of scores on one attribute in a table is independent of the distribution on another attribute. In other words, we are testing whether or not the two attributes or variables are related in the population. We do so by examining and comparing the observed bivariate cell frequencies with the cell frequencies we would expect if the two variables were unrelated. A test of goodness of fit is asking whether or not an observed distribution of scores "fits" a theoretically expected distribution. A significant chi-square indicates a poor fit between theoretical expectations and empirical actuality. A nonsignificant chi-square indicates a good fit.

The significance of the chi-square statistic depends on the value of the computed statistic and its associated degrees of freedom. Since chi-square is very sensitive to sample size, the larger the sample the more likely we are to observe a statistically significant difference if a difference actually exists in the population. Phi is a statistic suitable for 2×2 tables that measures the strength of association between two variables. When squared, phi gives the proportion of variance in the dependent variable accounted for by the independent variable.

The odds ratio is a useful statistic for reporting results to laypersons since everyone understands odds for or against an outcome. Yule's Q is a measure of association also suitable for 2 × 2 tables, and it is easily computed from the odds ratio. Chi-square is very sensitive to sample size, the probability of rejecting the null increasing in proportion to increasing sample size, given constant cell percentages.

The Krusal-Wallis one-way analysis of variance test is a nonparametric version of ANOVA suitable for ordinal-level data. This test tells us of any significant difference among two or more groups rank-ordered on some attribute using the chi-square distribution. Eta squared can be computed directly from H, giving us the proportion of variance in the dependent variable accounted for by the independent variable.

PRACTICE APPLICATION: CHI-SQUARE

We ask a sample of 89 residents of an upper-middle class apartment complex to identify themselves as being primarily either liberal or conservative in their political orientation. We also ask them their opinion on an issue raging on the university campus at present: "Do you think that the university should be allowed to fire a professor who advocates a communistic form of government for the United States." The answer categories are no and yes. We place their answers into a 2 × 2 table and compute chi-square, phi, the odds ratio, and Yule's Q.

Fire Profs.	Ideology		Totals
	Conservative	Liberal	
Yes	40 (75.5%)	12 (33.3%)	52 (58.4%)
No	13 (24.5%)	24 (66.7%)	37 (41.6%)
	53	36	89

Compute χ^2.

$$\chi^2 = \Sigma \frac{(O - E)^2}{E}$$

expected A = 53 × 52/89 = 31.0

expected B = 36 × 52/89 = 21.0

expected C = 53 × 37/89 = 22.0

expected D = 36 × 37/89 = 15.0

$$\chi^2 = \overset{\mathbf{A}}{\frac{(40 - 31)^2}{31}} + \overset{\mathbf{B}}{\frac{(12 - 21)^2}{21}} + \overset{\mathbf{C}}{\frac{(13 - 22)^2}{22}} + \overset{\mathbf{D}}{\frac{(24 - 15)^2}{15}}$$

$$= \frac{81}{31} + \frac{81}{21} + \frac{81}{22} + \frac{81}{15}$$

$$= 2.61 + 3.86 + 3.68 + 5.4 = 15.55$$

Chi-square is significant at less than .001. We are confident that a person's opinion on this matter is not independent of his or her political orientation. We reject the null hypothesis.

Compute phi.

$$\phi = \sqrt{\frac{\chi^2}{N}} = \sqrt{\frac{15.55}{89}} = \sqrt{.175} = .418$$

Phi is moderately strong. Political orientation is moderately strongly associated with one's opinion about the university's right to fire professors who advocate the communistic form of government for the United States. The percentage of variance in a respondent's opinion accounted for by political orientation is .418 squared = .175, or 17.5 percent.

Compute the odds ratio.

$$\text{odds ratio} = \frac{(A)(D)}{(B)(C)} = \frac{(40)(24)}{(12)(13)} = \frac{960}{156}$$

$$= 6.15:1$$

The odds on holding the opinion that the university should be able to fire professors who advocate a communistic form of government for the United States among conservatives are more than six times greater than the odds of holding the same opinion among liberals.

Compute Yule's Q.

$$Q = \frac{\text{odds ratio} - 1}{\text{odds ratio} + 1} = \frac{6.15 - 1}{6.15 + 1} = \frac{5.15}{7.15} = .72$$

There is a strong relationship between political orientation and the opinion that universities should be allowed to fire leftward-leaning professors.

Let us assume that our class standing/general knowledge ANOVA example in Chapter 7 was based on rank order rather than raw scores and compute Kruskal-Wallis H. The scores follow and are converted into ranks.

x	Rank	x	Rank	x	Rank
73	17	72	18	83	6.5
75	14	78	10.5	86	4
77	12	74	16	89	3
75	14	80	8.5	85	5
78	10.5	83	6.5	90	2
75	14	80	8.5	95	1
	81.5		68.0		21.5

$$H_0 : H = 0$$

Compute *H*.

$$H = \frac{12}{N(N+1)} \left[\frac{S_1^2}{N_1} + \frac{S_2^2}{N_2} + \frac{S_3^2}{N_3} \right] - 3(N+1)$$

$$= \frac{12}{18(19)} \left[\frac{81.5^2}{6} + \frac{68^2}{6} + \frac{21.5^2}{6} \right] - 3(19)$$

$$= \frac{12}{342} \left[\frac{6642.25}{6} + \frac{4624}{6} + \frac{462.25}{6} \right] - 57$$

$$= (.0351)(1107.04 + 770.67 + 77.04) - 57$$

$$= (.0351)(1954.75) - 57 = 68.12 - 57 = 11.61$$

Entering the chi-square table with 2 *df*, we find that the critical value needed to reject the null at the .01 level of significance is 9.21. Our computed value exceeds the critical value: We reject the null.

Compute eta squared.

$$\eta^2 = \frac{H}{N-1} = \frac{11.61}{17} = .683$$

The percentage of variance computed from the *H* test for these data is 68.3, which is approximately 5 percent less than using ANOVA (73.4 percent). This result illustrates the greater utility of using interval-level statistics and measures over ordinal-level statistics and measures if it is valid to do so.

APPENDIX: Computer Instructions for Chi-Square Test for Independence

Command 9.1

SPSSx	SAS
RECODE VIOL (0 = 1) (1 THRU HI=2)	IF VIOL = 0 THEN VIOL = 1;
CROSSTABS TABLES = VIOL BY POS	IF VIOL > 1 THEN VIOL = 2;
OPTIONS 3 4	PROC FREQ;
STATISTICS ALL	TABLES VIOL * POS/ ALL;

The RECODE or IF statements are necessary because VIOL was coded as a continuous variable, and we wish only to determine whether or not our subjects had ever committed one or more violent crimes. The CROSSTABS or TABLES command informs the computer that you wish to crosstabulate VIOL, the dependent variable, with POS (birth rank), the independent variable. The OPTIONS command tells the computer that you want both row and column percentages reported. The STATISTICS ALL or ALL command instructs the computer to report all available statistics.

REFERENCE

Hacking, I. (1984). Trial by number. *Science, 84* (November), 69–72.

Chapter 10

Measures of Association with Nominal and Ordinal Data

10.1 THE IDEA OF ASSOCIATION

We have already discussed three measures of association (eta, phi, and Yule's Q) without fully developing the idea of **association.** Eta, a measure of association introduced in Chapter 7, requires at least one of the variables being tested to be measured at the interval or ratio level. Phi and Yule's Q are measures suitable for dichotomous, nominal-level variables. We will develop the idea of association in this chapter with nominal- and ordinal-level measures only. Measures based on higher-level data are discussed elsewhere in the text. The statistical tests in this chapter are all nonparametric.

In social science we ask such questions as "Why do religious fundamentalists tend to be more prejudiced than nonfundamentalists?" "Why do blacks make less money than whites?" "Why are sex offenders punished more harshly than other kinds of offenders?" Each of these questions deals with the issue of how variables are connected, related, or associated. We are saying that the condition "being black," for instance, is related to low income, and we saw in Chapter 6 that the condition "sex offender" was related to harsher punishment. Another way of phrasing this last sentence would be to say that income levels depend on race and that harshness of punishment depends on type of crime. Thus, income and harshness of punishment are dependent variables, and race and type of offense are independent variables. Three main questions arise in the assessment of association: (1) Does an association exist? (2) How strong is it? (3) What is its direction?

10.1.1 Does an Association Exist?

Before we can ask why blacks make less money than whites we first have to determine if they really do by subjecting the hypothesis to a test of association. An association exists if values of one variable vary systematically with variation in a second variable. When we ask why blacks make less money than whites we are taking for granted that the value of the variable *income* changes as we move across conditions of the second variable, *race*. As another example, if we had five conditions of a religious preference variable ranging from fundamentalists to Unitarians (a very liberal church), we would expect the values of the prejudice variable to vary across those conditions. More precisely, we would expect levels of prejudice to get smaller and smaller as we move farther away from the fundamentalist condition. If values of one variable do not change across conditions of another, there is no association between them.

Table 10.1 illustrates the presence and absence of an association between attending college and whether or not the respondent's father is a college graduate (hypothetical data). In distribution A we see that whether one attends college is largely a function of whether one's father is a college graduate. Ninety-five of the respondents who attended college had fathers who were graduates and 20 had fathers who were not. Among those respondents who did not attend college, 80 had fathers who were not college graduates and 45 had fathers who were. In other words, the distribution of frequencies of the variable *attend college* is conditional on the distribution of frequencies of the second variable, *father is graduate*. We call such a joint frequency distribution a **conditional distribution**.

Distribution B shows a table of joint frequencies in which no association exists between the two variables. Whether or not one attends college is not conditional on whether or not one's father is a college graduate. Exactly half of those who attended college had fathers who were graduates and half who did not attend college also had fathers who were graduates. The same is true for those who did not attend college. The values of the first variable do not vary across conditions of the second.

TABLE 10.1   HYPOTHETICAL CONDITIONAL DISTRIBUTIONS SHOWING
ASSOCIATION (A) AND NO ASSOCIATION (B)

	A Father Graduate				B Father Graduate		
Attend College	Yes	No		Attend College	Yes	No	
Yes	A 95	B 20	115	Yes	A 65	B 65	130
No	C 45	D 80	125	No	C 55	D 55	110
	140	100	240		120	120	240

10.1.2 What Is the Strength of the Association?

Once we have evidence of a conditional distribution, the next step is to quantify the strength of the association. This is essentially a matter of examining the magnitude of change by moving from one condition to another. A crude measure of the strength of the association would be the simple percentage of change across cells. Take distribution A for instance. We could compare the percentage of respondents who attended college and who had fathers who graduated ($95/115 \times 100 = 83\%$) with the percentage of respondents who attended college but whose fathers did not graduate ($20/115 \times 100 = 17\%$). In this case we have a difference of 66 percentage points, whereas in distribution B the difference would be zero. One problem with this strategy is that we would have to make multiple comparisons of the percentages from cell to cell. It would be much more efficient to have a single summary value of the strength of the association.

Another problem is that of evaluating the meaning of a variety of percentage differences whose values do not vary within fixed limits. Again, it would be much more efficient to have a measure of association that varies within fixed, or "normed," limits. Norming operations are not new. When we discussed percentages, ratios, and proportions, we were norming, or standardizing, the raw data. All of the statistics of association we will be looking at involve ratios of one quantity to another. The statistics we will discuss in this chapter have the efficient properties of being single summary indices of the strength of the association and of ranging within fixed limits. In addition, they have the property of indicating the direction of the relationship.

10.1.3 What Is the Direction of the Association?

Relationships or associations between variables can be either positive or negative. There is a **positive association** when the values of one variable increase with the increased values of another—the values of both variables vary positively. In other words, high scores on one variable are associated with high scores on the other, and low scores are associated with low scores. There is **negative association** when we observe the opposite pattern; that is, as the values of one variable increase, the values of the other decrease.

Table 10.2 illustrates positive and negative associations. In distribution A we see that income varies positively with level of education: High scores tend to go with high scores and low scores tend to go with low scores. In this distribution the highest category Ns are found on the main diagonal (top left-hand cell to bottom right-hand cell). In distribution B we have the opposite pattern, in which high scores on the education variable are negatively associated with low scores on TV watching, and low scores on education are associated with high scores on TV watching. In this distribution the higher category Ns are found in the secondary diagonal (top right-hand cell to bottom left-hand cell). Another way of stating a negative relationship is to say that the variables are inversely related.

A normed measure of association generally ranges between -1 and $+1$. An association of -1 is a perfect negative association, and a value of $+1$ is a perfect positive association. An association of zero means that there is no association

TABLE 10.2 HYPOTHETICAL CONDITIONAL DISTRIBUTIONS SHOWING POSITIVE (A)
AND NEGATIVE (B) ASSOCIATION

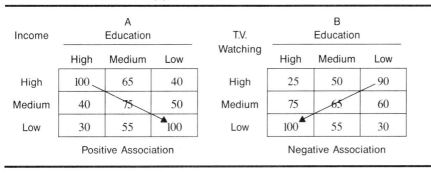

	A Education				B Education		
Income	High	Medium	Low	T.V. Watching	High	Medium	Low
High	100	65	40	High	25	50	90
Medium	40	75	50	Medium	75	65	60
Low	30	55	100	Low	100	55	30
	Positive Association				Negative Association		

between the two variables. Normed measures allow for the comparison of computed values across tables and across samples, something that could not be done
if the measures were not restricted to defined ranges. Let us suppose distribution
A was based on a sample of white respondents only, and the measure of association was +.60. We could take a sample of black respondents and also compute
the same measure of association between education level and income and compare the two values. If the value of the measure of association for blacks turned
out to be, say, +.40, we could validly say that the effect of education on income
is weaker for blacks than it is for whites because the strength of association in
both samples was measured by the same normed statistic.

Unfortunately, there are no hard rules for interpreting the numerical values
of the computed statistics. How strong does an association have to be before it is
considered worth attending to? And what do we mean by *strong,* anyway? The
answer to these questions depends really on the specific context of the research.
In one context an association of .50 might produce nothing more than a shrug of
the shoulders; in another it might set the heart pounding. Rules of thumb for
interpreting the strength of association, mindful of unspoken exceptions and
qualifications, are presented in Figure 10.1. Be aware that it only makes sense to
interpret a measure of association as weak, moderate, or strong if it is found to be
statistically significant.

We will now discuss some of these normed statistical techniques for assessing the existence, strength, and direction of association.

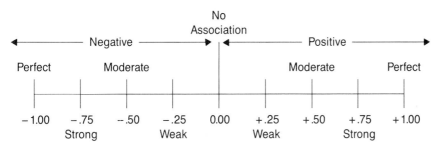

Figure 10.1 Rule-of-thumb scale for interpreting statistically significant strength of association for measures with fixed limits of −1.0 and +1.0

10.1.4 Lambda

As you might have guessed, if two variables are associated we can use one of them to predict the other. We saw in the last chapter that males and females differed significantly in their willingness to vote for a female for president of the United States. This being the case, knowing a person's sex will help you predict his or her willingness to vote for a female president. Of course, your predictions will not be infallible. You will make a number of errors in your predictions since not all women indicated such a willingness, and not all males were unwilling to vote for a female. The point is, you will make fewer errors making predictions if you are armed with knowledge about the independent variable than you would without such knowledge. This is formally called **proportional reduction in error (PRE)**, which again, refers to the reduction of errors made as we move from predicting scores on the dependent variable without knowing the distribution of the independent variable to predicting scores on the dependent variable with knowing the distribution of the independent variable.

Lambda is very useful for gaining a grasp of the concept of PRE because it uses the general formula for PRE, which is

$$PRE = \frac{\text{errors using rule 1} - \text{errors using rule 2}}{\text{errors using rule 1}}$$

Rule 1 is simply predicting the values of the dependent variable while ignoring the independent variable, and rule 2 is predicting the values of the dependent variable with knowledge of the independent variable. If there is perfect association between the two variables, knowledge of the independent variable will reduce prediction errors to zero, and lambda will be 1. If there is no association, knowledge of the independent variable will be of no predictive value, and lambda will be zero.

Lambda is an asymmetric measure of association with values ranging between zero and $+1$, and it is best suited to distributions in which both variables are nominal level. Lambda is not a particularly popular statistic in actual research because it has a strange quirk, which will be discussed later. For now, let us compute lambda from the data in Table 10.3. Suppose that we want to determine the association between prison psychologists' recommendations that prisoners be either released or not released and the parole board's actual release decision. From the table we see that psychologists recommended release for 110 inmates, and the parole board released 85 of them, meaning that they disagreed with the psychologists in 25 cases. Psychologists recommended against releasing 85 inmates, and the parole board concurred in 75 instances. Altogether there are 195 inmates who went before the parole board, and the board agreed with the psychologists' recommendation in 160 cases (82 percent). These data are set up in a 2 × 2 table.

We are using psychologists' recommendations to predict parole board decisions. What if we attempted to predict parole board decisions without knowledge of the psychologists' recommendations? Under conditions of ignorance about the independent variable, our best guess would be the modal category of the dependent variable, that is, that the prisoner would not be released. The modal category

TABLE 10.3

Parole Board's Decision (Y)	Psychologists' Recommendations (X)		
	Release	No Release	
Release	A 85	B 10	95
No Release	C 25	D 75	100
	110	85	195

for the parole board's decision is the "no release" row ($N = 100$). We would make fewer errors if we predicted no release for every inmate than if we predicted release for every inmate. If we chose the modal category every time, how many prediction errors would we make? We would make 95 errors (the number of inmates who were released). Therefore, $E_1 = 95$. In symbolic form, E_1 is defined as

$E_1 = N -$ modal category of the dependent variable

$= 195 - 100 = 95$

Having found the number of prediction errors by using rule 1, we must now determine the number of errors by using rule 2. By using rule 2, we are now armed with the knowledge that psychologists recommended releasing 110 inmates and not releasing 85. Knowing that psychologists recommended releasing 110 inmates, we will make fewer errors if we predict that the parole board will release all 110 inmates who received such a recommendation. Similarly, knowing that psychologists recommended no release for 85 inmates, we will make fewer errors predicting that the parole board will not release any of the 85. The errors we will make now are simply for those cases in which the board disagreed with the psychologists' recommendations. Thus, to determine the number of errors if we take the independent variable into account (rule 2) we simply subtract the modal cell frequency from each of the column totals and sum the values.

for release $110 - 85 = 25$

for no release $85 - 75 = 10$

Total $E = 35$

A total of 35 errors are made when taking the independent variable into account. Since prediction errors have been reduced considerably, the variables are associated. To find the proportional reduction in error we substitute the values of E_1 and E_2 into the formula:

$$\frac{E_1 - E_2}{E_1} = \frac{95 - 35}{95} = \frac{60}{95} = .632$$

By using Lambda as our PRE statistic, we have reduced our error in predicting inmate release with knowledge of the psychologists' recommendations by 63.2 percent. In other words, if we know what the psychologists' recommended, we improve our ability to predict the parole board's decision by 63.2 percent. There is a moderate to strong association between the two variables.

10.2 THE CONCEPT OF PAIRED CASES

Because the remaining statistics to be discussed in this chapter rely on comparisons of various types of paired cases, we should discuss the topic before proceeding further. By *paired cases* we mean all possible pairs of cases that can be found in a given set of cases. Suppose we have the following small data set of ten students who are categorized according to whether they scored high or low on an IQ test and on the SAT test.

Student	IQ	SAT
Jim	high	high
Jean	low	low
Bill	low	high
Frank	high	high
André	low	low
Melissa	low	low
Max	high	low
John	high	high
José	low	low
Ann	high	low

The possible number of paired cases that could be made up from any data set is determined by the formula

$$\text{total pairs} = \frac{N(N-1)}{2}$$

For our student data there are

$$\frac{(10)(9)}{2} = 45 \text{ possible pairs}$$

Let us display the data in a bivariate table (Table 10.4).

Clearly, we could predict a student's SAT score from his or her IQ score from these data. A student who scores high on an IQ test is likely to score high on the SAT also. Similarly, a student who scores low on an IQ test is likely to score low on the SAT. The seven observations conforming to this pattern can be considered to be in agreement with what we might logically hypothesize from our knowledge of the similarity of the mechanisms underlying scoring high or low on

TABLE 10.4   CROSSTABULATION OF IQ AND SAT

SAT (Y)	IQ (X)	
	High	Low
High	Jim Frank John N = 3	Bill N = 1
Low	Max Ann N = 2	Jean André Melissa José N = 4

both tests. There are only three departures (Bill, Max, and Ann) from this general pattern. These three cases are discordant with our expectations. It is the comparison of agreement to disagreement (similar to dissimilar pairs) in a data set that constitutes the basis for assessing the degree of association that exists between two nominal or ordinal variables. Let us now see the various kinds of pairs we could make from this small data set. There are five possible pair combinations in any data set:

1. Similar pairs, denoted by Ns. These are pairs that are ranked in the same order on both variables. Jim, Frank, John, Jean, André, Melissa, and José constitute similar pairs (either high-high or low-low).
2. Dissimilar pairs, denoted by Nd. Bill (high-low) and Max and Ann (low-high) constitute dissimilar pairs.
3. Pairs tied on the independent variable but not on the dependent variable, denoted by Tx. Jim, Frank, John, Max, and Ann are tied on the high category of the independent variable, and Bill, Jean, André, Melissa, and José are tied on the low category.
4. Pairs tied on the dependent variable but not on the independent variable, denoted by Ty. Jim, Frank, John, and Bill are tied on the high category of the dependent variable, and the remaining six students are tied on the low category.
5. Pairs tied on both the dependent and independent variables, denoted by Txy. These are the pairs that can be formed from the cases in the same cell. For instance, from the three cases in the high-high cell we could obtain $3(2)/2 = 3$ pairs.

We will now compute all possible pairs of each type. As we have already determined, they must sum to 45. We must be sure to refer back to Table 10.4 to see where the values are coming from.

Ns	3×4		12
Nd	1×2		2
Tx	$(3 \times 2) + (1 \times 4)$	=	10
Ty	$(3 \times 1) + (2 \times 4)$	=	11
Txy	$3 + 1 + 2 + 4$	=	<u>10</u>
Total pairs		=	45

10.3 A COMPUTER EXAMPLE OF NOMINAL AND ORDINAL MEASURES OF ASSOCIATION

Computer programs for nominal- and ordinal-level variables supply a variety of statistics with a procedure called CROSSTABS in SPSSx language and PROC FREQ in SAS. We will run a crosstabs table, which will serve to illustrate some of the ordinal-level measures of association we will be discussing in this chapter. This crosstabs procedure is based on our multiple sclerosis (MS) data.

Suppose we hypothesize that an association exists between the degree of physical restrictiveness suffered by an MS patient and the level of social isolation he or she is experiencing; that is, the more physically restricted an individual is the more he or she is socially isolated. We divide the degree of physical restrictiveness into three conditions: (1) those who never use a walking aid, (2) those who occasionally use a walking aid, and (3) those who always use a walking aid or wheelchair. Our measure of social isolation is Neal and Groat's (1974) social isolation scale, a nine-item scale with a four-point continuum, from strongly agree to strongly disagree. The minimum score is zero, indicating a complete lack of social isolation, to 36, indicating a high level of social isolation. Social isolation is the dependent variable and physical restriction is the independent variable. The chapter appendix provides the computer instructions necessary to run this job.

10.3.1 The Computer Printout

Table 10.5 reproduces the SPSSx crosstabs printout minus those statistics not relevant to this chapter. Lambda, Somer's *d*, tau-*b*, tau-*c*, and gamma are PRE statistics and will be discussed first. The contingency coefficient and Cramer's *V* are chi-square-based statistics that do not have a PRE interpretation; they will be discussed after the PRE statistics. The table format has been altered slightly to accommodate understanding of the statistics to be discussed.

10.3.2 Gamma

We will begin our discussion of ordinal-level statistics with **gamma**, the last statistic in the printout. We start with gamma because it is perhaps the most popular statistic applied to this type of analysis. Gamma ranges between -1 and $+1$, and its logic is identical to that of Yule's Q (Q is a special case of gamma used in 2×2 tables) in that it compares similar pairs of scores with dissimilar pairs and ignores tied pairs. By ignoring tied pairs, gamma informs us that as one variable

TABLE 10.5 CROSSTABULATION OF SOCIAL ISOLATION BY USE OF WALKING AID

CROSSTABULATION OF ISOL BY WAID
WAID (use of walking aid)

ISOL Social Isolation)	Never 1.00	Occas- ionally 2.00	Always 3.00	ROW TOTAL
(Low) 1.00	A) 20	B) 14	C) 8	42
(Medium) 2.00	D) 14	E) 23	F) 14	51
(High) 3.00	G) 4	H) 24	I) 14	42
COLUMN TOTAL	38	61	36	135

CHI-SQUARE	D.F	SIGNIFICANCE	MIN E.F.	CELLS WITH E.F. < 5
15.10207	4	0.0045	11.200	NONE

STATISTIC	SYMMETRIC	WITH ISOL DEPENDENT	WITH WAID DEPENDENT
LAMBDA	0.08228	0.083330	.08108
SOMERS' D	0.24979	0.253320	.24636

STATISTIC	VALUE	SIGNIFICANCE
CRAMER'S V	0.23650	
CONTINGENCY COEFFICIENT	0.31719	
KENDALL'S TAU B	0.24981	
KENDALL'S TAU C	0.24527	0.0006
GAMMA	0.37231	0.0006
NUMBER OF MISSING OBSERVATIONS =	0	

increases in value the other increases, decreases, or stays the same. The either/or feature makes gamma less useful than other measures for some research purposes. The formula for computing gamma is

$$\gamma = \frac{Ns - Nd}{Ns + Nd} \qquad (10.1)$$

where Ns = number of similar pairs

Nd = number of dissimilar pairs

From a visual inspection of Table 10.5 we note that a low level of physical restriction (no walking aid) is associated with a low level of social isolation, and that a high level of restriction is associated with a high level of isolation. We would know before looking at the statistics, then, that the association is positive. If we were to predict a person's position in terms of low, medium, and high on social isolation, it helps to know his or her level of physical restriction. For those low on physical restriction we predict the same rank order on social isolation, that is, low. Of the 38 individuals who are low on physical restriction, 20 are low on social isolation (cell A). We cannot pair this group of 20 people with people in any of the other cells sharing the same row (low isolation) or column (no walking aid) because these cells are tied, and gamma does not consider tied pairs in its computation.

As with Yule's Q, the first thing to do is to determine the similar and dissimilar pairs. To reiterate, similar pairs are all pairs that are not tied on one or the other of the conditions of the two variables. Thus, all those cells that are below and to the right of the upper left-hand cell constitute similar pairs because they are not tied in any way with those cells. We compute the number of similar pairs by multiplying the value of the upper left-hand cell with the sum of all cells below and to the right of it. This procedure is repeated for every cell in the table that has cells both below it and to the right. The following table indicates the first set of pairs to be calculated, starting with the "target" cell (no walking aid/low social isolation) and the cells below and to its right that are to be summed.

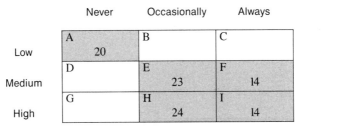

$$Ns \text{ for cell A} = (A)(E + F + H + I)$$

$$= (20)(23 + 14 + 24 + 14) = (20)(75) = 1500$$

The next step uses cell D as the target cell:

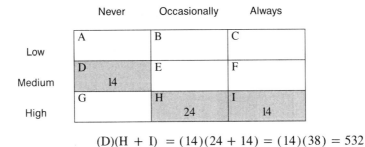

$$(D)(H + I) = (14)(24 + 14) = (14)(38) = 532$$

The next step uses cell B as the target cell:

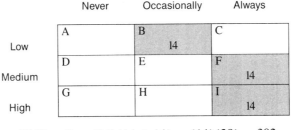

$$(B)(F + I) = (14)(14 + 14) = (14)(28) = 392$$

The final step uses cell E as the target cell (the only cell left with a cell that is both below and to the right of it):

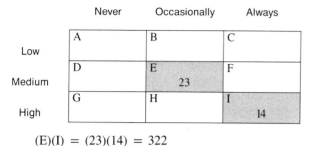

$$(E)(I) = (23)(14) = 322$$

We now sum these quantities and call the total *Ns*:

$$Ns = 1500 + 532 + 392 + 322 = 2746$$

We now have to find the dissimilar pairs by working in reverse. This time we start with the upper right-hand cell (cell C) and sum the values found in the cells below and to the left of it.

Target Cell

cell C = $(8)(23 + 14 + 24 + 4) = (8)(65) = 520$

cell B = $(14)(14 + 4) = (14)(18) = 252$

cell F = $(14)(24 + 4) = (14)(28) = 392$

cell E = $(23)(4) = 92$

We sum these quantities and call the total *Nd*:

$$520 + 252 + 392 + 92 = 1256$$

We now put the values of *Ns* and *Nd* into the formula for gamma:

$$\gamma = \frac{Ns - Nd}{Ns + Nd} = \frac{2746 - 1256}{2746 + 1256} = \frac{1490}{4002} = .372$$

There is a weak to moderate positive relationship between the degree of physical restriction and feelings of social isolation. Since we are dealing now with ordinal variables with an inherent ordered structure, direction of association has a definite meaningful interpretation. We are saying that as physical restriction gets more severe on an ordered scale, there is a tendency for MS patients to feel a greater degree of social isolation. We test this association for significance by using the *z* distribution. The null hypothesis is

$$H_0: \gamma = 0 \tag{10.2}$$

STEP 1.   Substitute the appropriate values into the formula.

$$z = \gamma\sqrt{\frac{Ns + Nd}{N(1 - \gamma^2)}} = .372\sqrt{\frac{4002}{135(1 - .372^2)}}$$

STEP 2. Square the value of gamma ($.372 \times .372 = .1384$). Subtract .1384 from 1 ($1 - .1384 = .8616$).

$$= .373\sqrt{\frac{4002}{135(1 - .1384)}} = .373\sqrt{\frac{4002}{(135)(.8616)}}$$

STEP 3. Multiply 135 by $.8616 = 116.316$. Divide 4002 by $116.316 = 34.406$. Take the square root of $34.406 = 5.866$.

$$= .372\sqrt{\frac{4002}{116.316}} = (.372)\sqrt{34.406} = (.372)(5.886)$$

STEP 4. Multiply .372 by $5.866 = 2.18$.

$$z = 2.18, \, p < .05$$

A z value of 2.18 is sufficient to reject the null at the .05 level of confidence. We conclude that it is unlikely that our data come from a population in which gamma equals zero.

10.3.3 Lambda

As we see from the computer printout, the value of **lambda** varies with which variable is taken as dependent. Because the degree of physical restriction is obviously not dependent on social isolation, we calculated lambda with social isolation as the dependent variable. Lambda is thus an asymmetric statistic. The third value of lambda in the computer printout, "symmetric" lambda can be thought of as an average of the two asymmetric lambdas. There is no simple test of statistical significance for lambda.

We will not repeat the computation of lambda with these data. Instead we will consider a particularly vexing liability. The problem is that lambda can yield a value of zero when there is, in fact, an association between the variables. This result occurs when the category modes of the independent variable occur in the same category of the dependent variable. Take the following bivariate distribution in which all modal column scores occur in the same row:

100	90	60	250	$E_1 = 400 - 250 = 150$
40	50	60	150	$E_2 = 40 + 50 + 60 = 150$
140	140	120	400	

$$\text{Lambda} = \frac{150 - 150}{150} = 0.00$$

Gamma for these data is

$$
\begin{array}{ll}
Ns = 100(50 + 60) = 11000 & Nd = 60(40 + 50) = 5400 \\
 (90)(60) = 5400 & (90)(40) = 3600 \\
 \text{Total} = 16400 & \text{Total} = 9000
\end{array}
$$

$$\text{gamma} = \frac{16400 - 9000}{16400 + 9000} = \frac{7400}{25400} = .291$$

If you compute z for this gamma you will find it is significant at $< .05$ ($z = 2.42$). Thus, even with a significant gamma it is possible to get a lambda of zero.

10.3.4 Somer's d

Somer's d is a measure of association that, although quite similar to gamma, is more restrictive in that it takes into account pairs that are tied on the dependent variable. Taking the tied pairs into account has the effect of weakening the numeric value of the association, as will be readily seen from the formula. By taking into account pairs tied on the dependent variable, we gain more information than gamma reveals to us. Somer's d has no either/or feature. It tells us that as X increases so does Y, but since it is an asymmetric statistic, not vice versa.

$$d = \frac{Ns - Nd}{Ns + Nd + Ty} \tag{10.3}$$

where Ty = tied on the dependent variable

Since the dependent variable is arrayed across the rows, pairs that are tied on Y are located across the rows. Taking cell A as our first target cell, we find that pairs to the right of it with values of 14 and 8 are tied with it. Taking cell B as the target cell we find that only cell C is tied with it. We calculated Ty by multiplying the value of the target cell by all tied cases to the right of it.

Target Cell

cell A = (20)(14 + 8) = 440
cell B = (14)(8)   = 112
cell D = (14)(23 + 14) = 518
cell E = (23)(14)   = 322
cell G = (4)(24 + 14) = 152
cell H = (24)(14)   = 336

total Ty = 1880

We already have Ns and Nd values from gamma so all that we have to do is put Ty into the formula:

$$d = \frac{Ns - Nd}{Ns + Nd + Ty} = \frac{2746 - 1256}{2746 + 1256 + 1880} = \frac{1490}{5882} = .2533$$

Like lambda, Somer's d is an asymmetric statistic that can also be computed as a symmetrical statistic. The value of Somer's d can vary between -1.0 and $+1.0$ and can be interpreted as a PRE statistic. Somer's d is tested for significance with the same formula as for testing gamma.

10.3.5 Tau-*b*

Tau-*b* is even more restrictive than Somer's *d* in that it includes pairs tied on *X* but not on *Y* and pairs tied on *Y* but not on *X*, that is, ties on one variable or the other but not on both. What this means it that tau-*b* can only reach -1.0 or $+1.0$ when all the frequencies fall on the diagonal, indicating that when *X* increases, *Y* increases, and similarly, when *Y* increases, *X* increases. Like gamma and Somer's *d*, tau-*b* uses the difference between *Ns* and *Nd* as the numerator. The formula for tau-*b* is

$$\text{tau-}b = \frac{Ns - Nb}{\sqrt{(Ns + Nd + Ty)(Ns + Nd + Tx)}} \tag{10.4}$$

We have alreaedy calculated all values except *Tx*. *Tx* is calculated just like *Ty* except that now we work down the columns of the independent variable instead of across the row of the dependent variable. Again taking cell A as the target cell, we multiply cell A by the pairs in each cell immediately below it.

Target Cell

$$
\begin{aligned}
\text{cell A} &= (20)(14 + 4) &&= 360 \\
\text{cell B} &= (14)(23 + 24) &&= 658 \\
\text{cell C} &= (8)(14 + 14) &&= 224 \\
\text{cell D} &= (14)(4) &&= 56 \\
\text{cell E} &= (23)(24) &&= 552 \\
\text{cell F} &= (14)(14) &&= 196 \\
&\text{total } Tx &&= 2046
\end{aligned}
$$

Putting in the values we get

$$\text{tau-}b = \frac{Ns - Nd}{\sqrt{(Ns + Nd + Ty)(Ns + Nd + Tx)}} = \frac{1490}{\sqrt{(5882)(2746 + 1256 + 2046)}}$$

$$= \frac{1490}{\sqrt{(5882)(6048)}} = \frac{1490}{\sqrt{35574336}} = \frac{1490}{5964.422} = .2498$$

Tau-*b* is also a PRE statistic that ranges between -1.0 and $+1.0$. Its use, however, is limited to square tables (equal numbers of rows and columns) such as we have here. We can test tau-*b* for significance by using the *z* distribution.

$$H_0: \text{tau-}b = 0 \tag{10.5}$$

$$z = \frac{\text{tau-}b}{\sqrt{\dfrac{4(r + 1)(c + 1)}{9Nrc}}}$$

where   *r* = number of rows

   c = number of columns
   and 4 and 9 are constants

Putting in the numbers we get

$$z = \cfrac{\text{tau-}b}{\sqrt{\cfrac{4(r+1)(c+1)}{9Nrc}}} = \cfrac{.2498}{\sqrt{\cfrac{(4(3+1)(3+1)}{9(135)(3)(3)}}}$$

$$= \cfrac{.2498}{\sqrt{\cfrac{4(16)}{9(1215)}}} = \cfrac{.2498}{\sqrt{\cfrac{64}{10935}}} = \cfrac{.2498}{\sqrt{.005853}} = \cfrac{.2498}{.0765} = 3.26$$

A z of 3.26 is associated with an area of .4994. Adding this figure to the other side of the curve, we get .9994; $1 - .9994$ leaves only .0006, or .06 percent of the area under the normal curve beyond a z of 3.26. Note that this value of .0006 is the significance level for tau-b given in the computer printout.

10.3.6 Tau-c

As mentioned, tau-b is not appropriate for tables with unequal rows and columns. **Tau-c** is a rarely used statistic but will be briefly discussed since it is given in the printout. Like gamma, tau-c takes only untied pairs into consideration. Unlike tau-b, it does not take the size of the table (the number of rows and columns) into account. The formula for tau-c is

$$\text{tau-}c = \frac{2m(Ns - Nd)}{N^2(m-1)} \tag{10.6}$$

where $m = $ the minimum (smaller of) r or c

   $N^2 = $ sample size squared

We already have all the values necessary to compute tau-c so we can simply substitute:

$$\text{tau-}c = \frac{2m(Ns - Nd)}{N^2(m-1)} = \frac{(2)(3)(1490)}{135^2(2)} = \frac{8940}{(18225)(2)}$$

$$= \frac{8940}{36450} = .2453$$

The test for significance of tau-c is the same as for tau-b.

10.3.7 Which Test of Association Should We Use?

Herbert Costner has written, "We suffer an embarrassment of riches with regard to measures of association" (1965, p. 341). He believes that whenever possible a PRE measure is preferable to any other kind. But all the statistics examined so far are PRE statistics; how do we decide which one to use? We have seen that the primary differentiation among them concerns whether and which ties are included in the denominator. The inclusion of ties weakens the value of the measure of association since their inclusion increases the magnitude of the denominator while the numerator (the similar minus the dissimilar pairs) remains constant for all measures.

Gamma, by ignoring ties altogether, yields the strongest measure of association. This probably accounts for its popularity, but it should not be seen as a positive feature. When a table has a large number of ties it is particularly inadvisable to use gamma. Tau measures (tau-*b* with square tables and tau-*c* with rectangular tables) are more conservative than gamma, and thus preferable. Lambda is rarely the preferred statistic because of the quirk we noted. To summarize briefly the issue of the choice of a statistic with data at this level we quote Kohout (1974, p. 231):

> Given that a researcher has ordinal data arrayed in a contingency table, where tau, gamma, and Somer's d may be applied, he must decide which one of the three measures is appropriate for his research problem. This decision should be made on the basis of the type of relationship his research hypothesis involves. If his theory concerns merely a "weak monotonic relationship," gamma would be the best choice. If his theory concerns a "strictly monotonic asymmetric relationship," Somer's d would be best. Finally, if his theory concerns a "category-rank linear relationship," tau [*b*] would be the appropriate index to use.

That is, you should choose your measures of association according to the theoretical context and meaning rather than their popularity or ease of computation. All of these measures are valid, but they differ in the form or nature of the association as well as in their strength. In our example of physical restriction and social isolation, the best measure would be Somer's *d* because the relationship is consistent with a "strictly monotonic asymmetric relationship." That is, one of the variables (social isolation) is clearly dependent and the other is clearly independent.

10.4 MEASURES OF ASSOCIATION BASED ON CHI-SQUARE

If the chi-square test of independence leads to the rejection of the null, the two variables are not independent of one another and are therefore associated. But chi-square does not reveal the strength of the relationship. As well as knowing if there is a real difference between variables, we would also like to know how strongly they are related to one another. As we have seen, chi-square is very sensitive to sample size. The larger the sample the more likely we are to get a significant chi-square if there is an actual difference in the population. This result is intuitively reasonable because the larger the sample the more likely we are to capture the true situation in the population from which the sample was drawn. It is quite possible with very large samples to attain a high level of significance when the variables are so weakly related that we are tempted to ask "so what?" The chi-square-based measures of association help us to decide if the significant difference is really worth attending to.

Chi-square-based measures of association standardize χ^2 by the maximum attainable χ^2. The maximum attainable χ^2 in a 2 × 2 table is directly proportional to N (the sample size) and is only attained when all cases fall in one of the diagonals, as in the following example:

50	0	50
0	50	50

50 50 100

expected for each cell $= \dfrac{50 \times 50}{100} = 25$

$$\chi^2 = \frac{(50 - 25)^2}{25} \cdots \frac{(50 - 25)^2}{25} \cdots$$

$$= \frac{625}{25} \cdots \frac{625}{25} \cdots$$

$$= 25 + 25 + 25 + 25 = 100 = N$$

The maximum attainable chi-square in a table greater than 2×2 is $N(k - 1)$, where k is the smaller of the number or rows or columns in a table. By dividing χ^2 by its maximum attainable value, we standardize it to a true range (between zero and 1) to render different values based on different Ns comparable (just as we did with crime figures in Chapter 2 in standardizing them by city size to obtain comparable rates).

10.4.1 Contingency Coefficient

We discussed phi as a chi-square-based measure in Chapter 9. Another chi-square-based measure of association is the **contingency coefficient** (C), which is appropriate for categorized variables having more than two categories. C is not a PRE measure (phi squared, however, does have a PRE interpretation) and therefore lacks a strict interpretation. Another problem with C is that its upper range is not 1 but, rather, depends on the size of the table. The upper limit of C is determined by the formula $\sqrt{(r - 1)/r}$, where r equals the number of rows in the table. In a 3×3 table, for instance, the upper limit of C is $\sqrt{2/3} = \sqrt{.666} = .816$. Even in a 10×10 table the upper limit is only .949. The interpretation of C does not go beyond that given by chi-square, that is, the concept of deviation from independence. Thus, it is often more advisable to use a PRE measure whenever possible. Nevertheless, there may be occasions when C might be useful, and it does have the advantage of being quickly and easily computed from the chi-square value. The formula for the contingency coefficient is as follows:

$$C = \sqrt{\frac{\chi^2}{\chi^2 + N}} \tag{10.7}$$

For our walking aid/social isolation data,

$$C = \sqrt{\frac{15.10}{15.10 + 135}} = \sqrt{\frac{15.10}{150.10}} = \sqrt{.1006} = .317$$

The computed value matches the printout. Since the chi-square on which it is based is significant, C is significant.

10.4.2 Cramer's *V*

Cramer's *V* is the final chi-square-based measure given in the printout. This statistic is a modification of the phi statistic that allows for the analysis of tables that are greater than 2×2. Like *C*, Cramer's *V* is not a PRE statistic. You will note from Formula 10.6 that *V* is identical to phi except that *N* is multiplied by $L - 1$, where *L* is the lesser of either the number of rows or columns.

$$V = \sqrt{\frac{\chi^2}{N(L-1)}} \tag{10.8}$$

where $L - 1$ = lesser of $(r - 1)$ or $(c - 1)$

We have $3 - 1 = 2$ rows and $3 - 1 = 2$ columns; thus we multiply *N* by 2. For our walking aid/social isolation data,

$$V = \sqrt{\frac{15.10}{(135)(2)}} = \sqrt{\frac{15.10}{270}} = \sqrt{.05592} = .236$$

10.4.3 Spearman's Rank Order Correlation

Sometimes social science data are in the form of rankings. **Spearman's rank order correlation (rho)** is ideal for measuring association between two variables with values that have been ordered into ranks on a case-by-case basis rather than into categories, as are the other measures discussed here. We are essentially asking if a case's rank on one variable can predict its rank on another variable.

Suppose that we have ten high school students who have taken the ACT college entrance exam in math and English and have obtained the scores in Table 10.6. Our first task is to rank order these scores from highest to lowest. Jane's score of 20 on the math test is the highest, so she is ranked number 1 on this variable. Her score of 17 on the English is the third highest, so she is ranked number

TABLE 10.6 RANK-ORDER OF STUDENTS ON ACT ENGLISH AND MATH SCORES

	Math		English			
	x	Rank	*x*	Rank	*D*	D^2
Jane	20	1	17	3	−2	4
Frank	19	2	20	1	1	1
José	17	3	13	4	−1	1
Ray	14	4	18	2	2	4
Sheila	12	5	8	7.5	−2.5	6.25
Tony	11	6	8	7.5	−1.5	2.25
Kurt	10	8	10	5	3	9
Ahmed	10	8	9	6	2	4
Joyce	10	8	6	10	−2	4
Martin	7	10	7	9	1	1
Sums					0.00	36.50

3 on this variable. Each student is so ranked. Kurt, Ahmed, and Joyce all scored 10 on the math exam. In the case of tied ranks such as these, we assign each case the average of the three ranks they would have occupied had their scores not been tied. These three subjects would have occupied ranks 7, 8, and 9. The average of these three ranks is 8, so they are all assigned this rank. Similarly, Sheila and Tony both scored 8 on the English test and are assigned the average of the two ranks they would have occupied had they not tied: $(7 + 8)/2 = 7.5$.

After we have determined the appropriate rankings we subtract the rank on the English exam from the rank on the math exam for each case and enter that value under D for "rank difference." Note that the sum of D is always zero. This is analogous to subtracting the mean from each raw score, as we did in Chapter 3. The positive and negative differences will cancel each other out. We then square the differences to arrive at the D squared values, which are then summed. This value is entered into Formula 10.9 for computing Spearman's rho. The 6 in the formula is a constant; it does not vary across computations.

$$r_s = 1 - \frac{6(\Sigma D^2)}{N(N^2 - 1)} = 1 - \frac{(6)(36.5)}{10(100 - 1)} = 1 - \frac{219}{990} \tag{10.9}$$

$$= 1 - .2212 = .779$$

Spearman's rho ranges from -1.0 to $+1.0$ and is an index of the strength of association between two rank-ordered variables. A perfect positive association would exist in the case of perfect agreement among the ranks, and a perfect negative association would exist for perfect disagreement among the ranks. Rho has a PRE interpretation when squared. If we square .779 we get .607, which means that our error is reduced by 60.7 percent when predicting rank with knowledge of one variable from rank on the other, as compared to predicting rank without knowledge of the other variable.

Assuming that these ten cases are a random sample from the population, we can determine whether the sample finding can be generalized to the population. Since we have only ten cases, the z distribution would not be appropriate for our test of significance. Fortunately, when the number of cases is ten or more, the distribution of rho approximates the t distribution. We now test for significance with the t distribution.

$$H_0 : r_s = 0. \tag{10.10}$$

$$t = r_s \sqrt{\frac{N - 2}{1 - r_s^2}} = .779 \sqrt{\frac{8}{1 - .607}} = .779 \sqrt{\frac{8}{.393}}$$

$$= .779 \sqrt{20.356} = (.779)(4.512) = 3.51$$

Turning to the t distribution table with 8 df ($N - 2$), we see that a t value of 2.896 is required to reject the null hypothesis with a one-tailed test and alpha set at .01. Our computed t exceeds this critical value, and we can thus reject the null and conclude that it is unlikely that these data came from a population in which $r_s = 0$.

The computer value of r_s for these data is .7754 (not shown). The reason for the slight difference is that the computer program uses a correction factor when it encounters tied ranks. However, unless there are an extensive number of tied ranks (25 percent or more) the difference is so slight that it can be safely ignored. For instance, the difference between our calculation and the computer's is only .0036.

10.5 SUMMARY

Association refers to the connectedness or relatedness of two or more variables. We use various statistics to determine whether or not an association exists, its strength, and its direction. We have examined various techniques for making these determinations in cases where the variables are measured at the nominal and interval levels. Most of these techniques are based on simple ratios of similar and dissimilar pairs (agreement to disagreement) of cases. Lambda is rarely used, but it is useful for illustrating the logic of proportional reduction in error. Basically, PRE means that knowing how one variable is distributed improves our ability to predict values on another variable. Any PRE measure is a ratio of errors made in predicting values of one variable made without knowledge of a second variable to errors made with knowledge of the second variable.

The gamma, Somer's *d,* and the tau measures differ in their computations depending on how they deal with tied cases. Gamma ignores them completely, and thus yields the most liberal index of association, and tau-*b* yields the most conservative index. All the measures are valid, but before choosing one you should be concerned with the theoretical context of your research and with the form and nature of the association. Choosing a measure simply to "maximize" the strength of the association is dishonest, and choosing one for no other reason than to be conservative is naive.

Chi-square-based measures of association (phi, contingency coefficient, and Cramer's *V*) standardize chi-square to its maximum attainable value. When squared, phi has a PRE interpretation, but *C* and *V* do not. Phi is used for 2 × 2 tables, *C* and *V* are used for larger tables.

Spearman's rho is an index of the strength of association between two variables that have been rank-ordered on a case-by-case basis on some attribute. When squared it is a PRE measure. All measures of association should be tested for statistical significance.

PRACTICE APPLICATION:
NONPARAMETRIC ORDINAL-LEVEL ASSOCIATION

What difference does the victim's sex make in the sentencing of sex offenders? We have 368 offenders who offended against females and 63 who offended against males. A low sentence is defined as one in which the offender was placed on probation with from zero to 90 days in jail. A medium sentence is defined as probation with any jail sentence less than six months, and a high sentence is defined as any prison sentence. We find the following conditional distribution:

	Victim's Sex		
Sentence	Female	Male	
Low	128	8	136
Medium	57	13	70
High	183	42	225
	368	63	431

$$\chi^2 = 12.15$$

Calculate lambda.

Since all the modal cell category scores are in the same category of the independent variable, lambda will be zero.

$$E_1 = 206 \qquad E_2 = 185 + 21 = 206 \qquad 206 - 206/206 = 0$$

Compute gamma.

$$Ns = \begin{aligned} 128(13 + 42) &= 7040 \\ (57)(42) &= 2394 \\ \text{total} &= 9434 \end{aligned} \qquad Nd = \begin{aligned} 8(57 + 183) &= 1920 \\ (13)(183) &= 2379 \\ \text{total} &= 4299 \end{aligned}$$

$$\gamma = \frac{Ns - Nd}{Ns + Nd} = \frac{9434 - 4299}{9434 + 4299} = \frac{5135}{13733} = .374$$

Test gamma for significance, with alpha = .05, two-tailed test.

$$H_0 : \gamma = 0$$

$$z = \gamma \sqrt{\frac{Ns + Nd}{N(1 - \gamma^2)}} = .374 \sqrt{\frac{13733}{431(1 - .374^2)}}$$

$$= .374 \sqrt{\frac{13733}{(431)(.86)}} = (.374)(6.087) = 2.27$$

Critical $z = 1.96$, computed $z = 2.27$; reject the null hypothesis.

Compute Somer's d. We have Ns and Nd; compute Ty.

$$(128)(8) \quad = 1024$$
$$(57)(13) \quad = \quad 741$$
$$(183)(42) = 7686$$
$$\text{total } Ty = 9451$$

$$d = \frac{Ns - Nd}{Ns + Nd + Ty} = \frac{9434 - 4299}{9434 + 4299 + 9451} = \frac{5135}{23184} = .221$$

Compute tau-b. We have Ns, Nd, and Ty; compute Tx.

$$128(57 + 183) = 30720$$
$$(57)(183) \qquad = 10431$$

$$8(13 + 42) \quad = \quad 440$$

$$(13)(42) \quad = \quad 546$$

$$\text{total } Tx = 42137$$

$$\text{tau-}b = \frac{Ns - Nd}{\sqrt{(Ns + Nd + Ty)(Ns + Nd + Tx)}} = \frac{5135}{\sqrt{(23184)(13733 + 42137)}}$$

$$= \frac{5135}{\sqrt{(23184)(55870)}} = \frac{5135}{\sqrt{1295290080}} = \frac{5135}{35990.1} = .143$$

Test tau-b for significance, with alpha $= .05$, two-tailed test.

H_0: tau-$b = 0$

$$z = \frac{\text{tau-}b}{\sqrt{\dfrac{4(r + 1)(c + 1)}{9Nrc}}} = \frac{.143}{\sqrt{\dfrac{4(3 + 1)(2 + 1)}{9(431)(3)(2)}}}$$

$$= \frac{.143}{\sqrt{\dfrac{4(12)}{9(2586)}}} = \frac{.143}{\sqrt{\dfrac{48}{23274}}} = \frac{.143}{\sqrt{.0020624}} = \frac{.143}{.0454} = 3.15$$

Reject the null: Computed z (3.15) exceeds critical z (1.96).

Compute tau-c. We have all values to compute tau-c already.

$$\text{tau-}c = \frac{2m(Ns - Nd)}{N^2(m - 1)} = \frac{(2)(2)(5135)}{431^2(1)} = \frac{20540}{(185761)(1)}$$

$$= \frac{20540}{185761} = .1106$$

Test tau-c for significance, with alpha $= .05$, two-tailed test.

H_0: tau-$c = 0$

$$z = \frac{\text{tau-}c}{\sqrt{\dfrac{4(r + 1)(c + 1)}{9Nrc}}} = \frac{.1106}{\sqrt{\dfrac{4(3 + 1)(2 + 1)}{9(431)(3)(2)}}}$$

$$= \frac{.1106}{\sqrt{\dfrac{4(12)}{9(2586)}}} = \frac{.1106}{\sqrt{\dfrac{48}{23274}}} = \frac{.1106}{\sqrt{.0020624}} = \frac{.1106}{.0454} = 2.44$$

Reject the null: Computed z exceeds critical z.

Compute the chi-square-based measures, C and V ($\chi^2 = 12.15$).

$$C = \sqrt{\chi^2/\chi^2 + N} = \sqrt{\frac{12.15}{443.15}} = \sqrt{.0274} = .165$$

$$V = \sqrt{\chi^2/N(L-1)} = \sqrt{\frac{12.15}{441}} = \sqrt{.0282} = .168$$

All computed measures indicate a weak but statistically significant association between the victim's sex and sentence type.

A researcher asks a number of men and women to rank the seriousness of 1J crimes. The researcher notes that although males tend to rank property crimes higher, females tend to rank personal crimes as more serious. Compute Spearman's rho to determine how these rankings agree or disagree.

Crime	Males Rank	Females Rank	D	D^2
Robbery	1	6	−5	25
Burglary	2	7	−5	25
Child molesting	3	2	1	1
Auto theft	4	11	−7	49
Rape	5	1	4	16
Drug trafficking	6	10	−4	16
Assault (fighting)	7	8	−1	1
Indecent exposure	8	9	−1	1
Trafficking in pornography	9	5	4	16
Wife beating	10	3	7	49
Dog fighting	11	4	7	49
		Sums	0	248

$$r_s = 1 - \frac{6(\Sigma D^2)}{N(N^2-1)} = 1 - \frac{(6)(248)}{11(121-1)} = 1 - \frac{1488}{1320}$$

$$= 1 - 1.127 = -.127$$

Test r_s for significance, with alpha = .05, two-tailed test.

$H_0 : r_s = 0.00$

$$t = r_s \sqrt{\frac{N-2}{1-r^2}} = -.127\sqrt{\frac{9}{1-.0161}} = -.127\sqrt{\frac{9}{.9839}}$$

$$= -.127\sqrt{9.1473} = (-.127)(3.024) = -0.384$$

Do not reject null: Computed t (−0.384) is less than critical t (2.08).

APPENDIX: Computer Instructions for Table 10.5

Command 10.1

SPSSX

```
COMPUTE ISOL = ISOA + ISOB + ISOC + ISOD + ISOE + ISOF + ISOG + ISOH + ISOI
RECODE ISOL (LO THRU 18=1)(19 THRU 23=2)(24 THRU HI=3)
SELECT IF (MSCON EQ 0)
CROSSTABS TABLES = ISOL BY WAID
STATISTICS ALL
```

SAS

```
IF ISOL <=18 THEN ISOL=1;
ELSE IF ISOL => 19 AND ISOL <= 23 THEN ISOL=2;
ELSE IF ISOL => 24 THEN ISOL=3;
IF MSCON=0;
PROC FREQ;
   TABLES ISOL*WAID/ALL;
```

Since each item on the social isolation scale was entered individually into the computer, we have to compute the total social isolation score by using the COMPUTE command. We then recode these scores into low, medium, and high levels of social isolation, trying to ensure that each level has approximately one-third of the cases, by using the RECODE command. We only want the MS cases, so we eliminate the control group by using the SELECT IF (MSCON EQ 0) command. We then ask the computer for a crosstabulation of our two variables, putting the dependent variable (ISOL) first and asking for all available statistics.

REFERENCES AND SUGGESTED READING

Costner, H. (1965). Criteria for measures of association. *American Sociological Review,* 30:341–353.

Gibbons, J. (1971). *Nonparametric statistical inference.* New York: McGraw-Hill: An excellent treatment of most nonparametric tests, but definitely not for those who suffer from math anxiety.

Kohout, F. (1974). *Statistics for social scientists.* New York: Wiley. Contains a very good treatment of nominal and ordinal association.

Neal, A., and Groat, H. (1974). Social class correlates of stability and change in levels of alienation: A longitudinal study. *Sociological Quarterly,* 15:548–558.

Chapter 11

Elaboration of Tabular Data

11.1 CAUSAL ANALYSIS

In statistical analysis we never uncover "real" causes but we do perform causal analysis. We say such things as "*A* is assumed to be a causal factor of *B* if the presence of *A* increases the probability that *B* will occur." We are not saying in statements of this kind that changes in *A* will cause changes in *B* in a completely prescribed way. We operate in a probabilistic, not deterministic, world. I agree with Blalock that causality is really a theoretical construct that cannot be demonstrated empirically: "But this does not mean that it is not helpful to think causally and to develop causal models that have implications that are indirectly testable" (1972, p. 6). We will examine this important concept of causality within the framework of the elaboration of tabular data.

11.2 CRITERIA FOR CAUSALITY

11.2.1 Association

The following discussion of the criteria for causality is indebted to Hirschi and Selvin (1966). The first criterion for causality is that an association must exist between presumed cause and effect. It is obvious that if two variables do not covary, neither can be considered to be a candidate for exerting causal influence on the other. For example, sexual intercourse increases the probability that conception will occur. That is, if sexual intercourse is associated with conception, conception must at least occasionally occur when sexual intercourse occurs. Conversely, if sexual intercourse can occur infinitely and conception has never been known to follow, it cannot be said to be a cause of conception. The sexual intercourse/conception association is a very good example for examining the concept of causality because almost everyone seems to think that the relationship between them is very strong. Actually there is a very weak association because there are numerous intercourse events that are not followed by conception.

As we saw in Chapter 10, variables are related to one another in varying degrees—which underscores the probabilistic nature of causality. A perfect positive relationship exists when we observe a one-to-one correspondence between the two variables being explored. A perfect relationship between sexual intercourse and conception would be one in which every act of intercourse, without exception, resulted in conception. A perfect negative association would be one in which every increase in event *A* produced a corresponding decrease in event *B*. The overwhelming majority of the time, however, events occur that only occasionally result in the occurrence of other events. But as long as some sort of consistency is observed between events *A* and *B*, we have a candidate for causal inference.

11.2.2 Temporal Order

For variable *A* to be considered a causal candidate for the occurence of *B*, it must occur before *B* in time. Causal order does not present much of a problem in the physical sciences. We can say without fear of contradiction that the sun shining on the window causes the glass to be warm, but it would be absurd to say that the warmth of the glass causes the sun to shine on it. It is not so easy in the behavioral sciences because of the reciprocal feedback nature of many of the phonemena we study. Consider the relationship between achievement and self-esteem. It has been well demonstrated that these two variables vary positively together. But which is causally prior? Each variable can cause an increase in the other in a felicitous spiral of achievement and self-esteem without ever actually determining which was ultimately responsible for setting the spiral in motion.

11.2.3 Spuriousness

The third criterion is that the relationship must not statistically disappear when the influence of other variables are considered. Someone once calculated a fairly high positive association between ice-cream consumption and rape. I have often used this example in my classes to demonstrate spuriousness. When I ask students to offer explanations, I have received some interesting ones, ranging from the possible aphrodisiac effect of ice cream to more sophisticated explanations of how the sugar in ice cream can affect a person's hypoglycemia and lead to aggression. Only occasionally do I get a student who realizes that the relationship is spurious in that a third variable, hot weather, leads to an increase in both the rate of ice cream consumption and rape. Ice cream consumption, although associated with the rape rate, has no causal influence on it; the two variables are associated but not causally connected. The relationship is explained away by considering a third variable, which is prior to both and influences the increase in both.

Do note that although a variable can be dismissed as a causal explanation because it is spurious, we need not dismiss it as a predictor. Because a correlation is spurious it does not mean that it is false; a measure of association is what it is. Spuriousness means that the interpretation of the association, not the association itself, is false. If one were so inclined, the rate of ice cream consumption could be used to predict fluctuations in the rape rate. This variable might serve as a better quantifiable predictor of the phenomenon than any other variable offering a theoretical adequate explanation, such as male sexual politics, alcohol abuse, and so on.

It would be useful at this point to examine some of the misunderstandings revolving around the concepts of "variables" and "constants" as they apply to causality. As we have seen, a variable is a factor that takes on a range of different values. A constant is a factor that does not vary across the phenomenon of interest. Scientific research is interested in exploring how factors that vary either qualitatively or quantitatively across a dependent variable produce changes in that dependent variable. If a factor is absolutely necessary to the viability of the dependent variable, but that factor does not vary, that is, it is always present in conjunction with the dependent variable, then that factor can be safely ignored in research as a cause. For instance, if we set out to do research into what makes a "great professional football player," we can safely ignore the variable of gender. Although gender is a variable, in this case it is a constant because all professional football players, great or otherwise, are males. Put otherwise, although up to the present time it has been absolutely necessary to be a male to be a professional big-league football player, we cannot include gender as a factor in determining what goes into making a great one precisely because of this nonvariability. Being a male is thus a necessary condition for being a great football player, but it is hardly a sufficient condition. Let us see what we mean by *necessary* and *sufficient*.

11.2.4 Necessary Cause

The substance of the following discussion is that a variable does not have to be a necessary or sufficient cause or condition of an event to be a causal candidate. A **necessary cause** or condition is one that must be present for an effect to follow. That is, if *A* is not present, there is no known incidence in which *B* has occurred. "Immaculate conception" and the newly developed technique of in vitro fertilization notwithstanding, intercourse is a necessary cause of conception. Certainly, being a female is necessary to being pregnant. And being a native-born white male over 35 with a well-padded wallet appears thus far to be a necessary cause of becoming president of the United States. Note that being a woman and experiencing intercourse does not mean that a woman will become pregnant any more than a man who fits the preceding profile will become president. They are merely necessary preconditions for the possibility and not sufficient per se.

11.2.5 Sufficient Cause

A **sufficient cause** is a cause or condition that by itself is able to produce an event. If other causal agents are needed to augment the nominated cause, it is not a sufficient cause. This does not mean that a sufficient cause is also a necessary cause. For instance, being a convict or ex-convict is sufficient to cause stigma, discrimination, and a "spoiled identity." But there are many other achieved and ascribed statuses, such as being a victim of some kind of deforming disease, being a carrier of AIDS, being "crazy," and so on, that are themselves sufficient ways of acquiring a spoiled identity. Likewise, a cause can be necessary without being sufficient. Sexual intercourse is a necessary cause of pregnancy but it is not a sufficient one. There are other variables in combination, such as the chemical environment of the womb, the absence of a contraceptive device, the fecundity of the female and the potency of the male, and so on, that are required to produce conception.

11.2.6 Necessary and Sufficient Cause

A cause is a **necessary and sufficient cause** if, and only if, it must be present for the effect to occur and has no help from other variables. Can you think of any nominated cause in behavioral science that meets this rigorous requirement for establishing a causal relationship between two variables? Neither can I. Yet this is the impied demand of laypersons who point out exceptions to causal statements made by social scientists when they assert a causal connection between two variables. "Poverty, prejudice, unemployment, and a brutal childhood are not causes of crime because there are millions who suffer these privations without resorting to crime," they say. What they are really saying is that if we cannot produce necessary and sufficient causes of the phenomena we study, the whole enterprise of social science is useless and cannot tell us anything of value. We cannot satisfy the necessary and sufficient criterion of causality and we never will.

11.3 STATISTICAL DEMONSTRATION OF CAUSE-AND-EFFECT RELATIONSHIPS

The following is a statistical illustration of a wholly mythical necessary and sufficient cause. Suppose we obtain a sample of 500 women who have experienced sexual intercourse and 500 women who have not. We then ask each woman if she had ever been pregnant. Having obtained the data, we array them in a 2 × 2 table and discover the bivariate distribution in Table 11.1. When we examine

TABLE 11.1 HYPOTHETICAL NECESSARY AND SUFFICIENT CAUSE

Ever Pregnant	Experienced Intercourse		Total
	Yes	No	
Yes	A 500	B 000	500
No	C 000	D 500	500
Total	500	500	1000

$$\chi^2 = 1000 \qquad \phi = 1.0$$

the relationship between just two variables, as we are doing in this case, the relationship is known as a **zero-order relationship**.

Such a table tells us the following:

1. Every woman who had intercourse got pregnant (cell A).
2. No woman got pregnant who never had intercourse (cell B).
3. No woman who had experienced intercourse did not get pregnant (cell C).
4. No woman who never had intercourse got pregnant (cell D).

The conclusion that must be reached from this example is that sexual intercourse is a cause or condition that will bring about the effect (pregnancy) entirely by itself and without which the effect cannot occur. The computed statistics support the conclusion. We have "maximum" significance in that chi-square is equal to $N = 1000$, and perfect association in that phi equals 1.0. Having sexual intercourse, then, explains 100 percent of the variance in the pregnancy variable, leaving no variance to be accounted for by any other variables. This, of course, is nonsense, as is any other "cause" nominated as necessary and sufficient—no one thing is *the* cause of anything.

Let us consider a much more plausible example of what a tabular analysis would look like with the same sample of women, where sexual intercourse is a necessary but not sufficient cause of pregnancy (Table 11.2).

We observe the following:

1. Twenty percent of the women who had intercourse got pregnant, indicating that the state of pregnancy does not characteristically follow an act of intercourse (cell A).
2. No woman who never had intercourse got pregnant, indicating that intercourse is perhaps a necessary cause of pregnancy (cell B).
3. Of the women who had intercourse, 80 percent did not get pregnant, indicating that although intercourse is a necessary condition it is far from sufficient (cell C).
4. No woman who never had intercourse got pregnant, which reinforces the notion that intercourse is a necessary condition for pregnancy (cell D). (Of course, in these days of artificial insemination, sexual intercourse is no longer a necessary cause of pregnancy in an absolute sense).

TABLE 11.2 HYPOTHETICAL NECESSARY CAUSE

Ever Pregnant	Experienced Intercourse		Total
	Yes	No	
Yes	A 100	B 000	100
No	C 400	D 500	900
Total	500	500	1000

$$\chi^2 = 111.05 \qquad \phi = .333$$

The statistics illustrate two important concepts, one statistical and the other methodological/theoretical. First, the large computed chi-square indicates that the probability of randomly selecting such a sample from a population where the probability for getting pregnant for both groups is equal is about 1 million to one. Despite this extremely high probability level, the association between the two variables is only weak to moderate. The magnitude of the computed chi-square is a function of the sample size; the magnitude of the computed phi is a function of the distribution of the cases in the cell diagonals and would not be affected by sample size given constant cell percentages. I know that I have already made this point, but I feel that I cannot make it too often. Far too much rope has been given to those who blithely compute chi-squares and consider significance levels to be sacred.

The second point is aimed at those who dismiss any variable as a cause when it is not characteristic. For instance, unemployment is often disparaged as a cause of crime (one among many) because the vast majority of those who become unemployed do not commit crimes; that is, it is not "characteristic" of the unemployed to commit crimes. As we have just seen, intercourse is not characteristically followed by pregnancy, but who among us who would dismiss sexual intercourse as *the* cause of pregnancy would also dismiss it as *a* cause? The importance of one variable in explaining another lies not in whether or not it is characteristic but rather in how much of the variance it can uniquely account for in the dependent variable or how much it reduces prediction error.

The whole point of the preceding discussion is to demonstrate that although there are few, if any, variables in social science that must necessarily be present to produce a specific effect, we are not precluded from causal analysis. What we can do is intelligently and accurately identify clusters of variables that in combination increase the probabilty of an event's occurrence. This observation leads into the next topic—the elaboration of bivariate tables, or multivariate contingency analysis.

11.4 MULTIVARIATE CONTINGENCY ANALYSIS

If no one independent variable satisfactorily accounts for all the variance observed in the dependent variable, it is obvious that other variables as yet unexamined must be also affecting the distribution of the dependent variable. Perhaps it is even the case that the association observed in the bivariate table is spurious, meaning that some third variable affects both the dependent and the independent variables in such a way that if its effects were to be removed, any observed relationship between the initial two variables would disappear. The classic example of **spuriousness** is the strong association between the number of firefighters at a fire and the magnitude of the dollar loss incurred by the fire (the more firefighters at the fire the greater the dollar loss). Does this strong association mean that there is a cause-and-effect relationship operating? Of course not. A third variable, namely, the size of the fire, determines both the number of firefighters attending the fire and the magnitude of the dollar loss. The initial relationship, therefore, is spurious in a causal sense.

Taking the size of the fire into account is an example of what is known as controlling for, or holding constant, the effects of a third variable. We accomplish the task of controlling for the effects of third variables by physically dividing our sample into subsamples based on categories of the control variable. We then examine the relationship between the original two variables within the categories of the control variable. By *controlling for* or *holding constant,* we mean that categories of the third variable are fixed so that they are no longer free to vary. The size of fire variable, for instance, is free to vary between large and small, or perhaps small, medium, and large. But once we determine categories of the third variable and then reexamine the bivariate relationship within those categories, we have essentially "controlled" its variability by changing a variable into a constant. More correctly perhaps, we have created as many constants as we have categories of the control variable. When reexamining the basic bivariate relationship within any given category of the third variable, now no longer free to vary, we have in effect eliminated the influence of the third variable. The influence of the third variable can be ascertained only when we compare the outcomes of the bivariate relationship across its categories.

To illustrate this process, let us consider an example from our offender data. Let us suppose we want to examine the effects of the relationship of the offender to the victim on the type of sentence (probation or prison) among sex offenders. We divide these offender/victim relationships into two gross categories, strangers and acquaintances, and compute chi-square and gamma for this zero-order bivariate relationship. The results are given in part A of Table 11.3. We observe that this relationship is highly significant and fairly strong. We then ask ourselves what else besides victim/offender relationship could influence sentence type. The most obvious answer is the seriousness of the crime. To convince ourselves of this possibility, we crosstabulate sentence type with crime seriousness (recoded into two categories by low and high) and obtain the zero-order results in Part B of the table. These results show a much stronger association between crime seriousness and sentence type than between offender/victim and sentence type. (See the chapter appendix for recode instructions.)

We can now examine the association between sentence type and offender victim/relationship within the two categories of crime seriousness, a variable that is now no longer free to vary. Part C presents two tables assessing this association within low and high categories of crime seriousness. We see that when crime seriousness is taken into account, the association between sentence type and offender/victim relationship is nonsignificant (both conditional chi-square values are far from the critical value of 3.841). Thus, the initially observed relationship was spurious in a causal sense. It appears that strangers are sentenced more harshly because they commit more serious crimes (they tend to use force and to harm their victims more so than offenders who are known to their victims). The bivariate table in part D assessing the association between offender/victim relationship and crime seriousness confirms this proposition. We see that 67 of the 115 stranger assaults (58.3 percent) are in the high crime seriousness category as opposed to only 62 of the 316 acquaintance assaults (19.6 percent).

In this example, the variable crime seriousness has explained away the initially observed bivariate relationship. Strangers are not punished more severely

TABLE 11.3 DEMONSTRATING A SPURIOUS RELATIONSHIP

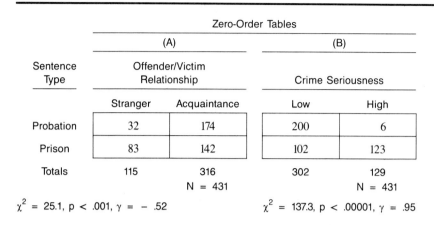

Zero-Order Tables

	(A) Offender/Victim Relationship		(B) Crime Seriousness	
Sentence Type	Stranger	Acquaintance	Low	High
Probation	32	174	200	6
Prison	83	142	102	123
Totals	115	316	302	129
		N = 431		N = 431

$\chi^2 = 25.1$, p < .001, $\gamma = -.52$ 　　　　$\chi^2 = 137.3$, p < .00001, $\gamma = .95$

Conditional (First-Order) Tables (C)

	Low Crime Seriousness Offender/Victim Relationship		High Crime Seriousness Offender/Victim Relationship	
Sentence Type	Stranger	Acquaintance	Stranger	Acquaintance
Probation	30	170	2	4
Prison	18	84	65	58
Totals	48	254	67	62
		N = 302		N = 129

$\chi^2 = 0.35$, n.s., $\gamma = -.09$ 　　　　$\chi^2 = 0.87$, n.s., $\gamma = -.38$

(D) Association between Offender/Victim Relationship
and Crime Seriousness

	Offender/Victim Relationship	
Crime Seriousness	Stranger	Acquaintance
Low	48	254
High	67	62
Totals	115	316

N = 431

$\chi^2 = 60.0$, p < .0001, $\gamma = -.70$

just because of their relationship with their victims but because they commit more serious crimes. Note that the Ns in the two conditions of crime seriousness sum to the N for the zero-order table ($302 + 129 = 431$). Note also that the cell frequencies in each of the conditional tables sum to the cell frequency of their respective zero-order cells. Tables produced in this manner are called *conditional* or *partial* tables, and the observed relationships are called *partial relationships*.

Of course, the results of the elaboration process are never this neat. If bivariate relationships were always explained away by the introduction of third variables, social science would be in a lot of trouble. There are a number of possible outcomes derived from the introduction of a third variable.

11.4.1 Explanation and Interpretation

Spuriousness occurs when a bivariate relationship disappears (or becomes nonsignificant) after a third variable is controlled for. The only reason for the initially observed relationship is that it is "caused" by one or more other variables. The spurious outcome can be subdivided into outcomes known as explanation and interpretation. A spurious outcome is called **explanation** when the original relationship is "explained away" by an **antecedent variable**, that is, a variable that precedes both the dependent and independent variables in time. In the classical example of the number of firefighters and dollar loss, the relationship is explained away by a variable that clearly occurred before both the dollar loss and the number of firefighters dispatched, the size of the fire. The following figure illustrates the relationship between an antecedent control variable and the dependent and independent variables in the context of this example.

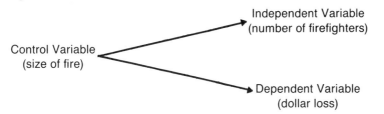

Interpretation occurs when the initial bivariate relationship is rendered spurious by an intervening variable. In the sentence type and offender/victim relationship it is obvious that crime seriousness is not an antecedent variable. The relationship between the two parties involved in the crime existed before the crime occurred. Crime seriousness is therefore an intervening variable between relationship and sentence type. Note that the association between crime seriousness and victim/offender relationship goes a long way in helping us to interpret the association between victim/offender relationship and sentence type; that is, those who offend against strangers commit more serious crimes, and more serious crimes result in more punitive sentences. In that the introduction of an intervening variable specifies a process by which the independent variable affects the dependent variable, many researchers do not consider an interpretation outcome to be a spurious one. It is argued that the independent variable "causes" the intervening control variable, which "causes" the dependent variable. In the present example, offender/victim relationship would be seen as "causing" crime seriousness, which then "causes" sentence type. The following figure illustrates the relationship between an intervening variable and the independent and dependent variables in the context of this example.

Independent Variable ————▶ Control Variable ————▶ Dependent Variable
   (relationship)   (crime Seriousness)   (sentence type)

The difference between explanation and interpretation are theoretical assumptions relating to the time ordering of the test variable. If a test variable exerts influence before both the independent and dependent variables, it is antecedent; if it exerts influence after the independent variable but before the dependent variable, it is intervening. To give a further simple example, suppose we find a significant relationship between broken homes and delinquency rates among a sample of schoolchildren. We then introduce a theoretical variable we shall call "quality of relationship with parent(s)" as a test variable and find the initial relationship to be spurious. We might then say that among children who enjoy a good relationship, delinquency rates are not affected by whether or not they come from a broken home. Similarly, we might find among children with a poor relationship that delinquency rates do not differ across categories of broken/intact homes. We thus conclude that it is the association between broken homes and quality of relationship that produced the original bivariate association; that is, poor-quality relationships increase the probability of delinquency and the probability that the home will be broken. Such a conclusion would mean that we have an explanation outcome: The initial relationship is explained away by an antecedent variable, that is, quality of relationship.

Let me emphasize here that the difference between explanation and interpretation is theoretical, not statistical. Researchers decide what type of outcome they observe according to their understanding of what is going on theoretically within the data. The statistics will only inform the researcher that the bivariate relationship disappears or becomes nonsignificant when the control variable is introduced, not why it disappeared. For instance, the data on delinquency, broken homes, and quality of relationship could reflect processes going in any and all directions. Delinquency could actually be the cause of poor relationships between child and parents rather than the other way around. Further, a child's delinquency could lead to a broken home because of mutual parental recriminations regarding the child's behavior. Only a strong sense of theoretical ordering and the ability to dig deeply into the data will lead researchers to a reasonable conclusion.

11.4.2 Replication

Replication occurs when the partial relationships are essentially of similar magnitude as the bivariate relationship, meaning that the third variable has no effect on the relationship between the zero-order variables. For example, suppose we observe a strong association of .75 between gender and amount of time spent watching sports on television among a sample of men and women, with men watching significantly more often. We then divide the sample into subsamples based on race (white/black) and reexamine the relationship, finding an association of .73 in the white category and one of .76 in the black category. In such a case we would have replicated our original finding, controlling for race. The race variable did not affect the relationship between gender and television sports watching in any way, men still watch significantly more sports on television regardless of whether they are white or black.

11.4.3 Specification

Specification occurs when the introduction of a third variable enables the researcher to specify under what conditions the bivariate relationship is "true" and when it is not "true." In such a case, one partial relationship may result in the replication of the bivariate correlation or even in a dramatic increase, whereas the other partial relationship is near zero or may even have changed direction (from positive to negative or vice versa). It is important to note that the specification of an intervening variable does not negate any assumed causal relationship between A and B. Rather, the intervening variable (C) specifies a process by which A influences B.

Some researchers use the term interaction to describe a specification outcome. We saw that interaction, discussed in great detail in Chapter 8 in the context of two-way ANOVA, means that the effects of the independent variable on the dependent variable differ considerably over categories of the third variable. Phrased differently, the effect of A on B depends on the level of C. *Specification* and *interaction* are really identical, but it is preferable to reserve the use of the term *interaction* for ANOVA outcomes, and to use the term *specification* when referring to crosstabulated data.

Earl Babbie (1975) provides a useful guide to the elaboration of tabular analysis in the form of Table 11.4. The "test" variable is what we have referred to as the control variable, and the column designations indicate whether it is antecedent or intervening. The rows on the left of the table contain the outcome designations after the control variable has been introduced, and the body of the table contains the technical notations for each outcome.

11.4.4 Illustrating Elaboration Outcomes

We can illustrate these outcomes from our data on the sentencing of sex offenders. We will first examine the bivariate relationship between offender type

TABLE 11.4 THE ELABORATION PARADIGM

Partial relationship Compared with original	Test variable	
	Antecedent	Intervening
Same relationship	REPLICATION	
Less or none	EXPLANATION	INTERPRETATION
Split*	SPECIFICATION	

*One partial the same or greater, while the other is less or none.
Source: Earl Babbie, *The Practice of Social Research* (Belmont, CA: Wadsworth, 1975), p. 393. Reprinted with permission of Wadsworth Publishing Company, Inc.

(sex and non-sex) and sentence (probation and prison). Our elaboration of this basic relationship will illustrate the advantages of elaboration and will point out a serious disadvantage. The joint distribution of offender group and sentence type produced by command 11.1 is shown in Table 11.5. Only the phi and gamma measures of association are given in the table.

11.4.5 Controlling for One Variable

We see from the output that sex offenders are significantly more likely to be sentenced to prison than are non-sex offenders. The probability of a convicted criminal being sent to prison is $281/637 = .441$. The probability of imprisonment for a sex offender is $225/637 = .522$, and for a non-sex offender it is .272. Computing the odds ratio as explained in Chapter 9, we find that sex offenders are 2.9 times more likely than non-sex offenders to be sent to prison.

Does this mean that sex offenders are the victims of discriminatory sentencing? The correct answer to this question has to await further analysis because there are other variables besides the type of offense that influence sentencing. Crime seriousness is certainly one of them. We saw earlier that the crime seriousness measure used in the jurisdiction from which our sample was taken is an ordinal measure ranging from 1 to 10 points. Since we do not want to get involved in the messiness of a 10×2 table, we divide our crime seriousness scores into

TABLE 11.5 CROSSTABULATION OF SENTENCE TYPE BY OFFENDER GROUP (ZERO-ORDER)

```
SENT CATEGORIZED SENTENCE  BY GROUP  WHAT GROUP DOES OFFENDER BELONG TO

            COUNT       GROUP
          ROW PCT
          COL PCT                            ROW
                      Non-Sex     Sex       TOTAL
  SENT    ─────────
          Probation    150        206        356
                       42.1       57.9       55.9
                       72.8       47.8

          Prison        56        225        281
                       19.9       80.1       44.1
                       27.2       52.2


          COLUMN       206        431        637
          TOTAL        32.3       67.7
                       100        100       100.0

CHI-SQUARE    D.F.    SIGNIFICANCE    MIN E.F.    CELLS WITH E.F. < 5
34.38336       1        0.0000        90.873           NONE
35.39094       1        0.0000        (BEFORE YATES CORRECTION)
STATISTIC              VALUE
   PHI                0.23571
   GAMMA              0.49053
```

approximately two equal categories based on a split at the median value of this variable. Those offenders who scored 3 or below are placed into a low seriousness category, and those who scored 4 or above are placed into a high seriousness category. We then recompute our statistics within the separate categories by using command 11.2. The separate tables produced by command 11.2 are presented in Table 11.6. For the sake of brevity, we have produced the tables as they would appear in a research report rather than as they would appear in the computer printout. We have also omitted percentages.

We are now examining the bivariate relationship between offender type and sentence under conditions of one control variable, an operation referred to as examining the **first-order partial relationship**. The partial relationship shows that within the low seriousness category we have replicated the original zero-order bivariate relationship. Phi has increased slightly, and gamma has increased for this conditional table from the zero-order value of .49 to .645. Note that although phi has increased, the chi-square value has decreased from 35.4 to 26.6 (the chi-square values before the Yate's correction are used here) because the sample size has decreased. This result illustrates the principle that given a constant strength of relationship, the larger the same size the more likely one will be to reject the null hypothesis of no relationship.

The association between offense type and sentence type becomes much stronger within the high seriousness category, and slightly higher within the low seriousness category when compared with the zero-order association between sentence type and offense type. This result indicates that crime seriousness has been acting as a **suppressor variable**, "hiding" the true relationship between offense type and sentence type. Sex offenders tend to receive harsher sentences, but they also tend to commit less serious crimes as seriousness is defined in this jurisdiction. The sentence type/offense type relationship is suppressed unless crime seriousness is controlled for. The outcome of this elaboration is both a replication (the original relationship and its direction remain) and a specification (we have specified that the relationship is particularly true within one of the categories of the control variable).

TABLE 11.6 BIVARIATE RELATIONSHIP BETWEEN OFFENDER TYPE AND SENTENCE CONTROLLING FOR CRIME SERIOUSNESS

	Low Seriousness				High Seriousness		
Sentence	Offender Type			Sentence	Offender Type		
	Non-Sex	Sex	Totals		Non-Sex	Sex	Totals
Probation	118	200	318	Probation	32	6	38
Prison	13	102	115	Prison	43	123	166
Totals	131	302	433	Totals	75	129	204

$\chi^2 = 26.6$, $p < .0000$, $\phi = .25$
$\gamma = .645$

$\chi^2 = 45.2$, $p < .0000$, $\phi = .47$
$\gamma = .877$

Note that although we have substantially decreased our sample size from 637 in the bivariate table to 204 in the high seriousness partial table, our computed chi-square has increased this time from 35.4 to 45.2, thus a reduced sample size does not necessarily result in a lower probability of rejecting the null hypothesis. This result illustrates another principle of chi-square: Given a constant sample size, the stronger the relationship the more likely one is to reject the null hypothesis.

Criminal record is another variable that is considered in sentencing decisions. Criminal record is measured in this jurisdiction by an ordinal measure ranging from 0 to 27. If we did not want a 2 × 10 table, we surely do not want a 2 × 27 table! So again we collapse our ordinal variable into two dichotomous variables: first offenders and repeat offenders. We then repeat the same procedure with prior record that we went through with crime seriousness. The computer commands are given in command 11.3, and the output is reported in Table 11.7.

From Table 11.7 we observe a specification outcome. That is, we have specified that the relationship between type of offender and type of sentence is true only among repeat offenders. The low prior record partial relationship is nonsignificant, and the high prior record partial relationship has increased in magnitude over the computed bivariate phi. In other words, we observe an interactive effect because the effect of offender group on sentence type differs markedly over the two categories of the control variable. The small observed effect of offender group on sentence for first offenders could be the result of chance.

11.4.6 Further Elaboration: Two Control Variables

Knowing the seriousness of the crime committed and the offender's criminal record will improve your ability to predict the sentence he will receive over what you would have predicted knowing only his offense type. However, each person is sentenced according to his joint distribution on both of these variables, not on either one of them alone. It is somewhat artificial, therefore, to attempt to predict sentence by either of these variables in isolation. To examine the joint effects of

TABLE 11.7 BIVARIATE RELATIONSHIP BETWEEN OFFENDER TYPE AND SENTENCE CONTROLLING FOR PRIOR RECORD

	Low Prior Record				High Prior Record		
Sentence	Offender Type			Sentence	Offender Type		
	Non-Sex	Sex	Totals		Non-Sex	Sex	Totals
Probation	69	112	181	Probation	81	94	175
Prison	12	32	44	Prison	44	193	237
Totals	81	144	225	Totals	125	287	412

$\chi^2 = 1.8$, n.s., $\phi = .09$ $\chi^2 = 36.6$, $p < .0000$, $\phi = .30$
$\gamma = .243$ $\gamma = .530$

these variables on the offender type/sentence type relationship requires the computation of four partial relationships: (1) low crime seriousness/low prior record, (2) high crime seriousness/low prior record, (3) low crime seriousness/high prior record, and (4) high crime seriousness/high prior record. These four partial tables are obtained by command 11.4 and are presented in Table 11.8.

When the basic bivariate relationship is examined under the various conditions of two control variables, it is called **second-order partial relationship**. Having controlled for the two legally relevant variables that are supposed to influence sentencing, we can now assess the effects of offense type, a variable that is not supposed to influence sentencing, on sentence type. Basically, we have replicated the initial bivariate relationship. Sex offenders are significantly more likely than non-sex offenders to be imprisoned regardless of which of the four partial relationships we examine. However, we are now able to be more precise in our predictions. For instance, the relationship is particularly strong in the high crime seriousness/high prior record category but quite weak (taking phi as the measure of association) in the low crime seriousness/low prior record category. The computed odds ratio for the high/high category indicates that sex offenders are about 32 times more likely to be sent to prison than are non-sex offenders.

TABLE 11.8 BIVARIATE RELATIONSHIP BETWEEN OFFENDER TYPE AND SENTENCE CONTROLLING FOR PRIOR RECORD AND CRIME SERIOUSNESS

Low Crime Seriousness
Low Prior Record

Sentence	Offender Type		
	Non-Sex	Sex	Totals
Probation	56	108	164
Prison	1	16	17
Totals	57	124	181

$\chi^2 = 5.7, p < .02, \phi = .18$
$\gamma = .785$

High Crime Seriousness
Low Prior Record

Sentence	Offender Type		
	Non-Sex	Sex	Totals
Probation	13	4	17
Prison	11	16	27
Totals	24	20	44

$\chi^2 = 5.4, p < .02, \phi = .35$
$\gamma = .651$

Low Crime Seriousness
High Prior Record

Sentence	Offender Type		
	Non-Sex	Sex	Totals
Probation	62	92	154
Prison	12	86	98
Totals	74	178	252

$\chi^2 = 22.7, p < .0000, \phi = .30$
$\gamma = .657$

High Crime Seriousness
High Prior Record

Sentence	Offender Type		
	Non-Sex	Sex	Totals
Probation	19	2	21
Prison	32	107	139
Totals	51	109	160

$\chi^2 = 38.2, p < .0000, \phi = .49$
$\gamma = .939$

This finding makes a powerful statement about the attitudes of the U.S. criminal justice system toward sex offenders.

11.4.7 Partial Gamma

To summarize the relationship between offender group and type of sentence received, we have had to make four separate statements with reference to four sets of computed statistics. It would be nice if we could boil these statements down to one succinct statement about the relationship between offender group and type of sentence controlling for crime seriousness and prior record. One technique that allows us to do so is known as **partial gamma**, which is obtained by the simple method of combining the separate computations from each conditional table into a single measure of association. Recall that the formula for gamma is

$$\gamma = \frac{Ns - Nd}{Ns + Nd}$$

The formula for partial gamma is

$$\gamma_p = \frac{\Sigma Ns - \Sigma Nd}{\Sigma Ns + Nd} \tag{11.1}$$

where ΣNs = the similar pairs summed across all conditional tables

ΣNd = the dissimilar pairs summed across all conditional tables

The zero-order gamma for our offender type/sentence type data was .490. The respective gammas for the low crime seriousness and the high crime seriousness conditional relationships were .645 and .877. We now wish to transform these separate gammas into a single summary statistic. The computations for the two separate gammas were

$$\text{low crime seriousness} = \frac{12036 - 2600}{12036 + 2600} = \frac{9436}{14636} = .645$$

$$\text{high crime seriousness} = \frac{3936 - 258}{3936 + 258} = \frac{3678}{4194} = .877$$

To obtain partial gamma we sum as directed:

$\Sigma Ns = 12306 + 3936 = 15972$

$\Sigma Nd = 2600 + 258 = 2858$

Therefore,

$$\gamma_p = \frac{15972 - 2858}{15972 + 2858} = \frac{13114}{18830} = .70$$

The first-order gamma of .70 indicates that knowledge of the distribution of crime seriousness, as well as knowledge of type of offense, improves our ability to predict the type of sentence by 70 percent over what our predictions would be without knowledge of these two variables. It is important to note, however, that crime seriousness has been "controlled for" in an arbitrary fashion. If we had used more categories of this variable, somewhat different results may have been obtained.

We will not compute the first-order partial for prior record. Rather, now that the student is aware of the logic involved, we will proceed directly to the computation of the second-order gamma. The computations of gamma for the four separate tables are as follows:

<table>
<tr><td align="center">Low Crime Seriousness/
Low Prior Record</td><td align="center">High Crime Seriousness/
High Prior Record</td></tr>
</table>

$$\frac{896 - 108}{896 + 108} = \frac{788}{1004} = .785 \qquad \frac{208 - 44}{208 + 44} = \frac{164}{252} = .651$$

<table>
<tr><td align="center">Low Crime Seriousness/
High Prior Record</td><td align="center">High Crime Seriousness/
High Prior Record</td></tr>
</table>

$$\frac{5332 - 1104}{5332 + 1104} = \frac{4228}{6436} = .657 \qquad \frac{2033 - 64}{2033 + 64} = \frac{1969}{2097} = .939$$

Summing,

$$\Sigma Ns = 896 + 208 + 5332 + 2033 = 8469$$

$$\Sigma Nd = 108 +\ \ 44 + 1104 +\ \ 064 = 1320$$

Therefore,

$$\gamma_p = \frac{8469 - 1320}{8469 + 1320} = \frac{7149}{9789} = .730$$

We have now arrived at a single statistic summarizing the relationship between sentence type and offender type, controlling for crime seriousness and prior record as we have measured and categorized these variables. Since gamma is a PRE measure, we may conclude that we have reduced our error in predicting type of sentence by 73 percent given our knowledge of offense type, crime seriousness, and prior record. Note that with knowledge of offense type only we were able to reduce prediction errors by 49 percent (zero-order gamma). With the additional information provided by crime seriousness we were able to reduce errors by 70 percent (first-order gamma). With knowledge of prior record we were able to reduce errors by another 3 percent. Knowledge of offense type, crime seriousness, and prior record reduces the errors we would make in predicting an offender's sentence type without this information by 73 percent.

A word of warning: In Table 11.8 all partial tables convey essentially the same information: Sex offenders are significantly more likely to be sent to prison than non-sex offenders. Given this consistency, partial gamma is a useful summary statistic. However, we would not want to compute partial gamma if significant interaction (specification) is discovered. The major reason for bivariate elaboration analysis is precisely to uncover interesting specifications. Having gone through the process of elaboration and discovering that your control variable has an interactive effect on the bivariate relationship, we would not want to cover it up again by simply reporting partial gamma.

Let me illustrate what I mean. Suppose we have the bivariate relationship shown in Table 11.9, in which the zero-order gamma is .263. We then elaborate this relationship and find that under condition A of the control variable we obtain a gamma of .756, and under condition B we obtain a gamma of $-.317$. It is obvious that the independent variable has very different and interesting effects on the dependent variable under the two conditions of the control variable. Under both conditions the strength of the association increases, and the relationship runs in opposite directions. Computing partial gamma, we obtain .219. Just reporting this partial gamma would totally mislead readers about the nature of the relationship between the independent and the dependent variables—it tells us nothing. They might even conclude that the initial relationship is replicated, though attenuated, when controlling for the third variable.

11.4.8 Problems of Bivariate Elaboration

As we moved from an examination of the zero-order to the second-order relationship we noted a rather severe diminution in the number of cases in each cell. For instance, 4 of our 16 cells in the second-order examination of offender type and sentence type contained fewer than five cases despite the fact that we have a relatively large sample. If we wished to add a further dichotomous control variable (third-order), each of our four partial relationships would have to be examined

TABLE 11.9 ZERO-ORDER BIVARIATE RELATIONSHIP

80	70	150
20	30	50
100	100	200

$$\gamma = \frac{2400 - 1400}{2400 + 1400} = .263$$

Conditional (First-order) Relationships

Condition A

45	25	70
5	20	25
50	45	95

Condition B

35	45	80
15	10	25
50	55	105

$$\gamma = \frac{900 - 125}{900 + 125} = .756 \qquad \gamma = \frac{350 - 675}{350 + 675} = -.317$$

$$\Sigma Ns = 900 + 350 = 1250 \qquad \gamma_p = \frac{1250 - 800}{1250 + 800} = .219$$

$$\Sigma Nd = 125 + 675 = 800$$

under the two conditions of the added control variable. Instead of 16 cells, we would now have 32. The effect of this change on cell frequency is obvious. Results would become increasingly less meaningful as our cells became increasingly deprived of adequate frequencies. Even if we doubled our sample size—a costly and time-consuming strategy—the task of summarizing so many tables into a succinct statement of how the variables are related would be a messy one. The logistic problems of elaboration render it a relatively inefficient method of multivariate analysis for all but the most simple substantive problems.

A further problem arises when we collapse interval-level data into a limited number of categories. Although collapsing was necessary in order to arrive at manageable tables, doing so cost us a loss of information. Taking crime seriousness, for instance, offenders who had 4 crime seriousness points were categorized with those who had 10 crime seriousness points. Our statistics were then computed as if these people had committed crimes of equal gravity, which they had not. In other words, it is reasonable to suppose that an offender with 10 crime seriousness points will receive a harsher sentence than will an offender with 4 crime seriousness points. However, we cannot determine this result from the analysis we have conducted because we have artificially placed them (along with offenders with 5, 6, 7, 8, and 9 points) into a single category.

It is for this reason that collapsing data measured at a higher level into limited categories to accommodate weaker methods of statistical analysis, when the data are suitable for more efficient and powerful techniques, is considered a statistical "mortal sin." Multiple regression analysis, to be examined in Chapter 13, or logit regression, to be examined in Chapter 15, are far more efficient methods of multivariate analysis because they do not require the physical placement of cases into subtables, and because they utilize all cases simultaneously. However, students get a better intuitive grasp of multivariate analysis if it is first presented in this fashion. They are able to see how the cases are physically moved around into the various categories of the control variable(s). And, after all, there are many instances in which only categorical analysis is suitable for our data.

11.5 SUMMARY

The concept of causality is a difficult one. There are three basic criteria for establishing causality: (1) a statistically significant association, (2) temporal order, and (3) nonspuriousness. There are various types of causality, such as necessary, sufficient, and necessary and sufficient causes. It is almost impossible to satisfy such stringent criteria for causality, because no one thing is the cause of anything; variables often act in conjunction to bring about an effect. To explore the effects of an independent variable on a dependent variable when performing tabular analysis, we have to examine the association within categories of a theoretically meaningful control variable in a process called elaboration.

When we examine the effects of additional variables on the basic bivariate relationship we observe various kinds of elaboration outcomes: replication, spuriousness, explanation, or specification. Replication means that the addition of another variable did not appreciably alter the zero-order outcome. Spuriousness means that the addition of another variable completely eliminates the initially observed relationship. Spuriousness is subdivided into explanation and interpretation depending on whether the control variable was antecedent or intervening.

Partial gamma, which we examined with our sex offender data for first-order and second-order elaboration tables, is an index of the strength of association between two variables, controlling for the effects of one or more other variables. If interesting specifications are uncovered by the elaboration method they should be noted, however, and not covered up again by partial gamma.

Some of the problems of bivariate elaboration include rapid depletion of cell sizes as more control variables are added and the somewhat arbitrary categories that sometimes have to be created.

PRACTICAL APPLICATION: BIVARIATE ELABORATION

Let us turn back to our 3 × 2 chi-square in Table 9.9. In it we found that birth order was significantly related to having committed a violent crime among a sample of 585 juvenile delinquents. We now wish to go a little further and see if this result is true for both boys and girls. We have to make two 3 × 2 tables now, one for the boys and one for the girls. We go back into the data to find the distributions on birth order/violent crime for each sex and we compute chi-square for each separate table.

Boys						Girls				
Violent Offence	Birth Order					Violent Offence	Birth Order			
	First	Middle	Last	Total			First	Middle	Last	Total
No	69	65	50	184		No	32	17	6	55
Yes	79	174	74	327		Yes	6	10	3	19
Total	148	239	124	511		Total	38	27	9	74

Compute chi-square.

$$\chi^2 = \Sigma \frac{(O-E)^2}{E} \quad \text{where } E = \frac{R \times C}{N}$$

Expected Frequencies, Boys

A. 148 × 184/511 = 53.29
B. 239 × 184/511 = 86.06
C. 124 × 184/511 = 44.65
D. 148 × 327/511 = 94.71
E. 239 × 327/511 = 152.94
F. 124 × 327/511 = 79.35

Expected Frequencies, Girls

A. 38 × 55/74 = 28.24
B. 27 × 55/74 = 20.07
C. 9 × 55/74 = 6.69
D. 38 × 19/74 = 9.76
E. 27 × 19/74 = 6.93
F. 9 × 19/74 = 2.31

Chi-square boys

$$\frac{(69 - 53.29)^2}{53.29} + \frac{(65 - 86.06)^2}{86.06} + \frac{(50 - 44.65)^2}{44.65} + \frac{(79 - 94.71)^2}{94.71}$$

$$+ \frac{(174 - 152.94)^2}{152.94} + \frac{(74 - 79.35)^2}{79.35}$$

$$= 4.63 + 5.15 + 0.64 + 2.61 + 2.90 + 0.36 = 16.29$$

$$\chi^2 = 16.29$$

Is it significant? With 2 degrees of freedom $[(R - 1)(C - 1) = 2]$, it exceeds the critical value for significance at .05 (5.99). It also exceeds the critical value for the .01 level (9.210). Therefore, it is highly unlikely that our sample comes from a population where the probabilities of commiting a violent crime is the same for each birth-order group.

Chi-square girls

$$\frac{(32 - 28.24)^2}{28.24} + \frac{(17 - 20.07)^2}{20.07} + \frac{(6 - 6.69)^2}{6.69} + \frac{(6 - 9.76)^2}{9.76}$$

$$+ \frac{(10 - 6.93)^2}{6.93} + \frac{(3 - 2.31)^2}{2.31}$$

$$= 0.50 + 0.47 + 0.07 + 1.45 + 1.36 + 0.21 = 4.06$$

$$\chi^2 = 4.06$$

With 2 df we need a chi-square value of 5.991 to reject the null hypothesis. Our computed value of 4.06 falls below this figure. Therefore, we fail to reject the null. The sample could have come from a population in which the probability of committing a violent crime is the same for all three female birth-order groups. We have a specification result: The association between birth order and violent crime is true only for delinquent boys.

Compute the contingency coefficient for both subsamples:

Boys

$$C = \sqrt{\chi^2 / \chi^2 + N} = \sqrt{16.29/16.29 + 511} = \sqrt{16.29/527.29}$$

$$= \sqrt{.0309} = .1758$$

Girls

$$= \sqrt{4.06/4.06 + 74} = \sqrt{4.06/78.06} = \sqrt{.0520} = .228$$

The contingency coefficient is actually stronger for girls than it is for boys. If we had an equal number of boys and girls, and assuming constant cell percentages, we would conclude that the relationship between birth order and the commission of a violent offense is stronger for girls than for boys. This does not mean that girls are more violent than boys. The percentage of girls convicted of a violent offense is 25.7, but for boys it is 64. It simply means that whether or not one has ever been convicted of a violent crime is more dependent on birth order for girls than it is for boys. Remember also that this could possibly be a simple chance finding since we have a chi-square that did not attain statistical significance

Compute partial gamma.

Boys _Ns_

$$\gamma_p = \frac{\Sigma Ns - \Sigma Nd}{\Sigma Ns + \Sigma Nd}$$

$$69 \times (174 + 74) = 17112$$
$$65 \times 74 = 4810$$
$$Ns = 21922$$

Boys _Nd_

$$50 \times (174 + 79) = 12650$$
$$65 \times 79 = 5135$$
$$Nd = 17785$$

Girls _Ns_ **Girls _Nd_**

$$32 \times (10 + 3) = 416 \qquad 6 \times (10 + 6) = 96$$
$$17 \times 3 = 51 \qquad 17 \times 6 = 102$$
$$Ns = 467 \qquad Nd = 198$$

$$\Sigma Ns = 21922 + 467 = 22389$$

$$\Sigma Nd = 17785 + 198 = 17983$$

$$\gamma_p = \frac{22389 - 17983}{22389 + 17983} = \frac{4406}{40372} = .109$$

Controlling for sex, we obtain a partial gamma of .109 between birth order and the commission of a violent crime. In Chapter 9 we saw that the zero-order correlation was .194. Controlling for sex diminishes the strength of the relationship.

APPENDIX: Computer Instructions for Table 11.5

For this particular task the RECODE command is necessary to get a 2 × 2 table because SENT was originally coded as a trichotomous variable (probation, probation with jail time, prison).

Command 11.1

SPSSx	SAS
RECODE SENT (1,2=1)(3=2)	IF SENT <=2 THEN SENT=1;
CROSSTABS SENT BY GROUP	IF SENT >2 THEN SENT=2;
OPTIONS 3,4	PROC FREQ;
STATISTICS ALL	TABLES SENT*GROUP/ALL;

APPENDIX: Computer Instructions for Table 11.6

Command 11.2

SPSSx

```
RECODE CRSER (LO THRU 3=1)(4 THRU HI=2)
RECODE SENT (1,2=1)(3=2)
CROSSTABS VARIABLES = SENT (1,2), GROUP (1,2), CRSER (1,2)/
        TABLES = SENT BY GROUP BY CRSER
OPTIONS 3,4
STATISTICS ALL
```

SAS

```
IF CRSER <=3 THEN CRSER = 1; IF CRSER >=4 THEN CRSER = 2;
IF SENT <=2 THEN SENT = 1; IF SENT >2 THEN SENT = 2;
PROC FREQ;
TABLES CRSER*SENT*GROUP/ALL;
```

The RECODE CRSER command in command 11.2 tells the computer to take all of the cases it finds with values of 1 through 3, inclusive, on crime seriousness and place them in one category, and all those who had crime seriousness points of 4 or more into another category. The CROSSTABS VARIABLES command alerts the computer that you are asking for a first-order partial and gives it the conditions or categories (1,2) of all variables to be examined. The tables command SENT BY GROUP BY CRSER tells the computer to examine the relationship between sentence and offender group twice: once in the low category of crime seriousness and once in the high category of crime seriousness. The printout will provide you with two bivariate tables assessing the relationship between SENT and GROUP within the two conditions of CRSER. It will provide two conditional gammas, the zero-order gamma, and the first-order partial gamma.

SAS does not provide partial gamma at present. The SAS notation TABLES CRSER*SENT*GROUP/ALL; is interpreted simply as a request for tables examining the relationship between SENT and GROUP under both conditions of CRSER. Conditional gammas are given, but partial gamma must be calculated by the student.

The computer instructions for Table 11.7 are exactly the same except PRREC is substituted for CRSER. The recode instructions for PRREC are RECODE PRREC (LO THRU 0=1)(1 THRU HI=2).

APPENDIX: Computer Instructions for Table 11.8

Command 11.3

SPSSx

```
RECODE CRSER (LO THRU 3=1)(4 THRU HI=2)
RECODE PRREC (LO THRU 0=1)(1 THRU HI=2)
RECODE SENT (1,2=1)(3=2)
```

```
CROSSTABS VARIABLES = SENT(1,2), GROUP(1,2), CRSER(1,2) PRREC(1,2)/
          TABLES  =  SENT BY GROUP BY CRSER BY PRREC
OPTIONS 3,4
STATISTICS ALL


                               SAS

IF CRSER <=3 THEN CRSER = 1; IF CRSER >=3 THEN CRSER = 2;
IF PRREC =0 THEN PRREC =1; ELSE PRREC=2;
IF SENT <=2 THEN SENT = 1; IF SENT >2 THEN SENT = 2;
PROC FREQ;
TABLES SENT*GROUP*CRSER*PRREC/ALL
```

These commands tell the computer to examine the bivariate relationship between sentence and offender types under four separate control conditions: (1) low crime seriousness/low prior record, (2) high crime seriousness/low prior record, (3) low crime seriousness/high prior record, (4) high crime seriousness/high prior record. The printout will provide the zero-order gamma, four conditional gammas, and the second-order gamma. Again, SAS does not offer partial gamma.

REFERENCES AND SUGGESTED READINGS

Babbie, E. (1975). The practice of social research. Belmont, CA: Wadsworth. Good discussion of causal analysis in terms of tabular data.

Blalock, H. (1972). Causal inferences in nonexperimental research. New York: W. W. Norton. An excellent book on the logic and process of causal analysis based on correlation and regression techniques.

Hirschi, T., and H. Selvin. (1966). False criteria for causality in delinquency research. *Social problems,* 13:254–268. This excellent article should be read by every researcher in the behavioral sciences.

Chapter 12

Bivariate Correlation and Regression

This chapter presents two powerful techniques for analyzing the linear relationship between two variables measured at the interval or ratio levels. Although these techniques differ somewhat in logic from those we have examined so far, they are designed to answer much the same questions. Correlation and regression are the "meat and potatoes" of contemporary social science. Open almost any social science journal and you are likely to find that correlation and regression techniques are used to analyze data more than all other techniques combined. Therefore, I feel that it is imperative to introduce students to these methods as soon as possible. It is also for this reason that I devote proportionately more space to these than to other techniques.

Basically, **regression** techniques are used to predict the value of one variable from knowledge of another. **Correlation** tells us how accurate these predictions are and describes the nature of the relationship (Blalock, 1972, p. 51). The indispensable nature of regression to scientific research has been aptly put by Pedhazur (1982, p. 42): "The regression model is most directly and intimately related to the primary goals of scientific inquiry: explanation and prediction of phenomena." Correlation and regression techniques are more powerful than the statistics discussed in Chapter 10. Statistics such as gamma allow us only to predict a case's category on one variable given knowledge of its category on another. Correlation and regression are more precise in that they enable us to predict the specific value or score of a case on one variable from a value or score on another. Since the purpose of regression is essentially prediction, many researchers use the term *predictor variables* for independent variables and *criterion variable* for the dependent variable.

As we saw in Chapter 10 there is a positive relationship between two variables when high scores on variable Y are associated with high scores on variable

X and low scores on Y are associated with low scores on X. Conversely, there is a negative relationship when high scores on Y are associated with low scores on X. With continuous data, these relationships can be approximated by a straight line. Any straight line is given by the equation $Y = a + bX$. I will comment further on this concept shortly, but now, for you to gain a preliminary understanding of linear relationships, I will present an idealized example in which the relationship between two scores is perfect.

Consider the example of workers earning \$4 per hour. A worker who works zero hours gets paid zero money, who works two hours gets \$8, and so on. The dependent variable is dollars earned and the independent variable is hours worked. We can graph this relationship as in Figure 12.1.

The relationship is linear and perfect—as X increases so does Y in a perfectly linear fashion; for example, a 1.5 increase in X is associated with an increase of 6 in Y. In regression analysis, such straight lines are called **regression lines**. Depending on the bivariate distribution of the data, these lines have different **regression slopes**. Trigonometrically, the slope of a line is defined as the vertical distance divided by the horizontal distance between any two points on the line. Symbolically, it appears as Formula 12.1.

$$b = \frac{\text{vertical distance}}{\text{horizontal distance}} = \frac{Y_1 - Y_2}{X_1 - X_2} \tag{12.1}$$

Referring to Figure 12.1, we let $Y_1 = 10$ and $Y_2 = 4$. These values are associated with X values of 2.5 and 1, respectively. We substitute these values into the formula to obtain the slope:

$$b = \frac{10 - 4}{2.5 - 1} = \frac{6}{1.5} = 4$$

The slope of the line is 4; it will be 4 for this data set regardless of which two reference points we may choose. For the present example, the slope, also known

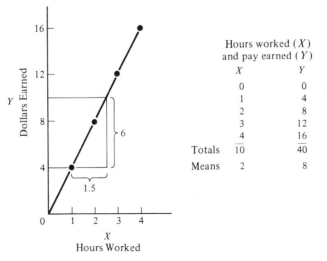

Figure 12.1

as the regression coefficient or beta, informs us that for each unit increase in the independent variable there is a four-unit increase in the dependent variable.

We said that the equation for a straight line is $Y = a + bX$. We have b and must now calculate a, which is the **Y-intercept**, or the point at which the line intersects the Y-axis. We can determine visually from Figure 12.1 that $a = 0$ because both Y and X scores have values of zero in the distribution and because a score of zero on X corresponds exactly with a zero score on Y. Nevertheless, we will demonstrate that $a = 0$ by the following:

$$a = \bar{Y} - b\bar{X} \qquad (12.2)$$

where a = the intercept

       $\bar{Y}$ = mean of Y

       $\bar{X}$ = mean of X

       b = the slope

Therefore,

$$a = 8 - (4)(2) = 8 - 8 = 0$$

Once we have the slope (b) and the intercept (a) for any set of data we can use the formula for a straight line to predict a Y value for any given value of X. The a and b values are constants, so all we have to do to determine a predicted Y (symbolized as Y' for "Y prime") value is to specify a value of X. To predict the Y value for a worker who works eight hours we would calculate

$$Y' = a + bX = 0 + (4)(8) = \$32 \qquad (12.3)$$

This looks like a horribly complicated way to arrive at a value that you could easily calculate in your head (8 hours at \$4 per hour = \$32). However, realize that this is a "perfect" example designed to convey the logic of linear prediction. Real social science data are never as cooperative. The intersection of Y and X scores never rise uniformly, as in this example. In other words, the plotted points representing the complexity of the real world will never fall on a straight line but will be scattered around it, meaning that any predictions we make will be subject to error. We will now more fully examine the concepts just presented in the context of an example more representative of this complexity.

12.1 PRELIMINARY INVESTIGATION: THE SCATTERGRAM

When we began examining the associations between variables measured at the nominal and ordinal levels, we noted that a useful preliminary technique was to examine the pattern of frequencies and percentages in each cell of the table. A similarly helpful technique when examining the association between two interval/ratio variables is to examine their joint distribution in a scattergram. A **scattergram** is a plot in which the position of each observation is designated at the point corresponding to its joint value on the dependent and independent variables. The independent variable is arrayed on the horizontal axis, and the dependent variable on the vertical axis. If these plots bunch together like a thin tube along a steeply angled line, the association is strong. If they bulge out at all sides like a balloon, the association is weak or nonexistent. If the plots appear to be rising from the lower left-hand corner to the upper right-hand corner, the association is positive. If they appear to be going from the top left-hand corner to the lower right-hand corner, the association is negative. Presented in Figure 12.2 are three scattergrams illustrating possible patterns of associations between two interval/ratio-level variables. Other patterns that are nonlinear are possible, but we will not examine them here. Part of the value of examining the scattergram is to check for linearity.

We begin by constructing a scattergram for some very simple data on the number of prior felony convictions and years of imprisonment for the latest offense. Suppose we have a sample of ten convicted felons with different criminal histories who received different sentences. We want to determine the impact that criminal record has on sentence severity. Our first task is to make a list of our ten cases, noting the number of prior felony convictions for each individual along with the sentence he received in years for the latest offense. These data are shown in Table 12.1.

The data are plotted on the scattergram shown in Figure 12.3 according to their joint position on both variables. This pattern of dots summarizes the nature of the relationship between the two variables. We can see that the relationship is positive and that it is linear; that is, as the number of prior convictions goes up, the number of years to which an individual is sentenced to prison also goes up in a constant manner. The pattern can be further clarified by drawing a straight line through the cluster of dots so that the line comes as close as possible to touching every dot. This is called "fitting the line." To draw a line we need two reference points, the first of which is the Y intercept, a. The value of a has been calculated to be .86 (we will see the calculations later). The second reference point is the intersection of the means of the two variables. Regardless of the value of the slope, the means of the two variables are always on the regression line. The mean

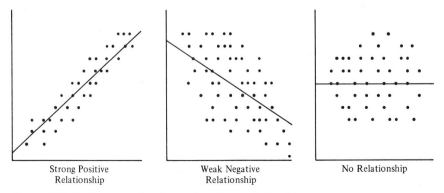

Strong Positive Relationship   Weak Negative Relationship   No Relationship

Figure 12.2 Scattergrams showing various linear relationships

TABLE 12.1   RAW DATA ON PRIOR CONVICTIONS AND SENTENCES

Case	Number of prior convictions (X)	Sentence in years (Y)
a	1	1
b	1	3
c	2	3
d	2	4
e	2	2
f	3	3
g	3	4
h	4	6
i	5	7
j	5	5
	28	38
	$\bar{X} = 2.8$	$\bar{Y} = 3.8$

of Y is 3.8 and the mean of X is 2.8. When we connect the two reference points with a straight line we have what is called the *least squares regression line*.

The least squares regression line is the line that "best fits" the data in that it comes closer than any other possible line to touching every data point on the scattergram. This is of great importance in terms of our ability to make predictions because the least squares line $Y = a + bX$ is the line with such values of a and b that $\Sigma(Y - Y')^2$ is minimized. Different lines will give different residuals $(Y - Y')$ or errors from the regression line. We want the line placed where, if each residual is squared and summed, we will get the smallest value and hence the smallest prediction errors. In other words, the squared distance between the regression line and each observation is the error we make in pediction; hence the term *least squares*.

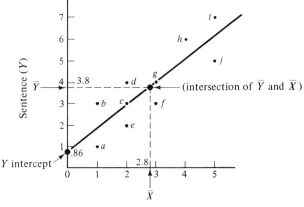

Number of Prior Convictions (X)

Figure 12.3 Scattergram of prior convictions and sentences

This is a variation of a concept we addressed in Chapter 3 when we discussed the mean. Recall that the mean of any distribution of scores is the point around which the variation is minimized. The regression line functions as a kind of "floating mean" in that the sum of the squared deviations off the regression line is less than off any other point. I will demonstrate this to be true later in this chapter, but now we will continue with the computation of b and a.

12.1.1 Computing b and a

Since we need the value of b in order to compute a, we will begin by computing b. In addition to conceptualizing b as a ratio of vertical to horizontal distance we also conceptualize it as a ratio of the sum of squares of the cross-products of Y and X to the sum of squares of X.

$$b = \frac{SS_{yx}}{SS_x} \tag{12.4}$$

The computational formula for b, however, is easier to work with:

$$b = \frac{N\Sigma XY - (\Sigma X)(\Sigma Y)}{N\Sigma X^2 - (\Sigma X)^2} \tag{12.5}$$

where N = number of cases (pairs of scores)

ΣXY = sum of the cross-products of the scores

ΣX = sum of the X scores

ΣY = sum of the Y scores

ΣX^2 = sum of the squared X scores

$(\Sigma X)^2$ = sum of the X scores squared

We will now compute b from our data on years' imprisonment per felony conviction, which requires five columns of figures in Table 12.2. The first two columns reproduce the original X and Y scores for each case. The third column lists the squared scores on X, and the fourth column lists the squared scores on Y. The fifth column lists the cross-products of X and Y (X multiplied by Y for each case). Each column is then summed and labeled. We do not need the sum of Y squared to compute b, but we will need it later to compute the correlation coefficient.

Putting the numbers into Formula 12.5, we get

$$b = \frac{(10)(127) - (28)(38)}{(10)(98) - (784)}$$

$$= \frac{1270 - 1064}{980 - 784} = \frac{206}{196} = 1.05$$

We know that b gives an average estimate of how much change in the dependent variable accompanies a one-unit change in the independent variable. There-

TABLE 12.2   COMPUTATIONS FOR b AND r

Case	X	Y	X^2	Y^2	XY
a	1	1	1	1	1
b	1	3	1	9	3
c	2	3	4	9	6
d	2	4	4	16	8
e	2	2	4	4	4
f	3	3	9	9	9
g	3	4	9	16	12
h	4	6	16	36	24
i	5	7	25	49	35
j	5	5	25	25	25
	$\Sigma X = 28$	$\Sigma Y = 38$	$\Sigma X^2 = 98$	$\Sigma Y^2 = 174$	$\Sigma XY = 127$

fore our computed slope of 1.05 tells us that for each unit change in X there is an associated average change of 1.05 units of Y. In this example, it means that for every additional felony conviction, an offender can expect, on the average, an additional 1.05 years of imprisonment. Take note of the repetition of the term *average*. We do not expect that an additional conviction for any particular offender will result in exactly 1.05 years of imprisonment.

12.1.2 The Intercept

We now have to find the intercept (a). To do so we need two additional computations, the mean of X and the mean of Y. The mean of X is 2.8, and the mean of Y is 3.8. Along with our computed b, these figures are put into Formula 12.2:

$$a = \bar{Y} - b\bar{X}$$

$$a = 3.8 - (1.05)(2.8) = 3.8 - 2.94 = .86$$

The regression line "intercepts" the Y ordinate at a value of .86. The a value is interpreted as the estimated average value of Y when X equals zero. It is a fixed or constant effect, which must be added to the constant effect of the slope times the varying value of X. In our example an offender without any prior convictions can expect, on the average, to receive .86 years imprisonment. Unfortunately, we have no offender in our sample with no prior convictions. Thus we are making predictions beyond the range of the data—often a risky business. We would be on much safer ground if we had in the sample data on offenders without any prior convictions.

The computer commands required to produce these statistics, as well as some we have yet to examine, are given in command 12.1 We will not reproduce the scattergram provided by the computer, but all the statistical output from the SPSSx program is seen in Table 12.3.

TABLE 12.3   PARTIAL COMPUTER PRINTOUT FROM SPSSx SCATTERGRAM
PROGRAM

```
STATISTICS...
CORRELATION (R)    .85525  R SQUARED       .73145  SIGNIFICANCE   .00080
STD ERR OF EST     .99681  INTERCEPT (A)   .85714  SLOPE (B)     1.05102
PLOTTED VALUES    10       EXCLUDED VALUES  0      MISSING VALUES  0
```

Now that we have all of the values for the regression line, we can use it to predict scores on the dependent variable (Y) for a given value on the independent variable (X). Since both the a and b values are constants (a is even called the "constant" in SPSSx regression), the only unknown value is X. We can give X any value that may be of interest to us. Suppose we wanted to predict the number of years that an individual with six prior convictions would be sentenced to (designated by Y' to indicate that it is a predicted value of Y rather than an actual value of Y). The formula for Y' is Formula 12.3.

$$Y' = a + bX$$
$$= .86 + (1.05)(6) = .86 + 6.3 = 7.16$$

Our hypothetical offender would expect to get 7.16 years imprisonment. Note that for an offender with nor prior convictions the b value would drop out of the equation, leaving .86 [.86 + (1.05)(0)]. = .86 + 0 = .86.

Obviously, our predictions will never be completely accurate for every case. They represent only our "best guesses" derived from the sample data we have available. For instance, we note that three of our ten felons had two prior convictions each, but they received sentences of 2, 3, and 4 years. If we used the formula to predict their sentences we would have computed $Y' = .86 + (1.05)(2) = 2.96$. For the first individual we would have been off by .96 years, for the second by .04 years, and for the third by 1.04 years. We would have had slightly less total error had we simply added the three sentences together and taken the mean ($2 + 3 + 4 = 9/3 = 3$). Using this method, we would have been off by 1 year for the first individual, on target for the second, and off by 1 year for the third. Thus, we would have had a total prediction error of 2 years as opposed to 2.04 years from the more complicated method.

However, as we will see later, regression minimizes the prediction error over all cases. In general, prediction error will decrease in proportion to the increase in sample size. Prediction error is also decreased when there are strong correlation coefficients. The strength of a linear relationship is measured by the Pearson product moment correlation coefficient (r).

12.1.3 The Pearson Correlation Coefficient (r)

Now that we have learned how to fit a regression line to paired data, our next step is to determine how well the line actually fits. Since b is a measure of the effect of X on Y, we already have some idea about the nature of the relationship. We know, for instance, that the relationship between prior convictions and sentence is positive, and we can assume with confidence that once we have computed the **correlation coefficient (Pearsons r)**, it will be quite strong because we have minimal scatter around the regression line. Why, then, do we bother to compute yet another statistic? Well, although the value of b is a function of the strength of the relationship, it cannot be used as a measure of the relationship per se for important reasons. The computed value of b depends on how we have measured our variables. For instance, if we had measured sentence severity in months instead of years, the value of b would be quite different. The correlation coefficient, however, would be the same regardless of how we measured sentence severity. In other words, r is independent of the scales of measurement of Y and X, but b is not.

Figure 12.4 shows graphically how computed bs can be quite different whereas the correlation coefficients remain the same. This is intuitively reasonable when we realize that the value of b is determined by the steepness of the line and the value of r is determined by the amount of scatter around the line. That is, the steeper the regression line, the greater the change in the dependent variable produced per unit change in the independent variable. If we would have measured sentence severity in months, the value of b would have been 12.6 ($1.05 \times 12 = 12.6$ months) instead of 1.05. It is important to realize that whereas b takes on a different value according to how we measure the dependent variable, they are really equivalent. This equivalence is recognized by r since the scatter around the regression line would be exactly the same. The function of r is to indicate the strength of the relationship so that we can predict, and our prediction would be

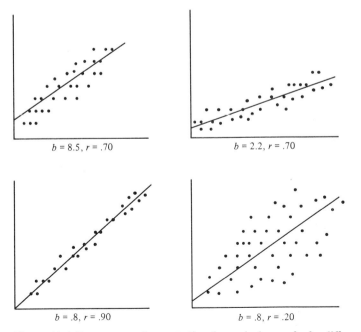

$b = 8.5, r = .70$ $b = 2.2, r = .70$

$b = .8, r = .90$ $b = .8, r = .20$

Figure 12.4 Scattergrams demonstrating the equivalence of r for different values of b and equivalence of b for different values of r

exactly the same whether we called it 1.05 years, 12.6 months, 54.6 weeks, or 382.2 days.

Another reason for computing Pearson's r in addition to b is that we cannot directly compare slopes for a number of different variables if they are all measured in different units, as we will see in the next chapter. We can compare correlation coefficients, however, regardless of how the variables they describe are measured because the squared correlation coefficient is interpreted in terms of the amount of variance explained in the dependent variable by the independent variable. This is a roundabout way of saying that bs do not vary between -1 and $+1$, as do correlations. This important property of correlation coefficients renders them comparable. It is also possible, of course, to have identical slopes but different correlations.

I mentioned that correlations range between -1 and $+1$. A negative correlation simply means that as the value of one of the variables increases, the value of the other variable decreases. A correlation of $-.70$ is just as strong as one of $+.70$. The positive or negative signs in front of the correlation indicate only the direction of the relationship.

12.1.4 Covariance and Correlation

Formula 12.6 is the computational formula for the Pearson correlation coefficient.

$$r = \frac{N\Sigma XY - (\Sigma X)(\Sigma Y)}{\sqrt{[N\Sigma X^2 - (\Sigma X)^2][N\Sigma Y^2 - (\Sigma Y)^2]}} \qquad (12.6)$$

Note that the numerator of r is the same as the numerator of b, which is the **covariance** of Y and X. The covariance is the covariation of two sets of scores from their respective means. The more the two variables covary (vary together) the stronger will be r, providing that the standard deviations of the two variables remain constant. The standard deviations of the two variables being correlated constitute the denominator of the formula for r. Thus, r is defined as the ratio of the product of the standard deviations of Y and X to the covariance of Y and X.

$$r = \frac{\text{covariance of } Y \text{ and } X}{(\text{standard deviation } Y)(\text{standard deviation } X)}$$

In Chapter 3 we defined the variance as the sum of the squared deviations of a set of scores off their mean divided by $N - 1$:

$$s^2 = \frac{\Sigma X^2 - \dfrac{(\Sigma X)^2}{N}}{N - 1}$$

Similarly, covariance is defined as

$$s^2 xy = \frac{\Sigma XY - \dfrac{(\Sigma X)(\Sigma Y)}{N}}{N - 1} \qquad (12.7)$$

where $\Sigma XY = $ sum of the cross-products of X and Y

Calculating the covariance (s^2xy) from the data in Table 12.2, we get

$$s^2xy = \frac{127 - \dfrac{(28)(38)}{10}}{9} = \frac{127 - 106.4}{9} = 2.2889$$

The standard deviations of Y and X have been calculated (not shown) and found to be 1.8135 and 1.4757, respectively. Therefore

$$r = \frac{2.2889}{(1.8135)(1.4757)} = \frac{2.2889}{2.6762} = .855$$

The correlation coefficient is .855. The definitional formula, although very useful in explaining the concept of covariance and the interrelatedness of many of the techniques we have discussed, is quite cumbersome. You will find the computational formula easier to work with. Substituting the information from Table 12.2, we get

$$r = \frac{(10)(127) - (28)(38)}{\sqrt{[(10)(98) - 784][(10)(174) - 1444]}}$$

$$= \frac{1270 - 1064}{\sqrt{(980 - 784)(1740 - 1444)}}$$

STEP ONE
Work everything within the parentheses: $10 \times 127 = 1270$; $28 \times 38 = 1064$; $10 \times 98 = 980$; $10 \times 174 = 1740$.

$$= \frac{206}{\sqrt{(196)(296)}}$$

STEP TWO
Do all subtractions: $1270 - 1064 = 206$; $980 - 784 = 196$; $1740 - 1444 = 296$.

$$= \frac{206}{\sqrt{58016}}$$

STEP THREE
Multiply: $196 \times 296 = 58016$.

$$= \frac{206}{240.86}$$

STEP FOUR
Take the square root of $58016 = 240.86$.

$$= .855$$

STEP FIVE
Divide: $206/240.86 = .855$.

A mathematically equivalent formula for computing r that requires less calculation if we have already computed a and b is Formula 12.8.

$$r = \sqrt{\frac{a\Sigma Y + b\Sigma YX - N(\bar{Y})^2}{\Sigma Y^2 - N(\bar{Y})^2}} \qquad (12.8)$$

$$= \sqrt{\frac{.86(38) + 1.05(127) - 10(3.8)^2}{174 - 10(3.8)^2}}$$

$$= \sqrt{\frac{21.63}{29.6}} = \sqrt{.731} = .855.$$

Our computed correlation coefficient of .855 indicates that there is a strong positive linear relationship between the number of prior felony convictions and the number of years sentenced to prison. That is, as the number of prior convictions increases, the severity of the sentence imposed increases. I remind you again at this point that a correlation never proves causality. It is a mathematical relationship that may or may not be indicative of some underlying causal relationship. What a correlation coefficient does do is support (or fail to support) an explanation that the researcher can justify on logical grounds.

12.1.5 The Coefficient of Determination and PRE

We can go beyond the somewhat arbitrary and ambiguous method of interpreting a computed correlation as strong, moderate, or weak by calculating the **coefficient of determination** directly from it. The coefficient of determination is simply the square of the correlation coefficient ($r^2 = r \times r$). Therefore, the coefficient of determination for our data is .731 (.855 $\times$ .855 = .731). This value can be interpreted as proportional reduction in error. That is, we can say that when knowledge of the independent variable (prior felony convictions) is taken into account, we improve our ability to predict values on the dependent variable (sentence in years) by a factor of 73.1 percent. We will now show this statement to be true.

Without knowledge of the independent variable our best prediction of the number of years a given offender would receive would be the mean of the sentence distribution. As we saw earlier, the scores vary less around the mean than around any other point. In other words, we would predict a sentence of 3.8 years for all offenders, and our line of prediction would run parallel with the abscissa starting from the mean of Y. To find out how much prediction error we would have, we must compute the total variation in the same way as in computing ANOVA. These errors for each case are found by $Y - \bar{Y}$ because they are the difference between each person's actual sentence and our best prediction (the mean), given that we have no knowledge of the distribution of the independent variable. The total variation is the sum of all the squared errors or deviations: $\Sigma(Y - \bar{Y})^2$. In Figure 12.5 we have drawn in the line of best prediction for the data, given ignorance of the independent variable, and we have computed the total variance. To compute the total variance we have subtracted the mean sen-

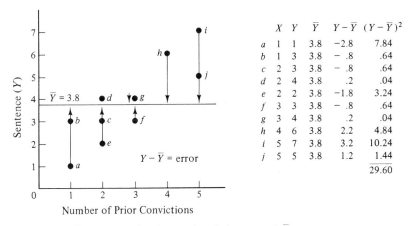

	X	Y	$\bar{Y}$	$Y-\bar{Y}$	$(Y-\bar{Y})^2$
a	1	1	3.8	-2.8	7.84
b	1	3	3.8	$-.8$	.64
c	2	3	3.8	$-.8$	.64
d	2	4	3.8	.2	.04
e	2	2	3.8	-1.8	3.24
f	3	3	3.8	$-.8$	.64
g	3	4	3.8	.2	.04
h	4	6	3.8	2.2	4.84
i	5	7	3.8	3.2	10.24
j	5	5	3.8	1.2	1.44
					29.60

Figure 12.5 Scattergram showing total variation around $\bar{Y}$

tence in years (Y) from each person's actual sentence (Y) to get the deviation ($Y - \bar{Y}$); we then squared this figure $(Y - \bar{Y})^2$ and summed to get $\Sigma(Y - \bar{Y})^2$. The total variance in Y is 29.6 years. In ANOVA we called this value the total sum of squares.

We will now compute the error based on the regression equation, that is, the error we will make in predicting sentence severity given that we now have knowledge of the distribution of the independent variable. These errors are labeled ($Y - Y'$) and are known as residuals. The sum of these squared residuals, noted by $\Sigma(Y - Y')^2$, is known as the unexplained variance. To obtain this value we have to compute the predicted value for each case by using the formula $Y' = a + bX$. We have computed this value in Figure 12.6 and found it to be 7.95. Thus, knowing the distribution of X has enabled us to make smaller prediction errors. It is for this reason that some statisticians have referred to the regression line as a "floating mean."

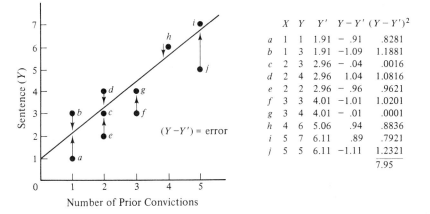

	X	Y	Y'	$Y-Y'$	$(Y-Y')^2$
a	1	1	1.91	$-.91$	.8281
b	1	3	1.91	-1.09	1.1881
c	2	3	2.96	$-.04$	.0016
d	2	4	2.96	1.04	1.0816
e	2	2	2.96	$-.96$	.9621
f	3	3	4.01	-1.01	1.0201
g	3	4	4.01	$-.01$	.0001
h	4	6	5.06	.94	.8836
i	5	7	6.11	.89	.7921
j	5	5	6.11	-1.11	1.2321
					7.95

Figure 12.6 Scattergram showing error variation around Y'

We now have the total sum of squares and the error sum of squares. We could calculate the explained sum of squares (the variance explained by the regression) by the same logic. But this is not necessary since once we have calculated the total sum of squares and the error sum of squares we automatically have the explained sum of squares since $SS_{explained} = SS_{total} - SS_{error}$:

$$\Sigma(Y' - \bar{Y})^2 = \Sigma(Y - \bar{Y})^2 - \Sigma(Y - Y')^2$$

$$SS_{explained} \qquad SS_{total} \qquad SS_{error} \text{ or } SS_{residual}$$

The coefficient of determination represents the proportion by which error is reduced by moving from estimating the mean of Y for all Y values to predicting each Y value from the regression equation. We are now in a position to determine how much we have reduced our prediction error when knowledge of the independent variable is taken into consideration. We just take the two components we have just computed and put them into the standard PRE formula already given in Chapter 10 as

$$\text{PRE} = \frac{E_1 \text{ (total variation)} - E_2 \text{ (error variation)}}{E_1 \text{ (total variation)}}$$

$$= \frac{29.6 - 7.95}{29.6} = \frac{21.65}{29.6} = .731$$

Thus, we have shown how the coefficient of determination is a PRE measure since our computed PRE is exactly the same value as r squared; in fact it is r squared determined by another method. The proportion of variance in the dependent variable left unexplained by the independent variable is known as the **coefficient of alienation**, which is simply $1 - r^2$. In our present example the coefficient of alienation is $1 - .731 = .269$. In ANOVA we called the variance left unexplained by the independent variable the within-group sum of squares or the error sum of squares. The intimate relationship between correlation and regression and ANOVA is further illustrated as follows.

12.1.6 Partitioning r Squared and Sum of Squares

To reiterate, we calculated r squared for our number of convictions and sentence data to be equal to .731. The coefficient of determination is interpreted as the percentage of the total variance in the dependent variable (Y) that is explained by the independent variable (X). This is determined by the second step in the PRE formula for r squared, namely, the explained variation (21.65) divided by the total variation (29.6). Thus, 73.1 percent of the variation in sentence severity is explained by the number of prior felony convictions in our hypothetical example. This means that 29.9 percent ($100 - 73.1$) of the variance is explained by variables other than the number of prior convictions.

Again, we can think of the coefficient of determination in ANOVA terms as the main effects sum of squares, and the squared coefficient of alienation as the residual (unexplained) sum of squares. Think of the total sum of squares as unity, and the coefficient of determination ($SS_{between}$) as a proportion of unity. The coefficient of alienation (SS_{within}) is the residual sum of squares ($1 - r^2 = .269$).

Dividing these values (.731 and .269, respectively) by their associated degrees of freedom (1 and 8), we obtain mean square values. The ratio of the mean square values is the F ratio. Table 12.4 summarizes the computation of the F ratio test of significance for the coefficient of determination by using the logic of ANOVA.

TABLE 12.4   SIGNIFICANCE OF r^2 BY USING THE LOGIC OF ANOVA

Source of variation	Sum of squares	Sum of squares as proportion of unity	df	Mean square	F Ratio
Number of convictions	21.65	.731	1	.731	.731/.0336
Unexplained	7.95	.269	8	.0336	$F = 21.756$
Total	29.60	1.000	9		$p < .01$

The F ratio (21.756) with 1 and 8 df exceeds the critical F at $< .01$.

12.1.7 Standard Error of the Estimate

A statistic for assessing the accuracy of predictions is called the **standard error of the estimate**. This statistic informs you of the average prediction error in predicting Y from X. The definitional formula for the standard error of estimate is

$$sy.x = \sqrt{\frac{\Sigma(Y - Y')^2}{N - 2}} \tag{12.9}$$

where $sy.x$ = the standard error of the estimate of Y from X

$\Sigma(Y - Y')^2$ = the sum of the squared differences between the predicted scores on Y from the actual scores on Y (computed in Figure 12.6)

The formula for $sy.x$ is quite similar to the formula for the standard deviation except that we divide by $N - 2$ rather than $N - 1$. It is conceptually similar also in that it reflects variability, but variability around the regression line rather than about a mean. Because $sy.x$ involves fitting the data to a straight line, which requires the estimation of the slope and the intercept and thus the calculations of $\overline{Y}$ and $\overline{X}$, we lose 2 df (N $-$ 2). Since we already have all of the values necessary to compute $sy.x$, we will simply put them in as follows:

$$sy.x = \sqrt{\frac{7.95}{8}} = \sqrt{.99375} = .997$$

Under the assumption that the array of Y scores associated with each value of X forms a normal distribution, the standard error of the estimate may be interpreted in terms of area under the normal curve. Thus, we can say that about 68 percent of our predictions will be within plus or minus 1 $sy.x$, and that 95 percent will be within plus or minus 2 $sy.x$'s. Be aware, however, that we are talking about average error, not the error for any particular prediction of Y from X. A moment's reflection should convince you that $sy.x$ will underestimate the error in predicting Y from X values as X departs markedly from the mean of X. There are formulas that adjust for this error, but as with many other adjustments for error we have looked at, the amount of error becomes negligible with large samples.

A less cumbersome method of calculating $sy.x$, which does not require the calculations in Figure 12.6 but uses previously calculated values of a and b, is given by Formula 12.10.

$$sy.x = \sqrt{\frac{\overline{\Sigma Y^2} - a\Sigma Y - b\Sigma XY}{N - 2}} \qquad (12.10)$$

$$= \sqrt{\frac{174 - (.86)(38) - (1.05)(127)}{8}}$$

$$= \sqrt{\frac{174 - 32.68 - 133.35}{8}}$$

$$= \sqrt{\frac{7.97}{8}} = \sqrt{.99625} = .998$$

12.1.8 Standard Error of *r*

If we drew ten further samples of ten convicted felons we would not expect to get a correlation between the number of convictions and the years of imprisonment of exactly .855. This value is simply an estimate of the population correlation coefficient (symbolized as ρ, the Greek letter rho), and other rs will vary as a result of sampling variation. As is the case with sample means, if we draw an infinite number of random samples from the same population and computed r for the two variables of interest, we would have a sampling distribution of rs. Just as 68 percent of sample means will lie within plus or minus 1 standard error of the true population mean, 68 percent of sample correlations will be within 1 standard error of the true population correlation. Thus, our sample standard error of .085, calculated below, means that 68 percent of the samples of the same size taken from the same population will yield a correlation of .855 plus or minus .085, or between .94 and .77.

Suppose rather than .855 we found a correlation of .20. Squaring .20 we get .04, and subtracting from 1 we get .96. Dividing this number by the square root of 10 we arrive at a standard error of .30. Clearly, a standard error that is larger than its correlation could be obtained from a population in which $\rho = 0$. If we take the 95 percent confidence level and say that we are 95 percent confident that ρ is somewhere between $+.80$ and $-.40$, clearly we have said nothing.

On the other hand, a correlation of .20 obtained from a sample of 1000 would result in a standard error of .0096. Since the population is 99.7 percent sure to lie within 3 ss of the sample r, with a sample of this size we can say that we are quite confident that ρ lies between $.20 + .0288$ ($3 \times .0096 = .0288$) and $.20 - .0288$, or between $.2288$ and $.1712$.

How well the sample r serves as an estimate of the population depends on two factors: the size of the correlation and the size of the sample. The bigger the sample r, the less likely it could have been obtained by chance. Similarly, the larger the sample the more likely we are to find a similar r in other samples and in the population as a whole. We can make use of these two factors to estimate the **standard error of r** in Formula 12.11.

$$s_r = \frac{1 - r^2}{\sqrt{N}} \qquad (12.11)$$

For our example,

$$s_r = \frac{1 - .855^2}{\sqrt{10}} = \frac{.269}{3.162} = .085$$

Note the mathematical effects of the size of r and of the sample. The larger the r the larger the value subtracted from 1 and, consequently, the smaller the value into which the square root of N is divided. Similarly, the larger the sample the larger the value we divide by. We have a small sample and thus a small denominator, but we have a large r and thus a small numerator.

12.1.9 Significance Testing for Pearson's r

As with other measures of association, we need to determine if the observed sample relationship can be assumed to exist in the general population from which the sample was drawn ($H_0: \rho = 0$). Although we already know from Table 12.4 that r is significant at $< .01$, the usual method of testing r for statistical significance is the t distribution, which is given by Formula 12.12.

$$t = r\sqrt{\frac{N - 2}{1 - r^2}} \qquad (12.12)$$

where $N - 2 = $ degrees of freedom

$$= (.855)\sqrt{\frac{10 - 2}{1 - (.855)^2}} = (.855)\sqrt{\frac{8}{1 - (.731)}} = (.855)\sqrt{\frac{8}{.269}}$$

$$= (.855)\sqrt{29.74} = (.855)(5.45) = 4.66$$

Turning to the distribution of t in Appendix B with 8 degrees of freedom, we find that our computed t of 4.66 exceeds the value for significance at the .05 level. We thus reject the null hypothesis and conclude that the variables are also related in the population from which our sample was drawn. Note that a t value of 4.66, when squared, results in the F value computed earlier, with tolerance for rounding.

We can rearrange Formula 12.11 to determine the minimum r necessary to reject the null hypothesis that the population $\rho = 0$. The first thing we must do is turn to Appendix B and find the critical t value required to reject the null with 8 degrees of freedom and a given alpha level. Let us say that we are conducting a two-tailed test and that we set alpha at .05. You will find the critical t value under these conditions to be 2.306. We then put this value into Formula 12.13 to determine the critical r:

$$r = \frac{t}{\sqrt{t^2 + df}} = \frac{2.306}{\sqrt{5.3176 + 8}} = \frac{2.306}{\sqrt{13.3176}} = \frac{2.306}{3.649} \qquad (12.13)$$

$$= .632$$

Thus, the minimum value of r required to reject the null at the .05 level (two-tailed test) with a sample of 10 is .632. We leave it to you to determine what the value of r should be to reject the null with a sample of 100, given the same t ratio.

12.1.10 The Interrelationship of b, r, and β

It is interesting to note that the regression slope can be expressed by

$$b = r \left(\frac{sy}{sx} \right) \qquad (12.14)$$

In prose, the regression slope is equal to the correlation between Y and X multiplied by the standard deviation of Y divided by the standard deviation of X. We substitute the previously calculated values into the formula and get

$$b = .855 \left(\frac{1.8135}{1.4757} \right) = .855(1.229) = 1.05$$

We can also utilize the standard deviations and the regression slope to calculate the standardized beta. The standardized beta, more fully explained in the next chapter, is a very useful statistic in multivariate regression analysis. One basic difference between the unstandardized and standardized beta that we can introduce at this point is that the former is presented in actual units of the dependent variable and the latter is given in standard deviation units. For the time being, just think of it as being analogous to the correlation coefficient. It is calculated by the following formula:

$$\beta = b \left(\frac{sx}{sy} \right) \qquad (12.15)$$

In prose, the standardized regression slope, or standardized beta, is equal to the unstandardized regression slope multiplied by the standard deviation of X divided by the standard deviation of Y. Let us put in these values:

$$\beta = 1.05 \left[\frac{1.4757}{1.8135} \right] = 1.05(.8137) = .855 \qquad (12.16)$$

This demonstrates that r and β are equivalent to the two-variable case.

SUMMARIZING PROPERTIES OF r, b, AND β

r ranges between -1 (perfect negative relationship) and $+1$ (perfect positive relationship). A value of zero indicates no linear relationship between Y and X.

The value of r is independent of the scale of measurement.

When squared, r is a PRE measurement indicating the proportion of variance in Y accounted for by X.

b indicates the change in Y per unit change in X.

The value of b depends on the scale of measurement.

β indicates the change in standard deviation units of Y per standard deviation unit change in X.

r and β are identical in a simply bivariate regression.

r, b, and β must have the same sign. When $r = 0$, b and $\beta = 0$.

12.1.11 Summarizing Prediction Formulas

Table 12.5 summarizes the operations we would perform in making predictions for any score with and without knowledge of the distribution of an independent variable. Without knowledge of the independent variable the best prediction would always be the mean since it minimizes the sum of squares. With knowledge of the distribution of the independent variable the regression equation provides the best prediction since it minimizes the sum of squares around the regression line (the "floating mean"). The error in making any prediction other than the mean in a univariate distribution is simply the deviation from the mean. In a bivariate distribution the error is known as a residual—the deviation of the predicted score from the regression line. The error averaged over all predictions in a univariate distribution is the standard deviation. In a bivariate distribution, the average error in predictions is the standard error of the estimate. We have shown that for any two variables that are linearly related, knowledge of their joint distributions improves our ability to predict one variable from the other.

TABLE 12.5 SUMMARY OF PREDICTION COMPUTATIONS WITH AND WITHOUT KNOWLEDGE OF THE INDEPENDENT VARIABLE

Operation	Without knowledge of X	With knowledge of X
Best prediction of a score	$\bar{Y} = \dfrac{\Sigma Y}{N}$ (the mean)	$Y' = a + bX$ (the regression equation)
Error of prediction of a score	$Y - \bar{Y}$ (deviation)	$Y - Y'$ (residual)
Average error in predicting a score	$\sqrt{\dfrac{\Sigma(Y - \bar{Y})^2}{N - 1}}$ (standard deviation)	$\sqrt{\dfrac{\Sigma(Y - Y')^2}{N - 2}}$ (standard error of estimate)

12.2 A COMPUTER EXAMPLE OF BIVARIATE CORRELATION AND REGRESSION

We will use our sex offender data to demonstrate bivariate correlation and regression. We will use the example given in Chapter 6 to demonstrate the t test to show the versatility of regression. Since we saw in Chapter 6 that the variances of the two offender groups were unequal, it is technically incorrect to perform regression with these data because regression analysis assumes equal variances. A transformation of the data such as weighted least squares (WLS) is the usual method of handling this problem. A discussion of WLS is beyond the scope of this book. However, I have used various transformation techniques and found the differences in results obtained between these methods and **ordinary least squares** (OLS) to be negligible. This demonstrates once again the remarkable robustness of OLS regression against the violation of its assumptions. In fact, when the larger sample has the greatest variance, as is the case here, regression is conservative with respect to committing type I errors.

We will first run a Pearson correlation program and then a bivariate regression program. Since we will be using these programs again in the next chapter, we will not give the computer commands here. Table 12.6 presents the correlation between sentence severity and group.

12.2.1 Interpreting the Output

The first piece of information is the number of cases and the means and standard deviations of each variable. We are then given the cross-product deviation and the covariance. The cross-product deviation (the numerator in Formula 12.7) is divided by $N - 1$ to yield the covariance ($34584.5275/636 = 54.3782$). Utilizing the information in this section of the printout, we can calculate r.

$$r = \frac{\text{cov}.YX}{(sy)(sx)} = \frac{54.3782}{(727.3945)(.4681)} = \frac{54.3782}{340.4934} = .1597$$

TABLE 12.6 PARTIAL COMPUTER PRINTOUT FOR SPSSx PEARSON CORRELATION
PROGRAM

VARIABLE	CASES	MEAN	STD DEV
SENSEV	637	492.0220	727.3945
GROUP	637	.6766	.4681

VARIABLES	CASES	CROSS-PROD DEV	VARIANCE-COVAR
SENSEV GROUP	637	34584.5275	54.3782

PEARSON CORRELATION COEFFICIENTS

	SENSEV	GROUP
SENSEV	1.0000 (637) P= .	.1597 (637) P= .000
GROUP	.1597 (637) P= .000	1.0000 (637) P= .

(COEFFICIENT / (CASES) / 1-TAILED SIG)

This matches the value given in the printout. The value beneath the coefficient is
the number of cases on which the calculation is based, 637, and the P= gives the
exact one-tailed significance of r. We will now examine the printout in Table
12.7 for the bivariate regression.

We note from this printout that a one-unit change in the variable offender
group (coded 0 for non-sex offenders and 1 for sex offenders) results in a 248.128
unit change in the dependent variable (sentence severity). Note that it now
becomes necessary to change the coding of the group variable. Formerly, non-sex
offenders were coded 1 and sex offenders were coded 2. As we will see later, this
0 and 1 convention is important in regression analysis for ease of interpretation.
If you turn back to the t test of significance for the difference between sentence
severity means for the two offender groups in Table 6.3, you will see that this
beta value is exactly the value of the difference between the means of the two
groups. Also note that the t value based on the assumption of equal variances is
the same.

TABLE 12.7 PARTIAL PRINTOUT FOR BIVARIATE REGRESSION FOR THE EFFECTS
OF OFFENDER GROUP ON SENTENCE SEVERITY (SPSSx)

	VARIABLES IN THE EQUATION				
VARIABLE	B	SE B	BETA	T	SIG T
GROUP	248.128579	60.869511	.159691	4.076	.0001
(CONSTANT)	324.135922	50.068978		6.474	.0000

Another quality of regression analysis is that we can use the standard error to establish confidence intervals for the differences between the group means represented by the *b* value. Our *b* value in a bivariate regression is a specific value or point estimate. The confidence band around that estimate is an interval estimate, indicating that *b* lies within a range of values. The logic of setting confidence intervals around the regression slope is identical to setting confidence intervals around the mean:

$$C.I. = b \pm (t)(sb)$$

where t = tabled two-tailed value for given df and alpha level

sb = standard error of b

Setting alpha at .05 with $df > 120$, we get t critical $= 1.96$. Therefore,

$$C.I. = 248.128 \pm (1.96)(60.87) = 119.3$$

We can therefore state with 95 percent confidence that the parameter lies somewhere between 248.128 plus or minus 119.3, that is, between 128.828 and 367.428.

The next value is the standardized beta (BETA in the printout). In a bivariate regression the standardized beta is analogous to the zero-order Pearsonian *r* between these two variables. Note that it is also the same as the eta value we computed for the same data in Chapter 7. This equivalence of *r* and eta only holds, however, when there is a dichotomous independent variable. Squaring the standardized beta yields the same variance-explained interpretation as the squares of eta and the correlation coefficient.

The standardized beta is followed by the *t* value and the significance of *t*. In Chapter 6 we defined *t* as the difference between means divided by the standard error of the difference. The unstandardized beta is the difference between the means of our dichotomous variable. Therefore,

$$t = \frac{\text{diff. of means}}{\text{s.e. of diff.}} = \frac{\text{unstandardized beta}}{\text{s.e. of unstan. beta}} = \frac{248.128}{60.869} = 4.076$$

It follows that if we are computing by hand we can save ourselves some time by computing only the standard error or *t* by the long method. If we had computed only *t* for this problem, for instance, we could simply divide the unstandardized beta (*B* in printout) by *t* to arrive at (s.e.b) SE B to get 248.1/4.076 = 60.869.

You might protest that although regression analysis reports the slope, the standard error, the standardized slope (beta), a significance test, and the *Y* intercept, it does not give the respective means for each of the offender groups. Won't we have to run a *t* test to get this information? The answer is no. Recall that the *Y* intercept *a* is the average value of *Y* when *X* equals zero. Since we have coded non-sex offenders as 0, the constant (*a*) is equal to the mean sentence severity for the non-sex offenders. This is the rationale for coding dichotomous variables in a regression equation as 0 and 1. The formulas for calculating the respective means are as follows.

$$\bar{Y}_0 = a + b_0 \quad \text{and} \quad \bar{Y}_1 = a + b_1 \qquad (12.17)$$

where $\bar{Y}_0$ = the mean sentence severity for non-sex offenders

$\bar{Y}_1$ = the mean sentence severity for sex offenders

b = the regression slope

a = the Y intercept

Putting in the numbers, we get

$$\bar{Y}_0 = 324.134 + 0 = 324.134$$

and

$$\bar{Y}_1 = 324.134 + 248.128 = 572.262$$

Almost before you can say t test, we have determined the respective group means from the regression analysis. Go back to Table 6.3 and check these means with those obtained from the t test procedure. This illustrates that for a dichotomous independent variable subjected to bivariate regression, the difference between the means of the two categories is the unstandardized beta. We can calculate the means of a dichotomous variable in a multiple regression after adjusting for the effects of a number of other independent variables in similar fashion. Analysis of variance (ANOVA) will also provide category means adjusted for the effects of independents. However, ANOVA requires the independent variables to be categorical. As you will see in Chapter 14, where we discuss dummy variables, regression does not have this restriction. Regression, in all its forms, is an incredibly powerful tool for statistical analysis.

Because we will need to refer back to bivariate regression values for crime seriousness and prior record when we discuss multivariate correlation and regression in the next chapter, I will present these values in the partial printouts in Table 12.8. Note that both crime seriousness and prior record are more powerfully related (as indicated by their respective standardized betas) to sentence severity than is offender group. Further discussion is deferred until Chapter 13.

TABLE 12.8 PARTIAL PRINTOUTS FOR BIVARIATE REGRESSION FOR THE EFFECTS OF CRIME SERIOUSNESS AND PRIOR RECORD ON SENTENCE SEVERITY (SPSSx)

VARIABLE	B	(Crime Seriousness) SE B	BETA	T	SIG T
CRSER	265.640540	10.272805	.716179	25.859	.0000
(CONSTANT)	−303.231569	36.756259		−8.250	.0000

VARIABLE	B	(Prior Record) SE B	BETA	T	SIG T
PRREC	64.392124	5.298170	.434416	12.154	.0000
(CONSTANT)	235.060001	33.495415		7.018	.0000

12.3 SUMMARY

Correlation and regression techniques are used to analyze linear relationships between interval or ratio variables. Regression is a method of predicting values on the dependent variables from knowledge of the independent variable by using the linear equation. Correlation tells us how accurate these predictions are. The regression line functions as a kind of floating mean in that predictions made on the basis of the line minimize prediction error (residuals).

A preliminary stage in regression analysis is the examination of plotted values on a scattergram. The regression is a function of a (the Y intercept) and b (the slope). The Y intercept is the value of Y when $X = 0$, and the slope reveals how much the dependent variable increases or decreases in a constant manner per unit increase in the independent variable. The slope and the intercept are constants in the prediction equation and are used to make predictions about Y from a given value of X.

The correlation coefficient, an index of the strength and direction of the association, ranges from -1 to $+1$. The correlation coefficient is defined as the ratio of the covariance of Y and X to their respective standard deviations. When squared, the correlation is interpreted as a PRE statistic. The standard error of r is an estimate of the population (rho), and it is tested for statistical significance by the t distribution.

The standard error of the estimate tells us the average prediction error in predicting Y from X. It functions similarly to the standard deviation in a univariate distribution in that it gives the average deviation of scores from the regression line.

We concluded the chapter by demonstrating the diversity and usefulness of bivariate regression when we have a dichotomous independent variable.

PRACTICE APPLICATION:
BIVARIATE CORRELATION AND REGRESSION

A researcher wants to determine if self-esteem is related to social distance from homosexuals. Two scales are administered to six subjects. The self-esteem scale ranges from zero (low esteem) to 40 (high esteem). The social distance scale ranges from zero (total nonacceptance of homosexuals) to 10 (complete acceptance). Compute the slope (b), the Y intercept, and the correlation coefficient. The slope (b) is

$$b = \frac{N\Sigma XY - (\Sigma X)(\Sigma Y)}{N\Sigma X^2 - (\Sigma X)^2}$$

$$= \frac{(6)(986) - (153)(38)}{(6)(3999) - (23409)} = \frac{5916 - 5814}{23994 - 23409} = \frac{102}{585} = .174$$

The slope of .174 tells us that for each unit change in self-esteem there is a .174 unit change in the acceptance of homosexuals.

Case	Self-Esteem X	Social Distance Y	X^2	Y^2	XY
a	20	6	400	36	120
b	22	5	484	25	110
c	29	8	841	64	232
d	25	6	625	36	150
e	32	7	1024	49	224
f	25	6	625	36	150

$$\Sigma X = 153 \qquad \Sigma Y = 38 \qquad \Sigma X^2 = 3999 \quad \Sigma Y^2 = 246 \quad \Sigma XY = 986$$

$$\bar{X} = 25.5 \qquad \bar{Y} = 6.33$$

The Y intercept (a) is

$$a = \bar{Y} - b\bar{X}$$

$$= 6.33 - (.174)(25.5) = 6.33 - 4.437 = 1.89$$

If a person has a self-esteem score of 30, what level of homosexual acceptance would you predict for him or her?

$$Y' = a + bX = 1.89 + .174(30) = 1.89 + 5.22 = 7 \text{ (rounded)}$$

The correlation coefficient is

$$r = \frac{N\Sigma XY - (\Sigma X)(\Sigma Y)}{\sqrt{[N\Sigma X^2 - (\Sigma X)^2][N\Sigma Y^2 - (\Sigma Y)^2]}}$$

$$= \frac{(6)(986) - (153)(38)}{\sqrt{[(6)(3999) - 23409][(6)(246) - 1444]}}$$

$$= \frac{5916 - 5814}{\sqrt{(23994 - 23409)(1476 - 1444)}} = \frac{102}{\sqrt{(585)(32)}}$$

$$= \frac{102}{\sqrt{18720}} = \frac{102}{136.821} = .7455$$

Compute the significance level by using t.

$$t = r\sqrt{\frac{N-2}{1-r^2}} = (.7455)\sqrt{\frac{4}{1-.556}} = (.7455)\sqrt{\frac{4}{.444}}$$

$$= (.7455)\sqrt{9.01} = (.7455)(3.0) = 2.236$$

The variables have a strong positive association. Acceptance of homosexuals increases as self-esteem increases. The coefficient of determination is $.7455^2$, or

.556, indicating that 55.5 percent of the variance in the acceptance of homosexuals is explained by the self-esteem level. The computed t value (2.236) with 4 *df* exceeds the critical t in Appendix B (2.132) for a one-tailed test with alpha set at .05. The correlation is significant at less than .05.

APPENDIX: Computer Instructions for Table 12.3

Command 12.1

SPSSx	SAS
SCATTERGRAM SENT WITH CON	PROC REG; MODEL SENT = CON;
STATISTICS ALL	PROC PLOT; PLOT SENT * CON;

REFERENCES AND SUGGESTED READINGS

Achen, C. (1982). *Interpreting and using regression.* Beverly Hills, CA: Sage. A very useful and not too technical introduction to regression.

Beck, C. (1980). *Applied regression: An introduction.* Beverly Hills, CA: Sage. A good introduction to applied regression written with simplicity and clarity.

Blalock, H. (1972). *Causal inferences in nonexperimental research.* New York: W. W. Norton. Excellent book on prediction and causality couched in terms of correlation and regression.

Pedhazer, E. (1982). *Multiple regression in behavioral research: Explanation and prediction.* New York: Holt, Rinehart and Winston. This large volume is the definitive work on correlation and regression. Every aspect of these techniques is explored in detail.

Chapter 13

Multivariate Correlation and Regression

13.1 PARTIAL CORRELATION

This chapter introduces you to multivariate statistical techniques for interval/ratio variables: partial and multiple correlation and multiple regression. **Partial correlation** gives a single measure of association between two variables, taking into consideration the presence of one or more other variables. That is, partial correlation provides a single measure of association between two variables while adjusting for the effects of one or more other variables. The logic is the same as for crosstabulation with control variables. With crosstabulation we physically moved the distribution of our two variables into two categories of the control variable, as when we examined the association between sentence and offender group in the two categories (prior offense and no prior offense) of prior record. We noted then how our average cell frequencies were drained with this relatively simple control. What if we wanted to control for five other variables? Even our relatively large sample would have dwindled to the point at which our "results" would have been extremely difficult to summarize in any succinct manner. Even if we had a sample large enough for adequate cell frequencies, how would we be able to digest mentally such a large number of subtables in order to arrive at a meaningful interpretation? We simply would not be able to see the tree for the forest.

Partial correlation allows us to control for a number of other variables simultaneously without physically manipulating the raw data into separate categories. It does so by statistical rather than physical control. Let us see what happens to the zero-order correlation of .855 between the number of prior felony convictions and the number of years imprisonment when we control statistically for a third variable, seriousness of criminal charge. Let us say that this variable is coded 1 for the least serious charge, 2 for the next most serious, 3 for the next, and 4 for the most serious charge. The data from Table 12.1 are reproduced in Table 13.1, with the crime charge (V) variable added.

TABLE 13.1 RAW DATA FROM TABLE 12.1 WITH CRIMINAL CHARGE ADDED

Case	Number of Prior Convictions (X)	Sentence in Years (Y)	Criminal Charge (V)
a	1	1	1
b	1	3	2
c	2	3	2
d	2	4	4
e	2	2	1
f	3	3	3
g	3	4	3
h	4	6	4
i	5	7	4
j	5	5	3
	28	38	27
	$\bar{X} = 2.8$	$\bar{Y} = 3.8$	$\bar{V} = 2.7$

There are three correlations in this data set:

between number of convictions (X) and sentence (Y) $ryx = .855$
between number of convictions (X) and charge (V) $rxv = .675$
between sentence (Y) and charge (V) $ryv = .867$

13.1.1 The Logic of Partial Correlation

To explain the rather difficult logic of partial correlation we will examine the effect of the number of prior convictions on sentence length, controlling for the effects of crime charge. The formula for partial correlation is

$$ryx.v = \frac{ryx - (ryv)(rxv)}{\sqrt{1 - r^2yv}\sqrt{1 - r^2xv}} \tag{13.1}$$

As we have said, partial correlation enables us to control for a third variable without physically dividing the joint distribution of Y and X into categories of the control variable, as we do in the elaboration of crosstabulated data. A close examination of Formula 13.1 might provide a clue to how this is done. The numerator tells us that we subtract the combined effects of crime charge (v) on both sentence length and prior convictions (the product of ryv and rxv) from the effects of prior convictions on sentence length (ryx). In effect we are considering only the covariance of sentence length and prior convictions remaining after crime charge has operated on them both. This value is then divided by what we might consider the average value of the coefficient of alienation, where $1 - r^2yv$ equals the proportion of variance in sentence length not explained by crime charge, and $1 - r^2xv$ equals the proportion of variance in crime charge not explained by prior convictions.

13.1.2 Computing Partial Correlations

Using these three correlations, we can now determine what the effect of prior convictions is on sentence length, controlling for the effects of crime charge. Look back at the correlations for a moment and try to determine logically what you think might happen. Will the correlation remain roughly the same? Will it increase? Or will it decrease?

STEP ONE   From preceding correlations, put the appropriate values into Formula 13.1.

$$ryx.v = \frac{.855 - (.867)(.675)}{\sqrt{1 - (.867)^2}\sqrt{1 - (.675)^2}}$$

STEP TWO
Multiply .867 by .675 = .585. Subtract this value from .855 = .27.

$$= \frac{.27}{\sqrt{1 - (.867)^2}\sqrt{1 - (.675)^2}}$$

STEP THREE
Square .867 = .7517. Square .675 = .4556.

$$= \frac{.27}{\sqrt{1 - .7517}\sqrt{1 - .4556}}$$

STEP FOUR
Subtract .7517 from 1 = .2483, and .4556 from 1 = .5444.

$$= \frac{.27}{\sqrt{(.2483)}\sqrt{(.5444)}}$$

STEP FIVE
Take the square root of .2483 = .4983, and the square root of .5444 = .7378. Multiply .4983 by .7378 = .3676.

$$= \frac{.27}{.3676} = .734$$

STEP SIX
Divide .27 by .3676 = .734.

As I hope you anticipated from noting the high correlation between prior convictions and crime charge, the relationship between prior convictions and sentence length has diminished from .855 to .734. We will now explore partial correlation further with a more complex computer example using our sex offender data.

13.1.3 A Computer Example

The first step is to develop a correlation matrix of zero-order correlations between all the variables we are interested in, remembering that a zero-order correlation is simply the association between two variables without any controls for additional variables. A matrix is a row-by-column display of zero-order correlations for each pair of variables. Following is a matrix that includes the variables sentence severity, offender group (non-sex and sex), crime seriousness, and prior record. Such a matrix is produced when you ask the computer for a

PARTIAL CORR (partial correlation). To obtain the correlation matrix presented in Table 13.2, command 13.1 is required.

TABLE 13.2 SPSSx PRINTOUT FOR PEARSON CORRELATION

VARIABLE	CASES	MEAN	STD DEV
SENSEV (Y)	637	492.0220	727.3945
GROUP (X)	637	.6766	.4681
CRSER (V)	637	2.9937	1.9611
PRREC (W)	637	3.9906	4.9073

P E A R S O N   C O R R E L A T I O N   C O E F F I C I E N T S

	SENSEV (Y)	GROUP (X)	CRSER (V)	PRREC (W)
SENSEV (Y)	1.000	.1597	.7162	.4344
	(637)	(637)	(637)	(637)
	P = .	P = .000	P = .000	P = .000
GROUP (X)	.1597	1.0000	− .1666	.0582
	(637)	(637)	(637)	(637)
	P = .000	P = .	P = .000	P = .071
CRSER (V)	.7162	− .1666	1.0000	.3150
	(637)	(637)	(637)	(637)
	P = .000	P = .000	P = .	P = .000
PRREC (W)	.4344	.0582	.3150	1.0000
	(637)	(637)	(637)	(637)
	P = .000	P = .000	P = .071	P = .

(COEFFICIENT / (CASES) / 1-TAILED SIG)

CODING: Offender Group: non-sex = 0, sex = 1.

Interpreting the Printout   The top of the computer printout lists the variable code names, the number of cases, and the means and standard deviations of all variables. Note that the mean given for the group variable is simply the proportion of sex offenders in the data set (431/637 = .6766). This will be true only if you use the convention of coding dichotomous variables as 0 and 1. Below this we see the correlation matrix of zero-order Pearson correlation coefficients. Note that the matrix is a "mirror image." Information is repeated on both sides of the diagonal formed by the correlation of each variable with itself.

Reading along the top row, we learn that sentence severity is weakly but significantly related to offender group (.16 rounded, $p = .000$). We next see that the correlation between sentence severity and crime seriousness is strong at .7162, and the correlation between sentence severity and prior record is moderate at .4344. Given this information, we might be led to conclude that crime seriousness is the most important variable determining sentence severity, followed by prior record, and lastly by offender group. We shall see later that this conclusion is not necessarily true.

Tracing along the next row, we find that offender group is negatively and significantly related to crime seriousness ($-.1666$) and positive but non-significantly related to prior record (.058). That is, as these two legal variables are measured by the courts, sex offenders commit the less serious crimes but have the more serious prior records. However, since the correlation between offender group and prior record is not significant at less than 0.05, we cannot assume that this is the situation in the population of sex offenders in this jurisdiction.

We should point out that whether a correlation between two variables is positive or negative depends on how we code noninterval variables. If we had coded the offender group as sex $= 0$, non-sex $= 1$, the correlation between sentence severity and offender group would have been $-.1597$, the correlation between offender group and crime seriousness would have been $+.1666$, and the correlation between offender group and prior record would have been $-.058$. Thus, although the coding is arbitrary with nominal variables, such as offender group, and does not affect the statistical computations, it must be shown in the table so that the reader may properly interpret the results. Needless to say, our coding system does not affect the underlying relationship in any way.

The last correlation reported in the table is the one between crime seriousness and prior record (.315), indicating a moderate statistically significant tendency for those with the more serious criminal histories to commit the more serious crimes. We will now compute the partial correlation between offender group and sentence severity, controlling for crime seriousness.

Given that we know that sex offenders receive significantly harsher sentences than non-sex offenders ($r = .16$), but also that they commit significantly less serious crimes ($r = -.167$), what affect do you think that controlling for crime seriousness will have on the basic offender group/sentence severity relationship? Will the association increase or decrease? Before you go any further, try to think the question out logically.

STEP ONE From the correlation matrix, put the appropriate values into Formula 13.1.

$$r_{yx.v} = \frac{.16 - (.716)(-.167)}{\sqrt{1 - (.716)^2}\sqrt{1 - (-.167)^2}}$$

STEP TWO
Multiply .716 by $-.167$ = $-.1196$. Subtract this value from .16 = .2796 (do not forget that minus a minus is a plus).

$$= \frac{.2796}{\sqrt{1 - (.716)^2}\sqrt{1 - (-.167)^2}}$$

STEP THREE
Square .716 = .5127. Square $-.167$ = .0279.

$$= \frac{.2796}{\sqrt{1 - .5127}\sqrt{1 - .0279}}$$

STEP FOUR
Subtract .5127 from 1 = .4873, and .0279 from 1 = .9721.

$$= \frac{.2796}{\sqrt{.4873}\sqrt{.9721}}$$

STEP FIVE
Take the square root of
.4873 = .6981, and the
square root of .9721 =
.9859. Multiply .6981 by
.9859 = .6882.

$$= \frac{.2796}{.6882} = .406$$

STEP SIX
Divide .2796 by .6882 = .406.

If you thought that controlling for the effects of crime seriousness would increase the strength of the relationship between sentence severity and offender group, you were obviously right. It makes sense that this should be so since offenders who were already receiving harsher sentences also had lower crime seriousness scores, a variable that contributes powerfully to sentence severity. Crime seriousness is acting as a suppressor variable that has been masking the "true" strength of the relationship between offender group and sentence severity.

We previously discussed suppressor variables in Chapter 10, but just in case the logic is still a little fuzzy, let us try a simplified example. Suppose we have a group of 100 U.S. citizens and a group of 100 Canadians who bought a pair of shoes during the last month. We find out how much the members of each group paid for their shoes (converting the Canadian dollars to U.S. dollars) and correlate national group with cost of shoes. We find that the Canadian buyers pay a mean of $30 for a pair of shoes, and that the U.S. citizens pay a mean of $27. Canadians, therefore, pay an average of $3 more for their shoes. Does this small dollar amount represent the real "cost" of being a Canadian rather than a U.S. citizen when it comes to buying shoes? If both groups enjoyed the same mean income it would. But suppose that the U.S. citizens were found to enjoy an income that was an average of 10 percent higher than that of the Canadians. If we took the effects of this difference in income into account, the relationship between national group and cost of shoes would become stronger. Thus, the cost of being a Canadian rather than a U.S. citizen when it comes to buying shoes is much greater than an initial analysis might indicate because it hurts the Canadians' budget more to purchase a pair of shoes than it does the U.S. citizens' budget. Even if the shoes were equally priced on both sides of the border this statement would be true because of the Canadians' lower income. In a "fair" purchasing world, if Canadian income is 10 percent less than U.S. income, the Canadians would pay 10 percent less for their shoes than U.S. citizens. However, it was the U.S. citizens who paid 10 percent less for their shoes than the Canadians. Thus, taking the income differential into account actually compounds the cost of being a Canadian in real terms.

Similarly, the cost of being a sex offender rather than a non-sex offender is greater than the mean difference of 248.1 sentence severity points that separates the groups as determined by the t test in Chapter 6. Why? Because sex offenders, on the average, are getting more than they "fairly" deserve as determined by their average lower crime seriousness score.

13.1.4 Second-Order Partials: Controlling for Two Independent Variables

As stated in Chapter 11, controlling for crime seriousness or prior record alone leaves an incomplete picture of what is going on in the sentencing world. Since they operate together in the real world, we have to assess their joint effects in our statistical world. Before I show you how to compute a second-order partial correlation, let us quickly compute the correlation between sentence severity and offender group, controlling for prior record ($ryx.w$).

$$ryx.w = \frac{ryx - (ryw)(rxw)}{\sqrt{1 - r^2yw}\sqrt{1 - r^2xw}}$$

$$= \frac{.16 - (.434)(.058)}{\sqrt{1 - (.434)^2}\sqrt{1 - (.058)^2}}$$

$$= \frac{.16 - (.0252)}{\sqrt{1 - (.1884)}\sqrt{1 - (.0034)}}$$

$$= \frac{.1348}{\sqrt{.8116}\sqrt{.9966}}$$

$$= \frac{.1348}{(.9009)(.9983)}$$

$$= \frac{.1348}{.8994} = .150$$

We see that the first-order partial correlation between offender group and sentence severity is .150 when controlling for prior record. This slight drop in the correlation is to be expected, given that sex offenders as a group had slightly more serious prior records.

We now have first-order partials controlling separately for seriousness of crime and prior record. We wish to determine the offender group/sentence severity relationship, controlling for both legal variables at the same time. Statistically, this would be stated as $ryx.vw$. Before you could compute this second-order partial, two final first-order correlations must be computed: the relationship between sentence severity and prior record, controlling for crime seriousness ($ryw.v$), and the relationship between offender group and prior record, controlling for crime seriousness ($rxw.v$). These values have been computed as $ryw.v = .315$ and $rxw.v = .119$. We will just put them into the formula along with $ryx.v$ (.407) to demonstrate that the logic of computing second-order partials is the same as that for computing first-order partials.

$$ryx.vw = \frac{ryx.v - (ryw.v)(rxw.v)}{\sqrt{1 - r^2yw.v}\sqrt{1 - r^2xw.v}} \tag{13.2}$$

$$= \frac{.407 - (.315)(.119)}{\sqrt{1 - (.315)^2}\sqrt{1 - (.119)^2}}$$

$$= \frac{.369}{\sqrt{1-(.099)}\sqrt{1-(.0142)}}$$

$$= \frac{.369}{(.949)(.993)}$$

$$= \frac{.369}{.942} = .392$$

The relationship between offender group and sentence severity, controlling for crime seriousness and prior record, is .392. The simultaneous control of these two legally relevant variables with partial correlation analysis will allow us to make statements about the sentencing of sex offenders that other techniques just hint at. Since we have controlled for the only two variables that are legally supposed to influence sentencing decisions, we can state with confidence that sex offenders receive discriminatory sentencing relative to non-sex offenders in this jurisdiction.

If we were to ask the computer to give us the correlation between sentence severity and group, controlling for crime seriousness and prior record, we would need command 13.2. The output from these commands is reproduced in Table 13.3. We will receive a correlation matrix with the output, which is not reproduced because it is the same as the one in Table 13.2.

TABLE 13.3   SPSSx PRINTOUT FOR PARTIAL CORRELATION

```
       PARTIAL CORRELATION COEFFICIENTS
CONTROLLING FOR.. CRSER
       GROUP

SENSEV .4055
       (634)
       p = .000
(COEFFICIENT / (D.F.) / SIGNIFICANCE

       PARTIAL CORRELATION COEFFICIENTS
CONTROLLING FOR.. PRREC
       GROUP

SENSEV .1495
       (634)
       p = .000
(COEFFICIENT / (D.F.) / SIGNIFICANCE

       PARTIAL CORRELATION COEFFICIENTS
CONTROLLING FOR.. CRSER PRREC
       GROUP

SENSEV .3907
       (633)
       p = .000
(COEFFICIENT / (D.F.) / SIGNIFICANCE
```

Interpreting the Printout   The first section gives the coefficient between sentence severity and group, controlling for crime seriousness (.4055). The second figure (634) is the degrees of freedom, and the final figure ($p = .000$) is the probability that the population correlation equals zero (t test).

The second section repeats the process, using prior record as the control variable. The final section gives the coefficient between sentence severity and group, controlling for the effects of both crime seriousness and prior record (.391, rounded). Again, the practice of rounding accounts for the slight differences between our calculations and those of the computer.

13.1.5 The Multiple Correlation Coefficient

A partial correlation is an estimate of the correlation between two variables in a population with the effects of one or more other variables controlled for, or partialed out. In other words, it is the correlation between y and x uncontaminated by v, w, and so on. When using partial correlation we are only interested in the association of y and x among a population rendered homogeneous on other variables. When we use **multiple correlation**, on the other hand, we are interested in the combined effects of a set of independent variables on y. We allow the population to be heterogeneous on all variables of interest and calculate the increment in variances explained over the variance explained by x.

In Chapter 12 we noted that the squared zero-order correlation coefficient is the proportion of variance in the dependent variable accounted for by the independent variable. In terms of our offender data, crime seriousness explains 51.3 percent of the variance in sentence severity (.716 squared $=$ .513) and offender group explains 2.56 percent (.16 squared $=$ .0256). You might think that all you have to do to determine the percentage of the variance that they jointly account for is to add their separate percentages (51.3 + 2.56) to arrive at 53.86. But things are not that simple. We have already seen that when we take crime seriousness into account, the correlation between sentence severity and offender group increases. Therefore, the percentage of variance in sentence severity jointly accounted for by these two independent variables should be greater than the sum of their zero-order contributions. Formula 13.3 is used to calculate the multiple correlation coefficient (capital R).

$$Ry.xv = \sqrt{\frac{r^2yx + r^2yv - 2ryxryvrxv}{1 - r^2xv}} \tag{13.3}$$

where $Ry.xv =$ the multiple correlation coefficient (R)

$r^2yx =$ the zero-order correlation between sentence severity and offender group squared

$r^2yv =$ the zero-order correlation between sentence severity and crime seriousness squared

$rxv =$ the zero-order correlation between offender group and crime seriousness

We put in the values from Table 13.2.

$$Ry.xv = \sqrt{\frac{.160^2 + .716^2 - 2(.16)(.716)(-.167)}{1 - (-.167)^2}}$$

STEP ONE
Perform all squaring and multiplication functions.

$$= \sqrt{\frac{.0256 + .5126 - 2(-.01913)}{1 - (.027889)}}$$

STEP TWO
Add .0256 and .5126. Multiply −.01913 by 2, and subtract .027889 from 1.

$$= \sqrt{\frac{.5382 - (-.03826)}{.972}}$$

STEP THREE
Subtract −.03826 from .5382 (this is the same as an addition problem, minus a minus = a plus).

$$= \sqrt{\frac{.57646}{.972}} = \sqrt{.539} = .77$$

STEP FOUR
Divide and take the square root of the quotient.

The multiple correlation coefficient is .77, and its squared value (.593) is the percentage of the variance in sentence severity accounted for by both variables operating jointly. Note that if the correlation between offender group and crime seriousness had been zero ($rxv = 0$), the multiple correlation coefficient obtained from this laborious process would have been exactly the value obtained from simply adding together the zero-order contributions (53.86 percent). Thus, in terms of accounting for variance in the dependent variable, the correlation between the predictor variables x and v is redundant information.

A diagrammatic illustration of a simple example may help you to visualize the nonadditivity, and hence redundancy, of variance explained in y by two correlated independent variables. In situation A in Figure 13.1 both x and v are correlated with y but are uncorrelated with each other. We can simply sum the separate proportions of variance explained by x and v to get 16 percent + 16 percent = 32 percent. In situation B, x and v are correlated. We cannot sum their contributions to variance in y because they account for a certain proportion of common variance. This shared variance, represented by the overlapped crosshatched area, is the redundant information that must be subtracted.

We can extend the multiple correlation coefficient to include any number of independent variables. But as you can imagine, it is a long and tedious process. As long as you understand the logic behind the process, you can safely leave the busy work to the computer.

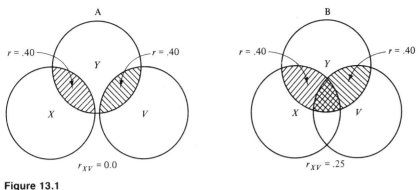

Figure 13.1

13.2 MULTIPLE REGRESSION

As neat and tidy as partial correlation is in summarizing complex relationships among a number of variables, it is far from comprehensive. For instance, how much extra time for the sex offender does that .392 correlation represent? What are the confidence intervals for that extra time? Which of the three variables (offender group, crime seriousness, or prior record) is of most or least importance in explaining variance in sentence severity, taking into consideration their simultaneous presence? How much of the variance in sentence severity do the three variables taken together explain? All of these questions, and more, can be answered by multiple regression. Basically, **multiple regression** is a tool for evaluating the overall dependance of a variable on a set of independent variables.

13.2.1 Extending the Regression Equation

We saw in Chapter 12 that the best way of describing the linear relationship between two interval level variables is the least-squares regression line: $Y = a + bX$. This regression line can be extended to include any number of other independent variables, even those that are measured at the nominal level by the use of "dummy variables," which are explained in Chapter 14. The relationship between the dependent variable sentence severity and our set of independent variables of offender group, crime seriousness, and prior record is defined by this formula:

$$Y = a + b_1 X + b_2 X + b_3 X + \cdots + b_k X \qquad (13.4)$$

where b_1 = the partial slope of the relationship between the first independent variable and sentence severity, with other independent variables being controlled

b_2 = the partial slope between the second independent variable and sentence severity, with other independent variables being controlled

b_3 = the partial slope between the third independent variable and sentence severity, with other independent variables being controlled

b_k = partial slope for any other independent variable(s) that may be added to the model

We saw in Chapter 12 that a regression slope shows the amount of change in the dependent variable per unit change in the independent variable. We also saw in the bivariate regression of crime seriousness on sentence severity that each unit increase in crime seriousness resulted in an increase of 265.6 days in prison. In the case of multiple regression, where we have more than one independent variable, the regression slope is an **unstandardized partial regression slope,** and indicates the amount of change in the dependent variable per unit change in the independent variable while controlling for the effects of one or more other independent variables in the equation.

13.2.2 The Unstandardized Partial Slope

The partial slopes for crime seriousness and group regressed on sentence severity are determined by the following formulas:

$$b_1 = \left(\frac{sy}{sv} \right) \left[\frac{ryv - (ryx)(rvx)}{1 - r^2vx} \right] \tag{13.5}$$

$$b_2 = \left(\frac{sy}{sx} \right) \left[\frac{ryx - (ryv)(rvx)}{1 - rvx} \right]$$

where b_1 = the partial slope of V (crime seriousness) on Y (sentence severity)

b_2 = the partial slope of X (offender group) on Y

sy = the standard deviation of Y (sentence severity)

sv = the standard deviation of V (crime seriousness)

sx = the standard deviation of X (offender group)

ryv = the zero-order correlation between sentence severity and crime seriousness

ryx = the zero-order correlation between sentence severity and offender group

rvx = the zero-order correlation between crime seriousness and offender group

All the relevant information needed to compute the partial slope is reproduced in Table 13.4.

TABLE 13.4 INPUT DATA FOR THE CALCULATION OF THE PARTIAL SLOPE

Sentence Severity (y)	Crime Seriousness (v)	Offender Group (x)	Correlations (r)
$\bar{X} = 492.0$	$\bar{X} = 2.99$	$\bar{X} = .667$	$ryv = .716$
$s = 727.39$	$s = 1.96$	$s = .468$	$ryx = .160$
			$rvx = -.167$

The partial slope for the crime seriousness (V) is

$$b_1 = \left(\frac{sy}{sv}\right)\left[\frac{ryv - (ryx)(rvx)}{1 - r^2vx}\right] \tag{13.6}$$

$$= \left(\frac{727.39}{1.96}\right)\left[\frac{.716 - (.16)(-.167)}{1 - (-.167)^2}\right]$$

$$= (372.1)\left[\frac{.716 - (-.0267)}{1 - .0279}\right] = (372.1)\left(\frac{.743}{.972}\right)$$

$$= (371.1)(.764) = 283.5$$

The partial slope for offender group (X) is

$$b_2 = \left(\frac{sy}{sx}\right)\left[\frac{ryx - (ryv)(rvx)}{1 - r^2vx}\right]$$

$$= \left(\frac{727.39}{.468}\right)\left[\frac{.16 - (.716)(-.167)}{1 - (-.167)^2}\right] = (1554.2)\frac{.16 - (-.1196)}{1 - .0279}$$

$$= (1554.2)\frac{.280}{.972} = (1554.2)(.288) = 447.6$$

Now that we have the partial slopes, what do they mean? The first partial slope (b_1) tells us that there will be a change of 283.5 units in the dependent variable (283.5 sentence severity points) per unit change in the first independent variable (per crime seriousness point) when the influence of the second independent variable (offender group) is held constant. When the influence of offender group is taken into account there is an increase of just under 20 points over the 265.6 value of the bivariate unstandardized slope.

In the second case (b_2), we are informed that there will be a change of 447.6 units in the dependent variable per unit change in offender group (moving from 0 = non-sex to 1 = sex) when the influence of crime seriousness is held constant. This figure is an increase over the bivariate slope for sentence severity and offender group $(b = 248.1)$ of 199.4.

13.2.3 The Standardized Partial Slope

As we have seen, partial regression slopes are marvelous tools for revealing the predicted change in the dependent variable associated with a unit change in the dependent variable, with other independent variables being controlled. However, we cannot determine from the partial slopes which of the independent variables in the model has the most powerful (is the most important) impact on sentence severity. If we look back to the bivariate regressions in Tables 12.7 and 12.8, we see that the slope for crime seriousness is 265.6; for offender group, 248.1; and for prior record, 64.4. We cannot assume from these figures that since the slopes for crime seriousness and offender group are almost equal, they are approximately of equal importance in determining sentence severity, nor can we assume that either one of them is about four times more important than the prior record. Why not? Simply because they are all measured differently. Recall that in Chapter 12 we explained how the value of b depends on how we measured the dependent variable. It also depends on the range of the independent variable. For example, the offender group only has to "split" the sentence severity variance it explains two ways—sex or non-sex offender. Crime seriousness points range from 1 to 10, and prior record points range from zero to 27, which means that they have to split the variance they account for 10 and 28 ways, respectively. If all of the independent variables had only two values (0 and 1), their slopes could be directly compared. Comparing partial regression slopes of independent variables that have different units of measurement is rather like comparing apples and oranges. To assess the relative importance of the independent variables, then, we have to convert them to a common scale, that is, standardize them.

To do so we draft the standard deviation back into service. When the standard deviation has worked its magic, we have what is known as the **standardized partial regression slope**. This slope shows how much a 1 standard deviation change in the independent variable will affect the dependent variable, controlling for all the other independent variables in the equation. The formula for standardizing a regression slope is as follows:

For the first independent variable:

Crime Seriousness

$$\beta_1 = b_1 \left(\frac{sv}{sy} \right) \tag{13.7}$$

where β_1 = the standardized slope of crime seriousness (V) on sentence severity (Y)

b_1 = the unstandardized slope of V on Y

sv = the standard deviation of crime seriousness

sy = the standard deviation of sentence severity

$$\beta_1 = 265.6 \left[\frac{1.96}{727.39} \right]$$

$$= 265.6(.002687)$$

$$= .714$$

For the second independent variable:

Offender Group

$$\beta_2 = b_2 \left[\frac{sx}{sy} \right]$$

where β_2 = the standardized slope of offender group (X) on sentence severity (Y)

b_2 = the unstandardized slope of X on Y

sx = the standard deviation of offender group

sy = the standard deviation of sentence severity

$$\beta_2 = 248.1 \left[\frac{.468}{727.39} \right]$$

$$= 248.1(.000643) = .1595$$

A similar computation of the standardized partial regression slope for prior record was .43. I hope you have noticed that our computed values for the standardized betas are, within the limits of rounding error, analogous to the zero-order correlations between these pairs of variables. But we still can not tell which of the three independent variables has the most important impact on sentence severity from these standardized betas, any more than we could from the zero-order correlations. To do so we must compute the standardized partial regression slopes for these variables.

The standardized partial regression slope, or *standardized beta,* as we will call it from now on, indicates the average standard deviation change in the dependent variable associated with a standard deviation change in the independent variable, holding constant all other variables in the equation. The formula for computing the standardized beta is as follows:

$$\beta yv.x = byv.x \left[\frac{sx}{sy} \right] \tag{13.8}$$

where $\beta yv.x$ = the standardized partial beta

$byx.x$ = the unstandardized partial beta

sx = the standard deviation of x (group)

sy = the standard deviation of y (sentence severity)

Substituting from values already computed, we get

$$\beta yv.x = 283.5 \left[\frac{1.96}{727.39} \right]$$

$$= (283.5)(.00269)$$

$$= .763$$

Note that this value of .763, with tolerance for rounding, is identical to the value we computed for the multiple correlation coefficient from Formula 13.3. In fact, Formula 13.8 is simply an alternative to Formula 13.3. A similarly computed partial standardized beta for offender group, controlling for crime seriousness, was .289. We are sure at this point that crime seriousness is more important to sentencing decisions than is being a sex offender. However, we still do not know whether offender group or prior record is the second most important variable in sentencing. The answer to this question requires us to extend the equation to include prior record. In the interest of brevity we will not compute this step. The logic, however, is analogous to that involved in computing second-order partial correlation coefficients. We will now discuss the computer readout for the regression model assessing the combined effects of offender group, crime seriousness, and prior record on sentence severity.

13.2.4 A Computer Example of Multiple Regression

We are finally in a position to assess the simultaneous effects of all three predictor variables on sentence severity. It will be useful to look at three separate printouts so that you can see the changes in the various statistics as we add new variables and to reinforce what you have learned about regression in the last two chapters. The first panel in Table 13.5 is a simple bivariate regression of crime seriousness on sentence severity. The second panel shows the regression results with offender group added to the equation, and the third panel shows the full three-variable model (crime seriousness, offender group, and prior record regressed on sentence severity). Computer instructions are given in command 13.3.

TABLE 13.5   THREE REGRESSION MODELS WITH VARIABLES ADDED
PROGRESSIVELY (SPSSx)

Panel 1. Bivariate Regression of Crime Seriousness on Sentence Severity

		Analysis of Variance			
Multiple R	.71618				
R Square	.51291		DF	SUM OF SQUARES	MEAN SQUARES
Adjusted R Square	.51215	Regression	1	172599964.05	172599964.05
Standard Error	508.06003	Residual	635	163909373.64	258124.99

F = 668.66815   SIGNIF F = .0000

Variable	B	SE B	BETA	T	SIG T
CRSER	265.640540	10.272805	.716179	25.859	.0000
(CONSTANT)	−303.231569	36.756259		−8.250	.0000

Panel 2. The Addition of Offender Group to the Equation

		Analysis of Variance			
Multiple R	.77006				
R Square	.59299		DF	SUM OF SQUARES	MEAN SQUARES
Adjusted R Square	.59171	Regression	2	199547814.06	99773907.03
Standard Error	464.78774	Residual	634	136961523.62	258124.99

F = 461.85714   SIGNIF F = .0000

Variable	B	SE B	BETA	T	SIG T
CRSER	283.378604	9.531104	.764002	29.732	.0000
GROUP	445.937607	39.927002	.286997	11.169	.0000
(CONSTANT)	−658.059821	46.260011		−14.225	.0000

Panel 3. The Addition of Prior Record to the Model

		Analysis of Variance			
Multiple R	.79265				
R Square	.62829		DF	SUM OF SQUARES	MEAN SQUARES
Adjusted R Square	.62653	Regression	3	211424782.77	70474927.59
Standard Error	444.52889	Residual	633	125084554.92	197605.93

F = 356.64379   SIGNIF F = .0000

Variable	B	SE B	BETA	T	SIG T
CRSER	258.685221	9.656112	.697427	26.790	.0000
GROUP	410.668415	38.456720	.264299	10.679	.0000
PRREC	29.548259	3.811352	.199345	7.753	.0000
(CONSTANT)	−678.185991	44.319758		−15.302	.0000

13.2.5 Interpreting the Printout

Summary Statistics: Multiple R, R, sy.x, and ANOVA We will begin the discussion with panel 2, the two-variable regression model. The first statistic encountered is multiple R, the correlation between a dependent variable and two or more independent variables. In the present case it is the correlation between sentence severity and crime seriousness and offender group. Please note that this value is identical to the value we computed for $Ry.xv$ on page 272.

The next statistic is R squared (given as R *square* in printout), which is simply the square of multiple $R(.77) = .593$ (three decimal places). It is important to note the change in the R squared value from that given in panel 1 to the value given in panel 2. It has increased from .51291 to .59299, an increment of .0801. This increase indicates that after crime seriousness has been allowed to explain all the variance that it can, offender group explains an additional 8 percent. In panel 3 you can see a further increase in R squared of .0353, for a total R squared for the model of .62829.

The next statistic is the **adjusted R squared**, a more conservative estimate of explained variance that is especially useful with a small sample and/or a large number of predictor variables. It adjusts for the number of independent variables in the equation and for the number of cases in the sample. It is always preferable to report this measure rather than the unadjusted R squared. The computation of the adjusted R squared found in panel 3 is illustrated by Formula 13.9.

$$\text{adjusted } R^2 = 1 - (1 - R^2)\frac{N - 1}{N - k - 1} \tag{13.9}$$

$$= 1 - (.37171)\frac{636}{633}$$

$$= 1 - (.37171)(1.004739) = .62653$$

where N = sample size

  k = number of independent variables in the model

Although the R squared value will always increase with the addition of further variables to the equation, the adjusted R squared may begin to decrease in value with the additional variables. When there is a serious decrease, we are being warned that we have added variables that are not useful in helping us to understand our data. Notice that the adjusted R squared value in panel 3 is only slightly less than the unadjusted R squared value.

Next comes the standard error, which is actually the standard error of the estimate. Recall from Chapter 12 that this is an estimate of the average prediction error, and it is defined as the standard error of actual Y values from the predicted Y' values based on the regression equation. The formula for the standard error estimate in panel 2 is simply an extension of Formula 12.10 (see Formula 13.10). In panel 3 the formula would be further extended to accommodate the third predictor variable.

$$Sy.xv = \sqrt{\frac{\Sigma Y^2 - a\Sigma Y - b_1\Sigma X_1 Y - b_2\Sigma X_2 Y}{N - 3}} \qquad (13.10)$$

Notice that the divisor is now $N - 3$ because three degrees of freedom are lost in estimating the multiple regression coefficients with two predictor variables.

To understand the standard error of the estimate further, recall that it is the standard deviation of the residuals. The residual or unexplained sum of squares is printed out as 125084554.9 in panel 3. If we divide this by the df for $SS_{residual}$, defined as $N - k - 1 = 633$, we get the variance of the residuals. The square root of the residuals is the standard deviation of the residuals, or the standard error of the estimate.

$$Sy.xvw = \sqrt{\frac{SS_{residual}}{df}} = \sqrt{\frac{125084554.9}{633}} = 444.53$$

To the right of these statistics is the familiar analysis of variance. The sum of squares explained by the regression is analogous to the term *explained sum of squares* in ANOVA, and the residual sum of squares means exactly the same as it does in ANOVA, that is, the variance in the model that is unexplained. The F ratio, obtained by dividing the regression mean square by the residual mean square, is shown for panel 3:

$$F = \frac{70474927.59}{197605.93} = 356.64379$$

Clearly, our regression model explains a highly significant proportion of the variance in sentence severity.

The Predictor Variables: *B*, SE *b*, beta, and *T* All of the reported statistics so far are those summarizing association and significance for the model, that is, all of the variables in the equation, however many there may be. Below the summary model statistics is information regarding the contributions of each specific variable in the model. Reading from left to right, we see the first statistic is the partial unstandardized beta (B in the printout) for sentence severity and crime seriousness, controlling for all other variables in the model, which happens to be only offender group at present. We note that the unstandardized beta has increased from 256.6 in panel 1 to 283.4 in panel 2. Within the limits of rounding error, this is the value we computed on page 275. In panel 3 the partial slope for crime seriousness declines somewhat to 258.68 because prior record is significantly and positively correlated with crime seriousness (those who commit the more serious crimes tend to have the more serious prior records).

The unstandardized partial slope of 258.68 in panel 3 means that for each unit increase in crime seriousness there will be an increase of 258.68 sentence severity points when the influence of offender group and prior record is held constant. This is just the best estimate derived from the regression. Obviously not all offenders will be similarly affected.

This observation brings us to the next reported statistic: the standard error of b (SE B). The standard error of b is used to establish confidence intervals for b.

Two standard errors (the reported standard error multiplied by 2) establishes the 95 percent confidence interval for *b*.

The next reported statistic is the standardized partial slope (BETA) for crime seriousness, reported as .697427 in panel 3. This value tells you how much a 1 standard deviation change in the independent variable will affect the dependent variable, also in standard deviation units, controlling for the effects of the other variables in the equation. This is an important statistic to reveal in any report because, unlike the unstandardized partial slope, it is a measure of the relative importance of the independent variables in the equation.

The next statistic is the *t* test (T). The *t* value is obtained by dividing the unstandardized partial slope value by its standard error. The *t* test in a multiple regression model tests the significance of the independent variable, given the other variables in the model. It follows that *t* is also a test of significance in the increment of the proportion of variance explained (*R* squared increment). All variables in the model are highly significant.

We now move down to the second row, containing the statistics relevant to offender group. The unstandardized partial slope of 410.7 given in panel 3 indicates that the effect on sentence severity of being a sex offender rather than a nonsex offender is 410.7 sentence severity points. This is a rather dramatic increase from the 248.1 sentence severity points difference observed when we did not take into account the two legally relevant variables.

With the addition of prior record to the equation, the betas, both standardized and unstandardized, for crime seriousness and offender group have diminished in size. Again, this is intuitively reasonable if we recall from the matrix of zero-order correlations that prior record is positively related to both crime seriousness and offender group. We finally know (within certain confidence intervals, of course) what being a sex offender versus not being a sex offender means in terms of sentence severity. It tells us more than a simple multiple correlation because we can easily "translate" the unstandardized partial slope into substantive terms by changing the sentence severity points into days' imprisonment.

Multiple regression has finally allowed us to determine the ranking of the independent variables in terms of how they affect sentencing. It is now obvious from the standardized betas that offender group ($\beta = .264$) has a more powerful effect than does prior record ($\beta = .199$). We would have been misled into thinking that prior record was the more important of the two had we not performed a regression analysis. The relative importance of these three predictor variables can be determined by taking the ratio of the squares of their standardized betas. The squares (rounded to two places) of our three predictors are crime seriousness = .49, offender group = .07, prior record = .04. Crime seriousness accounts for 7 times more of the variance (.49/.07 = 7) than offender group and just over 12 times more than prior record. Offender group accounts for 1.75 times more of the variance (.07/.04 = 1.75) than prior record.

The final statistic is the *Y* intercept (CONSTANT), which represents the value of *Y* when all of the independent variables are equal to zero. As we saw previously, we use the constant to predict the value of an individual score from given values of the independent variables in the equation. Suppose that we wished to predict the sentence severity of a sex offender with 4 crime seriousness points and 4 prior record points. We would use Formula 13.4:

$$Y' = a + b_1 X + b_2 X + b_3 X$$

where $a = Y$ intercept (constant)

b_1 = partial slope for group

b_2 = partial slope for crime seriousness

b_3 = partial slope for prior record

Putting in the values from panel 3 of Table 13.5, we get

$$Y' = -678.18 + 410.7(1) + 258.7(4) + 29.5(4)$$

$$= -678.18 + 410.7 + 1034.8 + 118 = 885.32$$

And for a non-sex offender with the same crime seriousness and prior record scores,

$$Y' = -678.18 + 410.7(0) + 258.7(4) + 29.5(4)$$

$$= -678.18 + 0 + 1034.8 + 118 = 474.62$$

13.2.6 A Visual Representation of Multiple Regression

To help you to grasp visually what is taking place in a multivariate regression analysis, the following diagram is offered (Figure 13.2). The circle labeled Y is the total variance in sentence severity. The first variable to enter the equation is crime seriousness (V). This variable takes a big bite out of the variance, accounting for, or explaining, 51.29 percent of it (visually represented by the shaded area). Since this proportion of the variance has been accounted for, it is removed from further consideration as far as the subsequent predictors are concerned. The next most powerful predictor, offender group (X), takes its bite out of the remaining variance, 8.01 percent. Finally, prior record (W) takes out 3.53 percent of the variance in Y after both X and V have taken their share. Thus, the three predictor variables have taken a combined bite of 62.83 percent of the variance in sentence severity, leaving 37.17 percent of the variance unexplained.

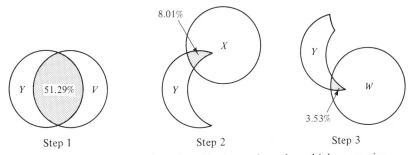

Figure 13.2 Visual representation of partitioning variance in multiple regression

13.2.7 Reporting Results

If we were submitting the results of our analysis to a research journal for possible publication, the format of our table describing the final model would be shown in Table 13.6.

Thus multiple regression is an excellent technique to examine relationships among variables when we have independent variables measured at different levels and an interval/ratio dependent variable. In addition to the comprehensive statistical information supplied by multiple regression, it has great resiliency. As Achen has put it, "As the consistency theorem shows, if the researcher sets up the problem correctly, regression will tend to give the right answer under any reasonable practical circumstances, even if a great many of the classical postulates are violated" (1982, p. 37).

TABLE 13.6 MULTIPLE REGRESSION OF CRIME SERIOUSNESS, OFFENDER GROUP, AND PRIOR RECORD ON SENTENCE SEVERITY

Variables	b	s.e.	β	t	sig.	R^2	R^2 change
Crime seriousness	258.7	9.7	.697	26.8	.000	.5129	.5129
Offender group	410.7	38.4	.264	10.7	.000	.5930	.0801
Prior record	29.5	3.8	.199	7.7	.000	.6283	.0353
(Constant)	−678.2	44.3		−15.3	.000		

Adjusted R squared $= .626$, $F = 356.6$, $p = .0000$, $N = 637$

13.3 SUMMARY

Partial correlation allows us to assess the association of two variables, controlling for the effects of one or more other variables. It does so mathematically rather than by physically moving cases around in table cells. As with tabular elaboration, partial correlation can result in replication, spurious, and specification outcomes.

Multiple correlation is an index of the combined association of three or more variables. Squaring the multiple correlation gives the percentage of the variance in the dependent variable explained by all of the independent variables in the equation. The squared multiple correlation is the multiple coefficient of determination.

Multiple regression is used to make predictions of the dependent variable from two or more independent variables. The unstandardized partial slope is an index of change in the dependent variable per unit change in one of the independent variables, controlling for the effects of the other independent variables in the equation. The unstandardized partial slopes are given in their original measurement units. The standardized partial slopes convey the same information in terms of standard deviation units rather than the original metric.

Multiple correlation and regression are remarkably powerful and robust techniques for assessing the combined effects of a series of independent or predictor variables on a dependent variable. They supply a wealth of information.

PRACTICE APPLICATION: PARTIAL CORRELATION

This problem continues with the topic explored in the last chapter. We know that acceptance of homosexuals is related highly to self-esteem. What would happen if we added educational level to the analysis? We will not go through the tedious task of computing additional zero-order correlations. Instead we will reproduce the correlation matrix for these three variables.

	Y	X	V	$\bar{X}$	s.d.
(Y) Social distance	1.000	.745	.548	6.333	1.033
(X) Self-esteem		1.000	.480	25.500	4.416
(V) Level of education			1.000	15.000	1.414

The formula for the first-order partial (the correlation between self-esteem and acceptance of homosexuals, controlling for education) is

$$ryx.v = \frac{ryx - (ryv)(rxv)}{\sqrt{1 - r^2yv}\sqrt{1 - r^2xv}}$$

Substituting,

$$ryx.v = \frac{.745 - (.548)(.480)}{\sqrt{1 - (.548)^2}\sqrt{1 - (.480)^2}} = \frac{.745 - .263}{\sqrt{.70}\sqrt{.77}}$$

$$= \frac{.482}{(.837)(.877)} = \frac{.482}{.734} = .657$$

Testing for significance (*note: df* = 3 because we are testing a first-order correlation and *N* = 6)

$$t = ryx.v\sqrt{\frac{N - 3}{1 - r^2}} = .657\sqrt{\frac{3}{.543}} = .657\sqrt{5.525}$$

$$= .657(2.35) = 1.54, \text{ n.s.}$$

Thus, the relationship between self-esteem and acceptance of homosexuals is weakened when controlling for educational level because of the moderately high correlations between the two independent variables. The computed *t* is far from the critical value of 2.353 required for significance at the .05 level with 3 degrees of freedom. As an additional exercise, compute *t* for *ryx.v,* assuming a sample size of 60.

PRACTICE APPLICATION: MULTIPLE REGRESSION

We will now apply multiple regression to the problem of self-esteem and acceptance of homosexuals. All the necessary information to make our computations is in the following matrix:

	Y	X	V	$\bar{X}$	s.d.
(Y) Social distance	1.000	.745	.548	6.333	1.033
(X) Self-esteem		1.000	.480	25.500	4.416
(V) Level of education			1.000	15.000	1.414

First we have to find the partial slopes. The partial slope for self-esteem is

$$b_1 = \left(\frac{sdy}{sdx} \right) \left[\frac{ryx - (ryv)(rxv)}{1 - r^2xv} \right]$$

$$= \left(\frac{1.033}{4.416} \right) \left[\frac{.745 - (.548)(.480)}{1 - (.480)^2} \right]$$

$$= (.234) \left[\frac{.745 - .263}{1 - .23} \right]$$

$$= (.234) \left[\frac{.482}{.77} \right]$$

$$= (.234)(.626) = .146$$

The partial slope for level of education is

$$b_2 = \left(\frac{sdy}{sdv} \right) \left[\frac{ryv - (ryx)(rxv)}{1 - r^2vx} \right]$$

$$= \left(\frac{1.033}{1.414} \right) \left[\frac{.548 - (.745)(.48)}{1 - (.48)^2} \right]$$

$$= (.73) \left[\frac{.548 - .358}{1 - .23} \right]$$

$$= (.73) \left[\frac{.19}{.77} \right]$$

$$= (.73)(.247) = .180$$

The Y intercept is

$$a = \bar{Y} - b\bar{X} - b\bar{V}$$

$$= 6.333 - (.146)(25.5) - (.180)(15.0)$$

$$= 6.333 - 3.723 - 2.7$$

$$= -.09$$

Compute the standardized partial slope. For self-esteem,

$$\beta_1 = b_1 \left(\frac{sdx}{sdy} \right)$$

$$= .146 \left(\frac{4.416}{1.033} \right)$$

$$= (.146)(4.275) = .624$$

For education,

$$\beta_2 = b_2 \left(\frac{sdv}{sdy} \right)$$

$$= .18 \left(\frac{1.414}{1.033} \right)$$

$$= (.18)(1.369) = .246$$

Self-esteem is a more powerful predictor of acceptance of, or social distance from, homosexuals. To assess their combined effects we compute the multiple correlation coefficient.

$$Ry.xv = \sqrt{\frac{r^2yx + r^2yv - 2ryxryvrxv}{1 - r^2xv}}$$

$$= \sqrt{\frac{.745^2 + .548^2 - 2(.745)(.548)(.48)}{1 - (.48)^2}}$$

$$= \sqrt{\frac{.555 + .30 - 2(.196)}{1 - (.23)}}$$

$$= \sqrt{\frac{.855 - .392}{.77}}$$

$$= \sqrt{\frac{.463}{.77}} = \sqrt{.601} = .775$$

Self-esteem and education jointly account for 60.1 percent of the variance in social distance from homosexuals. Self-esteem by itself accounted for 55.5 percent of the variance (.745 squared). We explained only an additional 4.6 percent of the variance by adding education to the model because education is rather highly correlated with self-esteem.

APPENDIX: Computer Instructions for Table 13.2

Command 13.1

SPSSx	SAS

```
                                   IF GROUP  =  1 THEN  GROUP  =  0;
RECODE GROUP (1=0)(2=1)            IF GROUP  >  1 THEN  GROUP  =  1;
PEARSON CORR SENSEV,CRSER,GROUP,   PROC CORR;
          PREEC
STATISTICS ALL                        VAR SENSEV GROUP CRSER PRREC;
```

APPENDIX: Computer Instructions for Table 13.3

Command 13.2

```
       SPSSx    (no analogous SAS program)*
RECODE GROUP (1=0)(2=1)
PARTIAL CORR SENSEV WITH GROUP BY CRSER, PRREC (1,2)
STATISTICS ALL
```

This command tells the computer that we want a set of partial correlation. The dependent variable is SENTENCE SEVERITY, the major independent variable is GROUP, and we wish to know how these two variables are related, controlling for the effects of CRIME SERIOUSNESS and PRIOR RECORD. The (1,2) command tells the computer that we want first- and second-order partials computed. Partials up to the fifth order can be requested. For instance, if we wanted to determine what additional effects race, class, and age had on the relationship, these variables could be added to the list, the order command being (1,2,3,4,5). Finally, we have told the computer to compute ALL relevant statistics.

* Although SAS has no specific partial correlation program at present, partial correlations are given in conjunction with other SAS programs such as factor analysis.

APPENDIX: Computer Instructions for Table 13.5

Command 13.3

SPSSx

```
RECODE GROUP (1=0)(2=1)
REGRESSION VARIABLES = SENSEV, CRSER, PRREC, GROUP/
                       DEPENDENT = SENSEV/
                       ENTER/
```

This command tells the computer (1) what variables are to be included in the regression model, (2) the dependent variable, and (3) the method of entry. The ENTER command is the simplest of all the available methods of entry in a regression model. Other methods of entering the variables, such as STEPWISE, BACKWARD elimation, and FORWARD selection can be used. In the stepwise method of entry, the computer first selects the variable with the strongest association with the dependent variable. It then goes back to the data and checks the remaining variables in the equation to see if they remain significant for the criteria we have specified. It then selects the next best variable and repeats the procedure until all variables that meet the specific criteria are included.

The backward elimination method starts with the r squared value of all of the independent variables in the model with the dependent variable and eliminates independent variables that do not meet the criteria for inclusion one at a time. If none is eliminated it means that they all contribute significantly to the prediction of the dependent variable.

Forward selection is analogous to stepwise selection in that the variable with the highest zero-order correlation with the dependent variable is selected for inclusion first. Variables already accepted for inclusion are not eliminated if the addition of another independent variable renders them insignificant (if they no longer contribute significantly to variance explained when the effects of the newly entered variable are present). For further information on methods of entry consult the SPSSx or SAS manual.

To obtain similar output from a SAS program, command 13.4 is required.

Command 13.4

SAS

```
PRO REG;
MODEL SENSEV=CRSER PRREC GROUP/ALL;
```

These commands, which are less complicated than SPSSx commands, ask the computer to run a regression (PROC REG;) using the same set of variables and to provide ALL pertinent statistics. The results obtained will, of course, be identical. However, SAS uses a terminology that departs somewhat from SPSSx's. Where SPSSx uses B (unstandardized beta), BETA (standardized beta), and CONSTANT (Y intercept), SAS uses PARAMETER ESTIMATE, STANDARDIZED ESTIMATE, and INTERCEPT, respectively. Both terminologies are valid, but SPSSx's is more consistent with that of social science.

REFERENCES AND SUGGESTED READINGS

Achen, C. (1982). *Interpreting and using regression.* Beverly Hills, CA: Sage.

Cliff, N. (1987). *Analyzing multivariate data.* New York: Harcourt Brace Jovanovich. An excellent and technically sophisticated approach to multivariate analysis. This text includes computer instructions in SPSSx, SAS, and BMDP.

Lewis-Beck, M. (1980). *Applied regression: An introduction.* Beverly Hills, CA: Sage.

Pehazur, E. (1982). *Multiple regression in behavioral research.* New York: Holt, Rinehart and Winston.

Chapter 14

Further Exploring Correlation and Regression

No other statistical techniques are as powerful, useful, and more generally applicable to social science data than correlation and regression. On the other hand, probably no other techniques have been so misunderstood, abused, and misued. This chapter points out some additional uses of correlation and regression as well as some common problems. Because this chapter is not essential to the understanding of correlation and regression, it may be omitted in some courses. However, if you are planning to go on to graduate school or further statistical studies, you will find these topics useful. We will begin with a discussion of dummy variable regression.

14.1 DUMMY VARIABLE REGRESSION

In Chapter 12 we looked at bivariate regression by using group as the independent variable. Group is a dichotomous variable that we dummy-coded 0 and 1. This section extends the discussion of dummy variables in regression. Some researchers have avoided the use of multiple regression under the mistaken impression that all variables must be measured at the interval or ratio level. Actually, the only requirement is that the dependent variable be an interval or ratio measure. Nominal variables, either dichotomous or multicategory (such as religious preference), can be used in a regression format when coded as dummy variables. **Dummy variables** are simply variables that are coded 1 in the presence of a given attribute and 0 in its absence. Offender type is a dummy variable because offenders who committed sex offenses were coded 1 and non-sex offenders were coded 0. In this case there are only two categories; the creation of dummy variables for multicategory nominal variables is just a little more complicated.

For instance, suppose that we wish to assess the sentences for sex and non-sex offenders according to the political party affiliations of the judges (Republican, Democratic, and independent). Although there is no natural ordering of party affiliation, if we entered this nominal variable into the regression model the computer would treat it as an ordered variable and would present meaningless and uninterpretable results. Dummy variable analysis gets around this problem by creating three separate dichotomous variables from the original variable containing three categories.

Dummy variable analysis is quite similar in logic to ANOVA and may, indeed, be considered a special case of ANOVA. The main difference between them is that with ANOVA, *judge* would be considered a single variable with three categories. In dummy variable regression, the nominal variable judge is treated as three separate dichotomous variables, scored 1 in the presence of an attribute and 0 in its absence. A Republican judge would be coded 1 on the Republican dummy variable and 0 on all others. A Democrat would be coded 1 on the Democratic dummy variable and 0 on all others. We do not need to create a dummy variable for the independent category since its value is completely determined by the first $k - 1$ dummies entered into the regression equation. The excluded category serves as a reference category whose mean on the dependent variable will be the Y constant (a). Dummy variable analysis, then, has $k - 1$ categories. That is, if we have three categories of an independent variable, we create $k - 1$, or two dummy variables. If we had five categories, we would create four dummy variables. The dummy variables for our categories of the judge's political affiliation are as follows:

Category	Dummies	
	D_1	D_2
Republican	1	0
Democrat	0	1
Independent	0	0 ◄——— (the reference category = the Y intercept)

To assess the effects of party affiliation on judges' sentencing of sex and non-sex offenders, command 14.1 is required. The output produced by this command is presented in Table 14.1.

TABLE 14.1 SPSSx DUMMY VARIABLE REGRESSION PRINTOUT

VARIABLE	B	SE B	BETA	T	SIG T
GROUP	249.483	60.884	.161	4.098	.0000
DUMMY1	93.456	81.125	.064	1.152	.2498
DUMMY2	−5.502	89.005	−.003	−.062	.9507
(CONSTANT)	273.166	83.919		3.255	.0012

Multiple R = .173, F = 6.5, sig = .0000

The important thing to note at this point is that the constant represents the reference dummy category, in this case the independent judges. The value of the constant (273.166) is the predicted mean sentence given by independent judges to non-sex offenders. To obtain the mean for sex offenders we simply add the constant to the beta value for group (273.166 + 249.483 = 522.65). The unstandardized beta for dummy 1 (93.456) indicates that the mean sentence severity of Republican judges is approximately 93 days more than the mean for the independent judges, and the unstandardized beta for dummy 2 indicates that the mean for Democratic judges is 5.5. days fewer. With some simple arithmetic we can determine the predicted mean sentence severity scores of each category of judge for our offenders. With the Republican judges, for example, the predicted means for non-sex and sex offenders are obtained as follows:

$$\bar{Y}' = a + b_1 d_1 + b_2 d_2$$

where $b_1 d_1$ = beta times dummy 1

$\qquad b_2 d_2$ = beta times dummy 2

For non-sex offenders, the predicted mean is

$$\bar{Y}' = 273.166 + 249.483(0) + 93.456(1)$$

$$= 273.166 + 0 + 93.456 = 366.362$$

For sex offenders the predicted mean is

$$\bar{Y}' = 273.166 + 249.483(1) + 93.456(1)$$

$$= 273.166 + 249.483 + 93.456 = 616.10$$

At this point you might well ask what the advantages of dummy variable analysis are in relation to ANOVA. There really aren't any at this juncture. In fact, ANOVA would probably be the choice of most researchers confronted with assessing the effects of two categorical variables on an interval-level dependent variable. So why bother with dummy variable regression? The answer is that ANOVA can deal only with categorical independent variables, whereas regression can deal with combinations of categorical and continuous variables in the model. Furthermore, ANOVA tends to get increasingly complicated and "messy" as we go beyond two or three independent variables. Regression analysis, on the other hand, can deal with a rather large number of independent variables, although there are limits.

If we do include additional predictor variables that are measured at higher levels, only minor additional calculations are required to arrive at category means. Of course, the regression results can stand by themselves as accurate assessments of the effects of the independent variables on the dependent variable. But there are times when it is considered important to report category means for each of the dummy categories. Suppose that we wanted to determine the sentence severity category means (sex and non-sex offenders) for Republican judges after adjusting for the effects of crime seriousness and prior record. When we run a regression of sentence severity containing the group, crime seriousness, prior record, and the dummy variables, we get the statistics reported in Table 14.2.

TABLE 14.2   DUMMY VARIABLES IN REGRESSION WITH A DICHOTOMOUS VARIABLE AND TWO INTERVAL VARIABLES

Variables	b	β	t	sig.
Crime seriousness	258.9	.70	27.0	.0000
Group	412.2	.26	10.8	.0000
Prior record	29.6	.20	7.8	.0000
Dummy 1	102.9	.07	2.1	.0396
Dummy 2	−7.3	−.00	−0.1	.8939
Constant	−734.8		−12.1	.0000

To find the mean for a particular category of judges, the constant is added to the unstandardized beta for that category and to the unstandardized betas of all nondummy variables in the model (crime seriousness, prior record, and offender group) multiplied by their respective mean values.

$$\bar{Y}' = a + b_1 d_1 + b_2 d_2 + b_{cs}\bar{X}_{cs} + b_G\bar{X}_G + b_{pr}\bar{X}_{pr}$$

where $\bar{Y}'$ = the predicted sentence severity mean

$\quad a$ = the Y constant

$\quad b_1 d_1$ = beta times dummy 1

$\quad b_2 d_2$ = beta times dummy 2

$\quad b_{cs}\bar{X}_{cs}$ = beta times crime seriousness mean

$\quad b_G\bar{X}_G$ = beta times offender group mean

$\quad b_{pr}\bar{X}_{pr}$ = beta times prior record mean

In Table 13.2 we saw that the mean value for crime seriousness is 3.0; for prior record, 4.0; and for group, 0.7 (all figures rounded). We use these numbers to determine the mean sentence severity score for sex offenders, adjusted for the influence of crime seriousness and prior record, when they are sentenced by Republican judges (dummy 1).

$$\bar{Y}' = -734.8 + 102.9(1) + 258.9(3) + 412.3(.7) + 29.6(4)$$

$$= -734.8 + 102.9 + 776.7 + 288.6 + 118.4 = 551.8$$

To determine the adjusted mean sentence severity for non-sex offenders sentenced by independent judges, the calculations would be

$$\bar{Y}' = -734.8 + 0(0) + 258.9(3) + (0)(.7) + 29.6(4)$$

$$= -734.8 + 0 + 776.7 + 118.4 = 160.3$$

I leave it to you as an exercise to compute predicted mean sentences for both offender groups by Democratic judges.

14.1.1 Dummy Variable Regression and Interaction

In Chapter 8 we illustrated the concept of interaction by looking at probation officers' sentencing recommendations for sex offenders with victim/offender relationship and probation officer ideology as independent variables. The ANOVA program indicated significant interaction between the two independent variables, thus suggesting further exploration of the data for a more meaningful interpretation of the effects of the two independent variables on recommendations. Dummy variable regression does not reveal explicitly the existence of interaction, as does ANOVA. Nevertheless, regression is superior to ANOVA for the complete exploration of sentencing recommendations because we can include the very important variables of crime seriousness and prior record in the equation. Significant interaction can be detected in multiple regression, however, with a little extra effort.

If preliminary statistical analyses of our theoretical knowledge of the subject under investigation leads us to suspect significant interaction, we cannot simply ignore it. What we can do is create a new variable that is a composite of the two interacting variables. This is easily accomplished with a series of compute statements (see the chapter appendix). For instance, we already know from the two-way ANOVA results in Chapter 8 that probation officers' sentencing recommendations are influenced by their ideology. Criminological theory tells us that conservatives are much more likely than are liberal officers to hold the position that punishment should fit the crime (Walsh, 1987). If this theory is correct, we would expect to find that crime seriousness is more important in the determination of conservative officers' recommendations than in liberal officers' recommendations. In other words, the effects of crime seriousness on recommendations will vary across officer category. To test this assumption we create an interaction term by multiplying ideology (PONAM) by crime seriousness (CRSER). This interaction term is entered into the regression equation in addition to its two composite variables. The regression model used to illustrate interaction in model C in Table 14.3 consists of one continuous dependent variable (POREC), one continuous independent variable (CRSER), one dummy independent variable (PONAM), and one interaction term (CRSER multiplied by PONAM). If the regression results indicate no significant interaction, the prediction equation is simply additive, with the form

$$Y' = a + b_1 X_1 + b_2 X_2$$

where X_1 = crime seriousness

   X_2 = officers' ideology

If interaction is significant, the additive model is no longer adequate to describe the data, and the equation must take the form

$$Y' = a + b_1 X_1 + b_2 X_2 + b_3 X_1 X_2$$

where $b_3 X_1 X_2$ = the interaction effect

Table 14.3 presents three separate regression models. Models A and B are simple bivariate regression models of the effect of crime seriousness on recommendations for sex and non-sex offenders for liberal and conservative officers, respectively. The adjusted r squared values (.325 for liberals and .594 for conservatives) support our contention that crime seriousness has more of an impact on the recommendations of conservative officers. The impact of one additional crime seriousness unit is associated with an increase of 290.89 recommendation units ($b = 290.89$) for conservative officers but only 178.75 units for liberal officers ($b = 178.75$). Subtracting the slope for the liberal officers from that of the conservative officers results in a difference of 112.14 recommendation units.

Let us now look at model C, which is a multiple regression including both independent variables and the interaction term CRSER × PONAM. Both independent variables are significant. The important point is the value of the unstandardized beta for the interaction term. We see that it is 112.14, the value we got from subtracting the b in model A from the b in model B. The test of statistical significance for the regression coefficient associated with the interaction term is a test of the statistical significance of the difference of the two slopes defined by the dummy variable (PONAM). The t value (5.18) for the interaction term is highly significant; thus the interaction effect is highly significant, and the additive prediction equation is inadequate. Note that the dummy independent variable PONAM has a significant effect on recommendation severity even after the effects of the interaction term have been accounted for.

TABLE 14.3 ILLUSTRATING INTERACTION

	(A) LIBERAL OFFICERS ONLY				
Variable	b	s.e.	β	t	Sig.
CRSER	178.75	14.66	.572	12.20	.0000
(CONSTANT)	−159.51	47.12		−3.38	.0008
ADJ. R Square	.325				
	(B) CONSERVATIVE OFFICERS ONLY				
Variable	b	s.e.	β	t	Sig.
CRSER	290.89	15.92	.772	18.27	.0000
(CONSTANT)	−318.56	64.28		−4.96	.0000
ADJ. R SQUARE	.594				
	(C) LIBERAL AND CONSERVATIVE OFFICERS AND IDEOLOGY × CRSER				
Variable	b	s.e.	β	t	Sig.
CRSER × PONAM	112.14	21.64	.352	5.18	.0000
CRSER	178.74	16.43	.502	10.87	.0000
PONAM	−159.04	77.64	−.111	−2.05	.0410
(CONSTANT)	−159.51	52.86		−3.02	.0027
ADJ. R. SQUARE	.528				

14.2 THE PROBLEM OF MULTICOLLINEARITY

Multicollinearity exists when there are high degrees of correlation among one or more independent variables in a regression equation. There is no commonly accepted standard of how high the correlation coefficient between two independent variables has to be before such a condition is said to exist. However, we should not get any argument if we state that a correlation of .70 or higher between two independent variables should give us cause for alarm (Hanushek & Jackson, 1977, p. 90). Pedhazur (1982, p. 235) points out, "High multicollinearity has extremely adverse effects on the standard errors of the regression coefficients, hence on tests of their statistical significance and their confidence intervals."

The greatest degree of correlation between two independent variables in the data sets provided with this text is the correlation of .59 between performance IQ (PIQ) and verbal IQ (VIQ) scores in the juvenile delinquency data. We may reason that these two separate measures of intelligence will be superior to a single measure (full-scale IQ: FIQ) in explaining variance in property crime scores. Although these two variables do not have extreme multicollinearity, we will regress them on property offense scores (boys only). We will then regress their composite (FIQ) on the same dependent variable and observe the effects of multicollinearity. Table 14.4 presents the results.

The first thing we notice is that the unstandardized and standardized coefficients have been "split" between the two measures of intelligence in regression A. Note that the standard errors for PIQ and VIQ are both larger than the standard error of their composite. Splitting the bs between the two measures has resulted in smaller values of b and larger standard errors, and hence smaller t values. In regression A, PIQ is not statistically significant, but in regression B it adds considerably to the t value assessing the significance of the impact of full-scale IQ on property crime. Unless we have good theoretical reasons for supposing that PIQ and VIQ have very different effects on property crime, it is clearly more meaningful statistically to enter them into the model as a composite. We must always be guided by theory and logic when doing research and evaluating statistical results.

TABLE 14.4   DEMONSTRATING THE EFFECTS OF MULTICOLLINEARITY

| A | | | | | B | | | | |
| Two Highly Correlated Measures Entered Separately, Regressed on Property Crime | | | | | Two Highly Correlated Measures Entered as a Composite, Regressed on Property Crime | | | | |
Variable	b	s.e.	β	t	Variable	b	s.e.	β	t
PIQ	.78	.44	.09	1.8	FIQ	2.3	.41	.25	5.7
VIQ	1.71	.52	.17	3.3					
	Adj. R^2 = .055					Adj. R^2 = .059			

Sometimes when multicollinearity is present a researcher will obtain regression coefficients that do not make sense. An interesting example is given by Groebner and Shannon (1981, pp. 483–484), who used a number of variables, such as age of house, number of bedrooms, number of bathrooms, and square footage, to predict housing sale prices. From their multiple regression results they obtained a regression coefficient of −2845.89 for number of bedrooms. This means that with all other variables held constant, an increase of one bedroom results in an average drop in price of $2,845.89! The zero-order correlation between sales price and number of bedrooms (+.494), as well as common sense, informs us that such a result is nonsense. It is obvious that number of bedrooms is highly correlated with the other variables in the model, especially square footage. The authors recognized this problem and suggested dropping number of bedrooms from the model as one method of dealing with multicollinearity. I would have suggested keeping this valuable predictor in the model but combining it with number of bathrooms to create a new variable, number of rooms. The two examples just given should convince you never to neglect searching for and dealing with any possible multicollinearity in your research data.

14.3 MEASUREMENT ERRORS

The term **measurement errors** basically refers to the reliability of the measured variables, that is, the consistency with which items on a scale measure the same concept. The reliability of a scale ranges between zero and 1, and the higher the reliability the more accurate the measure. The less reliability the measures have the more the correlations are underestimated. For instance, in our multiple sclerosis data we have measures of self-esteem and positive affect. These two scales have reliability coefficients of .866 and .907, respectively (Chapter 15 provides a brief discussion of how reliability coefficients are obtained). Although these coefficients are very respectable as social science scales go, they are not perfect. We will now demonstrate how we can correct for measurement error by a process known as *correction for attenuation*.

The uncorrected correlations between self-esteem and positive affect is .56. The formula for correcting correlations for attenuation is

$$rc = \frac{ryx}{\sqrt{r_1}\sqrt{r_2}} \tag{14.1}$$

where rc = corrected correlation

ryx = uncorrected correlation

r_1 = reliability of scale 1

r_2 = reliability of scale 2

Therefore, correcting r between self-esteem and positive affect, we get

$$rc = \frac{.56}{\sqrt{.907}\sqrt{.866}} = \frac{.56}{(.952)(931)} = \frac{.56}{.8862} = .632$$

The strength of correlation coefficients will always increase when corrected for attenuation as long as the variables being correlated are imperfectly measured. However, partial correlations can decrease, or even change signs (from positive to negative, or vice versa), when the control variable or variables are also corrected. That is, partial correlations can be seriously overestimated when variables are mismeasured. Whether we over- or underestimate in a multivariate analysis depends on the pattern of intercorrelations among the variables and the reliability of their measures. This is something to keep in mind when interpreting multivariate statistics.

14.4 SPECIFICATION ERRORS

Specification errors are errors that the researcher makes in specifying his or her model. These errors can be subsumed under three broad categories: (1) omitting theoretically relevant variables from the model, (2) including theoretically irrelevant variables in the model, and (3) specifying a linear regression model when it is curvilinear (Pedhazur, 1982, p. 35).

Suppose that we were to perform multiple regression with sentence severity as the dependent variable and crime seriousness and offender group as the independent variables. We know that prior record is a very important determinant of sentence severity, but we were unable to gain access to such records. To view the effects of the omission of this theoretically important variable, turn back to the regression results in Table 13.5 and compare model 2 with model 3. If prior record was not included, the analysis would have concluded with model 2. Concluding with model 2 would lead to overestimation of the effects of crime seriousness and group on sentence severity. Prior record is correlated significantly with sentence severity and with crime seriousness. By omitting prior record we have omitted the common variance (the overlap) that crime seriousness and prior record account for in sentence severity, thus biasing upward the effect of crime seriousness. Note that if prior record and crime seriousness were not correlated, no upward biasing of the crime seriousness regression coefficient would occur. However, such an omission would be reflected in a lower R square value.

Including irrelevant variables in a regression model is a result of theoretical ignorance and should not be done "just to see what happens." The problems involved with this type of misspecification are more the substantive meaninglessness of results than serious statistical biases.

Specifying a linear model when it is curvilinear requires a further look at eta squared.

14.5 NONLINEAR CORRELATION: ANOTHER LOOK AT ETA SQUARED

Regression analysis assumes that the relationships among variables are linear, that is, that they can be summarized by a straight line. However, there are times when the data are not "cooperative," and they assume other patterns. Some relationships between two variables are very strong, but the relationship may be curvilinear. For example, consider the set of scores in Figure 14.1, which constitutes a hypothetical index of muscular strength for five different age categories, ranging from very young to very old, arranged in a scatter diagram.

Just by examining the scores themselves we would guess that age and strength are strongly related, but the plotted scattergram shows these two variables to be related in curvilinear fashion. The intercept is exactly at the mean of the 25 scores, and the slope and the Pearson's *r* are zero. These values were computer generated. It might be a good idea for you to compute them for yourself as an exercise.

Having run these data through a correlation and regression program, the novice researcher might discard common sense and conclude that the two variables are unrelated. But if he or she had gone a step further and run a scattergram program, the existence of a relationship would be visually apparent. It should be obvious that this example is suited to ANOVA rather than correlation and regression since there is a categorized independent variable. It would not have been quite so obvious, however, had age been entered into the computer program in ungrouped form. Most researchers would enter the subjects' actual ages into the program because categorizing age (rendering a ratio measure as an ordinal measure) would cost them information. In the present case, not categorizing might lead to misinterpretation.

Using ANOVA on these data, we obtain a significant *F* ratio of 11.482 and an eta squared of .697, indicating that 69.7 percent of the variance in strength scores is accounted for by age. We will now demonstrate how eta can be so strong when *r* equals zero.

Figure 14.2 graphically illustrates the difference between the computations of *r* and η. Making predictions of *Y* from a linear function is no improvement over making the same predictions from the mean of *Y* when the *Y* intercept equals $\bar{Y}$. When computing eta we do not use the *X* scores, which are used only to define group boundaries. So, rather than using the grand mean or the "floating mean"

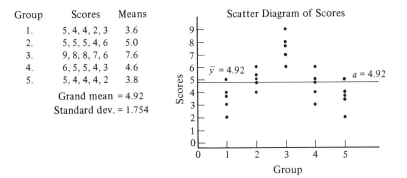

Group	Scores	Means
1.	5, 4, 4, 2, 3	3.6
2.	5, 5, 5, 4, 6	5.0
3.	9, 8, 8, 7, 6	7.6
4.	6, 5, 5, 4, 3	4.6
5.	5, 4, 4, 4, 2	3.8

Grand mean = 4.92
Standard dev. = 1.754

Pearson's *r* = 0   *r* squared = 0   significance .5000
std. err. of est. = 1.79177   intercept = 4.92   slope .0000

Figure 14.1

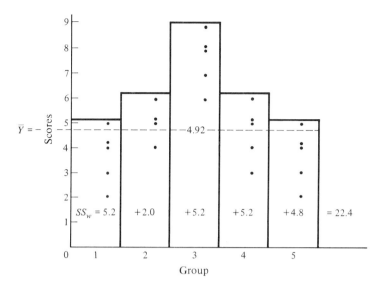

Figure 14.2 Scatter diagram of scores

(the regression equation), which in either case would predict a score of 4.92 for every subject, we compute five different sums of squares for each category. Just as in ANOVA, we add the separate variance estimates to obtain SS_{within}, which equals 22.4. We know from previous discussion that SS_{within} is the variance in Y that is unexplained by X, and that $SS_{between}$ is the proportion of variance in Y explained by X. The total variance is what we obtain if we try to predict Y from its grand mean. Therefore, if SS_{within} is smaller than SS_{total} we have improved our ability to predict Y from X. We have computed SS_{total} (not shown) to be 73.84. Subtracting SS_{within} from SS_{total}, we get $73.84 - 22.4 = 51.44$, which is $SS_{between}$, or the explained variance. Eta squared is defined as the ratio of the explained variance to the total variance. Therefore, $51.44/73.84 = .697$.

14.5.1 Eta Squared and Linearity

Eta squared is the sum of the linear and nonlinear variance in the dependent variable explained by the independent variable. It is a valuable statistic in its own right, but it can also be used to evaluate the linearity of the data in linear correlation analyses since it accounts for all variance, whereas R squared accounts only for linear variance. If eta squared is significantly larger than R squared we can conclude that our data do not describe a linear pattern.

We will use the data from our sentence length/number of convictions data from Chapter 12 to illustrate both the computation of eta squared and its utility for assessing linearity. Although the computation of eta squared can be rather cumbersome when computed from raw data, it is useful to do it to gain an understanding of its logic. The formula for the computation of eta squared is as follows:

$$\eta^2 = 1 - \frac{\Sigma(Y - \bar{Y}_i)^2}{\Sigma(Y - \bar{Y})^2} \quad \text{or} \quad \eta^2 = 1 - \frac{\text{within-category variance of } Y}{\text{overall variance of } Y} \quad (14.2)$$

Stated in prose form, eta squared is equal to 1 minus the within-category variance of Y divided by the overall variance of Y. The computational layout for eta squared is given in Table 14.5.

TABLE 14.5   COMPUTATION OF ETA SQUARED

Category	(Y) No. of years	Overall mean (Y)	Category mean (Y_i)	(Y − Ȳ)	(Y − Ȳ)²	(Y − Ȳ_i)	(Y − Ȳ_i)²
1	1	3.8	2.0	−2.8	7.84	−1.00	1.00
	3	3.8	2.0	−0.8	0.64	+1.00	1.00
2	3	3.8	3.0	−0.8	0.64	0.00	0.00
	4	3.8	3.0	+0.2	0.04	+1.00	1.00
	2	3.8	3.0	−1.8	3.24	−1.00	1.00
3	3	3.8	3.5	−0.8	0.64	−0.50	0.25
	4	3.8	3.5	+0.2	0.04	+0.50	0.25
4	6	3.8	6.0	+2.2	4.48	0.00	0.00
5	7	3.8	6.0	+3.2	10.24	+1.00	1.00
	5	3.8	6.0	+1.2	1.44	−1.00	1.00
					29.60		6.5

$(Y - \bar{Y}_1)^2$ is the within-category variance of Y, and $(Y - \bar{Y})^2$ is the total variance of Y. Using these values, we get

$$\eta^2 = 1 - \frac{6.5}{29.6} = 1 - .21959 = .7804$$

η = the square root of $\eta^2 = \sqrt{.7804} = .883$

Note that the overall variance (29.6) is the total variance we obtained when computing our PRE measure for these data in Chapter 12. Because of the relaxed restriction of assuming linearity, the computation of eta squared allows prior convictions to explain 5 percent more of the variance in years' imprisonment than R square (78 percent versus 73 percent). This result illustrates that eta squared will always be equal to or greater than R square. Two other important differences between eta and Pearson's r are these: (1) Unlike r, eta is nondirectional; that is, it indicates the strength of a relationship but no direction, positive or negative; (2) it doesn't assume a linear relationship.

To obtain the preceding information from the computer (only available in SPSSx), command 14.2 is required. The output produced by these commands is reproduced in Table 14.6.

TABLE 14.6 COMPUTER PRINTOUT FOR SUBPROGRAM BREAKDOWN

CRITERION VARIABLE	SEN			
BROKEN DOWN BY	CON			

VARIABLE	VALUE LABEL	MEAN	STD DEV	CASES
FOR ENTIRE POPULATION		3.8000	1.8135	10
CON	1	2.000	1.4142	2
CON	2	3.000	1.0000	3
CON	3	3.500	.7071	2
CON	4	6.000	.0000	1
CON	5	6.000	1.4142	2

TOTAL CASES = 10
MISSING CASES = 0

ANALYSIS OF VARIANCE

VALUE LABEL	SUM	MEAN	STD DEV	SUM OF SQ	CASES
1	4.0000	2.0000	1.4142	2.0000	2
2	9.0000	3.0000	1.0000	2.0000	3
3	7.0000	3.5000	.0701	.5000	2
4	6.0000	6.0000	.0000	.0000	1
5	12.0000	6.0000	1.4142	2.0000	2
WITHIN GROUPS TOTAL	38.0000	3.8000	1.1402	6.5000	10

ANALYSIS OF VARIANCE

SOURCE	SUM OF SQUARES	D.F.	MEAN SQUARE	F	SIG.
BETWEEN GROUPS	23.1000	4	5.7750	4.4423	.0667
LINEARITY	21.6510	1	21.6510	16.6546	.0095
DEV. FROM LINEARITY	1.4490	3	.4830	.3715	.7777

R = .8553   R SQUARED = .7315

WITHIN GROUPS	6.5000	5	1.3000		

ETA = .8834   ETA SQUARED = .7804

Notice that the F ratio for the variance explained by the between-group sum of squares is no longer significant. How can that be, given that the r squared and eta squared values remain the same? The answer lies in the fact that we can establish a relationship in regression with 1 degree of freedom rather than the 4 used here in the calculation of the sum of squares for $k - 1$ categories. This fact underscores both the importance of degrees of freedom in statistics and the general superiority of regression when we have linear data. The df for LINEARITY and DEV. FROM LINEARITY are simply a breakdown of the df for $SS_{between}$.

14.5.2 Do the Data Significantly Depart from Linearity?

Note that the value labeled linearity (21.65) is the value obtained when we subtracted the error variation from the total variation on page 250 in Chapter 12. The value labeled deviation from linearity (1.4490) is obtained by subtracting the within-group sum of squares (6.50) from the values we called the squared residuals (7.95) on page 249 (7.95 − 6.50 = 1.45). This difference is not significant (F = .3715, sig. = .7777). Hence, we can reject the null hypothesis and conclude that our data are linear.

Without immediate access to a computer, and assuming that you have R squared and eta squared values, it is a relatively simple operation to calculate the deviation from linearity by Formula 14.3. If you examine it closely, you will see that the "meat" of the formula is the strength of eta squared relative to r squared. The greater the relative strength of eta squared the less the data conform to a linear pattern.

$$F_{k - 2, N - k} = \frac{(\eta^2 - R^2)/(k - 2)}{(1 - \eta^2)/(N - k)} \qquad (14.3)$$

where $F = F$ ratio

N = sample size

k = number of categories

η^2 = eta squared

R^2 = coefficient of determination

Putting in the numbers, we get

$$F_{5 - 2, 10 - 5} = \frac{(.7804 - .7315)/5 - 2}{(1 - .7804)/10 - 5}$$

$$F_{3, 5df} = \frac{.0489/3}{.2196/5} = \frac{.0613}{.0439} = .3713$$

Setting alpha at .05 with 3 and 5 degrees of freedom, we find from the F ratio table that we would require a value of 5.79 to reject the hypothesis of a linear relationship. Since our computed F does not match this critical value, we can assume that the relationship between prior convictions and number of years sentenced to prison is linear.

14.6 THE PROBLEM OF HETEROSCEDASTICITY

We saw in Chapter 6 that the sentence severity variance associated with the sex offender and non-sex offender categories were heterogeneous and that the t test assumes homogeneity of variance, which the computer program tests for with the F ratio. The concept of **homoscedasticity** is closely related to the problem of homogeneity of variance. The assumption of homoscedasticity is that the variance of Y scores is uniform for all values of X. Homoscedasticity is important in terms of prediction accuracy in regression. Figure 14.3 illustrates homoscedastic and heteroscedastic distributions.

Although r_{xy} is roughly similar in both distributions, we are in a better position to make predictions from the data in distribution A because approximately 68

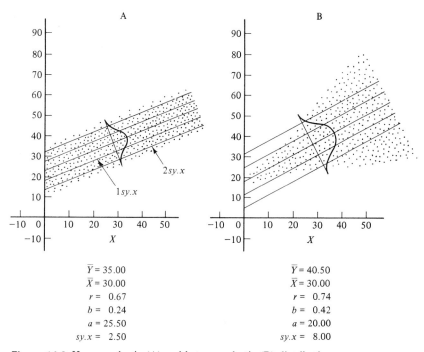

Figure 14.3 Homoscedastic (A) and heteroscedastic (B) distributions

percent of the observations lie within plus or minus 1 $sy.x$, and 95 percent lie within plus or minus 2 $sy.x$. In other words, the variance of Y is constant over different values of X. Now look at distribution B. Here we see that $sy.x$ is considerably larger and that 100 percent of the cases where $X = 10$ are within plus or minus 1 $sy.x$, and at $X = 50$ at least 50 percent of the cases lie outside 1 $sy.x$. Obviously, the variance of Y differs considerably over values of X in this distribution. Such a heteroscedastic distribution would lead to serious prediction errors should we attempt to predict from it.

Moderate departures from homoscedasticity can be tolerated in regression analysis. But when conducting research it is important to examine residuals (errors from the regression line) before making judgments based on the data. This step can be done with both SAS and SPSSx statistical packages.

14.7 ANALYSIS OF RESIDUALS AND THE OUTLIER PROBLEM

Recall that residuals are the prediction errors from a regression model and that they are obtained by $Yi - Y'$. The analysis of residuals allows us to determine if certain assumptions of regression, particularly homoscedasticity and linearity, are being met. When we use the regression program to obtain a scattergram of residuals it should show a fairly even scatter of residual values around the regression line. If it does not, one or more of the regression assumptions have been violated.

A fairly "healthy" pattern of residuals is seen in Figure 14.4, which is a plot of standardized residuals for the regression of crime seriousness on sentence severity. Residuals are standardized by dividing each residual by the standard error of the estimate. The standardization of residuals does not change their pattern on the plot.

Outliers are extreme residuals that can lead to serious misinterpretation of the relationship between variables. Consider the scattergrams in Figure 14.5. In distribution A there is a strong linear relationship between Y and X ($r = .81$). In distribution B there is a negative outlier, where $X = 7$ and $Y = 1$. We see that this one extreme case has attenuated the relationship rather drastically ($r = .45$). In the first instance X explains 66 percent of the variance in Y ($.81^2 = .66$), and in the second case X explains only 20 percent ($.45^2 = .20$). One extreme case has altered the relationship markedly by rotating the regression line toward it. In distribution C there is a positive outlier, where $X = 7$ and $Y = 14$. The correlation has again been decreased in the attempt to minimize the distance between the regression line and each data point.

Other statistics to note in Figure 14.5 are $sy.x$, b, and a. The slope (b) and the intercept (a) obviously have to change as the regression line is rotated toward the outliers. The $sy.x$ values in distributions B and C indicate how the outliers influence prediction errors.

If extreme outliers are found when examining residuals, they can be best dealt with by eliminating those observations from the data set. In the plot of residuals in Figure 14.4, for example, the computer program identifies the ten worst outliers for us (not shown). Most of the outliers in the offender data are positive (above the regression line) for high scores on crime seriousness. Having thus identified them we could discard them from the data set as being so atypical of the norm as not to be useful. Large samples tend to minimize the impact of

STANDARDIZED RESIDUAL (SPSSx Printout)

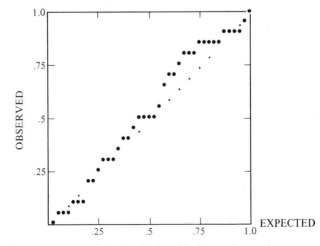

Figure 14.4 Plot of standardized residuals or crime seriousness regressed on sentence severity

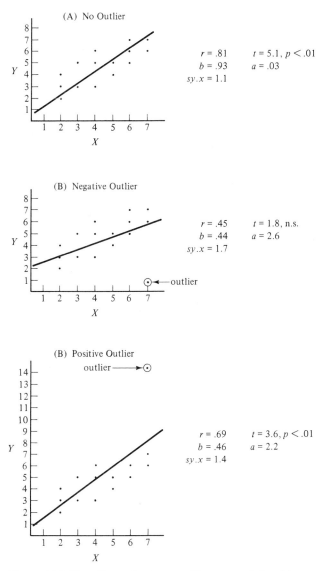

Figure 14.5 The effects of extreme outliers on a relationship

outliers, and those that are not too atypical can be dealt with by data transformation. We cannot get into this topic here, but see Pedhazur (1982) for a discussion. Computer instructions for the analysis of residuals are in the chapter appendix.

14.8 THE PROBLEM OF RESTRICTED RANGE

The problem of correlational analysis with variables whose range has been severely restricted is frequent in social science research. For example, suppose that we wished to estimate the correlation between sentence severity and prior record. Suppose further that the sample used to make this estimate was made up of prison inmates. The correlation between sentence severity and prior record we would obtain from such a sample would be lower than a correlation obtained from a sample of convicted felons whose sentences covered the entire range of sentencing possibilities. To understand why, consider the hypothetical distribution of sentence severity and prior record in Figure 14.6. If the distribution is fairly homoscedastic, the error variance around the regression line will remain relatively constant. However, the total variance in a truncated set of scores will be less than in the entire distribution, as you will readily see from Figure 14.6. Since the error variance remains more or less constant while the total variance gets smaller in a **restricted range** of scores, the correlation coefficient will be smaller.

As we saw in Chapter 12, the correlation coefficient squared can be expressed as the total variance minus the error variance divided by the total variance. Let us suppose that the total variance in an unrestricted sample is 20 and the error variance is 10. In this case the correlation coefficient will be

$$R^2 = \frac{20 - 10}{20} = \frac{10}{20} = .50$$

the square root of $.50 = .707$

$$r = .707$$

Now suppose that we take a subsample of cases from this sample. The error variance will remain roughly similar but the total variance will be less. In this case we may see something like the following:

$$R^2 = \frac{15 - 10}{15} = \frac{5}{15} = .333$$

the square root of $.333 = .577$

$$r = .577$$

Another example might make the point clearer. Suppose we wish to predict academic success from IQ. We would probably find a substantial correlation between the two variables from a large representative sample from the general population. Such a sample should contain a large range of IQ scores—say, from 70 to 135. However, we would obtain a smaller correlation if our sample consisted of only college students since, presumably, IQ operates as a factor in determining whether or not one goes to college. We might find IQ scores among college students ranging from 100 to 135. We would find an even smaller correlation if our sample consisted of graduate students because, again, IQ itself serves as one of the selection variables in the determination of graduate school attendance. With a sample of graduate students, the IQ range might be limited to 120 through 135, and the two variables might be distributed as in the subsample box in Figure 14.6. Remember that a correlation coefficient measures the covariance of two attributes. If either of the attributes being correlated does not vary, the correlation will be zero. If the attributes covary very little, the correlation will be small.

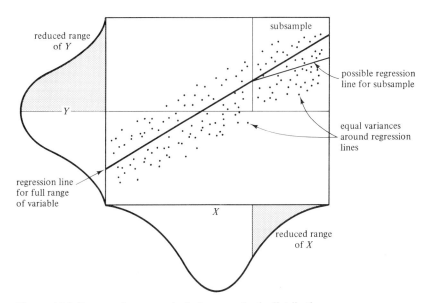

Figure 14.6 Truncated range and r in homoscedastic distribution

From this discussion we conclude that although information from selected subsets of the general population can be interesting, we have to be careful that we do not misinterpret the correlation between variables obtained from such samples as being accurate estimates of the "true" correlation between the two variables in the larger population. Be aware, however, that if the data are distributed heteroscedastically the correlation might actually be higher in a truncated sample than it is in the population. This observation underscores the importance of homoscedasticity.

14.9 POINT BISERIAL CORRELATION

In Chapter 12 we used the Pearson correlation coefficient to assess the relationship between sentence severity and offender group. Many texts assert that it is inappropriate to use this statistic unless both variables are measured at the interval or ratio levels, and that the appropriate statistic for calculating such a correlation is the **point biserial correlation**. If we take this dictum too literally we will be in trouble because we cannot mix statistics in a computer run. That is, if we are running a partial correlation program, for instance, the computer cannot suddenly switch to point biserial correlation when it encounters a dichotomous variable. To demonstrate that it does not need to, we will compute the point biserial correlation (Formula 14.4) with our sentence severity/offender type data.

$$r_{pb} = \frac{\bar{X}_1 - \bar{X}_2}{s_y}\sqrt{pq} \qquad (14.4)$$

where $\bar{X}_1$ = mean of group 1

$\bar{X}_2$ = mean of group 2

sy = standard deviation of the dependent variable

p = proportion of cases in group 1

q = proportion of cases in group 2

Recall from Table 6.3 that the mean sentence severity score for non-sex offenders is 324.1 and for sex offenders, 572.2, and from Table 13.2 that the standard deviation of sentence severity is 729.39. The number of non-sex offenders in the sample is 206, and their proportion is $206/637 = .3234$. Sex offenders number 431, and their proportion is .6766. Putting these values into Formula 14.4, we get

$$r_{pb} = \frac{\bar{X}_1 - \bar{X}_2}{sy} \sqrt{pq} = \frac{324.1 - 572.3}{727.39} \sqrt{(.3234)(.6766)}$$

$$= \frac{-248.1}{727.39} \sqrt{.2188} = (-.3411)(.4678) = -.16$$

This equation demonstrates the equivalence of r and r_{pb} when a continuous variable is correlated with a dichotomous variable. In fact, under such circumstances $r = r_{pb} = \eta = \beta = \phi$.

14.10 SUMMARY

This chapter has been a kind of potpourri of some advanced issues in correlation and regression. We first discussed multiple regression with dummy variables. A dummy variable is created from categorical variables lacking an inherent ordered structure. A dummy variable is coded 1 in the presence of an attribute and 0 in its absence. The number of dummy variables we create is $k - 1$, with the excluded category becoming the constant in the regression equation. The advantage of dummy variable regression over ANOVA is that we can include independent variables in the regression equation that are measured at all different levels rather than just categorical. The means for each dummy category can be calculated after adjusting for other variables in the equation.

Interaction is not made explicit for the researcher with multiple regression, but it presents the same interpretive problems as it does in ANOVA. If interaction is suspected it can be dealt with by creating a composite variable out of the two interacting variables. This new variable is entered into the regression equation along with its two component variables. If the interaction term is significant, interaction is present and must be considered in the prediction equation.

Multicollinearity exists when there are a high correlations among the predictor variables, leading to unstable regression coefficients and relatively large standard errors. The problem of multicollinearity can be overcome in many cases by combining highly correlated indicators of the same underlying variable into a single variable.

Measurement error refers to the reliability of measured variables. The lower the reliability of the measures the more the correlations will be underestimated. Measurement errors can result in wide fluctuations in multivariate analysis. In multivariate analysis, correcting correlations can lead to both under- and overestimation, depending on the pattern of the intercorrelations and their degrees of reliability. A correlation can be corrected for attenuation.

Specification errors are of three general kinds: (1) excluding relevant variables in a model, (2) including irrelevant variables, and (3) specifying a linear model when it is curvilinear. The first misspecification results in overestimating the effects of included variables if the excluded variable or variables are correlated with included variables. Including irrelevant variables results in theoretically meaningless results. The third error was dealt with by looking further at eta squared.

Eta squared is an excellent tool for assessing the relationship between variables that are nonlinear. Eta can be quite strong even when $r = 0$, and eta squared can be used to test the linearity of a set of data.

Homoscedasticity is the assumption that the variance in Y is uniform for all values of X. If homoscedasticity does not exist we obtain a large standard error of estimate, making predictions a risky business. The problem of outliers is somewhat related to homoscedasticity. An examination of residuals can alert us to the violations of regression analysis such as the assumptions of linearity and homoscedasticity. An outlier is an extreme residual that has the effect of rotating the regression line in its direction. Extreme outliers can cause a considerable decrease in the value of the correlation coefficient.

When the range of cases is restricted by sampling subsets of individuals, we almost always find a smaller correlation between two variables than if we had a more heterogeneous range of subjects. In a homoscedastic distribution the dispersion around the regression line remains fairly constant, whereas the total variation is truncated. In a highly heteroscedastic distribution, however, correlations can be stronger in a truncated sample than in the entire range.

The point biserial correlation is an index of association between a continuous and a dichotomous variable. We showed that under such conditions $r_{pb} = r = \eta = \beta = \phi$.

PRACTICE APPLICATION: DUMMY VARIABLE ANALYSIS

A researcher wants to determine the effects of broken homes and illegitimate births on violence (an interval-level variable) among male juvenile delinquents. An ANOVA is computed that shows significant interaction between these two variables. It is decided to compute a single composite variable from these two and enter it as $k - 1$ dummy variables. These dummy variables, mean violence scores, and category Ns follow:

DUMMY CODING AND VIOLENCE MEANS FOR FAMILY STRUCTURE/BIRTH STATUS
CATEGORIES

Categories	D_1	D_2	D_3	$\bar{X}$	N
Intact home/legitimate	1	0	0	55.45	170
Intact home/illegitimate	0	1	0	88.86	35
Broken home/legitimate	0	0	1	53.73	258
Broken home/illegitimate	0	0	0	109.16	50
			Grand mean	62.10	513

In addition to this composite variable, the researcher wishes to assess the effects of child abuse and birth order on violence. Determine the mean violence level for each category of the composite variable after adjusting for child abuse and birth order from the multiple regression results that follow. Birth order is coded 0 if firstborn and 1 otherwise.

MULTIPLE REGRESSION ON VIOLENCE

Variable	b	s.e.	β	t	sig.
Order	24.8	6.2	.16	4.00	.0001
Abuse	1.9	.2	.35	8.51	.0000
Dummy 2	2.7	14.2	.01	0.19	.8484
Dummy 3	−41.2	9.9	−.29	−4.14	.0000
Dummy 1	−30.6	10.6	−.20	−2.88	.0042
Constant	31.3	12.3		2.53	.0116

The constant represents the violence regression slope for delinquents who are illegitimate and from broken homes (the excluded category). To find the mean for a particular dummy category, the constant is added to the unstandardized beta for that category and to the unstandardized betas of all nondummy variables in the model (birth order and abuse) multiplied by their respective mean values, as in the formula

$$\bar{Y}' = a + b_1 d_1 + b_2 \bar{X}_2 + b_3 \bar{X}_3$$

The means of the nondummy variables are Abuse = 23.54 and Order = .71. The adjusted mean for dummy 1 (intact/legitimate) is

$$\text{adjusted } \bar{Y}_{D1} = 31.3 + (-30.6)(1) + 1.9(23.14) + 24.8(.71)$$

$$= 31.5 + (-30.6) + 43.96 + 17.36 = 62.02$$

The adjusted mean for dummy 2 (intact/illegitimate) is

$$\text{adjusted } \bar{Y}_{D2} = 31.3 + (2.7)(1) + 1.9(23.14) + 24.8(.71)$$

$$= 31.3 + 2.7 + 43.96 + 17.36 = 95.32$$

The adjusted mean for dummy 3 (broken/legitimate) is

$$\text{adjusted } \bar{Y}_{D3} = 31.3 + (-41.2)(1) + 1.9(23.14) + 24.8(.71)$$

$$= 31.3 + (-41.2) + 43.96 + 17.36 = 51.42$$

The adjusted mean for dummy 4 (broken/legitimate, the reference category) is

$$\text{adjusted } \bar{Y}_{D4} = 31.3 + 1.9(23.14) + 24.8(.71)$$

$$= 31.3 + 43.96 + 17.36 = 92.62$$

What violence score would you predict for a juvenile who is legitimate, is from an intact home, is firstborn, and has an abuse score of 30? Intact home/legitimate (dummy 1) is coded 1 in the presence of the attribute and zero in its absence. A beta of -30.6 is associated with the presence of the attribute, so this is included in the prediction equation. Being other than firstborn is associated with a beta of 24.8. Since the juvenile for whom we wish to predict a violence score is firstborn, beta drops out of the equation. The juvenile has an abuse score of 30, so this number is multiplied by the beta associated with abuse (1.9).

$$Y' = 31.3 + (-30.6)(1) + 24.8(0) + 1.9(30)$$

$$= 31.3 + (-30.6) + 0 + 31.9 = 32.6$$

What score would you predict for a juvenile coded 0 on dummy 1, who was also firstborn and who has an abuse score of zero?

$$Y' = 31.3 + (-30.6)(0) + 24.8(0) + 1.9(0)$$

$$= 31.3 + 0 + 0 + 0 = 31.3$$

Did you remember that the constant represents the value of Y when all other values in the model equal zero?

APPENDIX: Computer Instructions for Table 14.1

Command 14.1

SPSSx

```
RECODE JUDGE (1,2,6,7=1)(3,5,8=2)(4,9=3)
DO IF (JUDGE EQ 1)
COMPUTE DUMMY1 = 1
ELSE
COMPUTE DUMMY1 = 0
END IF
DO IF (JUDGE EQ 2)
COMPUTE DUMMY2 = 1
ELSE
COMPUTE DUMMY2 = 0
END IF
```

```
REGRESSION VARIABLES = SENSEV, GROUP, DUMMY1, DUMMY2/
                       DEPENDENT = SENSEV/
                       ENTER/
```

SAS

```
IF JUDGE=1 OR JUDGE=2 OR JUDGE=6 OR JUDGE=7 THEN JUDGE=1;
ELSE IF JUDGE=3 OR JUDGE=5 OR JUDGE=8 THEN JUDGE=2;
ELSE IF JUDGE=4 OR JUDGE=9 THEN JUDGE=3;
IF JUDGE=1 THEN DUMMY1=1;
ELSE DUMMY1=0;
IF JUDGE=2 THEN DUMMY2=1;
ELSE DUMMY2=0;
IF GROUP=1 THEN GROUP=0;
ELSE IF GROUP=2 THEN GROUP=1;
PROC STEPWISE;
MODEL SENSEV=GROUP DUMMY1 DUMMY2/SLE=.99 F;
```

These instructions first recode the judges into categories based on their party affiliation. We then create the two dummy categories (make sure also that GROUP is coded 0 and 1). They are then entered into the regression equation in which the third dummy category represents the excluded category, and which will be the constant in the printed results.

APPENDIX: Computer Instructions for Table 14.3

Command 14.2

SPSSx

```
SELECT IF (PONAM EQ 0 OR PONAM EQ 1)
COMPUTE FAIR = PONAM*CRSER
REGRESSION VARIABLES = PONAM, POREC, CRSER, FAIR/
                       DEPENDENT = POREC/
                       ENTER/
```

SAS

```
FAIR = PONAM * CRSER;
PROC REG ALL;
MODEL POREC = PONAM CRSER FAIR;
```

We first select only those officers identified as conservatives or liberals. We then create the interaction term by multiplying PONAM by CRSER to create a variable I have called FAIR. The name you give to the interaction term is, of course, arbitrary.

APPENDIX: Computer Instructions for Table 14.6

Command 14.3

      SPSSx   (no SAS equivalent)

```
BREAKDOWN TABLES = SEN BY CON
STATISTICS ALL
```

The first command instructs the computer to break down the sample into subgroups based on categories of the independent variable. The computer then calculates sums, means, standard deviations, and variances of the dependent variable among the various categories. Note that we are not introducing a new statistical technique here. BREAKDOWN is simply a classical ANOVA with the additional property of calculating the extent to which the data depart from linearity. The second command informs the computer that we want it to perform a one-way analysis of variance and the test for linearity.

APPENDIX: Computer Instructions for Figure 14.4

Command 14.4

      SPSSx

```
REGRESSION VARIABLE = SENSEV,CRSER/
         DEPENDENT = SENSEV/
         ENTER/
         RESID = DEFAULT SIZE (SMALL) ID (CRSER)/
```

      SAS

```
PROC REG;
MODEL SENSEV = CRSER/P R;
```

The RESID = DEFAULT command provides a scatterplot of residuals, a histogram of standardized residuals, and some other summary statistics. SIZE (SMALL) simply asks for a small scatterplot. The ID (CRSER) asks for an identification of outliers, which provides the case number, the score on the independent variable, and the standardized residual associated with it. In the SAS model the P R asks for predicted residuals. This SAS program provides a plot of unstandardized residuals.

REFERENCES AND SUGGESTED READING

Bund-Jackson, B. (1983). *Multivariate data analysis: An introduction*. Homewood, IL: Richard D. Irwin. Nicely written book on various multivariate techniques and their problems.

Groebner, D., and Shannon, P. (1981). *Business statistics: A decision-making approach.* Columbus, OH: Charles Merrill.

Hanushek, E., and Jackson, J. (1977). *Statistical methods for social scientists.* New York: Academic Press. A very good book for the more advanced student. See Chapter 4 for an excellent discussion of the multicollinearity problem.

Pedhazur, E. (1982). *Multiple regression in behavioral research: Explanation and prediction.* New York: Holt, Rinehart and Winston.

Walsh, A. (1987). The presentence process: Variables affecting conservative and liberal probation officers' decision making. *Journal of Justice Issues,* 2:1–17.

Chapter 15

A Brief Introduction to Some Advanced Statistics

This chapter introduces some of the more advanced statistical procedures as simply and as nonmathematically as possible. Emphasis is placed on understanding when these methods are applicable, obtaining the statistics from the computer, and being able to understand the output. It is possible to gain an appreciation and working knowledge of these techniques without a detailed knowledge of the mathematical intricacies involved. Many students will be able to execute a program with the data provided and to explain the findings without having a thorough understanding of the statistical theory underlying the procedures. We will begin with a discussion of path analysis.

15.1 PATH ANALYSIS

Regression analysis assesses the combined effects of a set of independent variables on the dependent variable. However, no causal ordering is assumed among the variables. Although statistically **path analysis** is nothing more than a series of multiple regression analyses, it has the additional advantage of allowing us to examine tentative causality in a way that regression per se does not. To utilize this technique properly, a theoretical understanding of the data is crucial. We must know how the variables in a path model fall into a specific causal order in terms of their effect on the dependent variable. The causal ordering could be of the type

$$A \longrightarrow B \longrightarrow C \longrightarrow D$$

That is, A causes B, B causes C, and C causes the dependent variable D. Of course, A can exert an effect on D without its connection to B and C. Such an effect is called the *direct* effect of *A* on *D*. It also has an effect on *D* through its association in the model with *B* and *C*. This is called the *indirect* effect of *A* on *D*. The total effect of *A* on *D* is the summation of its direct and indirect effects.

Let us consider a simple model from our offenders data assessing the causal effects of IQ, years of education, and occupational status on criminal history. What is the causal ordering here? Since criminal history is the dependent variable, it is placed to the right of each of the independent variables in a path diagram. Theoretical studies have informed us that all of the independent variables influence criminal history. Low occupational status, low education, and low IQ are all related to higher levels of criminality than are higher values on the same variables—as confirmed by the correlation matrix in Table 15.1.

We now have to decide the theoretical time ordering of the three independent variables. Although it is always possible to argue back and forth about causal ordering in the social sciences, we will assume that our causal order is as follows: IQ determines educational level, educational level determines occupational status, and occupational status determines level of criminal involvement. Is it possible that occupational status could determine one's education, that education has a causal influence on IQ levels, or even that criminal involvement could determine one's occupational status? Certainly, such possibilities, as well a reciprocal causation, are part of the fascination and challenge of social science. Each and every one of these conditions is a possibility. The researcher has to decide the most logical, likely, and general causal ordering of the variables from his or her knowledge of theory and prior research.

After deciding on the assumed causal ordering, the first step is to construct a **path diagram** by following certain rules.

1. Variables placed on the left of the diagram are assumed to be causally prior to those on the right.
2. Assumed causal relationships between variables are indicated by linking them by single-headed arrows running from the independent variable to the dependent variable.
3. Variables that are correlated but not assumed to be causally related are linked by a curved, double-headed arrow and are drawn parallel with each other on the horizontal axis.
4. The values entered on the direct paths are known as *path coefficients*. The path coefficients are the standardized betas (βs) obtained from multiple

TABLE 15.1 CORRELATION MATRIX OF THE VARIABLES IN PATH ANALYSIS EXAMPLE

	X_3	X_2	X_1	
X_4	−.319	−.359	−.183	X_4 = criminal history
X_3		.559	.441	X_3 = occupational status
X_2			.476	X_2 = educational level
X_1				X_1 = IQ

All correlations significant at < .001. $N = 376$

regression equations. (In some instances it might be preferable to use unstandardized betas.)

5. The values entered on a double-headed curved line linking noncausally related variables are zero-order correlations.

Figure 15.1 presents a **recursive path model** (one in which all the causal influences are assumed to be one-way) linking the variables together. Let us see how the model was constructed, one step at a time.

STEP ONE: We first asked the computer for a multiple regression model, just as we did in Chapter 13. The dependent variable is specified as prior record in the model, and the other three variables are specified as independent. The output from this computer job provides the direct influence of each of the independent variables in the model, adjusting for the effects of each of the other variables. Since we have only 376 cases for which IQ is reported, we have to use a SELECT IF (IQ LT 999)" command, which tells the computer to select out every case in which IQ is less than (LT) 999, the value assigned to missing values.

The results of this regression show that the variable years of education has a direct effect on criminal history of $-.270$, occupational status has a direct effect of $-.179$, and IQ has a direct effect of $.024$ (see Figure 15.1). The virtually nonexistent, nonsignificant direct effect of IQ on criminal history indicates that the zero-order correlation between the two variables was entirely a function of the relationship of IQ to the other two variables. The reported standardized beta values are known as *path coefficients.*

As we have said, the path coefficients are standardized betas, and thus reflect causal effects in terms of standard deviation units. For example, the reported coefficient of $-.179$ between criminal history and occupational status means that a 1 standard deviation unit increase in occupational status leads to a $.179$ standard deviation decrease in criminal history.

The adjusted R squared value for the model is a modest $.143$, indicating that 14.3 percent of the variance in criminal history is explained by the three independent variables.

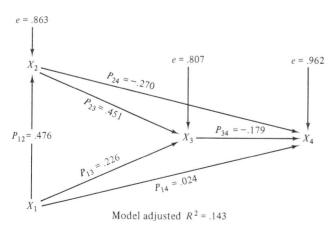

$e = .863$

X_2

$P_{24} = -.270$

$e = .807$ $e = .962$

$P_{23} = .451$

$P_{12} = .476$ X_3 $P_{34} = -.179$ X_4

$P_{13} = .226$

$P_{14} = .024$

X_1

Model adjusted $R^2 = .143$

Figure 15.1 Path analysis model for criminal history

STEP TWO: In this step we wish to explore the determinants of occupational status. To do so we run another multiple regression model with occupational status as the dependent variable and years of education and IQ as the independent variables. We do not, of course, include criminal record in this model. Note in Figure 15.1 that the path coefficients for education and occupational status and IQ and occupational status are .451 and .226, respectively. The R squared value for the model is .348, a much more satisfactory percentage of explained variance.

STEP THREE: The next task is to determine the effects of IQ on years of education. Since we have no other variables to consider at this point, it is not necessary to run another regression program. The zero-order Pearson correlation between these two variables is exactly the same as the standardized beta would be in a bivariate regression, .476. We now have paths linking all the variables in the model in an assumed causal order.

STEP FOUR: Our next task is to determine how much variance in the dependent variables remains unexplained. We ran three computer programs with criminal history, occupational status, and years of education taking their turns as the dependent variable. Thus, we have three R squared values reporting the proportion of variance explained. To get the proportion of variance left unexplained, we simply take the R squared value away from 1 to get the coefficient of alienation.

Percentage of Variance	
Explained	Unexplained
$R^2_{4.321} = .143$	$1 - R^2_{4.321} = .857$
$R^2_{3.21} = .348$	$1 - R^2_{3.21} = .652$
$R^2_{2.1} = .255$	$1 - R^2_{2.1} = .745$

$R^2_{4.321}$ is the percentage of variance in X_4 (criminal history) accounted for by X_3, X_2, and X_1, and so on. Thus, 85.7 percent of the variance in criminal history, 65.2 percent of the variance in occupational status, and 74.5 percent in years of education is left unexplained. We take the square root of the residuals and report this value by drawing an arrow from e (for error) to the dependent variable in question, for instance, .962 is the square root of .857, the unexplained variance in criminal history. These large residual values indicate, as one would expect, that many other variables contribute to the offenders' levels of criminal involvement. Think of residuals as variance explained by variables outside the model plus error in the measurement of those within it. Overall, the model is an unsatisfactory causal representation of criminal history. Many other variables have to be considered, and perhaps a reconsideration of the measure of criminal history used.

STEP FIVE: In this step we determine the estimated direct and indirect effects of the independent variables on criminal history. The direct effects are simply the effects indicated by the direct causal arrows linking each independent variable to criminal history. Thus, the direct effect of IQ on criminal history (P_{14}) is .024. Now, IQ affects educational level, which affects occupational status, which affects criminal history. This is known as the indirect effect of IQ on criminal history. The indirect effect is computed by tracing and multiplying the paths from IQ to criminal history through education and occupation ($P_{12}P_{23}P_{34}$), IQ to criminal history, passing through education only ($P_{12}P_{24}$), and IQ to criminal history passing through occupation only ($P_{13}P_{34}$). The indirect effects are the sum of the products of these paths.

There are three rules when tracing paths: (1) No path may pass through the same variable twice; (2) no path may go against the direction of an arrow after the path has been traced forward on a different arrow; (3) no path may be traced through a double-headed arrow (representing a zero-order correlation where no causal effect is assumed) more than once in a single path. The sum of the direct and all indirect paths linking any two variables should be equal to the zero-order correlation between them. Let us trace all the legitimate paths linking IQ and criminal history.

$$P_{14} = +.024 \text{ direct effect}$$

$$P_{12}P_{23}P_{34} = (.476)(.451)(-.179) = -.038 \text{ indirect effect via } X_2 \text{ and } X_3$$

$$P_{13}P_{34} = (.226)(-.179) = -.040 \text{ indirect effect via } X_3$$

$$P_{12}P_{24} = (.476)(-.270) = \underline{-.128} \text{ indirect effect via } X_2$$

$$\text{Total } r \quad -.182$$

Within rounding error, the sum of the direct and indirect paths do equal the zero-order correlation between IQ and criminal history. The total effect of IQ on criminal history for this model is the sum of the direct and indirect paths ($-.182$). The strongest indirect effect of IQ is its effect on criminal history via education ($-.128$).

If we trace the direct and indirect effects of education on criminal history we will find, within rounding error, that they do sum to the zero-order correlation. Tracing the indirect effect of education on criminal history via occupational status, we get $P_{23}P_{24} = (.451)(-.179) = -.0807$. The indirect effect ($-.0807$) plus the direct effect ($-.270$) $= -.3507$. Thus, IQ effects criminal history through its effects on education, which in turn effects occupational status.

Path analysis is a very useful tool for assessing the causal influence of a set of independent variables on a dependent variable. However, as we discussed extensively in Chapter 10, the kind of causality we are talking about is probabilistic, not deterministic. We can never prove causality; we can only bolster or support our hypothesis of a causal relationship. Further, we never really know what important causal variables have been left out of our models. In our example, for instance, social class origins could be expected to exert an influence causally prior to IQ, and therefore causally prior to all other variables. Perhaps not even social class is the crucial variable. It could be substance abuse, delinquent peers, patterns of child raising, or any number of other hypothesized variables. We thus repeat our counsel to be fully familiar with theory before asking the computer to work its wonders with the data.

15.2 LOGIT REGRESSION

Logit regression analysis is becoming an increasingly popular method of reporting research results in the more sophisticated journals. Therefore, students should have at least a modicum of understanding about its functional usage in research. The following discussion should be sufficient to give the student (1) a basic understanding of why it is a superior statistical tool in certain circumstances, (2) the necessary commands to run a logit program in both SPSSx and SAS, (3) the ability to interpret the output, and (4) the ability to calculate probabilities for a given variable profile from the computer readout.

Understanding logit analysis is not just adding another technique to our statistical repertoire. Logit (along with probit) is well suited to many kinds of data frequently found in social and behavioral research. So many of the dependent variables of interest in our discipline are dichotomous in nature, whereas many of the independent variables affecting them are measured at other levels. Adding to research woes are the nonlinear relationships between the dependent and independent variables in many instances. We have traditionally dealt with the analysis of variables measured at different levels by categorization of continuous variables, thereby losing a large amount of information. This strategy also necessitates using a weaker form of statistical analysis. As Kachigan (1986, p. 375) nicely put it, "If ever there is a cardinal sin in statistical analysis it is to use a weaker analysis when a more powerful and efficient analysis is readily available."

Logit circumvents these problems and should be used in many cases where researchers have used other, less appropriate techniques. No other technique will allow the researcher to analyze the effects of a set of independent variables on a dichotomous dependent variable (or a qualitative polytomous one) with such minimal statistical bias and loss of information.

15.2.1 The Rationale for the Use of Logit

Basically, logit regression allows the researcher to perform a regression like analysis of the data in cases where the dependent variable is qualitative rather than continuous. Although ordinary least squares (OLS) multivariate regression is remarkably robust in most of its assumptions—meaning that if an assumption is violated, the interpretation of the statistical results are not seriously in error—it is not robust against the assumption of the continuous linearity of the dependent variable.

15.2.2 An Example of Logit Regression

To illustrate logit, we will use our offender data to determine the probability of being sentenced to either probation or prison. The independent variables are race, crime seriousness, and prior record. Race is a dichotomy of white/black, and crime seriousness and prior record are continuous variables.

Assume that we want to assess the effects of crime seriousness on the dichotomous variable type of sentence, rendered in terms of probation or prison. That is, the offender is either placed on probation or sent to prison. If we were to use OLS regression with these data and produce a scattergram with crime seriousness as the independent variable, it would look like Figure 15.2, with a Y intercept of .055, a slope of .135, and a correlation of .510.

Whether or not the offender goes to prison is rather strongly associated with his crime seriousness score. The question we must ask ourselves is whether this association can be accurately described by a straight line. Ordinary least squares regression would fit the data to a straight line as in line A. Since, by definition, OLS regression fits a straight line that minimizes the sums of squares in the vertical dimension, the computed beta assumes a constancy of change. In other words, the computed beta tells the researcher that moving from 1 crime seriousness point to 2 has exactly the same effect on sentence type as moving from 3 to 4, 9 to 10, or any other one-unit increment in the independent variable.

The OLS predictions under such circumstances would be highly suspect, to say the least. Suppose we wanted to predict the probability of going to prison for someone with 8 crime seriousness points based on the OLS results. The prediction equation is

$$Y' = a + bX = .055 + .135(8) = .055 + 1.08 = 1.135$$

Since the probability of a dichotomous event coded 0 and 1 must range within those values (0 indicating zero probability and 1 indicating certainty), the computed probability makes no sense—one cannot be more certain than certain. Making predictions from OLS regression with a dichotomous dependent variable can often lead to predictions outside of the range of possibility, that is, less than zero or more than 1.

Note from the plotted values in Figure 15.2 that almost nobody goes to prison at the low end of the crime seriousness scale, and that almost everyone at the

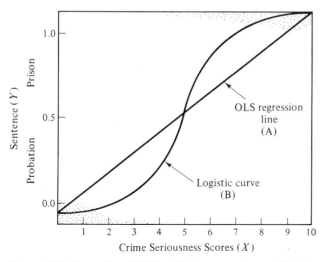

Figure 15.2 Illustration of OLS and logit regression specifications with a dichotomous dependent variable

high end does. The effect of moving from 1 to 2 crime seriousness points, or from 8 to 9, makes essentially no difference to an offender's probability of a probation or prison sentence. The distribution of scores indicates that there appears to be a "threshold" level on the crime seriousness scale when the addition of another point radically affects the offender's chances of prison versus probation. That is, the amount of change in the probability of going to prison at the low and high ends of the crime seriousness distribution is minimal, whereas in the middle of the range a change of 1 point has a much larger effect on the probability of going to prison. Thus, a true representation of the actual effect of crime seriousness is indicated by the *S*-shaped logistic line (line B) transposed on the scattergram in Figure 15.2.

15.2.3 A Computer Example of Logit Regression

We will now present a computer example comparing the effects of race on dichotomous sentence type, controlling for crime seriousness and prior record. Command 15.1 requests this logit regression with SPSSx. The important output is reproduced in Table 15.2.

Interpreting the Output   From the output presented in Table 15.2 we learn that our model "converged at iteration 6." This just means that the computer has used a repetitive process of orienting and reorienting the estimates until they converge. Because this is not a linear model, it takes this iterative technique to come up with the maximum likelihood estimates. The important thing for our purposes is that the estimates did converge. If a model does not converge, it means that the regression coefficients will not be reliable estimates. Models are inclined not to

TABLE 15.2 SPSSx LOGISTIC REGRESSION COMPUTER OUTPUT

637 UNWEIGHTED CASES ACCEPTED
0 CASES REJECTED BECAUSE OF MISSING DATA

ML CONVERGED AT ITERATION 6. THE CONVERGE CRITERION = .00001

PARAMETER ESTIMATES (LOGIT MODEL: (LOG(P/(1−P)/2 + 5 = INTERCEPT + BX)
NOTE 5 ADDED TO INTERCEPT AND LOGIT DIVIDED BY 2

	REGRESSION COEFF	STANDARD ERROR	COEFF/S E
RACE	− .42396	.11466	− 3.69751
CRSER	.37696	.03742	10.07299
PRREC	.15288	.01563	9.78185
	INTERCEPT	STANDARD ERROR	INTERCEPT/S.E.
	3.39735	.13603	24.97530

PEARSON GOODNESS OF FIT CHI SQUARE = 625.701   DF = 633   P = .574

CODING: SENT Probation = 0, Prison = 1. RACE white = 0,
Black = 1. CRSER (Crime Seriousness) = interval. PRREC
(Prior record) = interval.

converge if the sample size is small and/or there are too many predictor variables in the equation relative to sample size. A model is likely to converge (assuming that the statistical properties of the variables present no problems) if there are 50 or more cases per parameter (Aldrich & Nelson, 1984, p. 81).

We now look at the statistical output, leaving the discussion of the formula information preceded by the words "parameter estimates" until later. You will note that the statistical output looks quite like the output from a OLS regression. The regression coefficients and standard errors may be interpreted in a roughly analogous fashion. The COEFF/S E, although not strictly speaking a *t* test, can be interpreted as such. It is simply the regression coefficient divided by its standard error. All predictor variables are significant. No significance levels are given because the COEFF/S E is only "analogous" to *t* (the regression coefficient divided by its standard error), but we conservatively state that these values should not drop below 2 in order to consider a variable useful. We note that all three predictor variable coefficients are significant. Crime seriousness and prior record are positively related to sentence type, and race is negatively related. When the effects of crime seriousness and prior record are adjusted for (recall that SENT is coded 0 = probation, 1 = prison, and RACE is coded 0 = white, 1 = nonwhite), whites are significantly more likely to be sent to prison than are blacks.

The next statistic is the Pearson Goodness-of-fit chi-square. In the context of logistic regression, this statistic is not a real meaningful measure. It is meaningful in the context of the probit procedure, of which logit regression is a variant. SPSSx decided to leave this statistic in the logit design as a kind of "quick-and-dirty" indication of goodness of fit (personal communication with SPSSx statistician). With this in mind, and to the extent that it is useful, we note that this is nonsignificant ($p = .574$). Unlike other tests of significance, we actually want this to be nonsignificant to indicate that our model is a good fit (see Chapter 9 for a discussion of chi-square as a goodness-of-fit statistic). What this means is that the difference between the expected distribution of cases in this model and the actual observed distribution of cases is so slight as to be nonsignificant.

Going Beyond the Output   With some hand calculations we can gain much additional information that is useful in understanding and interpreting the data. When using SPSSx, we must first pay attention to the information given above the statistical output. The equation produced there indicates simply that the regression coefficients printed out must be multiplied by 2, and that the intercept must have 5 taken away from the printed value and the difference then multiplied by 2 (SAS users will find that they will not have to do this step). Computing these values, we get

$$\begin{array}{lrclr}
\text{RACE} & -.42396 & \times\ 2 & = & -.84792 \\
\text{CRSER} & .37696 & \times\ 2 & = & .75392 \\
\text{PRREC} & .15288 & \times\ 2 & = & .30576 \\
\text{INTERCEPT}\ (3.39735 & -\ 5) & \times\ 2 & = & -3.2053
\end{array}$$

We can now use this information to determine the probability of an offender being sent to prison given his race, his crime seriousness score, and his prior record score. We do so by substituting these parameter estimates and values for each of the variables into the logistic equation.

$$P(Y = 1) = \frac{_e a + b_1 X + b_2 X + b_3 X}{1 + _e a + b_1 X + b_2 X + b_3 X} \tag{15.1}$$

where $P(Y = 1)$ = the probability of going to prison

a = the intercept

e = the base of Naperian logarithms (2.71828)

$b_1 X$ = the race coefficient multiplied by the given race value (0 for white, 1 for black)

$b_2 X$ = the crime seriousness coefficient multiplied by the crime seriousness value determined by the researcher

$b_3 X$ = the prior record coefficient multiplied by the given prior record value determined by the researcher

Note that this is very like a prediction equation for ordinary least squares regression of the form $Y' = a + b_1 X + b_2 X + b_3 X \ldots b_k X$. However, instead of calculating the best prediction or "score" by Y', in logit we are calculating the best probability prediction (P').

Suppose that we wished to assess the probability of a white offender going to prison if he has 2 crime seriousness points and 4 prior record points. We perform the following calculations:

$$P(Y = 1) = \frac{_e 3.2053 + (-.84792)(0) + .75392(2) + .30576(4)}{1 + _e 3.2053 + (-.84792)(0) + .75392(2) + .30576(4)}$$

$$= \frac{_e 3.2053 + 0 + 1.50784 + 1.22304}{1 + _e 3.2053 + 0 + 1.50784 + 1.22304}$$

$$= \frac{_e 0.47442}{1 + _e 0.47442} = \frac{.662}{1.622} = .3835$$

Thus a white offender would have a .38 probability of being sent to prison. You might be puzzled about how to make the calculation involving the logarithmic e. It is very difficult to do so by hand, and it is certainly not necessary for the understanding of the technique. There are tables of logarithms that will help. However, most calculators easily perform this function. To obtain $_e 0.47442$, simply press the appropriate function button on your calculator and then the button marked "e E ln," or on some calculators, "log e" or "LN." This will provide the .622 solution ($-.47442 \log \ln = .622$).

In conducting evaluation research for various criminal justice agencies, it has been my experience that the consumers of this research more readily understand the results if probabilities are transformed into odds for or against the outcome of interest. The simple formula for computing odds is

$$\text{odds in favor of an outcome} = \frac{p}{q}$$

where p = probability of something occurring

q = the probability of it not occurring ($q = 1 - p$)

Thus, the odds of a white offender with the preceding variable profile being sentenced to prison = .38/.62 = .6129:1. Lay readers of research results may find the .6129:1 answer confusing. We get around this by reversing the formula to read q/p (.62/.38) and indicating that the results (1.63:1) are the odds *against* going to prison for a white offender with this variable profile.

A black offender with the same crime seriousness and prior record points would have the same probability plus the race coefficient. That is, $-.84792$ would be substituted in Formula 15.1 for 0. Making this calculation, we find that black offenders with the identical crime seriousness and prior record scores have a .22 probability of being sentenced to prison. The corresponding odds are 3.75:1 against.

15.2.4 The SAS Differences

The same logit regression model is obtained by using the SAS program with command 15.2. Logit is the one technique discussed in this book in which the printed output is so different in the two statistical packages that it warrants separate explanation.

Table 15.3 presents the logit regression output from the SAS program. The SAS output provides some information not found in SPSSx. In addition to the number of observations broken down by the categories of the dependent variable, it also gives the mean, standard deviation, and the minimum and maximum values of the predictor variables (not reproduced here). As indicated earlier, we do not have to make the calculations for the coefficients and the intercept as we did with the SPSSx printout because SAS has done it for us.

TABLE 15.3   SAS LOGISTIC REGRESSION COMPUTER PRINTOUT

MODEL CHI-SQUARE = 335.05 WITH 3 D F ($-2 \log L R$) P = 0 0

VARIABLE	BETA	STD. ERROR	CHI-SQUARE
INTERCEPT	-3.2053	.2721	138.80
RACE	-0.8479	.2293	13.67
CRSER	0.7539	.0758	101.46
PRREC	0.3057	.0313	95.67

C = 0.882   Somers DYX = 0.764   GAMMA = 0.769   TAU $-$A = 0.377

Although the SPSSx and SAS logit printouts differ more than they do for any other statistical procedure, it is important to realize that both provide exactly the same information in different forms. The model chi-square in SAS is based on the number of categories rather than the number of observations, that is, 3 degrees of freedom rather than 633. The chi-square test has a different interpretation in the SAS program than it does in SPSSx. We note that the probability for the model chi-square value of 335.05 is significant ($P = .00$, as printed out). The -2 log likelihood chi-square statistic is used to test the joint association of all variables in the model with the dependent variable. The significant chi-square value in the SAS program indicates that the independent variables have significant predictive value, whereas the nonsignificant chi-square value in SPSSx (interpreted with caution) indicates a good model fit. The significance tests for the betas (regression coefficients) are chi-squares rather than ts. If you take the square root of SAS's chi-square values we will get SPSSx's ts.

SAS also prints out the contingency coefficient, Somer's d, gamma, and tau-a. These may be interpreted in the usual fashion, that is, as the number of similar/dissimilar pairs. In the logit-specific instance, the computer classifies cases by comparing the predicted classification with the actual classification (prison/probation in the present example), and these statistics are numerical indices of how well the predicted outcomes maintain consistency with the actual observed outcomes. These values give us some additional information regarding the quality of the model's fit. SPSSx does not provide any such statistics because they are not universally accepted as appropriate. They have been proposed because somehow logit models do not seem "complete" without a single summary statistic in the same way that OLS multiple regression models are summarized by the R squared statistic.

Aldrich and Nelson (1984, p. 57) have proposed what they call **pseudo R squared** and characterize it as "being in the spirit of R^2." Its interpretation is not as simple as the OLS R squared, but it does have the useful quality of ranging between 0 and 1, approaching 1 as the quality of the fit improves. The formula for computing pseudo R^2 is simply

$$\text{pseudo } R^2 = C/(N + C) \tag{15.2}$$

where C is the likelihood ratio chi-square, and N is the sample size. Because only SAS gives us the likelihood chi-square, we cannot calculate pseudo R squared from SPSSx results. Calculating from the SAS results, we obtain

$$\text{pseudo } R^2 = 335.05/(637 + 335.05) = .345$$

It is hoped that this simplified explanation will enable you to grasp the meaning of logistic regression, which is really no more difficult than OLS regression. Indeed, the rendering of the results in terms of odds for or against an outcome on a dichotomous dependent variable, given a set of conditions determined by the researcher, can be much more intuitively understandable for the layperson than betas, correlations, and tests of significance. The beauty of logit regression is that it takes data that used to present formidable obstacles to analysis and renders them more intelligible to professional and layperson alike than any other method of reporting results.

15.3 FACTOR ANALYSIS

There are many kinds of factor analysis. The kind that we focus on here—principal component factor analysis—is the most straightforward and most popularly used. **Factor analysis** is a technique that analyzes the internal structure of a set of variables to identify any underlying constructs, called **factors**; that is, although we may have a set of variables measuring different things, subsets of these variables, or all of them together, may all be measuring a more general principle or principles.

Suppose that we have test grades for a number of students in math, English, history, French, physics, and chemistry. The grades on these six subjects could be seen as collectively representing a more general construct called *intelligence.* If all students taking these tests were equally able in all subjects, while differing in ability among themselves, we could indeed summarize their scores as indicators of degrees of the single factor of intelligence. However, it is possible to be quite good at some subjects, such as math, and quite bad at others, such as English. In such a case the correlation between one's math and English scores would be quite low. If an individual is good at math but poor in English, it is likely that he or she is good at physics and chemistry since they involve a great deal of mathematical thinking, and poor at history and French, since they involve the same sort of verbal skills required in English. Looking at a number of individuals of this type, we would observe a high correlation between their math, physics, and chemistry scores and a low correlation between these quantitative scores and their verbal scores. We would observe the opposite among individuals good at English but poor at math. A correlation matrix of the interrelationships of these six test scores might look like the matrix in Figure 15.3.

Since all the correlations in Figure 15.3 are positive, a single common factor represented in the data can be called *general intelligence,* that is, a mental attribute called on in the performance of any intellectual task. However, if general intelligence was the only factor determining test scores, the correlations between subtests should be perfect except for errors in measurement. Since they are not, the subtests tap some other ability specific to themselves. We have already supposed that these specific abilities represent quantitative and verbal abilities. The average correlation between the quantification-oriented scores (.843) and between the verbal-oriented scores (.786) supports our supposition. We have thus

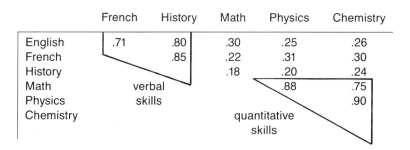

Figure 15.3 Correlation matrix of hypothetical test scores

identified two higher-level abstractions (factors) underlying these test scores—namely, quantification skills and verbal skills. Note that the average correlation between the separate subtest scores of these two identified factors is only .251.

This example gives an idea of what we try to do with factor analysis, but, although the logic remains the same, we are rarely confronted with anything quite so simple. For our computer example we will examine a study conducted by Corbin and Walsh (1988). We developed 9 hypothetical proposals for which a sample of older Americans was asked to indicate approval or disapproval (our Supreme Court data). Answer categories were in Likert format (strongly agree, agree, undecided, disagree, strongly disagree). The proposals were quite diverse, so we did not expect to observe any unidimensionality in the data. That is, we expected to find a number of components measuring different concepts among the nine-variable data set. However, we did not know what these underlying components would be. The use of factor analysis to discover these underlying dimensions is termed *exploratory factor analysis*. Some of these items could be expected to cluster together in the sense that they are highly correlated with one another; that is, they may be thought of as indicative of some underlying higher-order abstraction. The eight items in the data set follow. For reasons to be explained, one of the original nine items was deleted to illustrate factor analysis here, leaving eight items. Each item was preceded by the statement: "The Supreme Court has proposed" or "Congress has proposed" or "It has been proposed."

Questionnaire Items

LIE: that businesses cannot require employees or prospective employees to take lie detector tests.

MAT: new mothers be allowed maternity leave from their jobs for up to six months with pay and without loss of seniority or fringe benefits.

TRUST: that antitrust legislation is antibusiness and should be abolished.

HOMO: that homosexual acts between consenting adults should be illegal.

AIDS: that AIDS victims may have their movements legally restricted to protect others from the disease.

CHILD: that all children should receive equal funding for their education, even if it means moving tax funds from high- and middle-income neighborhoods to low-income neighborhoods.

SPORT: that funding for sports at universities should be distributed equally over all sports according to the number of players in that sport, rather than funds going overwhelmingly to traditional sports such as football and basketball.

COM: that it is permissible for colleges and universities to fire professors who advocate socialistic or communistic forms of government.

As previously stated, when we derive a subset of highly correlated variables from the complete set we call the subset of derived variables a factor. Although we can expect some overlap, in the sense that items in one factor may be marginally correlated with items in other factors, they are relatively independent of one another—in statistical language, they are orthogonal to one another. It is the function of factor analysis to form or identify factors that are as independent of one another as possible. Thus, factor analysis both summarizes data and identifies relationships among the variables. The commands required to obtain the information that will be used in the following discussion are given in command 15.3.

15.3.1 The Correlation Matrix

The first stage in factor analysis involves the creation of a correlation matrix. Suppose we had just five items in a scale and correlated with them one another to give us ten correlations. It would be possible to identify variables that are highly correlated with one another by visual inspection. However, with more variables the number of correlations starts accelerating rapidly. Ten variables would yield a matrix of 45 correlations. Our correlation matrix of eight variables yields 28 correlations. The number of correlations in a matrix is determined by the formula $[N][(N-1)/2]$. So you can appreciate why the computer is such a useful tool.

Printed below the correlation matrix in the computer output is a statistic called the Kaiser-Mayer-Olkin measure of sampling adequacy, or MSA, for short. This is an important statistic. It is a summary measure of how small partial correlations are relative to the simple correlations. If the MSA falls below .50, some sort of remedial action is called for. The MSA for our Supreme Court data with all nine items included was less than .50. The remedial action taken was to remove the item most responsible for the low MSA. The MSA in the eight-item model presented here is .58. This value is "adequate," but only barely so. A MSA of .80 or more is preferable.

15.3.2 The Factor Matrix

The computer takes the matrix of correlations and generates a *factor matrix*. (A computational example of how this is done is beyond the scope of this discussion and is not necessary to understand the procedure.) The computed values represent the *factor loadings*. Factor loadings range between -1 and $+1$ and indicate the strength of the association between each of the items and the derived factors. Hence, a factor loading is analogous to a correlation coefficient. The larger the factor loading the greater the degree of association between the variable and the factor. The matrix generated by this procedure is shown in Table 15.4. In the matrix, the rows represent the factors and the columns represent the input variables (the individual items).

The factor matrix in Table 15.4 indicates that the CHILD, SPORT, and MAT items cluster together ("load highly on") factor 1, the HOMO, AIDS, and COM items load highly on factor 2, and the TRUST and LIE items are isolated on factors 3 and 4, respectively. The derived factors have been boxed for ease of visual inspection. I will have more to say about what these clusterings mean in substantive terms later.

TABLE 15.4 FACTOR MATRIX (PRIOR TO ROTATION)

	FACTOR 1	FACTOR 2	FACTOR 3	FACTOR 4
CHILD	.66869	− .17240	− .41525	.06240
SPORT	.65323	.16255	− .27647	− .23408
MAT	.59499	.12098	.19195	− .59484
HOMO	− .05431	.74060	− .21132	.09267
AIDS	.12345	.68193	− .32858	.33670
COM	.10280	.65989	.49938	.11217
TRUST	.56812	− .00975	.57898	.27643
LIE	.42042	− .40231	− .01693	.61841

15.3.3 Communality

The most important determinant of the CHILD variable is factor 1. The variance in this variable accounted for by factor 1 is the square of the factor loading ($.66869^2 = .44715$), or 44.7 percent. The proportion of variance in CHILD accounted for by all four factors (see Table 15.5) is

$$h^2 = (.66869)^2 + (-.17240)^2 + (-.41525)^2 + (.06240)^2$$

$$= .44715 + .02972 + .17243 + .00389 = .65319.$$

This value is known as the **communality** of the variable and is designated by h^2. In other words, communality is the total variance accounted for by the combination of all common factors. We see this communality value for CHILD in Table 15.5. With principal component analysis, the communality of each item summed over all eight extracted factors would be 1. This table containing all eight factors demonstrating the unity of the communalities summed over all factors has been omitted for the sake of brevity. Principal component factor analysis will yield a communality of 1 regardless of the number of variables in the composite. There are odd cases in which the communality can be less than 1 or more than 1, but the problems associated with such occurrences are beyond the scope of the present discussion.

15.3.4 Extraction of Initial Factors

Table 15.4 presents initial extracted factors and associated statistics (factor loadings). The extraction of factors can be compared to multiple regression. The computer goes into the data and selects the linear combination of variables that accounts for more of the variance in the data than any other linear combination. This first factor is the principal component. The second component is the next best linear combination of variables in that it accounts for the largest amount of the variance remaining in the data after the effect of the first component is removed. The computer continues in this manner until all the variance in the data is accounted for.

Since we have pointed out the similarity of factor analysis and regression, we should also point out the difference between the two techniques. In regression we start with a single variable, defined as the dependent variable, and attempt to explain as much of its variance as possible with a linear set of independent variables. In factor analysis we attempt to explain a set of input variables by a linear set of factors that are unobserved and undefined until such time as the technique "discovers" them.

It is important to note that initially as many factors are extracted as there are variables. Our instrument contains eight variables, so eight factors are extracted. This does not seem much like data reduction at this point, but we will be discarding most of these factors later according to certain criteria. The first thing we note is a quantity called an **eigenvalue.** From Table 15.5 we see that the eigenvalue for factor 1 is 1.75613. This quantity corresponds to the percentage of variance explained by the equivalent number of variables, on the average, in the data. In other words, factor 1 accounts for as much variance in the data as 1.75613 variables. We can verify this result for ourselves. With eight variables, each one "on the average" will account for $100/8 = 12.5$ percent of the total variance. Thus, a factor with an eigenvalue of 1.75613 will account for $1.756 \times 12.5 = 22$ percent (rounded) of the variance. This is the value indicated in the table under PCT OF VAR. The eigenvalue for factor 2 is 1.68169, accounting for $1.68169 \times 12.5 = 21$ percent of the variance. These first two factors jointly account for 22 percent + 21 percent = 43 percent of the variance. This is the value found under CUM PCT (cumulative percentage of variance explained) next to factor 2. By the time we get to the final factor, the cumulative variance accounted for is 100 percent.

The eigenvalues are used to make our decision about how many factors are useful to us, and thus how many we will retain. A good rule of thumb is to eliminate those factors that account for less of the variance than the average variable, that is, less than 1 eigenvalue. Since we are concerned about data reduction, it would not make sense to retain factors that account for less of the variance in the data than the amount explained by a single variable. It is for this reason that the SPSSx program decided to retain only four factors in the factor matrix (Table 15.5). Obviously, we would like to account for as much variance as possible, but we also want to do so with as few factors as possible. We might say that the data

TABLE 15.5 INITIAL EXTRACT FACTORS (SPSSx)

VARIABLE	COMMUNALITY	*	FACTOR	EIGENVALUE	PCT OF VAR	CUM PCT
LIE	.72132	*	1	1.75613	22.0	22.0
MAT	.75933	*	2	1.68169	21.0	43.0
TRUST	.73448	*	3	1.02321	12.8	55.8
HOMO	.60468	*	4	1.00590	12.6	68.3
AIDS	.70160	*				
CHILD	.65319	*				
SPORT	.58436	*				
COM	.70798	*				

contain four fairly clear factors, which we assume to be indicative of underlying dimensions yet to be identified. To be more parsimonious we might even say that there are only two "real" clear factors (factors 1 and 2). However, these two factors account for only 43 percent of the variance in the data. Adding factor 3 would allow us to account for another 12.8 percent for a total of 55.8 percent. The four factors retained in Table 15.5 account for 68.3 percent. Herein lies part of the subjectivity of factor analysis: Do we opt for completeness or parsimony? Even when a factor is greater than 1 eigenvalue, it would not make much sense to retain it unless it was interpretable and substantively meaningful, a topic we will discuss after we discuss factor rotation.

15.3.5 Rotation of Factors

The initial extracted factors in Table 15.4 can be further simplified to determine more clearly separate dimensions in the data. That is, they can be rotated to a solution in which each variable will tend to load highly on only one factor and as low as possible on the others. In the initial extraction, the SPORT item, for instance, loads highest on factor 1. However, it can also be said to be "significantly" correlated with the other three factors in that with N of 150 (as is the case here), correlations $> .16$ are significant at $< .05$. Using this criterion, we see that seven of the nine factor loadings under factors 2, 3, and 4 correlate significantly with factor 1. For instance, SPORT is correlated with factor 2 (.162), factor 3 ($-.276$), and factor 4 ($-.234$). This situation exists because, although the initial factor extraction maximizes the independent source of variance in the data matrix, in doing so the factor will be distorted in order to accommodate some of the variance of the other variables that really do not belong to that factor. Rotation helps to correct this distortion by further delineating the factors.

There are a number of rotation methods, but the two most frequently used are *orthogonal* and *oblique.* Orthogonal rotation means that the factors will remain uncorrelated with one another; oblique rotation allows the factors to be correlated. Although the choice of rotation method depends on the needs of the researcher, we follow Zeller and Carmines's (1980, p. 44) belief that if "the researcher's concern is the parsimonious, interpretable identification of distinct, separable clusters of items, this purpose is frequently better served by orthogonal than by oblique rotation."

A computational example of rotation would require extensive space and would necessarily assume a grasp of trigonometry. It is enough to say that the computer uses a repetitive (iterative) process of orienting and reorienting the factors until it can no longer improve on the orthogonality of the loadings on the factors. As we see from Table 15.6, the computer took nine iterations to arrive at the terminal solution. It is important to note that rotation does not result in a change in the number of factors, in the percentage of variance explained, nor in the communalities of the variables. What rotation does do is refine the factors, making them more distinct from one another for ease of substantive interpretation.

Let us see what changes we observe in the rotated factor matrix in Table 15.6 from the initially extracted factors in Table 15.4. Factor 1 is still defined by the CHILD, SPORT, and MAT items, but MAT takes the place of CHILD as the strongest definer of the factor. How well has rotation redefined the data? In the initial extraction, MAT was almost equally defined by factors 1 and 4, each of them accounting for about 35.4 percent of the variance. The total variance in MAT accounted for by all four factors is 75.8 percent. In the unrotated matrix, factors 2, 3, and 4 accounted for .0146 + .0363 + .354 = 40.5 percent of the variance in MAT as opposed to 35.4 percent accounted for by factor 1. In the rotated solution, factors 2, 3, and 4 accounted for .0304 + .0692 + .0983 = 19.8 percent, and factor 1 accounted for 56.1 percent. With tolerance allowed for rounding, the variance accounted for in both cases is 75.8 percent, but the variance has been redistributed by rotation. The proportion of variance in the SPORT and CHILD variables accounted for by factor 1 has increased (albeit minimally for CHILD) under rotation.

Factor 2 was originally made up of the HOMO, AIDS, and COM variables. Under rotation, COM was dropped by factor 2 and picked up by factor 4. Factor 3 is still solely defined by LIE. If you spend a few minutes perusing the rotated factor matrix you will see that the computer has done a fairly good job of refining the dimensions that exist in the data.

15.3.6 Naming the Factors

This concludes the scientific aspect of factor analysis. Next comes the hard part—naming and making sense of the higher-order abstractions underlying the obtained factors. It is a commonly accepted rule of thumb that there should be at least three variables per factor for meaningful interpretation. We have only one factor (factor 1) that meets this criterion (but remember that we have only eight items in the data set).

Unlike the simple task of naming the obtained factors in our example of test

TABLE 15.6 ROTATED FACTORS (SPSSx)

VARIMAX CONVERGED IN   9 ITERATIONS.
ROTATED FACTOR MATRIX:

	FACTOR 1	FACTOR 2	FACTOR 3	FACTOR 4
MAT	.74924	−.17444	−.26309	.31356
SPORT	.73682	.17308	.10716	.00264
CHILD	.60695	.04803	.50296	−.17180
AIDS	.06756	.82859	.09543	.03708
HOMO	.02199	.74382	−.21882	.05520
LIE	−.00194	−.11115	.83568	.10299
TRUST	.16997	−.13083	.37512	.74011
COM	−.05106	.40477	−.22568	.70043

scores as "quantification" and "verbal" skills, the naming of the present factors requires real imagination, not to mention a firm grasp on substantive theory. We might call factor 1, consisting of the MAT, SPORT, and CHILD variables, "equality." Examining these questionnaire items shown earlier, it is fair to say that subjects who agreed with the proposals could be said to have a commitment to an egalitarian redistribution of resources. The concept of equality, then, can be seen as the higher-order abstraction underlying factor 1.

The factor defined by the AIDS and HOMO items could be labeled "homophobia/intolerance" for fairly obvious reasons. However, the factor defined by the COM and TRUST items requires a little more imagination. What would you label this factor? It seems to me that one common underlying theme is that of reactionary conservatism. We could test this supposition if we had administered a measure of reactionary conservatism to our sample and then correlated this factor with scores on the measure. But we did not have such a measure. Such is the frustration of social research, but also its challenge and joy.

15.3.7 Using Factor Analysis to Determine Scale Reliability

The reliability of our measuring instruments is an ever-present concern to social scientists. Many methods have been developed to assess the reliability of various scales. Principal component factor analysis allows us to determine the reliability (the consistency with which items on a scale or index measures the same underlying concept) of a scale with more precision than conventional methods. For instance, a colleague of mine, James Lee Christensen, has been attempting for some time to develop a scale to measure a form of love called *agape*. He factor-analyzed a large number of items, which he believes measures this concept, over and over again. He finally arrived at a 17-item scale. He subjected these 17 items to factor analysis to determine how reliable his measurement was, using a reliability measure called coefficient **theta.** Theta takes advantage of the fact that the first extracted factor accounts for the largest proportion of the variance in the composite. The first eigenvalue obtained from Christensen's data was 4.88, which is put into Formula 15.3 for calculating theta.

$$\theta = \left[\frac{n}{n-1} \right] \left[1 - \frac{1}{\lambda_1} \right] \tag{15.3}$$

where n = the number of items in the scale

λ_1 = the first (largest) eigenvalue

$$\theta = \left[\frac{17}{16} \right] \left[1 - \frac{1}{4.88} \right] = (1.02625)(1 - .2049) = (1.02625)(.7951)$$

$$= .845.$$

Since theta ranges between 0 and 1, the obtained coefficient of .845 is very respectable. Christensen can be quite confident that his scale is consistently (reliably) measuring the broad concept of love as he views that concept (see Zeller & Carmines, 1980, chap. 3).

15.4 SUMMARY

This chapter has introduced three commonly used advanced statistical procedures. We began with a discussion of path analysis, which is, statistically speaking, just a series of stepwise regression analyses. Path analysis attempts to discern possible causal explanations of phenomena in time-ordered fashion. The technique uses path diagrams linking the variables in the model. It assesses the direct and indirect effects of the independent variables in the model on the dependent variable. The causal ordering is represented by single-headed arrows from the variable assumed to be the cause to the variable assumed to be the effect. The direct effect is indicated by the standardized partial regression coefficient (sometimes the unstandardized coefficient is used) directly linking two variables. The indirect effect is determined by the products of all the variables traced from an independent variable passing through the chain of other intervening variables.

Logit regression is a regressionlike technique for assessing the combined effects of a set of independent variables on a qualitative dichotomous dependent variable. Ordinary least squares regression cannot be used in such instances because it tends to yield predictions beyond the range of possibilities and it assumes a constancy of change. Logit regression yields predictions in the form of probabilities of a dichotomous outcome ranging between 0 and 1. We can also report these probabilities in the form of odds for or against an outcome or event. This is a desirable quality for reporting results to lay readers.

Factor analysis is a data reduction device that enables us to uncover general underlying constructs from a set of data. The basic idea is that certain subsets of the data cluster together, and that clustering may be indicative of a general concept. These clusterings derived from the data set are called factors. Only those factors with an eigenvalue of more than 1 should be retained. After the extraction of the initial factors, the computer uses a process of rotating them in an attempt to discriminate further among them. At the completion of factor rotation (if an orthoganal rotation method is used), the factors will be as distinct from one another as possible. The final setup in factor analysis is to make sense of the derived factors. This step requires insight and theoretical knowledge.

Since the topics in this chapter are very involved mathematically, we will not present a practice application.

APPENDIX: Computer Instructions for Table 15.2

Command 15.1

SPSSx

```
COMPUTE ONECASE = 1
PROBIT SENT OF ONECASE WITH RACE,CRSER,PRREC/
  MODEL = LOGIT/
  LOG = NONE/
  PRINT/
```

The COMPUTE ONECASE = 1 and SENT OF ONECASE simply prepare the computer to accept SENT (for sentence type) as the dependent variable, after which comes the series of predictor variables to be used in the regression equation. The MODEL command tells the computer that we want a logit regression (we could also ask for a probit model, an alternative regression model not addressed in this book). The LOG command specifies the base of the logarithmic transformation of the predictor variables. By specifying NONE, no transformations are performed. The PRINT command in our example is specified without any key words in order to keep this discussion at a fairly simple and fundamental level.

APPENDIX: Computer Instructions for Table 15.3

Command 15.2

SAS

```
PROC LOGIST;
  MODEL SENT = RACE CRSER PRREC;
```

APPENDIX: Computer Instructions for Tables 15.4 Through 15.6

Command 15.3

SPSSx

```
FACTOR VARIABLES = LIE TO COM/
  PRINT = ALL/
  PLOT = ROTATION(1 2)/
  FORMAT = SORT/
  EXTRACTION = PA1/
  ROTATION = VARIMAX
```

SAS

```
PROC FACTOR ROTATE = VARIMAX ALL PLOT;
VAR LIE MAT TRUST HOMO AIDS CHILD
SPORT COM;
```

The FACTOR VARIABLES = LIE TO COM/ command instructs the computer to factor the variables from LIE to COM, inclusive. The PRINT = ALL/ command tells it that we want all variable statistics. The PLOT = ROTATION(1 2)/ tells it to print out a plot of the rotation of factors 1 and 2. The FORMAT = SORT/ command instructs the computer to order the factor loadings by magnitude. The EXTRACTION = PA1/ command tells the computer that we want to perform a principal component analysis. The ROTATION = VARIMAX command tells it that we want a varimax rotation of the extracted factors.

REFERENCES AND SUGGESTED READINGS

Aldrich, J., Nelson, F. (1984). *Linear probability, logit and probit models.* Beverly Hills, CA: Sage. The rationale behind the use of logit (and probit) regression is well explained in this monograph.

Asher, H. (1976). *Causal modeling.* Beverly Hills, CA: Sage. A very good introduction to the logic and complexities of path analysis.

Corbin, A., and Walsh, A. (1988). The U.S. Supreme Court and value legitimacy: An experimental approach with older Americans. *Sociological Inquiry,* 58:75–86.

Kachigan, S. (1986). *Statistical analysis.* New York: Radius Press.

Walsh, A. (1987). "Teaching understanding and interpretation of logit regression." *Teaching Sociology,* 15:178–185. The explanation of logit in the text is a modification of this paper.

Zeller, R., and Carmines, E. (1980). *Measurement in the social sciences: The link between theory and data.* Cambridge, England: Cambridge University Press. An excellent source on the many uses of factor analysis in social research. The best book I have seen on reliability and validity assessment.

Chapter 16

Introduction to the Computer and SPSSx and SAS Languages[1]

In computer-assisted statistical research, usually the biggest problem lies in using the computer. Most people who are unfamiliar with one are afraid that if they touch the wrong key or enter the wrong command, they will do some kind of damage. However, it takes a determined effort and some skill to be able to do any damage, and then it will be just the user's own data or programs that are altered or erased. Systems are designed so that the general user cannot harm the computer.

Most computer systems are designed around three basic areas, input devices, central processing units, and output devices. An input device can take several forms: a *card reader,* which reads computer cards that have holes punched in them to correspond with numbers or letters; a *terminal,* which is a televisionlike screen with a keyboard that can directly input data; and a *tape drive,* much like a reel-to-reel stereo player that reads information from a magnetic tape and inputs to the computer.

All the input will flow to the CPU (central processing unit), which is where all the real calculations are being carried out: adding, subtracting, dividing, and calling up other programs. In other words, this is where the real "thinking" takes place. When the CPU is done with your job it returns it to your *terminal* so that you can view the results, or it might send it to a *printer* to be printed on paper, depending on what it has been told to do. If it is printed on paper, it is known as *hard-copy,* or simply a printed form of your results.

The output device, like the *printer* or the *terminal,* is simply that, a device that receives the output from the CPU. A *tape drive* can also receive data from the CPU, and it would then become an output device. Some devices can be both

[1] By Marc R. Smith, Data Processing Department, Boise State University, Boise, Idaho.

input and output devices, which makes sense: If you can use a device to put something in, you can use the same device (in most cases), to get something out.

There is one other area that is closely linked to the CPU, the *storage device*. As you might have guessed, this is where data are stored. These devices can be peripheral to the CPU; that is, they can be machines that are physically set apart from the CPU. Usually they are called *disk drives,* large aluminum disks coated with a substance that can be magnetized. If the storage device is inside the CPU it is then referred to as *core* storage; usually this type of storage is temporary, used only while the CPU is briefly working on your job.

You as a researcher will utilize the computer by inputting your research data on an *input device*. Then the CPU will "think" about what you have requested and have the results come back to you through an *output device*. Now the real question is this: How do you ask the computer to do what you want it to do?

The computer can understand several different languages, but I will discuss only two: the Statistical Analysis System (SAS) and the Statistical Package for Social Sciences (SPSSx).

16.1 THE SPSSx LANGUAGE

The SPSSx language is "user friendly," and with just a little instruction you can be on your way to writing programs and getting statistical results. The internal programs for SPSSx, which you never see, are very complicated, yet the commands you use to write a program are very simple and are based on common sense. Let us dissect a simple program and explain what it does. Following is a small program consisting of five variables.

```
DATA LIST/
  ID 1-3 SEX 4, EDUC 5-6, INCOME 7, IQ 8-10, POL 11
VARIABLE LABELS
  ID 'SUBJECTS IDENTIFICATION NUMBER'
  SEX 'SUBJECTS SEX'
  EDUC 'YEARS OF EDUCATION'
  INCOME 'ANNUAL INCOME'
  IQ 'SUBJECTS IQ SCORE'
  POL 'POLITICAL PREFERENCE'
VALUE LABELS INCOME 1 'LOW' 2 'MIDDLE' 3 'HIGH'/
  SEX 0 'MALE' 1 'FEMALES'/
  INCOME 'LOW' 1 'MEDIUM' 2 'HIGH'/
  POL 1 'DEMOCRAT' 2 'REPUBLICAN' 3 'INDEPENDENT'/
BEGIN DATA
00111421051
00201211191
00311621112
00491210993
00509931312
00601831251
```

```
00711621333
00801321002
00910910872
01011511121
END DATA
MISSING VALUES SEX(9) EDUC (99)
COMPUTE CLASS = EDUC + INCOME
SELECT IF POL EQ 2
RECODE IQ (LO THRU 99=1)(100 THRU HI=2)
FREQUENCIES VARIABLES=SEX EDUC INCOME IQ COL FAC1/
   STATISTICS=ALL
```

The DATA LIST command directs SPSSx to read the data, the raw numbers. It is a preparatory type of command informing SPSSx to get ready to go to work. In this example DATA LIST is on line 1 and is followed by a back slash (/), which to SPSSx is much like a period in a sentence. It is telling SPSSx that this is all there is to this command. I could string these commands in one line as long as I knew where to end each command with a back slash (/). However, for ease of reading and simplicity I have separated each command by the mandatory back slash (/) and placed it on a separate line.

Line 2 is the variable definition for the data list; in other words I am now ready to tell the computer what the variable will be called and where it is in the data. For example, variable ID, which stands for identification number of the observation (observation 1, 2, 3, etc.), lies in columns 1 through 3. Remember columns run up and down. If you look at the first line of the data (raw numbers), columns 1–3, you will find the numbers 001—meaning that this is the first observation. Directly below in columns 1–3 are the numbers 002—meaning that this is the second observation in the data. In column 4 is a variable called SEX. Obviously this is the sex of the person I collected data from. I have decided to code males by the number 0 and females by the number 1. Since sex can be only one or the other, I need only one column for this variable. The variable EDUC, short for *education,* is in columns 5–6, and I have decided to code it by the number of completed years of education the person had. For example, if the person was a high school graduate, he or she was given the number 12, for 12 years of school. Notice that the column length must correspond to the maximum number of the datum. IQ has three columns because the average IQ has three numbers, as in 100. Nobody has a four-digit IQ, so I do not need four columns. If there is someone with an IQ of 98, I still must use all of the assigned columns and code it as 098. I have now told SPSSx (1) to read the data with the DATA LIST command and (2) where to find the values of a particular variable.

The VARIABLE LABELS statement comes after the DATA LIST statement. This command tells the computer the full names of the variables. Sometimes the variable name is quite clear, as in the variable SEX or INCOME. Yet other times it can be confusing. POL could stand for anything. With the VARIABLE LABELS command I can define exactly what the shortened form of a variable means. POL has been defined as POLITICAL PREFERENCE and EDUC has been translated as EDUCATION. I could have called these variables VAR1,

VAR2, and so on just as easily and then redefined them as SEX, EDUC, and so on. That particular SPSSx statement would look like this:

```
VARIABLE LABELS
  VAR1 'SEX'
  VAR2 'EDUCATION'
```

Next comes the VALUE LABELS command. This command assigns values to each variable. Do not get confused here. Look at the variable INCOME in column 7. If you look down this column you will find only the numbers 1, 2, or 3. I have coded the persons' income as low, medium, or high, and the VALUE LABELS statement will turn these numbers into words. A person with an income recorded as 1 is in the low income bracket, a middle-income person is coded 2, and so on. The variable POL, which stands for political preference, is coded in the same fasion: 1 = DEMOCRAT, 2 = REPUBLICAN, 3 = INDEPENDENT.

Sometimes you will not have to use a VALUE LABELS statement since what you have in numbers already makes sense. The variable IQ, for example, does not need to be labeled because an IQ of 100 is just that, 100. Age would be the same: 23 means 23. Height, weight, pounds, feet, all of these variables already make sense as pure numbers.

The BEGIN DATA statement is self-explanatory. It tells SPSSx that what follows are raw numbers, the actual data. As you can see from the program, this is where my data begin. If you count the lines, one for each person (observation), you will find that I have ten people in my survey. Also remember that the first variable was ID, or the identification number of the observation; you could look at the last line of the data and read the first three numbers—010. Thus you would know that there were only ten in the survey. The END DATA statement is a marker that defines where the data end. This statement must follow the very last line of data and must be included in the program.

The next line reads MISSING VALUES. Again SPSSx is very clear about what the command means. This is where I will assign a number to a piece of information that was not collected or was missing. SEX (9) indicates that if the person did not answer this question, this information is missing, and it will tell SPSSx that for this variable I do not have any information. The choice of the number is somewhat arbitrary since I could have coded it 8 just as easily. I could not have coded it SEX (99), however, because I have only one column for SEX: It is either 0 or 1. Remember that I assigned two columns to EDUC. Missing values for this variable must be coded with two digits since the column width is two digits long. In the program you will find that someone did not respond with educational level. I coded missing information for EDUC as 99.

The next statement is the COMPUTE command. This is an extremely useful and flexible tool. You can create new variables, as I have done with CLASS—the summation of two indices of social class (education and income). The COMPUTE command allows you to create one summary variable from many indices of that summary variable. The advantages in being able to do this are many, as you have seen in the text. You can also redefine an existing variable by using variables already in the DATA LIST. If, for example, you had the variable AGE, CURRYEAR (current year), and BIRTHDTE (birth date), you could verify age by checking it with existing information that you already have: COMPUTE AGE = CURRYEAR-BIRTHDTE.

The SELECT IF command allows you to examine your data selectively. In this program I have decided to look at only the data that pertain to REPUBLI-CANS. This was accomplished by telling SPSSx that I wish to look at the data only if POL equals 2 (recall that 2 is the code for Republican). Now you can pare your data to examine just those variables and categories of variables that are important to your research.

Sometimes it is important to transform your data from the existing code to another code, a step that can be done with the RECODE statement. For example, I wanted to dichotomize the variable IQ. With the RECODE command I took everything from the lowest (LO) IQ score up to and including 99 and recoded it as 1. All scores from 100 to the highest IQ score became 2. Thus this command allows you to change existing data or redesign the data to your specifications.

Now you are getting to the heart of the program, where you tell SPSSx what you want statistically. Until now I have described just what and where things are and have done a little "tailoring" on the data. The FREQUENCIES command generates the obvious, frequencies. This command will begin to give me some of the first impressions of my data: how many I have in each variable, whether there are more men than women, what the educational levels are, how many Republicans I have in my survey, and so on. With the FREQUENCIES command you can also check to see if you have entered your data correctly. From the partial listing that follows you can see that I have a (3) for sex. I have already decided that SEX can only be (0) or (1); I now know that I have a coding error and typed in a (3) instead of the correct number for SEX. I can backtrack through the data and find whre I made my mistake. Also notice that I have a (9); remember, this number indicates missing data and this is how it will be displayed in a print-out. The last line shows that I had nine valid cases and one missing, another way of giving me the same information.

With the STATISTICS = ALL command you can tell SPSSx that you want univariate statistics for each variable in your FREQUENCIES statement. This subcommand will generate the basic single variable statistics, mean, mode,

FREQUENCY TABLE OF SEX

SEX VALUE LABEL	VALUE	FREQUENCY	PERCENT	PERCENT	PERCENT
MALE	0	4	40.0	44.4	44.4
FEMALES	1	4	40.0	44.4	88.9
	3	1	10.0	11.1	100.0
	9	1	10.0	MISSING	
	TOTAL	10	100.0	100.0	
VALID CASES 9		MISSING CASES 1			

median, standard deviation, range, and other possibly important information. This differs from the SAS language. The Frequencies request in SAS will not supply univariate statistics, but it has other interesting capabilities. Let us now look at the same program in SAS.

16.2 THE SAS LANGUAGE

SAS frames the body of its programs differently than SPSSx. With the following SAS program, let us compare step by step the commands and describe the differences between the two languages.

```
DATA;
INPUT ID 1-3 SEX 4 EDUC 5-6 INCOME 7 IQ 8-10 POL 11;
LABEL EDUC = 'EDUCATION';
LABEL POL= 'POLITICAL PREFERENCE';
FAC1 = EDUC + INCOME + IQ;
IF POL=2;
IF IQ < =99 THEN IQ=1;
IF IQ = >100 THEN IQ=2;
CARDS;
00111421051
00201211191
00311621112
004 1210993
0050  31312
00601831251
00711621333
00801321002
00910910872
01011511121
;
PROC FORMAT;
VALUE INCOME 1='LOW' 2='MIDDLE' 3='HIGH';
VALUE SEX 0='MALE' 1='FEMALES';
VALUE POL 1='DEMOCRAT' 2='REPUBLICAN' 3='INDEPENDENT';
PROC FREQ;
TABLES SEX EDUC INCOME IQ POL FAC1/ALL;
FORMAT INCOME INCOME.;
FORMAT SEX SEX.;
FORMAT POL POL.;
```

The first step is known as the DATA statement, which is the same as the DATA LIST command in SPSSx. It commands SAS to build a data set with certain parameters and data. This data set is a "machine language" SAS creates from the data (raw numbers) it understands. In other words, it will turn the data from human understanding into data that SAS will understand. This is all done inside the CPU and the user never sees this process. SPSSx takes the same approach and accomplishes the same thing.

The next statement is the INPUT statement, which is analogous to the second line in the SPSSx program. It serves the same function, defining the variables' names and where they are in the data. Again, the first variable in the SAS program, ID, is located in columns 1–3. As you will notice, both of these INPUT statements are essentially the same. Each variable is in the same column in both programs. You may be wondering whether your data from a research project could be used in either language. The answer is yes; you would only have to know where each of the variables is in the data. For example, if you have a variable called DOB (date of birth) and it is in column 1–6, your data and input statement would look like this:

```
SPSSx

DATA LIST/
  DOB 1-6

SAS

DATA;
INPUT DOB 1-6;
```

The LABEL statement in SAS serves the same function as the VARIABLE LABELS command in SPSSx. It turns an abbreviated form of a variable into a name you can understand. Again POL was renamed POLITICAL PREFERENCE and EDUC was redefined as EDUCATION.

It is important to note that in this next area you will see for the first time where SAS and SPSSx differ in their construction of the basic program. You will notice that the COMPUTE statement in SPSSx is after the data, at the end section of the program. SAS has placed the same command before the data, in the beginning portion of the program. This command in SAS is not prefaced by the word COMPUTE but is simply stated (in the example on line 5).

```
CLASS = EDUC + INCOME;
```

This statement accomplishes the same computations as the SPSSx COMPUTE command.

The IF statement, on line 6, is much like the SELECT IF statement in SPSSx. It must be placed before the data and is not preceded by the word SELECT. It is very important to place the IF statement before the CARDS statement in the SAS program. Again, both statements have the same function, each able to separate selectively the variables and the categories of variables from the data. Using the same example as before, I wish to examine only data from Republicans, so I tell SAS IF POL = 2;—which will lock out every category except Republicans. The following two IF statements in the SAS program function exactly like the RECODE statement in SPSSx. I have decided to divide the variable IQ in two. The SAS IF statements does so in two steps, each a separate and individual statement. First I tell SAS to take all IQ scores equal to and less than 99 and recode them to the value of 1. Next I instruct SAS to group all IQ scores greater than 100 and recode them as 2. Now I have dichotomized my data from many different scores into only two levels or categories of the variable IQ. Remember that the IF type of statements in both languages is just a technique for changing or eliminating your data to suit your individual needs.

Next you will find the CARDS command, which simply alerts SAS to the fact that what will follow are data, just raw numbers. Although this is a simple command, it must be placed as the last line before the data. This statement is identical to BEGIN DATA in SPSSx.

Because data are data, and can be put into either language, there is not a lot to say about raw numbers, although there are a few key points to remember. Make sure that when you enter your data, they correspond to your input statement. If you tell both SAS and SPSSx that ID is in column 1–3, then in your data it must be in column 1–3. Although this advice appears to be obvious, you will often get results that do not make sense because you told the program to read data that were in the wrong column. Finally, if you are using SAS and you have missing data, make sure you leave a blank space or spaces. SAS will recognize this, just as SPSSx does with the MISSING VALUES command.

After the data you will see a single line with only a semicolon (;). Although I have successfully run programs with and without this marker placed here, I suggest you always put it in the program. It signifies that this is the end of the data. The END DATA statement in SPSSx has the same function.

Now this next part may appear somewhat confusing or complicated, but it really is not. SAS calls all of their procedures by the short form of PROC, and it has a PROC called FORMAT that does almost the same thing as the VALUE LABELS do in SPSSx. It is going to take a variable and a number and turn it into a word, and thereafter it will always associate that number and word with a specified variable. In the SAS program, the VALUE statement follows the PROC FORMAT command and simply says, "What will follow will be a variable that I will tie with the word INCOME and then relate numbers to words." Look at VALUE INCOME. INCOME is the word I have chosen to relate to the variable income. Remember that when SAS reads the data and finds the number 1 for INCOME it will remember to print the word LOW, if you tell it to. Just as SPSSx was told to remember that for the variable SEX the value 0 meant MALE. SAS and SPSSx differ here just a little. SAS must be told to do some number-word association. Skipping down to the last three lines in the SAS program you will find a statement that says FORMAT INCOME INCOME.;—which is where you tell SAS to relate the number 1 to the word LOW. If you don't put this statement in, you will get just numbers on your printout instead of words. Whereas SPSSx will put words in by default every time, SAS must be told by the FORMAT statement to connect numbers with their corresponding words.

Let us look a little deeper into the FORMAT statement. You will notice that it reads FORMAT INCOME INCOME.;. This first word after FORMAT must be a variable that SAS already knows, and by now it does recognize this variable. The next word is INCOME. This word must be the same word in the PROC FORMAT, VALUE statement relating the variable INCOME with its numbers,

1, 2, or 3. Notice that it has a period (.) after the second INCOME. This mark tells SAS to look for a VALUE named INCOME and associate the numbers to the words. To make this a little clearer I will give you an example. Say I have a variable called VISION, and because SAS has read this variable in the INPUT statement, SAS knows it. The PROC FORMAT and a PROC FREQ (frequencies) statement will look like the following:

```
PROC FORMAT;
VALUE V 1='EXCELLENT' 2='GOOD' 3='FAIR' 4='POOR';
PROC FREQ;
TABLES VISION;
FORMAT VISION V.;
```

You will notice that the value name is the letter *V*. If you connect that with the variable VISION in the FORMAT statement, you will be correct. Again, what I have done is tie some numbers to some words and then made SAS look for a value statement called V and hook the numbers to the words. I could have called the VALUE name VIS, and the two procedures would have looked like this:

```
PROC FORMAT;
VALUE VIS 1='EXCELLENT' 2='GOOD' 3='FAIR' 4='POOR';
PROC FREQ;
TABLES VISION;
FORMAT VISION VIS.;
```

The point here is that the VALUE name can be almost anything (with SAS restrictions), and as long as you remember what the value name is and what variable it is tied to, you will always be able to match your numbers with words.

You now have the basic information concerning how and what a computer system does. It is important to realize that every system is different. A good starting point, for the novice computer user, is to take a tour of your data center or have your instructor outline how your particular system is designed and works. Each system has its own commands and procedures. Becoming familiar with the system and the commands can save you hours of frustration. You also now have a rudimentary understanding of two statistical languages and how to use them for your research. Remember, once you have mastered the use of the system and the language, half the battle is over.

It is also important to note that both SAS and SPSSx periodically come out with new versions of their statistical programs. The commands associated with each statistical technique may change slightly with each new version. The computer commands given in the text are consistent with the versions of both languages that were up to date at the time of writing. If one or two of your programs do not run as indicated, it may well be that your computer center has purchased an updated program. In such an event, consult a SAS or SPSSx manual or your computer center.

Appendix A

Areas Under the Normal Curve

Values of $A(z)$ Between Ordinate at Mean (Y_0) and Ordinate at z

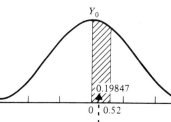

Example:
$z = 0.52$ (or -0.52),
$A(z) = 0.19847$ or 19.847%

$z = \left(\dfrac{x}{\sigma}\right)$	.00	.01	.02	.03	.04	.05	.06	.07	.08	.09
0.0	.00000	.00399	.00798	.01197	.01595	.01994	.02392	.02790	.03188	.03586
0.1	.03983	.04380	.04776	.05172	.05567	.05962	.06356	.06749	.07142	.07535
0.2	.07926	.08317	.08706	.09095	.09483	.09871	.10257	.10642	.11026	.11409
0.3	.11791	.12172	.12552	.12930	.13307	.13683	.14058	.14431	.14803	.15173
0.4	.15542	.15910	.16276	.16640	.17003	.17364	.17724	.18082	.18439	.18793
0.5	.19146	.19497	.19847	.20194	.20540	.20884	.21226	.21566	.21904	.22240
0.6	.22575	.22907	.23237	.23565	.23891	.24215	.24537	.24857	.25175	.25490
0.7	.25804	.26115	.26424	.26730	.27035	.27337	.27637	.27935	.28230	.28524
0.8	.28814	.29103	.29389	.29673	.29955	.30234	.30511	.30785	.31057	.31327
0.9	.31594	.31859	.32121	.32381	.32639	.32894	.33147	.33398	.33646	.33891
1.0	.34134	.34375	.34614	.34850	.35083	.35314	.35543	.35769	.35993	.36214
1.1	.36433	.36650	.36864	.37076	.37286	.37493	.37698	.37900	.38100	.38298
1.2	.38493	.38686	.38877	.39065	.39251	.39435	.39617	.39796	.39973	.40147
1.3	.40320	.40490	.40658	.40824	.40988	.41149	.41309	.41466	.41621	.41774
1.4	.41924	.42073	.42220	.42364	.42507	.42647	.42786	.42922	.43056	.43189

APPENDIX A (continued)

$z = \left(\dfrac{x}{\sigma}\right)$	.00	.01	.02	.03	.04	.05	.06	.07	.08	.09
1.5	.43319	.43448	.43574	.43699	.43822	.43943	.44062	.44179	.44295	.44408
1.6	.44520	.44630	.44738	.44845	.44950	.45053	.45154	.45254	.45352	.45449
1.7	.45543.	.45637	.45728	.45818	.45907	.45994	.46080	.46164	.46246	.46327
1.8	.46407	.46485	.46562	.46638	.46712	.46784	.46856	.46926	.46995	.47062
1.9	.47128	.47193	.47257	.47320	.47381	.47441	.47500	.47558	.47615	.47670
2.0	.47725	.47778	.47831	.47882	.47932	.47982	.48030	.48077	.48124	.48169
2.1	.48214	.48257	.48300	.48341	.48382	.48422	.48461	.48500	.48537	.48574
2.2	.48610	.48645	.48679	.48713	.48745	.48778	.48809	.48840	.48870	.48899
2.3	.48928	.48956	.48983	.49010	.49036	.49061	.49086	.49111	.49134	.49158
2.4	.49180	.49202	.49224	.49245	.49266	.49286	.49305	.49324	.49343	.49361
2.5	.49379	.49396	.49413	.49430	.49446	.49461	.49477	.49492	.49506	.49520
2.6	.49534	.49547	.49560	.49573	.49585	.49598	.49609	.49621	.49632	.49643
2.7	.49653	.49664	.49674	.49683	.49693	.49702	.49711	.49720	.49728	.49736
2.8	.49744	.49752	.49760	.49767	.49774	.49781	.49788	.49795	.49801	.49807
2.9	.49813	.49819	.49825	.49831	.49386	.49841	.49846	.49851	.49856	.49861
3.0	.49865	.49869	.49874	.49878	.49882	.49886	.49889	.49893	.49897	.49900
3.1	.49903	.49906	.49910	.49913	.49916	.49918	.49921	.49924	.49926	.49929
3.2	.49931	.49934	.49936	.49938	.49940	.49942	.49944	.49946	.49948	.49950
3.3	.49952	.49953	.49955	.49957	.49958	.49960	.49961	.49962	.49964	.49965
3.4	.49966	.49968	.49969	.49970	.49971	.49972	.49973	.49974	.49975	.49976
3.5	.49977	.49978	.49978	.49979	.49980	.49981	.49981	.49982	.49983	.49983
3.6	.49984	.49985	.49985	.49986	.49986	.49987	.49987	.49988	.49988	.49989
3.7	.49989	.499990	.49990	.49990	.49991	.49991	.49992	.49992	.49992	.49992
3.8	.49993	.49993	.49993	.49994	.49994	.49994	.49994	.49995	.49995	.49995
3.9	.49995	.49995	.49996	.49996	.49996	.49996	.49996	.49996	.49997	.49997
4.0	.49997									

Source: Table 6 of Dr. Stephen P. Shao's *Statistics for Business and Economics,* third edition. (Westerville, OH: Merrill Publishing Co., 1976). Reproduced by kind permission of Dr. Shao.

Appendix B

Values of *t* for Selected Probabilities

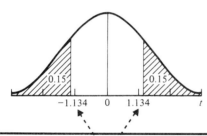

Example:
D (number of degrees of freedom) = 6:
   One tail above $t = 1.134$
   or below $t = -1.134$
   represents 0.15 or 15% of the area under the curve.
   Two tails above $t = 1.134$
   and below $t = -1.134$
   represent 0.30 or 30%.

				Probabilities (or areas under *t* distribution curve)				
One tail	.45	.35	.25	.15	.10	.05	.025	.01	.005
Two tails	.90	.70	.50	.30	.20	.10	.05	.02	.01
D					Values of *t*				
1	.158	.510	1.000	1.963	3.078	6.314	12.706	31.821	63.657
2	.142	.445	.816	1.386	1.886	2.920	4.303	6.965	9.925
3	.137	.424	.765	1.250	1.638	2.353	3.182	4.541	5.841
4	.134	.414	.741	1.190	1.533	2.132	2.776	3.747	4.604
5	.132	.408	.727	1.156	1.476	2.015	2.571	3.365	4.032
6	.131	.404	.718	1.134	1.440	1.943	2.447	3.143	3.707
7	.130	.402	.711	1.119	1.415	1.895	2.365	2.998	3.499
8	.130	.399	.706	1.108	1.397	1.860	2.306	2.896	3.355
9	.129	.398	.703	1.100	1.383	1.833	2.262	2.821	3.250
10	.129	.397	.700	1.093	1.372	1.812	2.228	2.764	3.169
11	.129	.396	.697	1.088	1.363	1.796	2.201	2.718	3.106

APPENDIX B (continued)

	Probabilities (or areas under *t* distribution curve)								
One tail	.45	.35	.25	.15	.10	.05	.025	.01	.005
Two tails	.90	.70	.50	.30	.20	.10	.05	.02	.01
D	Values of *t*								
12	.128	.395	.695	1.083	1.356	1.782	2.179	2.681	3.055
13	.128	.394	.694	1.079	1.350	1.771	2.160	2.650	3.012
14	.128	.393	.692	1.076	1.345	1.761	2.145	2.624	2.977
15	.128	.393	.691	1.074	1.341	1.753	2.131	2.602	2.947
16	.128	.392	.690	1.071	1.337	1.746	2.120	2.583	2.921
17	.128	.392	.689	1.069	1.333	1.740	2.110	2.567	2.898
18	.127	.392	.688	1.067	1.330	1.734	2.101	2.552	2.878
19	.127	.391	.688	1.066	1.328	1.729	2.093	2.539	2.861
20	.127	.391	.687	1.064	1.325	1.725	2.086	2.528	2.845
21	.127	.391	.686	1.063	1.323	1.721	2.080	2.518	2.831
22	.127	.390	.686	1.061	1.321	1.717	2.074	2.508	2.819
23	.127	.390	.685	1.060	1.319	1.714	2.069	2.500	2.807
24	.127	.390	.685	1.059	1.318	1.711	2.064	2.492	2.797
25	.127	.390	.684	1.058	1.316	1.708	2.060	2.485	2.787
26	.127	.390	.684	1.058	1.315	1.706	2.056	2.479	2.779
27	.127	.389	.684	1.057	1.314	1.703	2.052	2.473	2.771
28	.127	.389	.683	1.056	1.313	1.701	2.048	2.467	2.763
29	.127	.389	.683	1.055	1.311	1.699	2.045	2.462	2.756
30	.127	.389	.683	1.055	1.310	1.697	2.042	2.457	2.750
40	.126	.388	.681	1.050	1.303	1.684	2.021	2.423	2.704
60	.126	.387	.679	1.046	1.296	1.671	2.000	2.390	2.660
120	.126	.386	.677	1.041	1.289	1.658	1.980	2.358	2.617
∞	.126	.385	.674	1.036	1.282	1.645	1.960	2.326	2.576

Source: Table 6 of Dr. Stephen P. Shao's *Statistics for Business and Economics*, third edition. (Westerville, OH: Merrill Publishing Co., 1976). Reproduced by kind permission of Dr. Shao.

Appendix C

Values of *F* for Upper 5% Probability (or 5% Area Under *F* Distribution Curve)

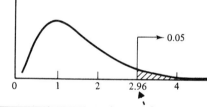

Example:
D_1 (degrees of freedom for numerator of *F* ratio) = 5,
D_2 (degrees of freedom for denominator) = 14:
The tail above $F = 2.96$ represents 0.05 or 5% of the area under the curve.

0.05

D_2 \ D_1	1	2	3	4	5	6	7	8	10	12
1	161	200	216	225	230	234	237	239	242	244
2	18.51	19.00	19.16	19.25	19.30	19.33	19.36	19.37	19.39	19.41
3	10.13	9.55	9.28	9.12	9.01	8.94	8.88	8.84	8.78	8.74
4	7.71	6.94	6.59	6.39	6.26	6.16	6.09	6.04	5.96	5.91
5	6.61	5.79	5.41	5.19	5.05	4.95	4.88	4.82	4.74	4.68
6	5.99	5.14	4.76	4.53	4.39	4.28	4.21	4.15	4.06	4.00
7	5.59	4.74	4.35	4.12	3.97	3.87	3.79	3.73	3.63	3.57
8	5.32	4.46	4.07	3.84	3.69	3.58	3.50	3.44	3.34	3.28
10	4.96	4.10	3.71	3.48	3.33	3.22	3.14	3.07	2.97	2.91
12	4.75	3.88	3.49	3.26	3.11	3.00	2.92	2.85	2.76	2.69
14	4.60	3.74	3.34	3.11	2.96	2.85	2.77	2.70	2.60	2.53
16	4.49	3.63	3.24	3.01	2.85	2.74	2.66	2.59	2.49	2.42
20	4.35	3.49	3.10	2.87	2.71	2.60	2.52	2.45	2.35	2.28
24	4.26	3.40	3.01	2.78	2.62	2.51	2.43	2.36	2.26	2.18
30	4.17	3.32	2.92	2.69	2.53	2.42	2.34	2.27	2.16	2.09
40	4.08	3.23	2.84	2.61	2.45	2.34	2.25	2.18	2.07	2.00
50	4.03	3.18	2.79	2.56	2.40	2.29	2.20	2.13	2.02	1.95
100	3.94	3.09	2.70	2.46	2.30	2.19	2.10	2.03	1.92	1.85
200	3.89	3.04	2.65	2.41	2.26	2.14	2.05	1.98	1.87	1.80
∞	3.84	2.99	2.60	2.37	2.21	2.09	2.01	1.94	1.83	1.75

APPENDIX C (continued)

D_2 \ D_1	14	16	20	24	30	40	50	100	200	∞
1	245	246	248	249	250	251	252	253	254	254
2	19.42	19.43	19.44	19.45	19.46	19.47	19.47	19.49	19.49	19.50
3	8.71	8.69	8.66	8.64	8.62	8.60	8.58	8.56	8.54	8.53
4	5.87	5.84	5.80	5.77	5.74	5.71	5.70	5.66	5.65	5.63
5	4.64	4.60	4.56	4.53	4.50	4.46	4.44	4.40	4.38	4.36
6	3.96	3.92	3.87	3.84	3.81	3.77	3.75	3.71	3.69	3.67
7	3.52	3.49	3.44	3.41	3.38	3.34	3.32	3.28	3.25	3.23
8	3.23	3.20	3.15	3.12	3.08	3.05	3.03	2.98	2.96	2.93
10	2.86	2.82	2.77	2.74	2.70	2.67	2.64	2.59	2.56	2.54
12	2.64	2.60	2.54	2.50	2.46	2.42	2.40	2.35	2.32	2.30
14	2.48	2.44	2.39	2.35	2.31	2.27	2.24	2.19	2.16	2.13
16	2.37	2.33	2.28	2.24	2.20	2.16	2.13	2.07	2.04	2.01
20	2.23	2.18	2.12	2.08	2.04	1.99	1.96	1.90	1.87	1.84
24	2.13	2.09	2.02	1.98	1.94	1.89	1.86	1.80	1.76	1.73
30	2.04	1.99	1.93	1.89	1.84	1.79	1.76	1.69	1.66	1.62
40	1.95	1.90	1.84	1.79	1.74	1.69	1.66	1.59	1.55	1.51
50	1.90	1.85	1.78	1.74	1.69	1.63	1.60	1.52	1.48	1.44
100	1.79	1.75	1.68	1.63	1.57	1.51	1.48	1.39	1.34	1.28
200	1.74	1.69	1.62	1.57	1.52	1.45	1.42	1.32	1.26	1.19
∞	1.69	1.64	1.57	1.52	1.46	1.40	1.35	1.24	1.17	1.00

Source: Reproduced by permission from *Statistical Methods,* fifth edition, by George Snedecor, © 1956 by the Iowa State University Press. Example by Dr. Stephen P. Shao, Table 9A, *Statistics for Business and Economics,* third edition. (Westerville, OH: Merrill Publishing Co., 1976).

Appendix C (continued)

Values of *F* for Upper 1% Probability (or 1% Area Under *F* Distribution Curve)

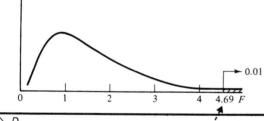

Example:
D_1 (degrees of freedom for numerator of *F* ratio) = 5,
D_2 (degrees of freedom for denominator) = 14:
The tail above $F = 4.69$ represents 0.01 or 1% of the area under the curve.

D_2 \ D_1	1	2	3	4	5	6	7	8	10	12
1	4,052	4,999	5,403	5,625	5,764	5,859	5,928	5,981	6,056	6,106
2	98.49	99.00	99.17	99.25	99.30	99.33	99.34	99.36	99.40	99.42
3	34.12	30.82	29.46	28.71	28.24	27.91	27.67	27.49	27.23	27.05
4	21.20	18.00	16.69	15.98	15.52	15.21	14.98	14.80	14.54	14.37
5	16.26	13.27	12.06	11.39	10.97	10.67	10.45	10.27	10.05	9.89
6	13.74	10.92	9.78	9.15	8.75	8.47	8.26	8.10	7.87	7.72
7	12.25	9.55	8.45	7.85	7.46	7.19	7.00	6.84	6.62	6.47
8	11.26	8.65	7.59	7.01	6.63	6.37	6.19	6.03	5.82	5.67
10	10.04	7.56	6.55	5.99	5.64	5.39	5.21	5.06	4.85	4.71
12	9.33	6.93	5.95	5.41	5.06	4.82	4.65	4.50	4.30	4.16
14	8.86	6.51	5.56	5.03	4.69	4.46	4.28	4.14	3.94	3.80
16	8.53	6.23	5.29	4.77	4.44	4.20	4.03	3.89	3.69	3.55
20	8.10	5.85	4.94	4.43	4.10	3.87	3.71	3.56	3.37	3.23
24	7.82	5.61	4.72	4.22	3.90	3.67	3.50	3.36	3.17	3.03
30	7.56	5.39	4.51	4.02	3.70	3.47	3.30	3.17	2.98	2.84
40	7.31	5.18	4.31	3.83	3.51	3.29	3.12	2.99	2.80	2.66
50	7.17	5.06	4.20	3.72	3.41	3.18	3.02	2.88	2.70	2.56
100	6.90	4.82	3.98	3.51	3.20	2.99	2.82	2.69	2.51	2.36
200	6.76	4.71	3.88	3.41	3.11	2.90	2.73	2.60	2.41	2.28
∞	6.64	4.60	3.78	3.32	3.02	2.80	2.64	2.51	2.32	2.18

APPENDIX C (continued)

D_2 \ D_1	14	16	20	24	30	40	50	100	200	∞
1	6,142	6,169	6,208	6,234	6,258	6,286	6,302	6,334	6,352	6,366
2	99.43	99.44	99.45	99.46	99.47	99.48	99.48	99.49	99.49	99.50
3	26.92	26.83	26.69	26.60	26.50	26.41	26.35	26.23	26.18	26.12
4	14.24	14.15	14.02	13.93	13.83	13.74	13.69	13.57	13.52	13.46
5	9.77	9.68	9.55	9.47	9.38	9.29	9.24	9.13	9.07	9.02
6	7.60	7.52	7.39	7.31	7.23	7.14	7.09	6.99	6.94	6.88
7	6.35	6.27	6.15	6.07	5.98	5.90	5.85	5.75	5.70	5.65
8	5.56	5.48	5.36	5.28	5.20	5.11	5.06	4.96	4.91	4.86
10	4.60	4.52	4.41	4.33	4.25	4.17	4.12	4.01	3.96	3.91
12	4.05	3.98	3.86	3.78	3.70	3.61	3.56	3.46	3.41	3.36
14	3.70	3.62	3.51	3.43	3.34	3.26	3.21	3.11	3.06	3.00
16	3.45	3.37	3.25	3.18	3.10	3.01	2.96	2.86	2.80	2.75
20	3.13	3.05	2.94	2.86	2.77	2.69	2.63	2.53	2.47	2.42
24	2.93	2.85	2.74	2.66	2.58	2.49	2.44	2.33	2.27	2.21
30	2.74	2.66	2.55	2.47	2.38	2.29	2.24	2.13	2.07	2.01
40	2.56	2.49	2.37	2.29	2.20	2.11	2.05	1.94	1.88	1.81
50	2.46	2.39	2.26	2.18	2.10	2.00	1.94	1.82	1.76	1.68
100	2.26	2.19	2.06	1.98	1.89	1.79	1.73	1.59	1.51	1.43
200	2.17	2.09	1.97	1.88	1.79	1.69	1.62	1.48	1.39	1.28
∞	2.07	1.99	1.87	1.79	1.69	1.59	1.52	1.36	1.25	1.00

Source: Reproduced by permission from *Statistical Methods,* fifth edition, by George Snedecor, © 1956 by the Iowa State University Press. Example by Dr. Stephen P. Shao, Table 9B, *Statistics for Business and Economics,* third edition. (Westerville, OH: Merrill Publishing Co., 1976).

Appendix D

Tabular Values of Q_α for Tukey's HSD Test

Example: $N = 15$, number of groups $= 3$. Therefore, $dfw = N - k = 12$; number of group means $= 3$, alpha $= .05$ $Q_\alpha = 3.77$.

| dfw | α | \multicolumn{11}{c}{k = number of group means} |
		2	3	4	5	6	7	8	9	10	11	12
1	.05	18.0	27.0	32.8	37.1	40.4	43.1	45.4	47.4	49.1	50.6	52.0
	.01	90.0	135	164	186	202	216	227	237	246	253	260
2	.05	6.09	8.3	9.8	10.9	11.7	12.4	13.0	13.5	14.0	14.4	14.7
	.01	14.0	19.0	22.3	24.7	26.6	28.2	29.5	30.7	31.7	31.6	33.4
3	.05	4.50	5.91	6.82	7.50	8.04	8.48	8.85	9.18	9.46	9.72	9.95
	.01	8.26	10.6	12.2	13.3	14.2	15.0	15.6	16.2	16.7	17.1	17.5
4	.05	3.93	5.04	5.76	6.29	6.71	7.05	7.35	7.60	7.83	8.03	8.21
	.01	6.51	8.12	9.17	9.96	10.6	11.1	11.5	11.9	12.3	12.6	12.8
5	.05	3.64	4.60	5.22	5.67	6.03	6.33	6.58	6.80	6.99	7.17	7.32
	.01	5.70	6.97	7.80	8.42	8.91	9.32	9.67	9.97	10.24	10.48	10.70
6	.05	3.46	4.34	4.90	5.31	5.63	5.89	6.12	6.32	6.49	6.65	6.79
	.01	5.24	6.33	7.03	7.56	7.97	8.32	8.61	8.87	9.10	9.30	9.49
7	.05	3.34	4.16	4.68	5.06	5.36	5.61	5.82	6.00	6.16	6.30	6.43
	.01	4.95	5.92	6.54	7.01	7.37	7.68	7.94	8.17	8.37	8.55	8.71
8	.05	3.26	4.04	4.53	4.89	5.17	5.40	5.60	5.77	5.92	6.05	6.18
	.01	4.74	5.63	6.20	6.63	6.96	7.24	7.47	7.68	7.87	8.03	8.18
9	.05	3.20	3.95	4.42	4.76	5.02	5.24	5.43	5.60	5.74	5.87	5.95
	.01	4.60	5.43	5.96	6.35	6.66	6.91	7.13	7.32	7.49	7.65	7.78
10	.05	3.15	3.88	4.33	4.65	4.91	5.12	5.30	5.46	5.60	5.72	5.83
	.01	4.48	5.27	5.77	6.14	6.43	6.67	6.87	7.05	7.21	7.36	7.48
11	.05	3.11	3.82	4.26	4.37	4.82	5.03	5.20	5.35	5.49	5.61	5.71
	.01	4.39	5.14	5.62	5.97	6.25	6.48	6.67	6.84	6.99	7.33	7.25

APPENDIX D (continued)

dfw	α	\multicolumn{11}{c	}{k = number of group means}
		2	3	4	5	6	7	8	9	10	11	12
12	.05	3.08	3.77	4.20	4.31	4.75	4.95	5.12	5.27	5.40	5.51	5.62
	.01	4.32	5.04	5.05	5.84	6.10	6.32	6.51	6.67	6.81	6.94	7.06
13	.05	3.06	3.73	4.15	4.45	4.69	4.88	5.05	5.19	5.32	5.43	5.53
	.01	4.26	4.96	5.40	5.73	5.98	6.19	6.37	6.53	6.67	6.79	6.90
14	.05	3.03	3.70	4.11	4.41	4.64	4.83	4.99	5.13	5.25	5.36	5.46
	.01	4.21	4.89	5.32	5.63	5.88	6.08	6.26	6.41	6.54	6.66	6.77
15	.05	3.01	3.67	4.08	4.37	4.60	4.78	4.94	5.08	5.20	5.31	5.40
	.01	4.17	4.83	5.25	5.56	5.80	5.99	6.16	6.31	6.44	6.55	6.66
16	.05	3.00	3.63	4.05	4.33	4.56	4.74	4.90	5.03	5.15	5.26	5.35
	.01	4.13	4.78	5.19	5.49	5.72	5.92	6.08	6.22	6.35	6.46	6.50
17	.05	2.98	3.63	4.02	4.30	4.52	4.71	4.86	4.99	5.11	5.21	5.31
	.01	4.10	4.74	5.14	5.43	5.66	5.85	6.01	6.15	6.27	6.38	6.48
18	.05	2.97	3.61	4.00	4.28	4.49	4.67	4.82	4.96	5.07	5.17	5.27
	.01	4.07	4.70	5.09	5.38	5.60	5.79	5.94	6.08	6.20	6.31	6.41
19	.05	2.96	3.59	3.98	4.25	4.47	4.65	4.79	4.92	5.04	5.14	5.23
	.01	4.05	4.67	5.05	5.33	5.55	5.73	5.89	6.02	6.14	6.25	6.34
20	.05	2.95	3.58	3.96	4.23	4.45	4.62	4.77	4.90	5.01	5.11	5.20
	.01	4.02	4.64	5.02	5.29	5.51	5.69	5.84	5.97	6.09	6.19	6.29
24	.05	2.92	3.53	3.90	4.17	4.37	4.54	4.68	4.81	4.92	5.01	5.10
	.01	3.96	4.54	4.91	5.17	5.37	5.54	5.69	5.81	5.92	6.02	6.11
30	.05	2.89	3.49	3.84	4.10	4.30	4.46	4.60	4.72	4.83	4.91	5.00
	.01	3.89	4.45	4.80	5.05	5.24	5.40	5.54	5.65	5.76	5.85	5.93
40	.05	2.86	3.44	3.79	4.04	4.23	4.39	4.52	4.63	4.74	4.82	4.91
	.01	3.82	4.37	4.70	4.93	5.11	5.27	5.39	5.50	5.60	5.69	5.77
60	.05	2.83	3.40	3.74	3.98	4.16	4.31	4.44	4.55	4.65	4.73	4.81
	.01	3.76	4.28	4.60	4.82	4.99	5.13	5.25	5.36	5.45	5.53	5.60
120	.05	2.80	3.36	3.69	3.92	4.10	4.24	4.36	4.48	4.56	4.64	4.72
	.01	3.70	4.20	4.50	4.71	4.87	5.01	5.12	5.21	5.30	5.38	5.44
∞	.05	2.77	3.31	3.63	3.86	4.03	4.17	4.29	4.39	4.47	4.55	4.62
	.01	3.64	4.12	4.40	4.60	4.76	4.88	4.99	5.08	5.16	5.23	5.29

Appendix E

Values of χ^2 for Selected Probabilities

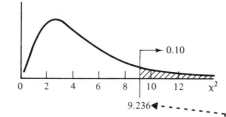

Example:
D (number of degrees of freedom) = 5, the tail above $\chi^2 = 9.236$ represents 0.10 or 10% of the area under the curve.

0.10

9.236

Probabilities
(or areas under χ^2 distribution curve above given χ^2 values)

D	.90	.70	.50	.30	.20	.10	.05	.02	.01
					Values of χ^2				
1	.016	.148	.455	1.074	1.642	2.706	3.841	5.412	6.635
2	.211	.713	1.386	2.408	3.219	4.605	5.991	7.824	9.210
3	.584	1.424	2.366	3.665	4.642	6.251	7.815	9.837	11.345
4	1.064	2.195	3.357	4.878	5.989	7.779	9.488	11.668	13.277
5	1.610	3.000	4.351	6.064	7.289	9.236	11.070	13.388	15.086
6	2.204	3.828	5.348	7.231	8.558	10.645	12.592	15.033	16.812
7	2.833	4.671	6.346	8.383	9.803	12.017	14.067	16.622	18.475
8	3.490	5.527	7.344	9.524	11.030	13.362	15.507	18.168	20.090
9	4.168	6.393	8.343	10.656	12.242	14.684	16.919	19.679	21.666
10	4.865	7.267	9.342	11.781	13.442	15.987	18.307	21.161	23.209
11	5.578	8.148	10.341	12.899	14.631	17.275	19.675	22.618	24.725
12	6.304	9.034	11.340	14.011	15.812	18.549	21.026	24.054	26.217
13	7.042	9.926	12.340	15.119	16.985	19.812	22.362	25.472	27.688
14	7.790	10.821	13.339	16.222	18.151	21.064	23.685	26.873	29.141
15	8.547	11.721	14.339	17.322	19.311	22.307	24.996	28.259	30.578

APPENDIX E (continued)

	Probabilities (or areas under χ^2 distribution curve above given χ^2 values)								
	.90	.70	.50	.30	.20	.10	.05	.02	.01
D					Values of χ^2				
16	9.312	12.624	15.338	18.418	20.465	23.542	26.296	29.633	32.000
17	10.085	13.531	16.338	19.511	21.615	24.769	27.587	30.995	33.409
18	10.865	14.440	17.338	20.601	22.760	25.989	28.869	33.346	34.805
19	11.651	15.352	18.338	21.689	23.900	27.204	30.144	33.687	36.191
20	12.443	16.266	19.337	22.775	25.038	28.412	31.410	35.020	37.566
21	13.240	17.182	20.337	23.858	26.171	29.615	32.671	36.343	38.932
22	14.041	18.101	21.337	24.939	27.301	30.813	33.924	37.659	40.289
23	14.848	19.021	22.337	26.018	28.429	32.007	35.172	38.968	41.638
24	15.659	19.943	23.337	27.096	29.553	33.196	36.415	40.270	42.980
25	16.473	20.867	24.337	28.172	30.675	34.382	37.652	41.566	44.314
26	17.292	21.792	25.336	29.246	31.795	35.563	38.885	42.856	45.642
27	18.114	22.719	26.336	30.319	32.912	36.741	40.113	44.140	46.963
28	18.939	23.647	27.336	31.391	34.027	37.916	41.337	45.419	48.278
29	19.768	24.577	28.336	32.461	35.139	39.087	42.557	46.693	49.588
30	20.599	25.508	29.336	33.530	36.250	40.256	43.773	47.962	50.892

Source: Table 6 of Dr. Stephen P. Shao's *Statistics for Business and Economics*, third edition. (Westerville, OH: Merrill Publishing Co., 1976). Reproduced by kind permission of Dr. Shao.

Glossary

abscissa The horizontal axis of a graph.

adjusted R squared The R squared value in a regression equation adjusted for sample N and for the number of independent variables in the equation.

alpha level The proportion of area that includes the critical region. Conventionally set at .05, .01, or .001. Also called a *significance level.*

alternative or **research hypothesis** A formal statement declaring that the sample value of an attribute is significantly different from the population value or that the value of sample 1 is significantly different from the value of sample 2.

analysis of variance (ANOVA) A statistical technique used for assessing significance of difference between three or more means by using the ratio of within-group variance to between-group variance.

antecedent variable A variable that precedes both the dependent and independent variable in time.

association The degree to which two variables are associated, related, or connected or vary together.

bar chart A graphic display for nominal and ordinal data or grouped interval or ratio data. Bars represent qualitatively different categories and are constructed to a height corresponding to the proportion of observations in the category.

between-group sum of squares Sum of squares based on the deviation of group means from the grand mean. When divided by df $(k - 1)$, it is the between-group variance estimate.

census A complete tabulation of a characteristic of interest for all elements of a population.

central limit theorem A principle asserting that a sampling distribution will approach a normal distribution as N gets large even if the population being sampled is not normally distributed.

chi-square distribution A positively skewed probability distribution, the shape of which is determined by degrees of freedom.

chi-square goodness-of-fit test A nonparametric test used to determine whether or not an observed set of frequencies fits the theoretically expected frequencies.

chi-square test of independence A nonparametric test used to determine whether or not the distribution of one variable in a table is independent of the distribution of another by comparing the observed frequencies with the frequencies expected under conditions of chance.

coefficient of alienation The proportion of variance in the dependent variable not accounted for by the independent variable.

coefficient of determination The Pearson correlation squared. A value that expresses the proportion of the variance in the dependent variable that is accounted for by the independent variable.

communality The total variance of a variable accounted for by the combination of all common factors.

conditional distribution The distribution of one variable in a table under a fixed value of a second variable. The joint frequency of conditions of two variables in a cell.

conditional odds The chances of being in a particular category of one variable given a particular category of another.

confidence interval A range of values constructed around a point estimate for which there is (conventionally) either 95 percent or 99 percent confidence that within this range lies the population parameter.

consistent estimate An estimate that is consistent with its parameter. The larger the random sample the greater the consistency of estimate and parameter.

contingency coefficient A chi-square-based measure of association for tables bigger than 2×2. No PRE interpretation.

continuous variable A variable that can potentially take on any value.

correlation Statistical techniques that, in the context of this chapter, are used to assess the accuracy of a prediction.

correlation coefficient (Pearson's *r*) An index of the strength and direction of linear association between two variables.

covariance The covariance of two sets of scores from their respective means.

Cramer's *V* A chi-square-based measure of association for tables bigger than 2×2. Preferable to the contingency coefficient, but no PRE interpretation.

critical region The area under the sampling distribution that contains unlikely sample outcomes.

data Information about some domain of interest expressed numerically (singular, *datum*).

degrees of freedom The number of values in a sample that are free to vary in the calculation of a statistic.

dependent variable A variable assumed to be influenced or predicted by another variable (the *independent variable*).

descriptive statistics Statistics that describe a data set in simple and direct ways.

discrete variable A variable that takes on only a finite number of values.

dummy variables Variables created for inclusion in a regression equation from a categorical variable. $K - 1$ variables are created and coded 1 in the presence of an attribute and 0 in its absence.

efficient estimate An estimate of a population parameter in which the distribution of a statistic is clustered around the parameter being estimated. The best ("most efficient") estimator of all possible estimators.

eigenvalue A measure of the amount of variance explained by a factor corresponding to the equivalent number of variables the factor represents.

eta squared The ratio of the between-group sum of squares and the total sum of squares. The proportion of variance in the dependent variable explained by the independent variable.

explained sum of squares Sum of squares explained by all independent variables in the model plus interaction.

explanation An elaboration outcome in which an initial relationship between two variables is explained away by an antecedent variable.

F distribution A theoretical distribution of the ratio of two independent sample variances used for assessing the significance of ANOVA results.

F ratio The ratio of MS_{within} to $MS_{between}$ tested for significance with the F distribution with df between and within.

factor A higher-order, unobserved construct derived from the observed interrelations in a data set. A general concept subsuming and summarizing a number of less general but related concepts.

factor analysis A technique for deriving underlying dimensions from a data set.

first-order partial relationship A relationship between two variables examined within categories of one control variable.

frequency distribution A distribution of observations indicating the number of times each score or value occurs.

gamma A measure of association for grouped data in ordered categories.

heterogeneity of variance A condition that exists when the variances of the two subsamples are not equal. Heterogeneity is tested with the F ratio.

histogram A graphic display of interval- or ratio-level data consisting of contiguous lines of a height corresponding to the number of observations in the interval.

homogeneity of variance In the context of this chapter, the assumption that the variances of two subsamples being tested for significance of difference are equal.

homoscedasticity The assumption that the variability in Y is constant over all values of X.

independent variable A variable assumed to influence or predict another variable (the *dependent variable*).

index of qualitative variation A measure of variation suitable for qualitative categorized data (nominal and interval data).

inferential statistics Statistical techniques whereby inferences about populations are based on information derived from samples.

interaction An effect that occurs when the relationship between two variables is significantly different within categories of a third variable. Similar to specification in tabular analysis.

interpretation An elaboration outcome in which an initial relationship is rendered spurious by an intervening variable.

interval estimate An estimate of a population parameter within a specified range of values.

interval level A measurement level of a continuous, quantitative variable that has equal unit intervals but no real zero point.

intervening variable A variable that mediates, or intervenes between, the independent and dependent variable.

Kruskal-Wallis one-way ANOVA An ordinal-level, nonparametric test of significance for three or more samples of rank-ordered data.

kurtosis The degree of curvedness or peakedness of a distribution.

lambda A nominal-level measure of association.

leptokurtic A curve that has the characteristic of thinness or peakedness—positive kurtosis.

line graph A graphic display of some quantitative variable indicating change over some time period.

logit regression A regressionlike technique for analyzing the effects of a set of independent variables on a qualitative, dichotomous dependent variable.

main effects The sum of squares explained by the independent variable, or joint effects of two or more variables, in ANOVA. Sometimes called model effects.

marginals The summations of column and row frequencies in a contingency table.

mean The arithmetic average of a distribution of data.

mean square A sum of squares divided by its degrees of freedom to yield a variance estimate.

measurement The assignment of numbers to observations according to a set of rules.

measurement errors Errors in measurement due to lack of complete reliability of variables. Correlations between variables can be "corrected for attentuation" if the scale reliabilities are known.

measures of central tendency Measures that locate the various ways (mean, mode, median) in which the data cluster at the center of a distribution.

measures of dispersion Measures that describe the amount of scatter or spread of a distribution of data about the mean.

median The point in a distribution of data below and above which half of the scores are located.

mesokurtic A curve that has the characteristic of normality; neither peaked or flattened— zero kurtosis.

midpoint The point of a class interval that is halfway between the interval's real lower and real upper limits.

mode The most common score in a distribution of data or the largest category of a variable.

multicollinearity A condition that exists when there are high correlations among the predictor variables in a regression equation.

multiple correlation The combined association between two or more independent variables and a dependent variable.

multiple regression The regression of two or more independent variables on a dependent variable.

necessary and sufficient cause A cause or condition that must be present for the effect to occur and that can cause the event all by itself.

necessary cause A cause or condition that must be present for the effect to occur.

negative association An association or relationship in which high values on one variable are associated with low values on another.

nominal level A measurement level of a discrete, qualitative variable whose categories do not bear any relationship of magnitude to one another.

normal curve A symmetrical bell-shaped curve based on a theoretical distribution of an infinite number of observations.

normal curve table A table supplying the area under the normal curve between a z score and the mean (Appendix A).

null hypothesis A formal statement declaring that the sample value is equal to the population value or that the value of sample 1 is equal to the value of sample 2. A statement of "no difference."

odds ratio The ratio of two conditional odds. Very useful for reporting results of bivariate tabular analyses to laypersons.

one-tailed test or **directional hypothesis** A hypothesis test used when a researcher has theoretical reasons for believing that any departure from the null hypothesis will occur in one tail of the distribution.

operational definition The definition of a concept in terms of the operations used to measure it.

ordinal level A measurement level of a discrete, qualitative variable whose categories do bear a relationship of magnitude to one another but do not have the property of equal intervals.

ordinary least squares A method used to determine the regression equation by minimizing the sum of squares around the regression line.

ordinate The vertical axis of a graph.

outlier An extreme residual that has the effect of increasing or decreasing the value of the correlation coefficient beyond what it would be with the outlier removed.

parameters Measurable characteristics of a population that are not known but that can be estimated by statistics.

parametric statistics A set of statistical techniques used under the assumptions that the populations from which samples are drawn are normally distributed and have a known standard deviation.

partial correlation The association between two variables, controlling for the effects of one or more other variables.

partial gamma An index of the strength of association between two variables, controlling for the effects of other variables.

path analysis A method of interpreting probabilistic causal relationships and causal ordering among a set of variables.

percentage The number of observations in a particular category divided by the number of observations in all categories; the quotient is then multiplied by 100.

phi A chi-square based measure of association for 2×2 tables.

pie chart A graphic display of categorical data in which a circle (the pie) is divided into segments proportional to the percentage of cases in each category.

platykurtic A curve that has the characteristic of flatness—negative kurtosis.

point biserial correlation An index of association between a continuous and a dichotomous variable.

point estimate An estimate of a population parameter at a specific single value.

polygon A graphic display of a distribution of observation in which adjacent class intervals marked by their midpoints are connected by a straight line.

population The totality of cases, subjects, events, or individuals who share some common characteristic.

positive association An association or relationship in which high values on one variable are associated with high values on another.

probability A mathematical tool for making predictions based on either a priori knowledge (classical probability) or previous observations (empirical probability). Probability is a ratio of events or outcomes to the total possible events or outcomes.

proportion The number of observations in a particular category divided by the number of observations in all categories.

proportional reduction in error (PRE) An interpretational feature of some measures of association. It is the reduction in errors that are made in predicting the dependent variable with knowledge of the independent variable over making predictions without knowledge of the independent variable.

pseudo *R* squared A summary statistic for logit regression "in the spirit of *R* squared."

range The difference between the highest and lowest scores in a distribution of data.

rate The actual number of occurrences of some phenomenon divided by possible occurrences of that phenomenon over a defined period of time.

ratio The number of observations in one category divided by the number of observations in some other category.

ratio level A measurement level of a continuous, quantitative variable that has equal unit intervals and a true zero point.

real lower and upper limits Those points of a particular number that fall one-half unit below and above their apparent limits.

recursive path model A path analytic model in which all the causal influences are assumed to be one-way (nonreciprocal).

regression Statistical techniques involving the prediction of one variable from another.

regression line The line describing the best linear fit between two interval or ratio variables.

regression slope A measure of the average amount of change in the dependent variable predicted per unit change in the independent variable. Also known as *beta*.

replication An elaboration outcome in which controlling for another variable does not change the nature of the original bivariate relationship.

restricted range A problem in correlation analysis that arises when we sample a homogeneous subsample of subjects from a heterogeneous population.

robustness The ability of a statistical test to withstand violations of its assumptions without seriously damaging the interpretation.

sample A subset of a population.

sampling distribution of means A theoretical probability distribution of an infinite number of sample means from a population

sampling error The difference between the value of a sample statistic and the value of its corresponding population parameter.

sampling frame A technical term for the actual list of the sampling units from which the sample will be drawn. The sampling frame should ideally correspond to the target population but rarely does.

scattergram A graphic representation showing the joint distribution of two interval or ratio variables.

Scheffe test A multiple comparison test of pairs of group means in an ANOVA test; used when the researcher has unequal sample sizes.

second-order partial relationship A relationship between two variables, controlling for two additional variables.

simple random sampling A method of selecting cases from a population in which every case has an equal probability of being selected.

size The magnitude of the size of a class interval obtained by subtracting its real lower limit of its interval from its real upper limit.

skewness A measure of asymmetry in a distribution curve in which the preponderance of scores are on one side of the mean or the other.

Somer's *d* An ordinal-level measure of association that is computed either symmetrically or asymmetrically according to which variable is considered dependent.

Spearman's rank order correlation (rho) A measure of linear association for rank-ordered data.

specification An elaboration outcome in which the researcher specifies under what condition(s) of the control variable the original relationship remains true. Also sometimes called interaction.

specification errors Errors made in specifying the nature of a statistical mode: (1) omitting theoretically relevant variables, (2) including irrelevant variables, and (3) specifying a linear model when the data are curvilinear.

spuriousness An elaboration outcome in which the bivariate relationship is shown to be false, being explained away or interpreted by the control variable.

standard deviation The square root of the variance. A measure of dispersion reflecting the extent to which the mean represents a population or sample.

standard error The standard deviation of a sampling distribution.

standard error of *r* A measure used to place confidence intervals around *r*; the standard deviation of a theoretical distribution of *r*s.

standard error of the difference The standard deviation of the sampling distribution of differences between means.

standard error of the estimate A measure of the variability around the regression line.

standard normal curve A theoretical normal curve that has been standardized to a mean of zero and a standard deviation of 1.

standardized partial regression slope An index of the amount of change in the dependent variable per unit change in an independent variable, controlling for one or more other independent variables where all variables have been standardized.

statistics Measurable characteristics of a sample used to infer population characteristics. Also, a set of mathematical techniques for collecting, analyzing, interpreting, and presenting quantitative data.

stratified random sampling A method of sampling by which cases are selected from sub-lists of the population either proportionally or disproportionately.

sufficient cause A cause or condition that is sufficent in itself to produce an effect.

sum of squares Sum of the squared deviations of scores around the mean. A measure of dispersion.

suppressor variable A control variable that hides or "masks" the true nature of an association between two variables.

t distribution A distribution used for significance testing when the population standard deviation is unknown and when sample size is small. It is a family of distributions defined by the number of degrees of freedom. Popularly used for large samples also because it becomes identical to the *z* distribution when $df > 120$.

t test Used to test a hypothesis about a mean and about the difference between two means. The *t* test formula differ according to whether variances of the two subsamples are equal or not.

tau-b An ordinal-level measure of association.

tau-c An ordinal-level measure of association.

theta An index of scale reliability derived from principal component factor analysis.

total sum of squares The sum of the squared deviations from the grand mean. Divided by df $(N - 1)$, it is a total variance estimate.

Tukey's honestly significant difference A test used to identify pairs of group means from an ANOVA test that differ significantly when the researcher has equal sample sizes.

two-tailed test or **nondirectional hypothesis** A hypothesis test used when the research hypothesis is concerned with outcomes in both tails of the distribution.

two-way ANOVA Analysis of variance between two or more categories of the dependent variables within categories of two independent variables. ANOVA can be extended to *N* way.

type I (or alpha) error An error that occurs when the null hypothesis is rejected when it should have been retained; that is, a significant difference is claimed when there is none.

type II (or beta) error An error that occurs when we retain the null hypothesis when it should have been rejected; there is a significant difference but we fail to claim it.

unbiased estimate An estimate of the population parameter that tends to be equal to the population parameter being estimated.

univariate analysis The analysis of a single variable in the form of frequencies, percentages, etc.

unstandardized partial regression slope An index of the amount of change in the dependent variable per unit change in an independent variable, controlling for one or more other independent variables where all variables are in their original metrics.

variable Any trait, characteristic, or attribute that can change from observation to observation.

variance Sum of squares divided by n for populations and $N - 1$ for samples. A measure of dispersion.

within-group sum of squares The sum of the squared deviations of scores from the mean within each group from the mean of each group. Divided by df $(N - k)$, it is the within-group variance estimate.

Y intercept The point at which the regression line crosses the Y-axis. The Y intercept (a) is the value of Y when the value of X is zero.

Yate's correction for continuity A method of "correcting" a 2×2 table when any cell's expected frequency is less than 5.

z score The expression of a raw score that has been standardized by subtracting the mean from a raw score and dividing the difference by the standard deviation.

zero-order relationship The relationship between two variables prior to instituting controls for other variables.

Index